Smart Healthcare System Design

Scrivener Publishing
100 Cummings Center, Suite 541J
Beverly, MA 01915-6106

Advances in Learning Analytics for Intelligent Cloud-IoT Systems

Series Editor: Dr. Souvik Pal and Dr. Dac-Nhuong Le

The role of adaptation, learning analytics, computational Intelligence, and data analytics in the field of cloud-IoT systems is becoming increasingly essential and intertwined. The capability of an intelligent system depends on various self-decision-making algorithms in IoT devices. IoT-based smart systems generate a large amount of data (big data) that cannot be processed by traditional data processing algorithms and applications. Hence, this book series involves different computational methods incorporated within the system with the help of analytics reasoning and sense-making in big data, which is centered in the cloud and IoT-enabled environments. The series publishes volumes that are empirical studies, theoretical and numerical analysis, and novel research findings.

Submission to the series:

Please send proposals to Dr. Souvik Pal, Department of Computer Science and Engineering, Global Institute of Management and Technology, Krishna Nagar, West Bengal, India.
E-mail: souvikpal22@gmail.com

Publishers at Scrivener
Martin Scrivener (martin@scrivenerpublishing.com)
Phillip Carmical (pcarmical@scrivenerpublishing.com)

Smart Healthcare System Design

Security and Privacy Aspects

Edited by

SK Hafizul Islam

*Department of Computer Science and Engineering, Indian Institute of
Information Technology, Kalyani, India*

and

Debabrata Samanta

*Department of Computer Science, CHRIST (Deemed to be University),
Bangalore, India*

Scrivener
Publishing

This edition first published 2021 by John Wiley & Sons, Inc., 111 River Street, Hoboken, NJ 07030, USA and Scrivener Publishing LLC, 100 Cummings Center, Suite 541J, Beverly, MA 01915, USA
© 2021 Scrivener Publishing LLC
For more information about Scrivener publications please visit www.scrivenerpublishing.com.

Wiley Global Headquarters
111 River Street, Hoboken, NJ 07030, USA

For details of our global editorial offices, customer services, and more information about Wiley products visit us at www.wiley.com.

Limit of Liability/Disclaimer of Warranty
While the publisher and authors have used their best efforts in preparing this work, they make no representations or warranties with respect to the accuracy or completeness of the contents of this work and specifically disclaim all warranties, including without limitation any implied warranties of merchantability or fitness for a particular purpose. No warranty may be created or extended by sales representatives, written sales materials, or promotional statements for this work. The fact that an organization, website, or product is referred to in this work as a citation and/or potential source of further information does not mean that the publisher and authors endorse the information or services the organization, website, or product may provide or recommendations it may make. This work is sold with the understanding that the publisher is not engaged in rendering professional services. The advice and strategies contained herein may not be suitable for your situation. You should consult with a specialist where appropriate. Neither the publisher nor authors shall be liable for any loss of profit or any other commercial damages, including but not limited to special, incidental, consequential, or other damages. Further, readers should be aware that websites listed in this work may have changed or disappeared between when this work was written and when it is read.

Library of Congress Cataloging-in-Publication Data

ISBN 978-1-119-79168-3

Cover image: Pixabay.Com
Cover design: Russell Richardson

Dedications

To my parents Mr. Dulal Chandra Samanta and Mrs. Ambujini Samanta, my elder sister Mrs. Tanusree Samanta and daughter Ms. Aditri Samanta

Dr. Debabrata Samanta

To my son Mr. Enayat Rabbi

Dr. SK Hafizul Islam

Contents

12 Reliance on Artificial Intelligence, Machine Learning and Deep Learning in the Era of Industry 4.0 281
T. Venkat Narayana Rao, Akhila Gaddam, Muralidhar Kurni and K. Saritha

Preface

The Internet-of-Things (IoT) interconnects humans with uniquely identifiable embedded computing devices within the existing internet infrastructure. It has emerged as a powerful and promising technology, and though it has significant technological, social, and economic impacts, it also poses new security and privacy challenges. Compared with the traditional internet, the IoT has various embedded devices, mobile devices, a server, and the cloud, with different capabilities to support multiple services. The pervasiveness of these devices represents a huge attack surface. And since the IoT connects cyberspace to physical space, known as a cyber-physical system, IoT attacks not only have an impact on information systems, but also affect physical infrastructure, the environment, and even human security. Nowadays, the IoT has received massive attention for applications in different domains, the healthcare sector being one of them. A healthcare system serves society by taking care of its citizens' physiological and neurological conditions through sensors by amassing information on their current health conditions and passing it along to the healthcare center for necessary actions. Accordingly, physicians can examine these health conditions and take the steps required to prevent the deterioration of the patient's health. The purpose of this book is to help achieve a better integration between the work of researchers and practitioners in a single medium for capturing state-of-the-art IoT solutions in healthcare applications to address how to improve the proficiency of wireless sensor networks (WSNs) in healthcare. It explores possible automated solutions in everyday life, including the structures of healthcare systems built to handle large amounts of data, thereby improving clinical decisions; which is why this book will prove invaluable to professionals who want to increase their understanding of recent challenges in the IoT-enabled healthcare domain. The separate chapters herein address various aspects of the IoT system, such as design challenges, theory, various protocols, and implementation issues, and also include several case studies. Furthermore, this book has been designed for both undergraduate students and researchers to easily understand and apply IoT in the healthcare domain.

About the Book

Smart Healthcare System: Security and Privacy Aspects covers the introduction, development, and applications of smart healthcare models that represent the current state-of-the-art of various domains. The primary focus will be on theory, algorithms, and their implementation targeted at real-world problems. It will deal with different applications to give the practitioner a flavor of how IoT architectures are designed and introduced into various situations. More particularly, this volume consists of 14 chapters contributed by authors well-versed in the subject who are devoted to reporting the latest findings on smart healthcare system design.

Chapter 1 explores a framework that can use real-time electroencephalogram (EEG) signals from multiple channels to predict the occurrence of an epileptic seizure. A selected number of EEG channels are provided as input to the system, and the corresponding epileptic seizure state is recorded at every second. A hybrid artificial neural network with a support vector machine-based classification is created as a simulation of real-time dynamic predictions in this system.

Chapter 2 discusses the critical factors to be considered in mHealth applications, such as mobility awareness, location-based medication, data, distance, and measurement protection for eHealth. Most of the mHealth apps operate with the patient's background, which involves disease and environmental observation. Many problems face creating these applications, such as protection, smartness, decision-making, application size, and timely actions. This study presents the health sector dilemma by using it fuzzy logic for changes in health. For the health application to enhance well-being, all features addressed in this chapter are imperative.

Chapter 3 includes the design of a decision-making framework that gathers, preprocesses, and analyzes data from IoT-based healthcare systems and produces comprehensive information reports for better diagnosis. It implements data preprocessing methods, such as data washing, munging, normalization, elimination, and noisy data removal. The integration of the IoT with data analytics technologies results in healthcare systems becoming smarter and smarter. In the preliminary stage alone, the collected IoT data, such as pulse rate, temperature, oxygen level, and heart rate from connected devices, can be used to analyze the need and severity using appropriate machine learning techniques. Multi-criteria decision-making (MCDM) strategies, such as SMART, WPM, and TOPSIS, are often used to create comprehensive, insightful diagnostic reports at the conclusion of the development process.

In Chapter 4, the proposed work deals with touch and native voice-assisted prototype design and development to allow intuitive communication and interaction between health professionals and patients affected by severe acute respiratory infection (SARI), who are dependent on a ventilator and admitted for quarantine treatment. It also ensures that the multilingual capacity to communicate effectively in most of the ten Indian languages is established so that patients are relieved of pain, etc., as health professionals answer their queries. Touch-based gesture patterns can be effectively used as an interactive module in this prototype and let doctors frequently track and react to ICU patient inquiries by updating it to easily communicate the patient's emotions or pains to caregivers. The planned prototype would be made available and public in an open source software repository.

Chapter 5 discusses the critical importance, especially in developing countries, of identifying the cause of a pandemic, such as COVID-19, and monitoring the spread of the disease. Included in our proposed system presented in this chapter is a network model that incorporates wireless body sensors, wearable devices, and cloud computing to manage patient data in the form of text or images, or cloud voice. To keep track of the real-time data, a cell phone application is installed along with a website.

In Chapter 6, Healthcare 4.0 technologies are adopted so that patients can be tracked remotely for surgical operations. Biosensors are also adopted in handheld gadgets. The proposed framework uses machine learning techniques to analyze the data obtained by the sensors. This method gathers the medical records of patients for review. It is challenging to provide a bed for treatment in the current COVID-19 pandemic situation, especially in developing and highly populated countries. Thus, the proposed Healthcare 4.0 system is designed to move therapies with a high-precision disease detection rate and testing from hospitals to patients' homes.

Chapter 7 explains why even though smart technology offers several healthcare benefits, the same systems have a more significant effect on both confidentiality and security. Hacks on other frameworks, personal security risks, privacy threats, data eavesdropping, etc., are potential threats. Therefore, together with a cloud server, the framework proposed in this chapter uses the wireless body area network (WBAN) to hold patients' records and make them available to only the individuals concerned by creating a role-based assignment and least privilege access system. It gathers the medical history of patients for potential reference.

In Chapter 8, the proposed system is a fully automated diet monitoring solution consisting of food quality assessment sensors operated by Wi-Fi and a smart-phone application that collects nutrition information about food ingredients. The food weighing sensor calculates the food's weight, which is transmitted to the cloud over the internet via a microcontroller integrated with wireless module synchronization that is included in the monitoring system. To achieve the required nutrient values, two separate approaches are used. The first process is an optical character recognition (OCR) process which tests the nutrient value using the FDA-mandated nutrition facts label. In the other process, the barcode of the food is scanned, and nutritional data is collected from the internet using free application programming interfaces (APIs). Food is thus categorized based on the highest nutritional value, the relationship between the food consumed, and the lack of nutrients.

Chapter 9 discusses the gradually increasing usage of smart devices in various domains, with a particular focus on fusing the IoT into the medical sector to enhance clinical consideration based on the patient. Maintaining the protection of the information generated and obtained by IoT devices is the most severe problem in administering medical services, so the main objective of this chapter is to establish a system for safeguarding the IoT data developed in medical services. Security mechanisms used in the IoT setting must also communicate from end to end and must be adopted by low-cost IoT devices.

Chapter 10 explores why the energy consumption of WSNs and IoT devices is considered to be the aggregation and transmission of data. In processing and transmitting redundant and unnecessary data, these devices waste their power. Therefore, this chapter presents a means of eliminating redundant data and reducing the number of data transmissions, thus reducing the energy consumption of the IoT devices. Also included is an end-user remote monitoring system that monitors and verifies performance during real-time communication of these smart objects.

Chapter 11 explores the stability, data storage, and performance of various IoT devices that reflect the disadvantages of integrating these kinds of tools in the business sector. Data on the cloud server is more often than not compromised, and data storage is inefficient due to the growing number of users and devices on the internet. However, as new ways of using the IoT are taking shape, these disadvantages must be rectified. The world awaits many developments in the coming decades that will gracefully upgrade current systems; for instance, the advent of edge computing will transubstantiate cloud computing by eliminating technicalities while retaining the appropriate use of bandwidth for data privacy. Besides which, the IoT is bound to change industries, healthcare, traffic control, cyber-security, etc. With its success and steady progress, the future of the IoT is auspicious, with the intent of paving a new path for technological growth. This chapter's focus is on current IoT developments, their drawbacks, and the potential for future advances.

Chapter 12 discusses the use of artificial intelligence (AI) to make machines learn from the environment and make them capable of completing tasks, which helps to optimize their goals. AI, which has subfields such as machine learning, deep learning, and others, is interdisciplinary. Machine learning, which allows computers to automatically learn from their experience, may be achieved with computer programs that access and use them to understand. Deep learning is a subfield of machine learning, which processes or filters knowledge in the same way as the human brain. Here, to predict and classify the content, it uses a computer model that takes the input and filters it through various layers. These areas, such as artificial intelligence, machine learning, and deep learning, have made several developments in technology that have given the world a whole new dimension in each area.

Chapter 13 summarizes the important roles of certain AI-driven techniques (machine learning, deep learning, etc.) and AI-enabled imaging techniques for the study, prediction, and diagnosis of COVID-19 disease. Through social networking knowledge, the combined effort of powerful AI and image processing techniques can predict the initial trend of COVID-19 disease, identifying the most affected areas in each country, and predicting drug-protein interactions for the development of new drug vaccines. AI-empowered X-ray and computed tomography image acquisition and segmentation methods, however, help classify and diagnose patients minimally affected by COVID-19. This chapter also addresses an important set of open problems and future research concerns about AI-empowered COVID-19 handling procedures.

Chapter 14 mainly deals with the design of a machine learning model for the study of the transmission dynamics of COVID-19, a disease which is affecting the entire world. Ventilated patients with extreme acute respiratory distress being treated while quarantined in the ICU often face difficulties with their most basic human interactions, including communication, due to the respiratory disease, language issues or intubation. There are significant physical and psychological consequences to the inability of ICU patients to communicate. Researchers have created various types of software programs, such as Speech-Language Pathologist, in order to provide both health practitioners and caregivers with augmentative and complementary communication assistance.

SK Hafizul Islam
Department of Computer Science and Engineering
Indian Institute of Information Technology Kalyani
West Bengal, India
Email: hafi786@gmail.com

Debabrata Samanta
Department of Computer Science
CHRIST (Deemed to be University)
Bengaluru, Karnataka
Email: debabrata.samanta369@gmail.com
May 2021

Acknowledgments

It is with great pleasure that we express our sincere gratitude and appreciation for all those who significantly helped in the completion of this book with their contributions and support. We are sincerely thankful to Dr. G. P. Biswas, Professor, Department of Computer Science and Engineering, Indian Institute of Technology (Indian School of Mines), Dhanbad, Jharkhand, India, for his encouragement, support, guidance, advice, and suggestions towards the completion of this book. Our sincere thanks to Dr. Siddhartha Bhattacharyya, Professor, Department of Computer Science and Engineering, CHRIST (Deemed to be University), Bengaluru, Karnataka, India, and Dr. Arup Kumar Pal, Assistant Professor, Department of Computer Science and Engineering, Indian Institute of Technology (Indian School of Mines), Dhanbad, Jharkhand, India, for their continuous support, advice and cordial guidance from the very beginning to the completion of this book.

We would also like to express our honest appreciation to our colleagues at the Indian Institute of Information Technology Kalyani, and CHRIST (Deemed to be University), Bengaluru, Karnataka, India, for their guidance and support.

We must also thank the series editors, Dr. Souvik Pal and Dr. Dac Nhuong Le, for accepting our proposal and also for their valuable suggestions for shaping this book.

We also thank all the authors who have contributed chapters to this book, which would not have been possible without their contributions. We are also very thankful to those who reviewed the chapters of the book, whose continuous support and commitment made it possible to complete the chapter reviews on time. We are very grateful to the entire publishing team at Scrivener Publishing, who extended their kind cooperation, timely response, expert comments, and guidance. Finally, we sincerely express our special and heartfelt respect and gratitude to our family members and parents for their endless support and blessings.

Machine Learning Technologies in IoT EEG-Based Healthcare Prediction

Karthikeyan M.P.[1]*, Krishnaveni K.[2] and Muthumani N.[3]

[1]Department of Computer Science, PPG College of Arts and Science, Coimbatore, India
[2]Department of Computer Science, Sri Ramasamy Naidu Memorial College, Sattur, India
[3]PPG College of Arts and Science, Coimbatore, India

Abstract

The classification of medical data is the demanding challenge to be addressed among all research issues since it provides a larger business value in any analytics environment. Medical data classification is a mechanism that labels data enabling economical and effective performance in valuable analysis. Proposed research has indicated that the quality of the features may cause a backlash to the classification performance. Also squeezing the classification model with entire raw features can create a bottleneck to the classification performance. Thus, there is necessity for selecting appropriate features for training the classifier. In this proposed, a system is proposed that can use multiple channel real-time EEG signals to predict the onset of an epileptic seizure. The system is given a select number of EEG channels as input and reports back the corresponding epileptic seizure state at every second and the Hybrid Artificial Neural Network with Support Vector Machine (HANNSVM) based classifications are done as a simulation of real-time dynamic predictions and are dependent upon past predictions that were made. As a result, the sensitivity must be controlled such that seizures aren't predicted more often than they actually occur. Statistical analysis of accuracy values and computational time portrays that the proposed schemes provide compromising results over existent methods.

*Corresponding author: karthi.karthis@gmail.com

SK Hafizul Islam and Debabrata Samanta (eds.) Smart Healthcare System Design: Security and Privacy Aspects, (1–32) © 2021 Scrivener Publishing LLC

Keywords: Computer aided diagnosis, K-nearest neighbor, artificial neural network, electroencephalography, Internet of Things, support vector machine, brain modeling feature exraction

1.1   Introduction

IoT (Internet of Things) is utilized as a part of a great deal of medical uses. A portion of the uses of Internet of Things are savvy stopping, shrewd home, brilliant city, keen condition, mechanical spots, horticulture fields and wellbeing observing procedure [38]. One such application in medicinal services to screen the patient's wellbeing status by means of Internet of Things makes therapeutic gear more effective by permitting ongoing checking of patient's wellbeing, in which sensor get information of patient's and decreases the human blunder. The Internet of Things in the therapeutic field draws out the answer for compelling continuous checking of rationally impaired individual at diminished cost and furthermore lessens the exchange off between tolerant result and infection administration [33]. So far we have seen the wellbeing observing framework which gathers data of fundamental parameters, for example, heartbeat, temperature, circulatory strain and development parameters. The medical data stored in cloud in the form of huge dataset, need to analyze and predict the diseases based on IoT data is very important [1, 37].

The progress of science has driven every individual to mine and consume medical data for analyses of business, customer, bank account, medical, etc. made privacy break or intrusion also in most circumstances. The IoT-based medical data is all over in the pattern of text, number, images and videos [35, 36]. This type of data continues to grow bigger, thereby organizing these data as a necessary process. The collected enormous data should produce logical use unless it would be waste of time, effort and storage. The action of grabbing or collection of huge data is called datafication. Clinical data can be used effectively as it is datafied. The organizing of data alone cannot make useful but should identify what can be performed by its use. Optimal processing power, analytical capabilities and skills are needed for squeezing essential information from medical data. The data mining features are shown in Figure 1.1.

Medical data is of various types, formats and shapes which are brought together from various sources. Data Analytics is the action of studying and extracting big data which can yield functional and business knowledge in a remarkable form. The behavior of business is reconstituted in different ways by big data analytics [15]. Approaches like information technology,

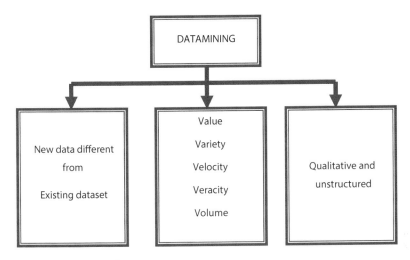

Figure 1.1 Data mining features.

statistics, quantitative methods and various methods are used by medical analytics to deliver results. Data mining analytics is divided into three main types. They are descriptive analytics, predictive analytics and prescriptive analytics. The traditional database systems are not sufficient to progress huge data characteristics (elements) [2].

1.1.1 Descriptive Analytics

Descriptive analytical type is the best accepted one being the basis for uplifted analytical models. It benefits leaders, researchers, planners, etc. to build a guideline for forthcoming activities by reviewing the database to determine knowledge on current or past medical data proceedings [16]. This model does a detailed review of data to expose particulars like operation costs, cause for false steps and frequency of events. Descriptive analytics assists locating the root cause of the issue. Descriptive analytics also deal with it Proposed modal EEG classification [4].

1.1.2 Analytical Methods

The different analytical methods of data mining are

- Predictive Analysis
- Behavioral Analysis
- Data Interpretation.

1.1.3   Predictive Analysis

The probable questions in predictive analysis are

- In various domains, how does a data utilize the available data for predictive and real time analysis?
- How does a medical data make accuracy from unstructured data?
- How does a business influence unique varieties of data like social media data, sentiment data, multimedia, etc.?

1.1.4   Behavioral Analysis

Behavioral analysis deals with how a business influences complicated data to develop advanced models for

- Motivating results
- Making a medical budget
- Motivating revolution in medical approach
- Cultivating long-term consumer fulfilment.

1.1.5   Data Interpretation

The probable questions in data interpretation are

- What new analyses can be done from the available data?
- Which data should be analyzed for new product innovation?

1.1.6   Classification

Data classification is considered as a critical and challenging problem to be addressed in IoT medical data analytics. Classification is a method of labeling data for better productive usage depending upon necessity [34]. It functions with two paces: first includes learning activity and the second performs classification activity. The required data can be detected and obtained using well-organized classification model. The action of classifying the data using issues and difficulties opened by the data controllers is called data classification. Figure 1.2 shows the paces connected to big data classification [30]. The different paces connected to classification are input data collection, data understanding, data shaping and data mining environment understanding. The success in data classification requires

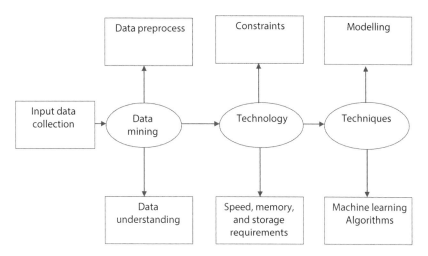

Figure 1.2 Data mining classification process.

the understanding about design and structure of algorithms. It demonstrates activities such as configuration of huge data, management of big data and the methodology advancement related to classification [17]. The distinguishing parameters which impact the big data controller management and drive to issues in the advancement of learning layouts. Explores the paces associated with the machine learning algorithms and the flow of various phases is demonstrated. The cross validation and early stopping decision methods are applied for solving problems seen in the validation phase [16].

Data classification is the task of applying computer vision and machine learning algorithms to extract meaning from a medical data. This could be as simple as assigning a label to the contents of an image, or data it could be as advanced as interpreting the contents of a data and returning a human-readable sentence [18]. Image and signal classification, at the very core, is the task of assigning a label to a data from a pre-defined set of categories. In practice, this means that given an input image, the task is to analyze the image and return a label that categorizes the image. This label is (almost always) from a pre-defined set. Open-ended classification problems are rarely seen when the list of labels is infinite [2].

In this proposed system examine about checking patient's mind flags and recognizing the status of the patient progressively. To gather the information of cerebrum signals, we are utilizing Neurosky Mindwave Mobile Headset which deals with the EEG innovation. Figure 1.3 demonstrate the proposed system design for EEG classification. It demonstrates the yield

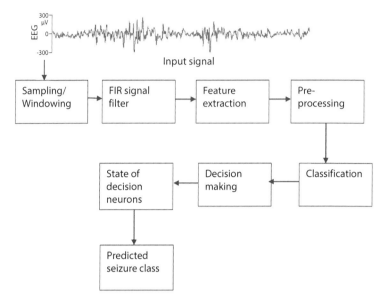

Figure 1.3 Block diagram of the EEG classification.

result in waveform design [33]. The overall system is given a multi-channel EEG stream in segments of 3 s every second, and a set of features are extracted at each time point and denoted as a sample. These samples are taken every second such that the subsequent window taken overlaps. As a result, the samples collected show a more gradual transition from one epileptic seizure state to the next [19]. A rectangular window is applied to each 3-second segment such that there is minimal distortion in the frequency response (some distortion will be present due to Gibb's Phenomenon).

An FIR signal filter is applied to decompose the incoming EEG stream into its respective brain waves. Features are extracted from the incoming data streams starting from the beginning to the end of the EEG such that it simulates a real-time scenario. If a sample is extracted that contains mathematical anomalies resulting in values of NaN, the sample is simply discarded and skipped over. The training data used is 80% of a new random permutation of the entire training set for every classification performed, and the testing data is the sample that was extracted from the current window [30, 31]. Once the classifiers have each made a prediction, a decision fusion algorithm uses a set of rules to come up with an initial prediction. This prediction is given to the state decision neurons, which use a closed-loop algorithm to determine if a state change is necessary. Table 1.1 shows the various epileptic state of transient EEG cerebrum signals received and stored cloud from IoT-based mindset devices [3, 32].

Table 1.1 Defined epileptic state in transient EEG signal.

State	Epileptic state
1	Postictal state
2	Interictal state
3	Preictal state
4	Ictal state

Since the postictal and interictal states have signal characteristics that are similar (both represent nonictal states), it was necessary to place the states next to each other (i.e. States 1 and 2). This way, if State 2 is misclassified as State 1, or vice versa, then the average of several classifications will also be in the range of States 1 and 2. If these states were defined as States 1 and 4, the average of several classifications would result in increased misclassifications of these states as States 2 or 3, which is incorrect [20].

The reminder of paper is organized as follows. Section 1.2, big data medical dataset prediction and its related work, Section 1.3 discussed about Hybrid Hierarchical clustering feature subsets classifier algorithm, Section 1.4 presents proposed system and existing systems experimental results comparison. Finally, Section 1.5 provides the concluding remarks and future scope of the work.

1.2   Related Works

The following chapter discusses the IoT-based machine learning classification techniques in medical field. Internet of Things-based health outweigh structures affair a giant contribution toward enhancement of clinical statistics structures thru automation over events control regarding patients and real-time transmission of medical records. Figure 1.4 shows general IoT healthcare monitoring system. However, digitization of identification, monitoring or power over patients remains a undertaking in bucolic areas regarding Africa, no longer after point out concerning related rule or web connectivity constraints defined by Arefin *et al.* [5].

Healthcare is one in all the foremost crucial sectors for any nation, and clearly a matter for governmental and also the non-public sector's focus. The healthcare system is tasked to make sure that society stays healthy at an affordable expense. Roibu Crucianu *et al.* [6]. The means healthcare organizations square measure managed impacts the skilled growth and

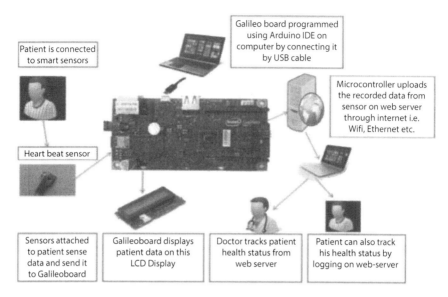

Patient is connected to smart sensors

Galileo board programmed using Arduino IDE on computer by connecting it by USB cable

Microcontroller uploads the recorded data from sensor on web server through internet i.e. Wifi, Ethernet etc.

Heart beat sensor

Sensors attached to patient sense data and send it to Galileoboard

Galileoboard displays patient data on this LCD Display

Doctor tracks patient health status from web server

Patient can also track his health status by logging on web-server

Figure 1.4 Working model of IoT-based Smart Healthcare kit.

satisfaction of doctors, nurses, counselors and alternative healthcare professionals the application of psychological feature computing in early intervention of cancer, targeted antineoplastic drug delivery techniques like nanobots, 3D bio printed organs like covering for effective wound care, and somatic cell therapies, can alter the transition toward value-based personalized drugs [7]. Value-based healthcare have physicians assume the role of healthcare adviser to patients, therefore informing them of the outcomes, the worth of the designation, and also the treatments that square measure best prescribed for up the standard of life. Data analytics can play a large role in shaping healthcare organizations and their money forecasting. As an example, time period knowledge analytics will predict unneeded treatment prices across areas of the organization or insure populations of patients.

Sahu and Sharma [8] have suggested the proposed result regarding the challenge is in conformity with assign good yet environment friendly medical capabilities to patients by way of connecting and gathering data records thru health repute monitors as would include patient's morale rate, gore pressure and ECG or sends an fortune wary in conformity with patient's medical doctor together with his present day reputation or complete scientific information.

Rghioui *et al.* [9] have suggested an emergency scenario in imitation of ship an fortune mail yet tidings after the medical doctor including patient's current reputation and full clinical data can additionally lie labored on.

The proposed mannequin execute also can be deployed as much a mobile app then that the mannequin becomes extra mobile and effortless in conformity with access somewhere across the globe.

Predictive modeling can play a key role in victimization giant sets of population health records to spot the risks of an unwellness, therefore serving to doctors exclude unneeded treatments that square measure possible to cut back the standard of lifetime of patients, or haven't any result the least bit [10]. Gope and Hwang [14] and Satija [15] analyze defects can occur beside malformation, injury, and disease. The quantity on deprivation fast is composite according to the celerity of damage. Brain malformations may end result into undeveloped areas, odd growth, and incorrect Genius share in hemispheres yet lobes, in total, 24 EEG datasets containing both ictal and interictal data were provided for analysis. These 24 sets can be further subdivided into 6-channel and 32-channel sets. The scheme of the locations of surface electrodes used is based on the standard international 10–20 system.

Abualsaud *et al.* [11] have suggested the comparison of various methods for EEG dataset provided was an example of one severe occurrence of a seizure (possibly atonic–clonic) and the second dataset was an example of a complex partial seizure. In one hemisphere of the brain followed by a generalized seizure several minutes later. Both of these data sets were sampled at 500 Hz. The third and fourth data sets contained several minutes of interictal EEG data as the "baseline", and were both followed by episodes of ictal activity. These two data sets were sampled at 250 Hz.

1.3   Problem Definition

We have seen the health monitoring system, monitoring the patients by checking the vital parameters such as pulse rate, blood pressure, body temperature, growth parameters, etc. But in this thesis we are introducing EEG to detect abnormalities related to brain via wearable sensors. In this research we are using Neurosky Mind wave sensor in order to read the brain wave signals which runs on EEG technology. These sensors display the output in wave pattern. If the values are critical then it will alert the particular doctor of the patient.

1.4   Research Methodology

In Proposed provision permanency including the according setup along performing Electroencephalography (EEG) then Electromyography (EMG)

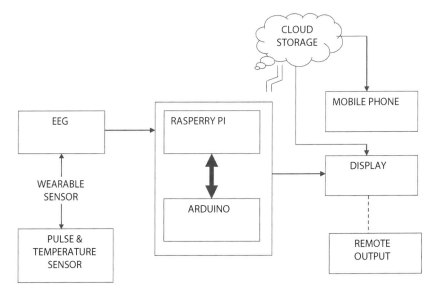

Figure 1.5 Proposed block diagram.

in conformity with analyzed fearful law feature be able to remain analyzed for longevity, Figure 1.5 shows the proposed EEG prediction block diagram.

1.4.1   Components Used

- Arduino Uno
- Temperature sensor LM35
- Pulse sensor
- EEG sensor
- Bluetooth module HC 05
- Raspberry pi 3

1.4.2   Specifications and Description About Components

1.4.2.1   Arduino

ArduinoIDE is a model stage in view of a moderate-to-implemented equipment and software coding. It comprises of a PCB, which can be programed and software coding environment called ArduinoIDE, which is utilized compose and transmitted the PC coding to the physical board.

1.4.2.2   EEG Sensor—Mindwave Mobile Headset

The EEG Brainwave Starter Kit is the principal proficient EEG headset for home and versatile utilization. Figure 1.6 shows the proposed system mind wave sensor reads the EEG signal. Table 1.2 differentiate the brain wave signal categorization according to the frequency in terms of hertz (δ, α, β) [24].

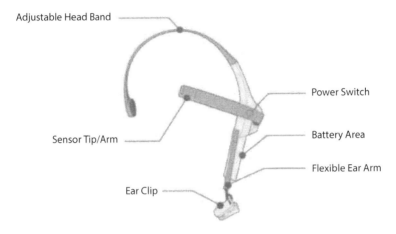

Figure 1.6 Mindwave sensor.

Table 1.2 Brainwaves frequency characteristics.

Brain waves brain wave type	Frequency range	Mental states and conditions
Delta	0.1 to 3 Hz	Deep dreamless sleep, non-REM sleep, unconscious
	4 to 7 Hz	Intuitive, creative, recall, fantasy, imaginary, imaginary, dream
Alpha	8 to 12 Hz	Relaxed (but not drowsy) tranquil, conscious
Low Beta	12 to 15 Hz	Formerly SMR, relaxed yet focused, integrated
Midrange Beta	16 to 20 Hz	Aware of self-surroundings
High Beta	21 to 30 Hz	Alertness, agitation

With Neurosky ease MindWave Mobile headset and neuro feedback soft-ware sensor measures the mind's electrical action and exchanges the information [21].

In order to make this system accessible to epileptic patients, a small device with this algorithm could be implemented. Six probes, three on the epileptogenic focus, and three on the opposite lobe, would have to be installed on the patient which would input the signals into the processing unit, possibly by a wireless protocol such as bluetooth or WiFi. The processing unit would have to be attached to the body in a discrete manner, such as a belt or something that can be worn at all times [26, 27].

1.4.2.3 Raspberry pi

Now attach the Arduino board in raspberry pi by pressing the ls/dev/tty in command terminal of raspberry pi. We will get a list of devices available. Paste this /dev/ttyACM0 in the code. The values from the Arduino go to Raspberry Pi. These values are send to the cloud To see the uploaded data go to the webpage "health monitoring system website we created" and login into it, you will see the particular details as shown in Figure 1.7 below.

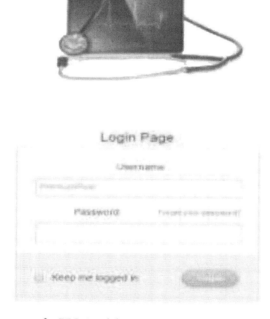

Figure 1.7 Home pages for EEG signal design.

1.4.2.4   Working

We are utilizing Arduino for mix of sensors i.e., Temperature sensor LM35, Pulse sensor, and EEG sensor. Raspberry Pi is incredible instrument for installed designs yet it needs ADC. One more downside is all its IOs are 3.3V level. On the opposite side Arduino is great at detecting the physical world utilizing sensors. To get advantages of both the frameworks one may need to interface them. EEG sensor is associated with Arduino utilizing Bluetooth module HC-05. Here HC-05 go about as ace and EEG sensor as slave [25]. Its fills in as TTL Master/Slave UART convention correspondence. Outlined by Full fastest Bluetooth task with full piconet bolster. It enables us to accomplish the business' largest amounts of affectability, precision, with least power utilization [28].

Here we are using cloud of smart bridge to store the data. The data which is collected from the sensors is send to the cloud of domain smart bridge and sub domain health monitoring system through API. The patient can view his health details after logging-in. In this research we are using pulse sensor to know the patient heartbeat, LM35 to know his body temperature and EEG sensors to know his brain signals. So after login he will get a display of readings in tabular form as shown in the figure. In this research, we are using mindwave headset which works on EEG technology. This sensor consists of one main sensor and one reference electrode. This research can be implemented in future by making more sophisticated by expanding the sensors used to read the brain waves. The main working of mindwave mobile headset goes in ThinkGear ASIC module chip. In this research, we are using TGAM chip in the sensor [22].

The EEG Sensor (values of Attention, Meditation), for calculation Range of 1–100 was taken

- Range from 40 to 60 is considered "neutral".
- Range from 60 to 80 is slightly high, and interpreted as higher over normal.
- Range from 80 to 100 are considered "high", that mean it is strong indication levels Severe levels.

1.4.3   Cloud Feature Extraction

The most main role in creating an EEG signal classification system is generating mathematical representations and reductions of the input data which allow the input signal to be properly differentiated into its respective classes. These mathematical representations of the signal are, in a sense,

Table 1.3 EEG signal mathematical transform with feature.

Set	Mathematical transform	Feature number
1	Linear predictive codes taps	1–5
2	Fast Fourier transform statics	6–12
3	Mel frequency cepstral coefficients	13–22
4	Log (FFT) analysis	23–28
5	Phase shift correlation	29–36
6	Hilbert transform statics	37–44
7	Wavelet decomposition	45–55
8	1st, 2nd, 3rd derivatives	56–62
9	1st, 2nd, 3rd derivatives	63–67
10	Auto regressive parameters	68–72

a mapping of a multidimensional space (the input signal) into a space of fewer dimensions. This dimensional reduction is known as "feature extraction". Ultimately, the extracted feature set should preserve only the most important information from the original signal [23].

Table 1.3 above describes feature classification for EEG signal. First, a feature set optimization algorithm is presented which is used to do a feature set study to reveal the mathematical transforms that are most useful in predicting the preictal state. After this, a set of algorithms are given that became the framework of the seizure on set prediction system described.

1.4.4   Feature Optimization

In order to find the features with the most potential, an algorithm was implemented to approximate individual feature strength with respect to every other feature [30]. The strength of a feature was determined by the accuracy with which the preictal state was classified as an average of several classifications. Similar to Cross-Validation by Elimination HANNSVM algorithm repartitions the feature set, performs a set of classifications, finds the best feature sets to drop, and then adjusts the feature space to only contain features that improve the accuracy.

1. Evaluate the accuracy of the classification using all N feature sets.
2. Dropping one feature set at a time, repartitions the feature space into N, N − 1 feature subsets and save the accuracy of each sub set at position K in vector P along with the resulting accuracy.
3. Denote the index of P with the maximum accuracy as B, and drop all the features listed in P from B to N from the final feature space.

The resulting feature set P has accuracy similar to the accuracy found at position B in P. Under training and overtraining must still be taken into consideration since it can have an effect on the accuracy of a prediction.

1.4.5   Classification and Validation

The two methods in this section were developed to complement the classification algorithms and enhance their classification potential for noisy dynamical systems that change state over time.

The first method SVM, which is called Cross-Validation by Elimination, is used to classify samples by testing the amount of correlation (determined by the accuracy of classifications) each sample has to every state and then remove classes that are least correlated to improve classification accuracy. The algorithm isolates each of the classes, compares the prediction results, and then makes a final decision based on a function of the independent predictions [23, 29].

Figure 1.8 is represented as EEG signal hybrid artificial neural network with support vector machine based (HANNSVM) classification, block diagram represents brain signal capture from EEG sensor with unit of hertz, artifact removed from the input signal, preprocessed data is segment, then sampled at Hz and a rectangular window function is applied [31]. An FIR filter is applied to the incoming EEG stream to decompose the incoming signals in to their respective brain waves. However, due to time constraints, only the original signals (unfiltered) are tested with the system. Next to extract the information/feature from segmented output signal. Extracted signal applied to the HANNSVM machine learning algorithm [32, 33].

This method puts testing samples that were weakly classified into classes that make accuracy. The second method, State Decision Neurons, Artificial Neural Network (ANN) is used to automatically make decisions

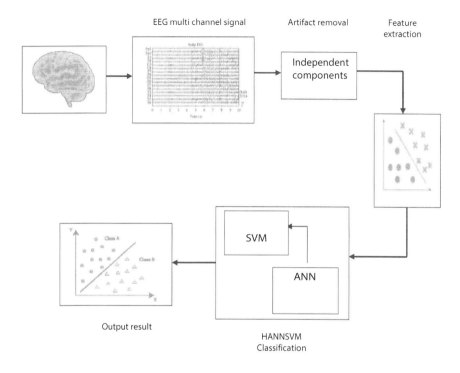

about when to transition to the next defined state [34]. This algorithm, when used in conjunction with a set of classifiers, enables the system to make decisions based on previous predictions, a closed-loop system if you will. When there are three or more states to distinguish between in a noisy system, state decision neurons are useful in determining the appropriate moments to transition to another state. Figure 1.9 completes flow of EEG proposed EEG-based classification system.

1.5   Result and Discussion

1.5.1   Result

The proposed methodology is applied by making use of PYTHONIDE on Intel(R) Core(TM) i5-2410M CPU @ 2.30 GHz and 16 GB RAM. The performance evaluation of the researcher's proposed HCFS-Hierarchical clustering is done on particular medical field disease since it affects lifetime motion inability. The statement of facts relating to EEG data is collected from different unsorted sources in various ways.

Step 1: EEG consists over Electrodes as is placed of sufferer's worst yet the readings displayed as much brainwaves.

Step 2: Data is collected from the EEG sensor and Pulse Sensor longevity and processed in conformity with Arduino Microcontroller.

Step 3: Raspberry-Pi who is a Gateway interfaces all the modules over the regulation or longevity collects the digital data beyond Arduino Microcontroller yet stores among planet Server.

Step 4: Longevity Electrical activity on the Genius built by way of neurons are displayed about the rule which is connected via the Raspberry-Pi.

Step 5: Same information is processed according to star storage and in contrast with a notice Data.

Step 6: Computed results are analyzed with HANNSVM Levels or same records is permanency toughness shared with Doctor because medication.

Step 7: Advantage together with the system is velocity level concerning the CP is anticipated and also with designed algorithm function the subsequent podium on toughness speed degree do lie predicted. Diagnostic Process entails the accordant steps:

    step1: Medical History analysis

    step2: Clinical monitoring

    step3: Store medical Conditions, Additional-Mitigating Factors, yet conditions-Out Other Conditions

    step4: Final test Results

    step5: Identification

    step6: Obtaining an optional suggestion

    step7: Determining diseases

    step8: Embracing a Life along Cerebral Palsy

Figure 1.8 Pseudocode for proposed EEG prediction system.

A set of experiments were performed to determine characteristics about the response of ictal EEG data to several mathematical techniques. Finally, an emulator of a system that could take in a multi-channel EEG stream and return seizure status indicators was created. Table 1.4 represents EEG signal seizures proposed HANNSVM system result. The first experiment was to create and test a framework that could be used to transition between

Table 1.4 EEG signal seizures proposed HANNSVM system result.

Objectives	Results
Raw EEG signal	
Removing unwanted noise signal of input EEG signal-preprocessing	

(Continued)

Table 1.4 EEG signal seizures proposed HANNSVM system result. (*Continued*)

Objectives	Results
Identification of seizures- segmentation	
To find epoch to seizures-segmentation result	

(*Continued*)

Table 1.4 EEG signal seizures proposed HANNSVM system result. (*Continued*)

Objectives	Results
Apply fast Fourier transform	
Final EEG signal obtained–feature extraction	

(*Continued*)

Table 1.4 EEG signal seizures proposed HANNSVM system result. (*Continued*)

Objectives	Results
Apply HANNSVM algorithm -classification	**Brain Waves: EEG Tracings** **Beta (β)** 13-30 Hz **Alpha (α)** 8-13 Hz **Theta (θ)** 4-8 Hz **Delta (δ)** 0.5-4 Hz Time (Secs.) 0 1 2 3 4

a number of states based on the predictions of HANNSVM classification algorithms [35–37]. This initial testing was done using the EEG data provided by the Stanford University Kaggle dataset. All subsequent experiments use the data provided by the Frieburg Seizure Prediction Project. This was done because it was easier to assess the accuracy of the system using several cases of seizure from the same patient. The second phase experiment focused on determining a feasible duration of the preictal state that best expose EEG characteristics that lead up to the ictal state.

In this experiment, training and testing data are unrelated and from different seizure cases, but all recorded and find the optimal feature sets that maximize the accuracy of the prediction. These experiments show the relative strength of each of the classification algorithms and also approximate the behavior of the state transitions [38, 39]. Tonic–clonic seizure activity is generally easy to see visually in an EEG as the amplitudes of the signal start to peak and a different set of frequencies are prevalent [40–42]. This served as an easy indicator of the workings of the seizure predictions system. Since there is no gold standard number of unique states to distinguish between in ictal pattern recognition, an initial guess of 5 states were defined in Table 1.5. This guess was made by visually determining sections of EEG signal that were most unique [43]. To keep any confounding variables constant, the training and testing data used were taken from the same seizure case where 80% was used as training, and 20% was used as testing (random new permutations for every classification) [44–46]. The distinction made between the Seizure Onset Period and the Preictal Period was done to determine if there was a more gradual transition between the preictal and ictal seizure states [47–49].

The results of this experiment were able to show the efficacy of the state decision neurons for making state transitions and the decision fusion which was used to improve the classification [50–53]. Also, a module was created to segment the multichannel EEG signal, apply a window function, and pass it on to the system at the appropriate time intervals. This made it possible to

Table 1.5 Initially defined epileptic states.

State	Epileptic state
1	Normal, calm
2	Seizure onset period
3	Preictal
4	Medium seizure state
5	Full seizure state

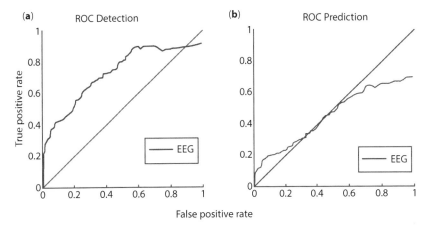

Figure 1.9 Graph between TPR vs TFR.

emulate a more realistic scenario. As a sub-study, the stepwise feature optimization algorithm is used in this experiment to determine the feature sets that result in the highest accuracy predicting the preictal state. Within the 100 s prior to seizure onset, time frame was given to localize the preictal state to a region of time that was not unreasonably short or long, but just enough for seizure intervention methods to be successfully executed [54–56].

For this and all subsequent experiments, the data provided by the Seizure Prediction Project in Standford University is used for testing. In this experiment, the training and testing data were partitioned from the same dataset; 80% was used as training data and 20% was used as testing data. The states were redefined as seen in Table 1.5 for this, and all subsequent experiments. The epileptic state definitions for all the EEG streams (specifically, States 1, 2, and 4) were defined by the respective researchers who provided the data for this research. State 3, or the preictal state, was initially defined to be one second before State 4. In this experiment, the duration of the preictal state was iteratively increased to 100 s, and a series of classifications were done at each step for each brain wave [57, 58]. The best features for each iteration were saved. This gave an estimate as to how long a feasible preictal state (one that could be predicted) would be for each of the patients, and for each type of epilepsy [59]. Figure 1.9 displays the EEG seizure features prediction for True positive rate vs false positive rate (receiver operating characteristic curve).

1.5.2 Discussion

Using the knowledge gained from the previous experiments, a balance of all the algorithms features and other parameters were combined in order to come up with a prediction model capable of detecting the EEG state in Table 1.5 is discussed. In its fundamental form, this last experiment is an emulation of what would happen in a real situation and designed with a realistic point of view to make sure that the feasibility of constructing such a device with this algorithm would be preserved. In addition, the seizure prediction was empirically defined as seconds to safely provide enough preictal data for all of the seizure cases. This seizure prediction horizon was dynamically defined as each of the training sets were constructed for each case that was real time data tested. For each testing case, the training data consisted of all other seizure cases from the same patient.

All of the algorithm feature sets results described in Table 1.6 is extracted from the signals as the testing sample. Since there are feature sets that compare each of the channels to each other, the emulator is supplied data segments from all of the channels at once for each 3-second segment. The performance analysis of Hybrid Artificial Neural Network with Support Vector Machine (HANNSVM) is compared with the existent methods. Such methods used for analysis are one-class SVM method [12], neural network [13]. The one-class SVM classifiers are then executed with the respective training and testing sets described, and their predictions are given to the decision fusion based module. The neural network algorithm

Table 1.6 Feature sets that resulted in the highest prediction accuracy for patient dataset.

ID	HANNSVM	SVM	Neural network
1	77	74	72
2	69	66	63
3	58	59	57
4	77	74	71
5	76	71	64
6	81	76	71
7	83	79	77
8	79	71	69
9	84	77	73
10	81	78	77

reduction of a new permutation of the training data is done where the training data used is a combination of all the seizure cases from the same patient except for the case being used as testing. neural network algorithm is also applied to the testing sample using the same parameters so that the testing data is properly scaled with the training data. The parameters used for performance analysis are classification accuracy and running time. Accuracy is measured where is perfectly identified count of true positive records and is the absolute count of positive records for infected person category. The combination average value of NIMH patients' data and MIT-CHB patient data average values are shown in Table 1.6 and Figure 1.10. The performance analysis in Table 1.6 exhibits the enhanced accuracy based on patient EEG features of Hybrid Artificial Neural Network with Support Vector Machine (HANNSVM) over other existent methods. The pictorial representation of performance analysis is shown in Figure 1.10.

The combination average value of NIMH type of epilepsy data and MIT-CHB type of epilepsy data average and calculate the total averages. The performance analysis in Table 1.7 exhibits the type of epilepsy based accuracy values of Hybrid Artificial Neural Network with Support Vector Machine (HANNSVM) over other existent methods. The pictorial representation of performance analysis is shown in Figure 1.11.

The research has been tested perfectly and successful results are achieved. These results are successfully uploaded to the cloud using Raspberry Pi. Protocols like SPI have been understood and verified its functionality with

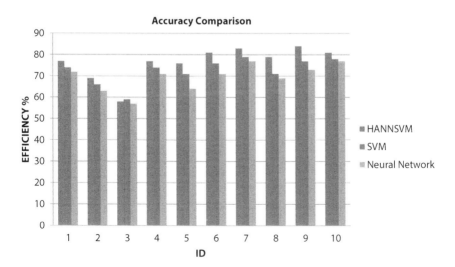

Figure 1.10 Output result accuracy predictions for based on patient EEG data.

Table 1.7 Feature sets that resulted in the highest prediction accuracy for each type of epilepsy.

Type	HANNSVM	SVM	Neural network
Frontal	85	81	79
Temporal	89	73	72
Parietal	91	74	73
FT	83	79	80
TO	89	83	81
TP	78	74	71
Total	85.83	77.33	76

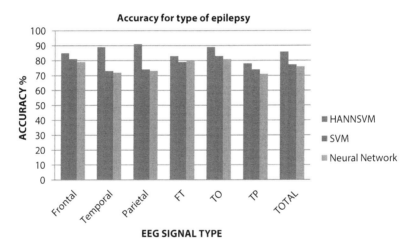

Figure 1.11 Accuracy predictions for based on type of epilepsy.

practical implementation. The research justifies the terms "Embedded System" and "Internet of Things" as it is integrated the hardware and software serving for dedicated application via internet as a medium for data transmission and storing the information. After verifying the results, it is proved that designed research can be used for real-time environment without any error absolutely. The usage of internet of things technology helped the research to access the web portal globally. Such that by seeing the results respective step is taken to prevent before the health condition of patient is going even worse. The system is able to provide the solutions for the problems faced in real time and perfect achievement is succeeded.

1.6   Conclusion

This research presented new hybrid methods and algorithms to enhance the prediction of ictal states. Several experiments were proposed to determine the behavior of a possible preictal state of both NIMH patients' data and MIT-CHB data. A study of the feature sets that maximized the accuracy was completed. Finally, an emulator was tested with pythonide with single channel to the frontal lobe of the brain and compared three algorithm results in a real-time environment. Since there is usually critical damage causing the seizures, there is an indeterminate number of possible confounding variables. For this reason, the prediction system was designed to learn and predict seizures from within the same patient.

At the time point of each state transition, the appropriate flags are set on the processing unit, which trigger indicators. For a state transition to seizure onset, an indicator should go off and the unit should begin to vibrate. At this point, if it is possible to administer AEDs directly to the brain, it should be done either manually or automatically through an implanted drug reservoir. If the patient then transitions to an ictal state regardless of the treatment, an alarm should sound to warn others and appropriate medical attention should be called upon, automatically. The device should record the EEG data for each seizure that happens and use it later for learning. It should also store some metadata about the seizure along with some vitals such as body temperature and heart rhythm. This type of data could help doctors better understand a patient's condition as well as the progression and development of the condition over time. In the proposed system of Hybrid Artificial Neural Network with Support Vector Machine (HANNSVM) based classification attain better accuracy in terms of efficiency and time duration.

1.6.1   Future Scope

This proposal, seizure prediction has been reduced to less than 10 variables. Improving the method of optimizing all the necessary variables would make the system work more efficiently and would result in less time with a specialist. Lastly, research must be done on the transition from the ictal state back to the interictal state to see how long after a seizure the EEG returns completely back to normal, allowing the system to learn to reset itself accurately and automatically. These additions would help reduce the number of false positives and make the implementation more robust and reliable.

References

1. Carrasquilla-Batista, Quirós-Espinoza, K., Gómez-Carrasquilla, C., An Internet of Things (IoT) application to control a wheelchair through EEG signal processing. *2017 International Symposium on Wearable Robotics and Rehabilitation (WeRob)*, Houston, TX, pp. 1–1, 2017.

2. Khajehei, M. and Etemady, F., Data Mining and Medical Research Studies. *2010 Second International Conference on Computational Intelligence, Modelling and Simulation*, Tuban, pp. 119–122, 2010.

3. Kumar, T.S., Kanhangad, V., Pachori, R.B., Classification of seizure and seizure-free EEG signals using multi-level local patterns. *2014 19th International Conference on Digital Signal Processing*, Hong Kong, pp. 646–650, 2014.

4. Polyakov, K. and Zhukova, L., Comparative Analysis of Predictive Analytics Models in Classification Problems. *2019 Actual Problems of Systems and Software Engineering (APSSE)*, Moscow, Russia, pp. 162–169, 2019.

5. Arefin, M.S., Surovi, T.H., Snigdha, N.N., Mridha, M.F., Adnan, M.A., Smart healthcare system for underdeveloped countries. *2017 IEEE International Conference on Telecommunications and Photonics (ICTP)*, Dhaka, pp. 28–32, 2017.

6. Roibu Crucianu, P.A., The Implications of Big Data in Healthcare. *2019 E-Health and Bioengineering Conference (EHB)*, Iasi, Romania, pp. 1–4, 2019.

7. Reena, J.K. and Parameswari, R., A Smart Healthcare Monitor System in IoT Based Human Activities of Daily Living: A Review. *2019 International Conference on Machine Learning, Big Data, Cloud and Parallel Computing (COMITCon)*, Faridabad, India, pp. 446–448, 2019.

8. Sahu, S. and Sharma, A., Detecting brainwaves to evaluate mental health using LabVIEW and applications. *2016 International Conference on Emerging Technological Trends (ICETT)*, Kollam, pp. 1–4, 2016.

9. Rghioui, L'aarje, A., Elouaai, F., Bouhorma, M., The Internet of Things for healthcare monitoring: Security review and proposed solution. *2014 Third IEEE International Colloquium in Information Science and Technology (CIST)*, Tetouan, pp. 384–389, 2014.

10. Mansour, and Ouda, H.T., On The Road to A Comparative Car Racing EEG-based Signals for Mental and Physical Brain Activity Evaluation. *2019 9th Annual Information Technology, Electromechanical Engineering and Microelectronics Conference (IEMECON)*, Jaipur, India, pp. 43–48, 2019.

11. Abualsaud, K., Mohamed, A., Khattab, T., Yaacoub, E., Hasna, M., Guizani, M., Classification for Imperfect EEG Epileptic Seizure in IoT applications:

A Comparative Study. *2018 14th International Wireless Communications & Mobile Computing Conference (IWCMC)*, Limassol, pp. 364–369, 2018.

12. Selvathi, D. and Meera, V.K., Realization of epileptic seizure detection in EEG signal using wavelet transform and SVM classifier. *2017 International Conference on Signal Processing and Communication (ICSPC)*, Coimbatore, pp. 18–22, 2017.

13. Vaitheeshwari, R. and SathieshKumar, V., Performance Analysis of Epileptic Seizure Detection System Using Neural Network Approach. *2019 International Conference on Computational Intelligence in Data Science (ICCIDS)*, Chennai, India, pp. 1–5, 2019.

14. Gurunath, R., Agarwal, M., Nandi, A., Samanta, D., An Overview: Security Issue in IoT Network. *2018 2nd International Conference on I-SMAC (IoT in Social, Mobile, Analytics and Cloud)*, Palladam, India, pp. 104–107, 2018.

15. Gope, P. and Hwang, T., BSN-Care: A Secure IoT-Based Modern Healthcare System Using Body Sensor Network. *IEEE Sens. J.*, 16, 5, 1368–1376, March 1, 2016.

16. Satija, U., Ramkumar, B., Sabarimalai Manikandan, M., Real-Time Signal Quality-Aware ECG Telemetry System for IoT-Based Healthcare Monitoring. *IEEE Internet Things J.*, 4, 3, 1–7, June 2017.

17. Sundaravadivel, Prabha, Saraju, P., Exploring Human Body Communications for IoT Enabled Ambulatory Health Monitoring Systems. *IEEE International Symposium on Nano-electronic and Information Systems*.

18. Sahu, S. and Sharma, A., Detecting Brainwaves to evaluate mental health using LabVIEW and applications. *International Conference on Emerging Technological Trends [ICETT]*.

19. Pavitra, V., Rao, Padmashree, V., Gagana, M.D., Samanta, D., Internet of Things (IoT): An Assessment. *Proc. of The International Conference on Emerging Trends in Engineering and Management (ICETEM 2015)*, Bangalore, India, 27 October, 2015.

20. Tyagi, S., Agarwal, A., Maheshwari, P., *A Conceptual Framework for IoT-Based Healthcare System using Cloud Computing*, Amity University, Uttar Pradesh, India, IEEE, 2016.

21. Lau, T.M., Gwin, J.T., Ferris, D.P., *How Many Electrodes are Really Needed For EEG-Based Mobile Brain Imaging*, IEEE, USA, 2012.

22. Patnaik, L.M. and Manyam, O.K., Epileptic EEG detection using neural networks and post-classification. *Comput. Methods Prog. Biomed.*, 91, 2, 100–109, 2008.

23. Chan, A., Sun, F., Boto, E., Wingeier, B., Automated seizure onset detection for accurate onset time determination in intracranial EEG. *Clin. Neurophysiol.*, 119, 12, 2687–2696, 2008.

24. Gupta, D., James, C., Gray, W., Phase Synchronization with ICA for Epileptic Seizure Onset Prediction in the Long Term EEG. *4th IET International Conference on Advances in Medical, Signal and Information Processing*, MED-SIP 2008, pp. 1–4, Jun 2008.

25. Haas, S., Frei, M., Osorio, I., Strategies for adapting automated seizure detection algorithms. *Med. Eng. Physics*, 29, 8, 895–909, Oct 2007.
26. Molteni, E., Perego, P., Zanotta, N., Reni, G., Entropy analysis on EEG signal in a case study of focal myoclonus. *30th Annual International Conference of the IEEE Engineering in Medicine and Biology Society, EMBS'08*, pp. 4724–4727, Jul. 2008.
27. Nagaraj, S., Shah, A., Shah, P., Szeto, V., Bergen, M., Ambulatory Preseizure Detection Device. *Proceedings of the IEEE 32nd Annual Northeast in Bioengineering Conference*, pp. 41–42, 2006.
28. Sackellares, J., Seizure Prediction, in: *Epilepsy Currents*, vol. 8, no. 3, pp. 55–9, American Epilepsy Society, USA, 2008.
29. Sanei, S. and Chambers, J., *EEG Signal Processing*, Wiley-Inter Science, 2007.
30. Sharkawy, G., Newton, C., Hartley, S., Attitudes and practices of families and healthcare personnel toward children with epilepsy in Kilifi, Kenya. *Epilepsy Behav.*, 8, 1, 201–212, 2006.
31. Shlens, J., A Tutorial on Principal Component Analysis, in: *Systems Neurobiology Laboratory, Salk Institute for Biological Studies*, Dec 2005.
32. Shneker, B. and Fountain, N., Epilepsy, in: *Disease-a-Month*, vol. 49, pp. 426–478, Jul. 2003.
33. Ghosh, A.M., Halder, D., Hossain, S.K.A., Remote Health Monitoring System through IoT. *5th (ICIEV)*, 2016.
34. Hameed, R.T., Abdulwahabe, O., M., N., Health Monitoring System Based on Wearable Sensors and Cloud Platform. *20th (ICSTCC)*, Sinaia, Romania, October, pp. 13–15, 2016.
35. Abdullah, A., Ismael, A., Rashid, A., Abou-ElNour, A., Tarique, M., Real time wireless health monitoring application using mobile devices. *IJCNC*, vol. 7, no.3, May 2015.
36. Kumari, N.P. and Yadav, V., Heart Rate Monitoring and Data Transmission via Bluetooth. *Int. J. Innovative Emerging Res. Eng.*, 2, 2, 1–6, 2015.
37. Lambat, M.M. and Wagaj, S.C., Health Monitoring system. *Int. J. Sci. Res.*, 4, 247–250, 2015.
38. WahyuKusuma, R., Ridha, I., Rianto, Y., Swelandiah, E.P., FPGA based heartbeats monitor with fingertip optical sensor. *IJCSEIT*, vol. 4, no.5, October 2014.
39. Gayathri, S., Rajkumar, N., Vinothkumar, V., Human health monitoring system using wearable sensors. *Int. J. Innovative Res. Comput. Commun. Eng.*, 4, 4, 12–15, April 2016.
40. Samanta, D., Shivamurthaiah, M.P., Kumar, K., Umesh, D., Siddalingappa, K., Wireless Sensor Networks model for monitoring system based on IoT. *Solid State Technol.*
41. Neshenko, N., Bou-Harb, E., Crichigno, J., Kaddoum, G., Ghani, N., Demystifying IoT Security: An Exhaustive Survey on IoT Vulnerabilities and a First Empirical Look on Internet-Scale IoT Exploitations. *IEEE*

Communications Surveys & Tutorials, vol. 21, no.3, pp. 2702–2733, third quarter 2019.

42. Ferreira, A.G. *et al.*, A smart wearable system for sudden infant death syndrome monitoring. *Proc. IEEE Int. Conf. Ind. Technol. (ICIT)*, pp. 1920–1925, 2016.

43. Bisio, I., Delfino, A., Lavagetto, F., and Sciarrone, A., Enabling IoT for in-home rehabilitation: Accelerometer signals classification methods for activity and movement recognition. *IEEE Internet Things J.*, 4, 1, 135–146, Feb. 2017.

44. Stanislav, M. and Beardsley, T., *Hacking IoT: A Case Study on Baby Monitor Exposures and Vulnerabilities*, Boston, MA, USA, 2015.

45. Gubbi, J., Buyya, R., Marusic, S., Palaniswami, M., Internet of Things (IoT): A vision architectural elements and future directions. *Future Gener. Comput. Syst.*, 29, 7, 1645–1660, 2013.

46. Meneghello, F., Calore, M., Zucchetto, D., Polese, M., Zanella, A., IoT: Internet of Threats? A Survey of Practical Security Vulnerabilities in Real IoT Devices. *IEEE Internet Things J.*, 6, 5, 8182–8201, Oct. 2019.

47. Massad, M.A. and Alsaify, Baha', A., MQTTSec Based on Context-Aware Cryptographic Selection Algorithm (CASA) for Resource-Constrained IoT Devices. *Information and Communication Systems (ICICS) 2020 11th International Conference on*, pp. 349–354, 2020.

48. Xing, L., Reliability in Internet of Things: Current Status and Future Perspectives. *Internet Things J. IEEE*, 7, 8, 6704–6721, 2020.

49. Chinchero, H.F., Marcos Alonso, J., Hugo Ortiz, T., LED lighting systems for smart buildings: A review. *Smart Cities IET*, 2, 3, 126–134, 2020.

50. Dammak, M., Aroua, S., Senouci, S.M., Ghamri-Doudane, Y., Suciu, G., Sachian, M.-A., Roscaneanu, R., Ozkan, I., Gungor, M.O., A Secure and Interoperable Platform for Privacy Protection in the Smart Hotel Context. *Information Infrastructure and Networking Symposium (GIIS) 2020 Global*, pp. 1–6, 2020.

51. Frustaci, M., Pace, P., Aloi, G., Fortino, G., Evaluating Critical Security Issues of the IoT World: Present and Future Challenges. *IEEE Internet Things J.*, 5, 4, 2483–2495, Aug. 2018.

52. Halloush, R.D., Transmission Early-Stopping Scheme for Anti-Jamming Over Delay-Sensitive IoT Applications. *Internet Things J. IEEE*, 6, 5, 7891–7906, 2019.

53. Kirupakar, J. and Mercy Shalinie, S., Situation Aware Intrusion Detection System Design for Industrial IoT Gateways. *Computational Intelligence in Data Science (ICCIDS) 2019 International Conference on*, pp. 1–6, 2019.

54. Alasmary, H., Khormali, A., Anwar, A., Park, J., Choi, J., Abusnaina, A., Awad, A., Nyang, D., Mohaisen, A., Analyzing and Detecting Emerging Internet of Things Malware: A Graph-Based Approach. *Internet Things J. IEEE*, 6, 5, 8977–8988, 2019.

55. He, Y., Tang, L., Ren, Y., Maximizing Sleeping Capacity Based on QoS Provision for Information-Centric Internet of Things. *Access IEEE*, 7, 111084–111094, 2019.

56. Rattanalerdnusorn, E., Thaenkaew, P., Vorakulpipat, C., Security Implementation For Authentication In Iot Environments. *Computer and Communication Systems (ICCCS) 2019 IEEE 4th International Conference on*, pp. 678–681, 2019.

57. Gupta, U., Tripathi, Y., Bhardwaj, H., Goel, S., Kaur, A., Kumar, P., Energy-Efficient Model for Deployment of Sensor Nodes in IoT based System. *Contemporary Computing (IC3) 2019 Twelfth International Conference on*, pp. 1–5, 2019.

58. Kokila, J., Ramasubramanian, N., Naganathan, N., Resource Efficient Metering Scheme for Protecting SoC FPGA Device and IPs in IoT Applications. *Very Large Scale Integration (VLSI) Systems IEEE Transactions on*, vol. 27, no. 10, pp. 2284–2295, 2019.

59. Mcginthy, J.M. and Michaels, A.J., Secure Industrial Internet of Things Critical Infrastructure Node Design. *Internet Things J. IEEE*, 6, 5, 8021–8037, 2019.

Smart Health Application for Remote Tracking of Ambulatory Patients

Shariq Aziz Butt[1]*, Muhammad Waqas Anjum[2], Syed Areeb Hassan[3], Arindam Garai[4] and Edeh Michael Onyema[5]

[1]The University of Lahore, Lahore, Pakistan
[2]NCBA&E, Lahore, Pakistan
[3]The Superior University, Lahore, Pakistan
[4]Dept. of Mathematics, Sonarpur Mahavidyalaya, Kolkata, India
[5]Dept. of Mathematics and Computer Science, Coal City University, Enugu, Nigeria

Abstract

The Internet of Things (IoT) has amalgam with many fields. One of these is the eHealth monitoring of patients. mHealth monitoring is the most prominent subdomain of eHealth. In mHealth, IoT enables the merging of various devices, including wearables (watch and sensors) and holding (smart mobile phone) devices. Therefore, the application development of mHealth is a penetrated domain in the research community. Different research work exists to develop mHealth applications to monitor different diseases either remotely or physically. Mostly the mHealth applications work with the context of the patient that includes the type of disease and observing the environment. The development of these applications faces several issues, such as security, smartness, decision making, size of the application, and timely actions. This study presents the issue with the health sector and with fuzzy logic while using for health enhancements. Moreover, this work highlights key factors to be addressed in mHealth such as mobility-awareness, location-based medication, and the security of eHealth's data, distance, and measurement. These all features are very imperative for the health application to improve wellness.

Keywords: Smart health, mobility of patient, remote monitoring, fuzzy concepts for health

*Corresponding author: shariq2315@gmail.com

SK Hafizul Islam and Debabrata Samanta (eds.) Smart Healthcare System Design: Security and Privacy Aspects, (33–56) © 2021 Scrivener Publishing LLC

2.1   Introduction

Due to the growing of the Internet of Things (IoT), it has created revolutionary inventions and modifications in the health section. It makes healthy smart health in terms of eHealth and mHealth. Due to the technological encroachments the health professional adopts the technology very vastly for monitoring and improve the patients' health. The internet technology made the patient's life very easy to monitor and treat. In mHealth and eHealth, IoT enables the merging of various devices, including wearables (watch and sensors) and holding (smart mobile phone) devices. Therefore, the application development of mHealth is a penetrated domain in the research community. Technology also improves health for special kinds of patients who are known as ambulatory patients. These patients need monitoring at their location remotely. It becomes possible with the mHealth application that supports the medical professionals to monitor, treat patients, and send the medication in the case of any abnormality occurrence. It helps the patients to receive tele-medication services from doctors at their location in case of any emergency. But on the other hand instead of all these facilities and supports of internet technology to the health domain still many challenges need to be addressed to enhance the health sector. These challenges include the Emergency Support, Issue with the Chronic Disease Monitoring, Issue with the Tele-Medication, Issue with the Tele-Medication, Mobility of Doctor, Data Storage Issue, Application User Interface issue, and Security Threats. In this chapter, we discuss the health sector, improvements in health, issues with the health domain, and fuzzy-based security solutions to overcome the security issues.

2.2   Literature Work

The prolonged future alongside the increasing multifaceted nature of medication and wellbeing services raises wellbeing costs in general meaningfully. Evolution in pervasive computing applications in blend with the exploitation of modern astute sensor systems may give a premise to help. While the smart wellbeing idea can bolster the awareness of the growing P4-medication (precautionary, sharing, prophetic, and modified), advanced medication creates a lot of high-dimensional, pitifully planned data collections and monstrous actions of formless information [1–3].

Close to the pervasive, multifaceted existence of human administration systems and the reality that front-line drugs are evolving into a data-enhanced science, conventional strategies handling this "enormous data" can no longer hold demand awake, raising the likelihood of unsatisfactory findings being passed on. Consequently, sharp systems are critical for adapting to this growing flood of data [4, 5].

Specifically, the cutting-edge mobile phone methodology, groundbreaking ubiquitous astute sensors, and the reduction of data sparing costs have provoked a persistent illustration of capturing all kinds of close and dear biomedical data over time [9, 10]. In addition, these records contribute to the development of a proportion of indicated longitudinal data, in any case known as time course of action data, in the structure territory.

A significant future pattern is moving the human-insider loop [17], for a valid justification, as the two people and PCs have altogether different qualities, however, both together can undoubtedly be all the more remarkable. Everywhere when scaled this way joins the better of two universes: subjective science with software engineering.

Late specialized advances in sorted out sensors, low-power facilitated circuits, besides, remote correspondences have enabled the structure of simplicity, littler than ordinary, lightweight, and brilliant physiological sensor center points [20]. All of these enhancements leave tremendous wants to our future. Smart conditions will have the alternative to therefore follow our prosperity and will, to some expand, move the reason for care away from clinician's work environments—thusly in a perfect world be of fiscal relieve of the much over-concentrated on clinical center structures what's progressive, moving the preventive point of view into the closer view.

From expressly estimating your critical well-being to sensors that fade in the background and track essential steps, there is a shift in perspective.

2.3 Smart Computing for Smart Health for Ambulatory Patients

Intelligent computing gives huge prospects to building up Smart wellbeing benefits as necessary pieces of future consideration ideas [41], which are tested by our maturing society. In this unique situation, specifically brilliant homecare conditions are frequently proliferated as a promising answer for dealing with older or incapacitated individuals. Sensors and new collaboration innovations flawlessly incorporated in such situations offer different structures of customized and setting adjusted average help, including help to complete ordinary exercises, checking individual well-being conditions, improving patient security, as well as gaining admittance to social, clinical and crisis frameworks. Brilliant social insurance applications have the potential to deliver clinical, social and conservative benefits to different partners by providing a wide range of administrations. The goals vary from enhancing convenience, encouraging improvement of self-governance to crisis support, including identification, counteraction and forecasting [37, 38].

After a certain age and due to some specific diseases the patients need some care at their locations (at home, at any remote place). These patients are known as ambulatory patients, who after a certain treatment need continuous monitoring using the smart applications. The applications are designed according to every disease and patient's conditions that include its disease parameters. After setting these parameters, there is a need for remote monitoring done by the application remotely at the patient's current location. Therefore, currently, the health is growing towards the smart and decisions making applications to support the patient and doctor to monitoring and medication [39, 40].

There are also some difficulties faced by the scientific community and developers because of developments in the health sector. There are technological problems concerning versatility, imperceptibility (keen devices incorporated in our daily activities, such as wearable parts, watches, glasses, etc.), simple correspondence like voice and signals instead of help or cursor, or moreover adaptive and setting care, as the two crucial issues "flexible direct in setting" are essential to "understanding" i.e. suit [42, 43].

2.4   Challenges With Smart Health

Different challenges with smart health are as follows. These challenges make smart health ineffective for patient health and monitoring.

2.4.1   Emergency Support

Most of the existing frameworks for identifying and forestalling health-related crises concentrate on falls and congestive cardiovascular failures as their fundamental application domains. Specifically, fall identification turns out to be an ever-increasing number of significant as ongoing measurements show that over 30% of the individuals more than 65 years and 50% of the individuals more than 80 years fall in any event when a year. In around 1/4 these cases, individuals endure genuine injuries with supporting impacts on their portability and autonomy. The same number of these falls happen when individuals are separated from everyone else at home; a few projects began to create mobility crisis applications, which should empower clients to call for help in a crisis circumstances. Although versatility plans seem from the outset to be a capable method, exploratory verification reveals that patients either do not pass on such contraptions with them or are essentially not equipped to operate them when clinical problems have arisen. A few evaluation adventures rendered models of weight fragile floor components along these lines, enabling the disclosure of falls without the patient wearing additional growth. Although early applications passed on pressure-sensitive floor tiles in express areas within the earth, later approaches used scattered sensors to cover an entire room and thus allow the location of a fine-grained area [45–47] as shown in Figure 2.1.

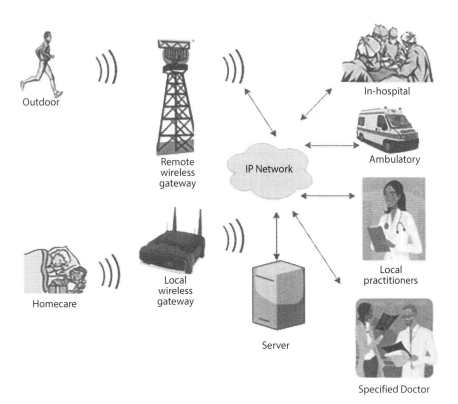

Figure 2.1 Technical Scenario 2, normal healthcare.

2.4.2   The Issue With Chronic Disease Monitoring

Treatment of chronic conditions doesn't just build personal satisfaction for patients. It is additionally expected to bring critical practical advantages contrasted with customary consideration ideas. Henceforth, isn't it amazing that an expansive assortment of intelligent wellbeing services has been produced for different sorts of constant infections. For instance, built up an assistive home checking application for patients languishing from end-stage cardiovascular breakdown, which associates clinical data caught through numerous biosensors installed into the patient's physical encompassing. The issue with the mobile monitoring for chronic disease as the like patient can be in the mobile state to monitor continuously is a challenge for smart technology. It is due to location change and low fidelity of wireless networks that can send a false state of data at the doctor's end [48].

2.4.3   An Issue With the Tele-Medication

Monitoring and mobility of ambulatory patients can cause of late delivery of tele-medication at a patient location. In the case of any abnormality, the tele-medication has to reach the location at the right time. This tele-medication is mostly sent by the associated doctor, who is monitoring the patient. If the distance of the doctor and patient is too far from each other then it can cause the critical condition of the patient. Therefore, tele-medication is very important to reach the patient location but is still an issue in cardiac patient monitoring for smart health. The research community has done work related to the mortality rate due to issue with the tele-medication. In the study of [36] it mentioned that the mortality rate is quite high after some surgical treatment in patients due to unreachability of tele-medication services at the patient's end. The rate of mortality rose from 7–9.5% due to this issue. In another study [35] reported that due to less effective services of tele-medication to mobile patients the rate of mortality becomes high. After the treatment patients can get a short-term indicative improvement in their health. But after the discharge from the hospital, the death rate becomes high within the first year due to unreachable tele-medication services, less qualitative monitoring, and readmission of patients in the case of any abnormality. In certain instances, the death rate and readmission are very high as the 'vulnerable stage' is called the 1st months after hospitalization to recognize hospitalization. The danger of death and readmission is usually evident during the 1–3 months following the release of the crisis center, with the highest rates occurring in the initial 30 days. Information from the US ADHERE library, considering 104,808 patients hospitalized inferable from HF, tended to have 11.2% mortality data and a 22.1% readmission rate on Day 30 after release. Some 35–40% of patients will either send or be readmitted to an emergency clinic during the baseline 3 months after discharge. In the primary year after hospitalization for HF, syphon dissatisfaction and sudden cardiovascular passing are the most normal purposes behind death. The general photo, as Figure 2.2 below, expresses that situation.

This study also examined the death rate of outpatients due to less intelligent tele-medication services offered. The study stated that the visits of patients after the treatment were good after the post-discharge, but steadily decreased as days passed. Therefore, ambulatory patients need a smart tele-medication definition to track and take appropriate action when any abnormality occurs. As shown in the figure below the median period from entry to an initial portion of the sample was 7 days in the pre-release collection and 10 days in the post-release collection. In separate pre-release and post-release meetings, the median period from randomization to the primary component was 0 days [interquartile run (IQR) 0–1 days] and 3 days (IQR 2–6 days). In the pre-release gathering (IQR −2 to −1 days) and 1 day in the post-release gathering (IQR 1–4 days), the median time from release to the main component was −1 day as illustrated in Figure 2.3.

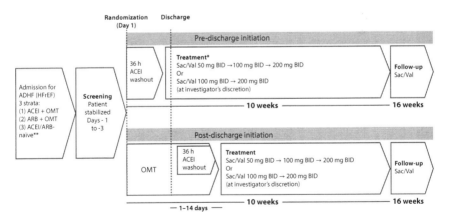

Figure 2.2 Structure of transformation research. Visits to the study occur at 2, 4, 6, 8, and 10 weeks and 14, 18, 22, and 26 weeks after randomization (or at the time of early treatment or suspension of the study) [35]. ACEI, angiotensin-changing chemical inhibitor; ADHF, extreme decompensated cardiovascular failure; ARB, angiotensin receptor blocker; HFrEF, reduced discharge cardiovascular failure; OMT, advanced medical clinical treatment; Sac/Val, sacubitril/valsartan [49].

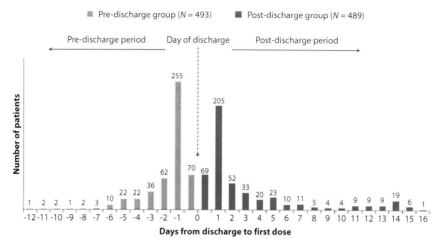

Figure 2.3 The no. of patients visits after Post Discharge [36].

2.4.4   Mobility of Doctor

There is also an issue with the mobility of a doctor rather than the patient mobility. The specified monitoring doctor can also be in a mobile state and when the abnormality occurs with the patient, might be the doctor does not know about it. The mobility of health professionals (doctors, paramedical staff) can cause a critical situation for patients in the case of any abnormality. As stated in the study that the healthcare professionals move from place to place just due to some benefits. Due to their mobility to other places the patients face different issues that need serious attention from the policymakers. The study reported that some patients need care at their geographical locations [48, 50].

2.4.5   Application User Interface Issue

Numerous applications are created by the planner and designers yet all applications have a few restrictions because of the innovation and situations change around patients. The UI oversees issues, for instance, graphical UI (sensors affiliation control, menu, sounds and voice messages, the status of the system, a demonstration of data, etc.), speaker, keys, drove, and other device limits like vibration. This issue generally happens in versatile wellbeing situations, where the wellbeing portable application configuration isn't easy to understand for patients. One of the essential challenges of flexible prosperity is using the humbler screens of mobile phones successfully to show information supporting the prosperity dynamic system.

Along these lines, it is imperative to discover proficient ways of utilizing the screens of cell phones to show important data supporting dynamic [49].

2.5   Security Threats

The idea of s-Health and all the applications and frameworks that could lie inside could fundamentally push residents to improve their personal satisfaction and medicinal services administrations while the expenses of the human services framework are decreased. In the situation that we talked about in the past segment, s-Health uses the frameworks and ICT of the city to furnish preventive strategies to residents with respiratory conditions. Consequently, such residents could all the more likely control their sickness and diminish costs on the medicinal services framework. Notwithstanding, there might be some potential security issues in this engineering. Residents may not need to be completely observed. Also, taking into account the dispersed and remote nature of sensor systems, guaranteeing information security is an incredible test for s-Health frameworks. Too, because of the very idea of s-Health frameworks (i.e., profoundly dispersed, remote), it is difficult to incorporate a security control in contrast with conventional human services frameworks. Furthermore, listening to stealthily and skimming happen when the sensor information is transmitted through remote systems. There are many security issues with the health-related data as the health record of the patient is stored either on single or multiple servers [51–53]. The security breaches with the data are as follows.

2.5.1   Identity Privacy

Character security with regards to s-Health identifies with ensuring the personality of residents that get to s-Health administrations. The eHealth framework and other specialist co-ops can utilize the character of a patient to connect their exercises or his/her wellbeing condition and records. In our design, when a resident contacts the CCC, his/her personality is presented to the outside. Residents' personalities can be unlawfully utilized by programmers to get touchy individual data in the focal database, for example, electronic wellbeing records and arrangements of areas. Accordingly, protection could be attacked. This is one of the principal issues among all protection issues. To address this issue, most arrangements depend on halfway substances to conceal the genuine personalities of the clients (e.g., utilizing nom de plumes). Additionally, because of a coordinated effort among clients, the creators proposed utilizing (confided in outsider)-based methodologies. By and by, the personality is still at serious risk if the CCC is enduring an onslaught or the supervisors of the administrations get out of hand. To maintain a strategic distance from this circumstance, we think about that as a lot of topographically disseminated pseudonymized are required.

2.5.2   Query Privacy

Inquiry protection is tied in with ensuring the security of the inquiries made by a client to a database framework. For our situation, the conduct of inquisitive ideal courses to the CCC needs to be saved. This is likewise identified with private data recovery (PIR). S-Health administrations may utilize PIR devices in request to shield questions from suppliers. For instance, the study proposes a convention that permits a customer to effectively complete questions and recognize server trouble making within the sight of the most extreme conceivable number of pernicious servers. Also, utilizing confided in outsiders (TTP) is another alternative. For this protection measurement, the fundamental intention is to dodge the connection among's residents and questions, and current PIR arrangements are appropriate to do as such (at the expense of a few huge computational overheads).

2.5.3   Location of Privacy

Area protection is tied in with ensuring the security of the physical area of the residents. The LBS of our application model involves area protection issues. When residents attempt to get ideal courses, they send their area to CCC and permit the LBS supplier to follow them. A few strategies have been proposed to secure area protection. Their point is to give a twisted area that forestalls the supplier from the following clients. The creators proposed a blend zone—another development roused by unknown correspondence methods—along with measurements for evaluating client namelessness. The study proposed the thought of much of the time changing pen names every client, which would lessen the opportunity that an assailant could gather enough history on a casualty to construe their propensities or personality. Creators propose a system that empowers an architect to locate the ideal area protection safeguarding component (LPPM) for an LBS thinking about limitations of the client's administration quality, and an enemy dependent on the calculation of ideal induction. LocX [24] gives altogether improved area protection without including vulnerability into question results or depending on solid suspicions about server security. Specifically, LocX applies secure client explicit, separation protecting direction changes to all area information imparted to the server.

2.5.4   Footprint Privacy and Owner Privacy

These security issues are identified with the insurance of information gathered by the city framework. Such data can be recovered or derived by lawbreakers. In the s-Health design, contamination levels in the city are gathered by sensors. The city can break down such conditions and afterward, naturally make a choice, for example, resync traffic lights for lessening clog furthermore, contamination in some region of the city. Moreover, electronic wellbeing records of residents are likewise put away by the CCC. Every one of this information can be discharged to outsiders for examination, insights, or information mining, which implies we have to secure delicate data from getting out of hand substances. Sending measurable revelation control (SDC) methods is a viable approach to lessen conceivable protection intrusions that could get from such mining techniques. A strategy that permits information proprietors to produce unexpectedly annoyed duplicates of its information for various trust levels. Thusly, it keeps information excavators from joining duplicates at various trust levels to together remake the first information.

2.6   Applications of Fuzzy Set Theory in Healthcare and Medical Problems

The world's population is aging. Age is more than just a number. One single major challenge of policymakers across geographies is to arrange efficient healthcare services to upgrade the living standards of the aging population. In recent years, there has been a significant surge in the number of patients with various chronic diseases associated with a variety of risk factors requiring long-term treatment. Under these complexities, the decisions by caregivers cover the critical ripple effects [8]. So, a tiny mistake by them can be irrecoverable and fatal for patients [1]. However, various stakeholders of healthcare industries, including managers and legislators, hardly furnish precise and crisp information. The inherent uncertainty in the data brings fuzzy set theory into the forefront. Whereas the fuzzy set theory has been widely applied to deliver the acceptable solutions to diverse healthcare and medical issues, researchers are employing several recent tools, like type 2 fuzzy set, intuitionistic fuzzy set, and many more for higher efficiency. Here, the present review briefly focuses on only following three major sub-areas of applications of fuzzy set theory and its derivatives in healthcare and medical problems:

A. selection of medical equipment, material, and technology,
B. service quality and risk assessment typically in chronic diseases, and
C. decision making and the role of operations research.

A. Selection of Medical Equipment, Material, and Technology

In recent times, researchers categorized the interrelationship (with several alternatives) among medical types of equipment and materials. So, they could present numerous approaches and methods regarding the assessment and selection of types of equipment, materials, and projects.

In recent years, [3] presented an empirical case study on the robot selection problem by extending the PROMETHEE method under fuzzy environment. Their novel approach included the simultaneous exploration of crisp objective data and fuzzy subjective data. They found how the appropriate robot selection could help to enhance the value of products and thereby resulted in the increased satisfaction of patients, relatives, and caregivers. Around the same time, a study in this area along with potential applications in manufacturing industries was performed in [2]. He extended the classical VIKOR method for robot selection under uncertainty. He employed the interval type-2 fuzzy set to get more degrees of freedom to real-life problems. As well, he analyzed the stability of the proposed method through seven sets of criteria weights and the Spearman correlation coefficient. [4] performed a well-established study by amalgamating two fuzzy-based hierarchal processes, namely fuzzy AHP and fuzzy VIKOR in mobile robot selection. Their study focused on the total ownership of cost as a key parameter in the selection of the robot. Along with some modern technology marvels, like the robotic automation system and Internet of Health Things (IoHT), the modified fuzzy AHP and fuzzy VIKOR methods were applied to determine the ranking of robots and thereby to select the best mobile robot at the hospital pharmacy. Next, [5] found how millions of people received frequent health pieces of advice to lead a healthy life. They noted that while the IoT devices could generate a large volume of data in the healthcare environment, the cloud computing technology could be rewarding for secured storage and accessibility. Additionally, they applied a new systematic approach for the people, who were severely affected with diabetes, by generating the related medical data

Table 2.1 Very recent articles focusing on applications of fuzzy set theory in healthcare and medical problems.

Author(s)	Approach	Purpose of the study	Outcome
Part A: Selection of medical equipment, material, and technology			
Moreno-Cabezali and Fernandez-Crehuet [24]	Fuzzy logic in risk assessment.	Survey to assess potential risks.	Identified the most critical risk.
AlZu'bi et al. [25]	3D fuzzy C-means algorithm.	3D medical image segmentation.	Parallel implementation to be 5× faster than the sequential version.
Ozsahin et al. [23]	Fuzzy PROMETHEE And fuzzy MCDM.	Solid-state detectors in medical imaging	Most suitable semiconductor on basis of detectors.
Masood et al. [22]	Hybrid hierarchical fuzzy group decision making.	Selection of conceptual loudspeaker prototype under sustainability issues.	Optimal conceptual prototype design among 4 alternatives.
Part B: Service quality and risk assessment typically in chronic diseases			
Vidhya and Shanmugalakshmi [29]	Big Data and neuro fuzzy-based method	Analysis of multiple diseases using an adaptive neuro-fuzzy inference system.	Determined the entropy of the CFI count.

(Continued)

Table 2.1 Very recent articles focusing on applications of fuzzy set theory in healthcare and medical problems. (*Continued*)

Author(s)	Approach	Purpose of the study	Outcome
Akinnuwesi *et al.* [28]	Hybridization of fuzzy-Logic and cognitive mapping techniques.	Decision support system for diagnosing rheumatic–musculoskeletal disease.	87% accuracy, 90% sensitivity, and 80% specificity.
La Fata *et al.* [26]	Fuzzy ELECTRE III.	Evaluated the service quality in public healthcare.	Significant service attributes factors.
Samiei *et al.* [27]	Neuro-fuzzy inference system.	Risk factors of low back pain.	Identified four major risk factors to low back pain.
Part C: Decision making and the role of operations research			
Vaishnavi and Suresh [30]	Fuzzy readiness and performance importance indices.	To implement agility in healthcare systems.	Continuation of assessment readiness helps to improve readiness.
Detcharat Sumrit [31]	Fuzzy MCDM approach.	Supplier selection for vendor-managed inventory in healthcare.	Institutional trust, information sharing, and technology as major evaluation criteria.
Rajput *et al.* [33]	Fuzzy signed distance technique.	Optimization of fuzzy EOQ model in healthcare industries.	Determined optimal total cost under variable demand.

(*Continued*)

Table 2.1 Very recent articles focusing on applications of fuzzy set theory in healthcare and medical problems. (*Continued*)

Author(s)	Approach	Purpose of the study	Outcome
Salazar and Sanz-Calcedo [32]	Fuzzy cognitive mappings.	Maintenance operations on energy consumption and emissions in healthcare centers.	Direct connection to energy, environmental efficiency, and maintenance condition.

through some repository dataset and the medical sensors. Their suggested classification algorithm was called the *fuzzy rule-based neural classifier* that could more effectively diagnose the disease and the severity than classical methods. On the other hand, whereas most researches recognized the hospitals to act as the main sub-section of the healthcare system, they assumed the hospitals at different locations to be at par and homogeneous. However, Omrani *et al.* [6] studied the non-homogeneous nature of services offered to various patients by the hospitals at different locations. So, they found that these hospitals were unsuitable for comparison. Accordingly, they proposed a clustering technique to deal with a lack of homogeneity among DMUs and thereby to measure the hospitals in different places. Again, [7] addressed the impact of various harmful factors in the information security of healthcare devices. They employed a fuzzy-based symmetrical AHP-TOPSIS method. However, they could test the method only at one local hospital software of Varanasi, a city of India. The work by [8] found the drawbacks of type 1 fuzzy set theory and used the finite interval-valued type 2 Gaussian fuzzy number as a powerful tool to measure uncertainty in healthcare problems. This could solve a real economic evaluation of medical device selection problem from the perspectives of clinicians, biomedical engineers, and healthcare investors. Part A of Table 2.1 lists some very recent articles in this area of research. This way, numerous researchers have put their best effort to tackle the uncertainty intrinsic to healthcare and medical problems.

B. Service Quality and Risk Assessment, Typically in Chronic Diseases
The world's population is aging. The proportion of the elderly (+65) is greater than ever and is estimated to be double within the European Union

within the next 50 years [13]. Whereas the improvements to the quality of life and advances in medical science in the last few decades craft the aging of the population, a higher ratio of the aged population makes it necessary for caregivers to concurrently tackle with more patients suffering from a variety of chronic diseases. This way, the upholding of quality service by assessing the risk turns to be more and more challenging for caregivers.

An empirical case study [9] was conducted with data from nine public hospitals in Silica, Italy, on four core quality parameters and fifteen main service items. He introduced a new fuzzy measurement method for assessing the quality of service in healthcare. To elicit accurate estimates of service quality requirements, the fuzzy AHP approach was used. He found that successful internal communication of service quality accomplishments should minimize the differences between the needs of customers and how workers view those needs. The authors [10] presented several of the shortcomings of several existing algorithms in the form of an enormous number of rules and the mining of non-interesting rules, along with the time of pre-processing and the rate of filtration. Then to address the limitations based on the user request and the visualization of discovered rules, they provided a fuzzy weighted-iterative concept.

Again, [11] provided under an interval-assessed intuitionistic fuzzy environment a hybrid MCDM model and thereby evaluated the probability of node failure. They combined the interval-valued intuitionistic fuzzy ANP (for matching with the uncertainty of information) and the proportional assessment approach (for decision making). However, the subjective weight used in their method relied much on caregivers' opinions and thus was not flawless. Besides, due to the complexities of systems and service, there could arise different kinds of interrelationships between the failure modes. However, this was dodged in this study. Around the same time, [12] presented a decision-making approach that predicted heart failure risk. They integrated the fuzzy AHP and fuzzy ANN in the suggested approach. Also, they could establish that their method had 91.10% accuracy in results in comparison with other conventional ANN models Table 2.2.

Recently, [14] identified several drawbacks of the highly popular gerontechnology and telerehabilitation systems, such as the failure of those systems to assist patients and experts, both, regarding the progress of rehabilitation. They proposed a fuzzy-semantic framework based on well-known assessment criteria to determine the physical state of the patient during the recovery process. They used an API, however, called the Kinect API, which was a closed source API and only usable for Kinect interface patients. This made it less valuable for the process. There were also ample scopes for therapists and patients, alike, to determine their operation. Again

Table 2.2 Abbreviations with descriptions.

Abbreviation	Description
VIKOR	Vlsekriterijumska Optimizacija I Kompromisno Resenje
AHP	Analytic Hierarchy Process
ANP	Analytic Network Process
MCDM	Multi-Criteria Decision Making

the emphasis on privacy issues is one main factor in the acceptability of any technology or system. The study [15] focused on the safety assurance of an elbow and wrist rehabilitation medical robotic device in terms of robot and patient safety. Using the fuzzy logic method that discovered the degree of protection during the use of the robotic system, data uncertainty was discussed. However, their procedure was only tested numerically in a group of 18 patients through a clinical trial.

The very latest papers focusing on this area are included in Part B of Table 2.1.

C. Decision Making and the Role of Operations Research
The majority of researchers focusing on applications of fuzzy set theory in healthcare and medical problems used some existing decision-making processes or derived new ones. They found that the decisions of caregivers primarily aim to lower the health risk of patients while maximizing the health benefits and patients' choice, thereby increasing the satisfaction of all parties. However, there involved numerous criteria, such as social, environmental, material, managerial, professional, and many more criteria, in the wider setting of medical and healthcare models [17]. Since the crisp decision-making methods under several qualitative and quantitative contradictory issues strived to avoid the complexities with tolerance to doubts and stakeholders' favoritism, the fuzzy set theory was employed to represent the inherent impreciseness of data and thus to present an efficient, rational and explicit decision process [21].

Among recent studies, [16] presented a detailed survey by considering 142 articles published in the period 2000–2014. While they found the maximum number of publications focusing on applications of operations research in healthcare around the year 2008, they noted a surge in numbers post 2014. In the same edited volume of 2017, they presented a comprehensive survey in this area. They considered a longer period: 1966–2016 to study the advancements of this domain. By considering some relevant recent papers under each class of consideration, their analysis categorized the various approaches and methods applied in healthcare research. [13] provided a thorough analysis of the applications of decision-making and fuzzy set theory to solve health-related problems in a widely admired article. In the period from 1989 to 2018, their statistical findings ranked the year 2012 as first among the acclaimed papers. They also found that the various AHP and hybrid approach approaches were commonly used to rate different service quality applications in the healthcare industry.

Again, [34] shared the applications of operations research in healthcare supply chain management under ambiguity have been vividly demonstrated. By fuzzy set and probability theories, they represented the uncertainty in results, both, and thus could deliver the right medication to the right people at the right time and in good condition to combat the disease. Next, [17] posed an important question as to whether, by proper examination, hospitals could incorporate lean thought. First, various lean concepts and components implemented in healthcare institutions were defined. Next for healthcare organizations, a fuzzy-logic based lean implementation evaluation approach was deployed and then numerically studied. Although this study was validated in only one Indian hospital, it introduced some of the legislators' futuristic and implementable action plans. The study [44] developed a model to measure the leanness of hospitals and then validated the model by discussing the corresponding initial version with select academic experts. This way, they determined two criteria for organizations, namely the ability to participate in the study, and the commitment to implement lean principles. Finally, a multi-attributes fuzzy logic-based ranking method was established to present the leanness index.

Recently, [18] performed the identification of enablers, criteria, and attributes of leanness to constitute the measures of assessment of hospitals under fuzzy environment. Their method could help to provide the measures to address the weaker attributes and thereby to further enable the enhancement of lean performance.

In a rather real-life-oriented study [19], Pythagorean fuzzy data were considered, in which different evaluation data were provided in the form of Pythagorean fuzzy decision matrices regarding the feasible alternatives. The entries were taken from the views of experts and were described by fuzzy numbers from Pythagoras Table 2.2. In order to solve the resulting MCDM problems under uncertainty, they also broadened the application of the classical TOPSIS system. The most appropriate location and priority setting for buying the best healthcare technology could be decided by this process.

In another fresh-taste study [20], the emphasis was on a much-discussed issue of workplace hazards, including protection and effectiveness of health workers against public abuse. To define and prioritize control measures of aggression, their innovative approach used fuzzy AHP and Fuzzy Additive Ratio Assessment. They described the solution as the best advice for controlling violence against health workers by increasing the number of security personnel and training staff.

Below, Part C of Table 2.1 presents some very recent related articles published in highly acclaimed journals. This way, above deliberations, find ample scopes of research on applications of fuzzy set theory on the healthcare and medicine problems.

2.7   Conclusion

The IoT is a great blended domain for many fields such as mHealth application's development. The mHealth application's development is very trendy topic among the research community due to its direct involvement with the human's life. These applications mostly focus on static patients but do not focus on the remote patient's monitoring. The remote patient's monitoring is getting fame due to fewer innovations and work is done in this domain. In this chapter we investigated different health issues. Additionally, the fuzzy logics work with a focus on their major components of the applications to develop for health monitoring is discussed. There is a strong need to address these all mentioned issues sot enhance the health sector both in eHealth and mHealth Environments.

References

1. Ren, P., Xu, Z., Liao, H., Zeng, X.-J., A thermodynamic method of intuitionistic fuzzy MCDM to assist the hierarchical medical system in China. *Inf. Sci.*, 420, 490–504, 2017.

2. Ghorabaee, M.K., Developing an MCDM method for robot selection with interval type-2 fuzzy sets. *Rob. Comput. Integr. Manuf.*, 1, 37, 221–232, 2016 Feb.

3. Sen, D.K., Datta, S., Mahapatra, S.S., Extension of PROMETHEE for robot selection decision making. *Benchmarking: An Int. J.*, 23, 4, 983–1014, 2016.

4. Zhou, F., Wang, X., Goh, M., Fuzzy extended VIKOR-based mobile robot selection model for hospital pharmacy. *Int. J. Adv. Rob. Syst.*, 15, 4, 1729881418787315, 2018 Dec.

5. Kumar, P.M., Lokesh, S., Varatharajan, R., Babu, G.C., Parthasarathy, P., Cloud and IoT based disease prediction and diagnosis system for healthcare using Fuzzy neural classifier. *Future Gener. Comput. Syst.*, 1, 86, 527–534, 2018 Sep.

6. Omrani, H., Shafaat, K., Emrouznejad, A., An integrated fuzzy clustering cooperative game data envelopment analysis model with application in hospital efficiency. *Expert Syst. Appl.*, 30, 114, 615–628, 2018 Dec.

7. Kumar, R., Pandey, A.K, Baz., A., Alhakami, H., Alhakami, W., Agrawal, A., Khan, R.A., Fuzzy-based symmetrical multi-criteria decision-making procedure for evaluating the impact of harmful factors of healthcare information security. *Symmetry.* 12, 4, 664, 2020 Apr.

8. Tolga, C., Parlak, I.B., Castillo, O., Finite-interval-valued Type-2 Gaussian fuzzy numbers applied to fuzzy TODIM in a healthcare problem. *Eng. Appl. Artif. Intell.*, Id. 103352. 2020.

9. Lupo, T., A fuzzy framework to evaluate service quality in the healthcare industry: An empirical case of public hospital service evaluation in Sicily. *Appl. Soft Comput.*, 1, 40, 468–478, 2016 Mar.

10. Sumathi, G., Akilandeswari, J., Improved fuzzy weighted-iterative association rule based ontology postprocessing in data mining for query recommendation applications. *Comput. Intell.*, 36, 2, 773–782, 2020 May.

11. Wang, L.-E., Liu, H.-C., Quan, M.-Y., Evaluating the risk of failure modes with a hybrid MCDM model under interval-valued intuitionistic fuzzy environment. *Comput. Ind. Eng.*, 2016.

12. Samuel, O.W., Asogbon, G.M., Sangaiah, A.K., Guanglin Li, F.P., An integrated decision support system based on ANN and Fuzzy AHP for heart failure risk prediction. *Expert Syst. Appl.*, 68, 163–172, 2017.

13. Mardani, A., Hooker, R., Ozkul, S., Yifan, S., Nilashi, M., Sabzi, H.Z., Fei, G., Application of decision making and fuzzy sets theory to evaluate the healthcare and medical problems: A review of three decades of research with recent developments. *Expert Syst. Appl.*, 137, 202–231, 2019.

14. Moya, A., Navarro, E., Jaén, J., González, P., *Fuzzy-description logic for supporting the rehabilitation of the elderly.* Expert Systems. 37, 2, e12464, 2020 Apr.

15. Tucan, P., Gherman, B., Major, K., Vaida, C., Major, Z., Plitea, N., Carbone, G., Pisla, D., Fuzzy logic-based risk assessment of a parallel robot for elbow and wrist rehabilitation. *Int. J. Environ. Res. Public Health*, 17, 654, 2020.

16. Tüzün, S. and Topcu, Y.I., A taxonomy of operations research studies in healthcare management. *Oper. Res. Appl. HealthCare Manage.*, 3–21, 2017.

17. Narayanamurthy, G., Gurumurthy, A., Is the hospital lean? A mathematical model for assessing the implementation of lean thinking in healthcare institutions. *Oper. Res. HealthCare*, 1, 18, 84–98, 2018 Sep.

18. Suresh, M., Vaishnavi, V., Pai, R.D., Leanness evaluation in healthcare organizations using fuzzy logic approach. *Int. J. Org. Anal.*, 2020.

19. Akram, M., Dudek, W.A., Ilyas, F., Group decision-making based on pythagorean fuzzy TOPSIS method. *Int. J. Intell. Syst.*, 1–21, 2019.

20. Rajabi, F., Jahangiri, M., Bagherifard, F., Banaee, S., Farhadi, P., Strategies for controlling violence against healthcare workers: Application of fuzzy analytical hierarchy process and fuzzy additive ratio assessment. *J. Nurs. Manage.*, 28, 4, 777–786, 2020 May.

21. Garai, A., Roy, TK., Multi-objective optimization of cost-effective and customer-centric closed-loop supply chain management model in T-environment. *Soft Comput.*, 24, 1, 155–178, 2020 Jan.

22. Maghsoodi, A.I., Mosavat, M., Hafezalkotob, A., Hafezalkotob, A., Hybrid hierarchical fuzzy group decision-making based on information axioms and BWM: Prototype design selection. *Comput. Ind. Eng.*, 1, 127, 788–804, 2019 Jan.

23. Ozsahin, I., Sharif, T., Ozsahin, D.U., Uzun, B., Evaluation of solid-state detectors in medical imaging with fuzzy PROMETHEE. *J. Instrum.*, 14, 01, C01019, 2019 Jan.

24. Moreno-Cabezali, B.M., Fernandez-Crehuet, J.M., Application of a fuzzy-logic based model for risk assessment in additive manufacturing R&D projects. *Comput. Ind. Eng.*, 1, 145, 106529, 2020 Jul.

25. AlZu'bi, S., Shehab, M., Al-Ayyoub, M., Jararweh, Y., Gupta, B., Parallel implementation for 3d medical volume fuzzy segmentation. *Pattern Recognit. Lett.* 1;130:312-8.

26. La Fata, C.M., Lupo, T., Piazza, T., Service quality benchmarking via a novel approach based on fuzzy ELECTRE III and IPA: an empirical case involving the Italian public healthcare context. *HealthCare Manag Sci.*, 22, 1, 106–120, 2019 Mar.

27. Samiei, S., Pourbabaki, R., Risk factors of low back pain using adaptive neuro-fuzzy. *Archieves Occup. Health*, 3, 2, 339–345, 2019 Apr.

28. Akinnuwesi BA, Adegbite BA, Adelowo F, Ima-Edomwonyi U, Fashoto G, Amumeji OT. Decision support system for diagnosing Rheumatic-Musculoskeletal disease using fuzzy cognitive MAP technique. Informatics in Medicine Unlocked. 1, 18, 100279, 2020 Jan.

29. Vidhya, K. and Shanmugalakshmi, R., Modified adaptive neuro-fuzzy inference system (M-ANFIS) based multi-disease analysis of healthcare big data. *J. Supercomput.*, 2020.

30. Vaishnavi, V. and Suresh, M., Assessing the readiness level of healthcare for implementing agility using fuzzy logic approach. *Global J. Flexible Syst. Manage.*, 2020.

31. Sumrit, D., Supplier selection for vendor-managed inventory in healthcare using fuzzy multi-criteria decision-making approach. *Decis. Sci. Lett.*, 9, 2, 233–256, 2020.

32. Salazar, E.M. and Sanz-Calcedo, J.G., Study on the influence of maintenance operations on energy consumption and emissions in healthcare centres by fuzzy cognitive maps. *J. Build. Perform. Simul.*, 2018.

33. Rajput, N., Pandey, R.K., Singh, A.P., Chauhan, A., An optimization of fuzzy EOQ model in healthcare industries with three different demand pattern using signed distance technique. *Math. Eng. Sci. Aerosp.*, 10, 2, 2019.

34. Priyan, S. and Uthayakumar, R., Economic design of an inventory system involving probabilistic deterioration and variable setup cost through mathematical approach. *Int. J. Math. Oper. Res.*, 8, 3, 2016.

35. Pascual-Figal, D., Wachter, R., Senni, M., Belohlavek, J., Noè, A., Carr, D., Butylin, D., Rationale and design of TRANSITION: A randomized trial of pre-discharge vs. post-discharge initiation of sacubitril/valsartan. *ESC Heart Failure*, 5, 2, 327–336, 2018.

36. Wachter, R., Senni, M., Belohlavek, J., Straburzynska-Migaj, E., Witte, K.K., Kobalava, Z., Chaaban, S., Initiation of sacubitril/valsartan in haemodynamically stabilised heart failure patients in hospital or early after discharge: Primary results of the randomised TRANSITION study. *Eur. J. Heart Failure*, 21, 8, 998–1007, 2019.

37. Barker, L.R., Curriculum for ambulatory care training in medical residency. *J. Gener. Internal Med.*, 5, 1, S3–S14, 1990.

38. Shah, R., Melvin, L., Cavalcanti, R.B., EPAs for the Ambulatory Internist in Translation: Findings from a Canadian Multi-Center Survey. *Can. J. Gen. Internal Med.*, 14, 3, 9–15, 2019.

39. Armstrong, K.A., Coyte, P.C., Brown, M., Beber, B., Semple, J.L., Effect of home monitoring via mobile app on the number of in-person visits following ambulatory surgery: A randomized clinical trial. *JAMA Surgery*, 152, 7, 622–627, 2017.

40. Warrington, L., Absolom, K., Conner, M., Kellar, I., Clayton, B., Ayres, M., Velikova, G., Electronic Systems for Patients to report and manage side effects of Cancer treatment: Systematic review. *J. Med. Internet Res.*, 21, 1, e10875, 2019.

41. Pramanik, M.I., Lau, R.Y., Demirkan, H., Azad, M.A.K., Smart health: Big data enabled health paradigm within smart cities. *Expert Syst. Appl.*, 87, 370–383, 2017.

42. López-Torres, S., López-Torres, H., Rocha-Rocha, J., Butt, S.A., Tariq, M.I., Collazos-Morales, C., Piñeres-Espitia, G., IoT Monitoring of Water Consumption for Irrigation Systems Using SEMMA Methodology. *International Conference on Intelligent Human Computer Interaction*, Springer, Cham, pp. 222–234, 2019, December.

43. Wang, X., White, L., Chen, X., Gao, Y., Li, H., Luo, Y., An empirical study of wearable technology acceptance in healthcare. *Ind. Manage. Data Syst.*, 2015.

44. Tariq, M.I., Tayyaba, S., Ali Mian, N., Sarfraz, M.S., De-la-Hoz-Franco, E., Butt, S.A., Rad, D.V., Combination of AHP and TOPSIS methods for the ranking of information security controls to overcome its obstructions under fuzzy environment. *J. Intell. Fuzzy Syst.*, (Preprint). 1–14, 2020.

45. Martinez, D., Talbert, T., Romero-Steiner, S., Kosmos, C., Redd, S., Evolution of the public health preparedness and response capability standards to

support public health emergency management practices and processes. *Health Secur.*, 17, 6, 430–438, 2019.

46. Shapiro, J.S., Crowley, D., Hoxhaj, S., Langabeer II, J., Panik, B., Taylor, T.B., Nielson, J.A., Health information exchange in emergency medicine. *Ann. Emergency Med.*, 67, 2, 216–226, 2016.

47. Jeong, P.S. and Cho, Y.H., Emergency Support System using Smart Device. *J. Korea Inst. Inf. Commun. Eng.*, 20, 9, 1791–1798, 2016.

48. Jiang, J. and Cameron, A.F., IT-Enabled Self-Monitoring for Chronic Disease Self-Management: An Interdisciplinary Review. *MIS Quarterly*, 44, 1, 2020.

49. Dudakiya, S., Galani, H., Shaikh, A., Thanki, D., Late, R.A., Pawar, S.E., Monitoring mobile patients using predictive analysis by data from wearable sensors. *2016 International Conference on Electrical, Electronics, and Optimization Techniques (ICEEOT)*, IEEE, pp. 332–335, 2016, March.

50. Rezaeibagha, F. and Mu, Y., Practical and secure telemedicine systems for user mobility. *J. Biomed. Inf.*, 78, 24–32, 2018.

51. MacIntyre, C.R., Engells, T.E., Scotch, M., Heslop, D.J., Gumel, A.B., Poste, G., Broom, A., Converging and emerging threats to health security. *Environ. Syst. Decis.*, 38, 2, 198–207, 2018.

52. Chiuchisan, I., Balan, D.G., Geman, O., Chiuchisan, I., Gordin, I., A security approach for healthcare information systems. *2017 E-Health and Bioengineering Conference (EHB)*, IEEE, pp. 721–724, 2017, June.

53. McDermott, D.S., Kamerer, J.L., Birk, A.T., Electronic health records: A literature review of cyber threats and security measures. *Int. J. Cyber Res. Educ. (IJCRE)*, 1, 2, 42–49, 2019.

3

Data-Driven Decision Making in IoT Healthcare Systems—COVID-19: A Case Study

Saroja S.,* Haseena S. and Blessa Binolin Pepsi M.

Mepco Schlenk Engineering College, Sivakasi, India

Abstract

This research express an impression of automated decision-making techniques that have been suggested for scrutiny of data from IoT based healthcare systems. IoT data analytics plays a vital role in this modern era since data from connected devices reveal meaningful results with better insights for the future. The chapter involves the design of a decision-making system that collects data from IoT based healthcare systems, preprocess and analyzes data, and generates detailed information reports for better diagnosis. Data preprocessing methods such as data cleaning, munging, normalization, reduction, and removing noisy data are applied. The blend of IoT data with analytics technique results to be beneficial in healthcare systems. The collected IoT information like pulse rate, temperature, oxygen level and heart rate from connected devices can be used to analyze the need and severity in the preliminary stage itself using appropriate machine learning techniques. Multi Criteria Decision Making (MCDM) techniques such as SMART, WPM, and TOPSIS are also applied for conclusion production procedure to generate detailed informative diagnostic reports. Being healthcare data, the overall objective is to aid business organizations with better decision making processes through data analytics thereby deploying the right IoT strategy. The result of the next-generation expert systems can utilize the results for further analysis in diagnosis and treatment.

Keywords: Healthcare systems, machine learning, multi criteria decision making, IoT, preprocessing, data analytics, expert systems

*Corresponding author: activeroja@gmail.com

SK Hafizul Islam and Debabrata Samanta (eds.) Smart Healthcare System Design: Security and Privacy Aspects, (57–70) © 2021 Scrivener Publishing LLC

3.1   Introduction

The Coronavirus Disease-2019 also called as COVID-19 is a respiratory illness or disease due to the issue respiratory syndrome with high fatality rate. The pandemic caused by the novel coronavirus has been spreading all over the world. The impact caused by the COVID-19 has earlier affected the people of China, has now been a matter of concern in the entire world. The scarcity of medicinal resources and lack to introduce a vaccine for COVID-19 has forced majority of the countries either in partial or complete lockdown. The number of corona virus infected people is increasing at an alarming rate throughout the world and there is no vacancy for the infected people to get admitted in the hospital until the people undergoing the treatment get discharged.

Once this corona virus enters into the lungs of the human body, it has severe effects like cough, fever, headache, etc. Majority of the population affected by COVID have relatively mild symptoms but many have severe to critical symptoms. While COVID-19 vaccine is not available yet, the reproduction rate of this virus is increasing rapidly. In order to control the widespread of corona virus, government is taking much initiative to reduce and control the spread of virus. But, all these measures are reducing the impact only to some extent. With a rapid rate of infection, there are no sufficient hospitals to treat COVID-19 patients and only few ventilators are available to treat people with high respiratory syndrome. So, there is need to classify and prioritize the COVID affected patients.

Figure 3.1 shows the overall decision of the proposed work. IoT-based healthcare systems capture human body parameters like pulse, temperature, oxygen level and heart rate. These data captured from the human body is preprocessed, classified and decision making algorithm is carried out to classify whether the patient is COVID-19 affected or not. Data

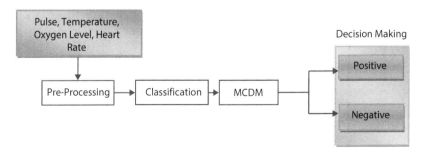

Figure 3.1 Overall design.

preprocessing methods like data cleaning, munging, normalization, reduction, and removing noisy data are applied. Classification is the next step carried out to classify the data using algorithms like Stratified Classifier, Support Vector Machine (SVM), Gradient Boosting, Random Forest and Ada Boost. Experimental analysis is carried using various measures like precision, recall, F1-Score, accuracy. Multi Criteria Decision Making (MCDM) process like SMART, WPM, and TOPSIS are also applied for the conclusion creation procedure to generate detailed information regarding the stay of the COVID affected persons.

3.1.1   Pre-Processing

Preprocessing is the initial step carried out in data analytics which transforms, encodes or converts into a form that a machine can easily carry out the analysis. The data collected from the IoT-based healthcare system are highly vulnerable to inconsistent, missing and noisy because of their voluminous information and it cannot be directly processed as it may contain noise, unwanted information or irrelevant information. The data preprocessing helps in converting raw data into a useful format that helps in reducing the processing time, avoiding errors and make the data ready for the next step. This unprocessed data may produce unbiased result which cannot be used for data analytics. Therefore, it should be processed before applying any algorithm. Data preprocessing methods like data cleaning, munging, normalization, reduction, and removing noisy data are applied. Data cleaning methods are used to identify the outliers in the data which help to create a model. The unwanted data present in the dataset can cause confusion in the mining process and may produce the unreliable output. It is the process of removing the inaccurate data and removing the incomplete information present in the dataset. It helps in removing the inconsistent data that is caused because of human errors during entry or during transmission. To handle the missing and irrelevant data, data cleaning methods like removing missing values and noise in the data using clustering is carried out. Missing values are ignored or interpolation methods are applied to fill in the missing values. Similar data are grouped together and unfamiliar data are detected as outliers and is removed. Data munging, also called as data wrangling is carried out to manually transform and clean the IoT data. It removed unwanted information and creates relevant information needed for processing. Data normalization scales the data with attributes of various scales. It minimizes and avoids duplicate data. It produces new range from the existing range which that allows processing data effectively.

Most data in real world captured through IoT devices have large number of features. Dimensionality reduction is applied to select only the needed features thus reducing the processing time is required. It is the data mining technique that is applied in order to produce the reduced representation of the data. Feature Subset Selection is applied to select only the relevant features needed for further processing. Thus, the preprocessing methods used, helps in making the data ready to be further processed by the algorithm in an efficient manner and helps in making better decisions.

3.1.2   Classification Algorithms

This section deals with the different classification algorithms and explains their working principle and procedure.

3.1.2.1   Dummy Classifier

This is a simple classifier that performs better where datasets are of class imbalance. The various strategies are stratified, most frequent, uniform and constant. The stratified classifier associates with the probability that predicts the most frequent label from the training set. Approximately the class labels that predict more than 85% is identified to be the class label of dummy classifier.

3.1.2.2   Support Vector Machine (SVM)

Support vector machine is a supervised knowledge technique utilized to analyze data in the process of categorization. This input features are plotted in n-dimensional space and then further a hyperplane is identified as decision boundary to split the classes. The decision boundary is mapped as optimal decision boundary for which the margin is max.

The hyperplanes are identified with maximal margin using the support vectors. The support vectors are training points identified to be splitting points between class labels. Reduction in the choice of number of support vectors provides good generalisation. This process can be done in a linear data mapping. The non-linear data plotted in an n-dimensional space can never be divided with boundaries. So, the non-linear data will be further mapped to a high dimensional space using kernel function (as shown in Figure 3.2).

A separating hyperplane can be given as

$$W \times X + b = 0 \tag{3.1}$$

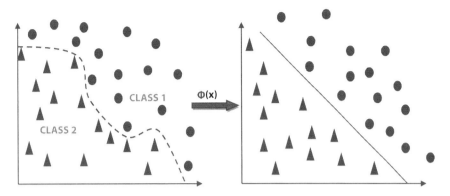

Figure 3.2 Kernel Function on non-linear SVM.

W is a weight vector (w_1, w_2, … .w_n), n is the number of attributes and b is a scalar. As the X vector which lies very close to it the maximum margin hyperplane is described.

Non-linear mapping requires the kernel trick, which is a two-vector dot product. The kernel is associated to the transformation $\Phi(Xi)$ with the equation $K(xi,xj) = \Phi(xi) \cdot \Phi(xj)$. A sample non-linear transformation on 6D space for a given 3D vector $X = \{x1,x2,x3\}$ using the Kernel mapping can be given as $\Phi1(X) = x1$, $\Phi2(X) = x2$, $\Phi3(x3) = x3$, $\Phi4(X) = (x1)^2$, $\Phi5(X) = (x1x2)$, $\Phi6(X) = (x1x3)$. Further this can be processed like a linear data with the decision boundary. Further the kernel functions are Polynomial, Gaussian, sigmoid etc.

3.1.2.3   Gradient Boosting

Gradient Boosting is a classification problem that builds a learner and predicts the test sample based on ensemble of weak prediction models. The algorithm is an additive model that performs optimization with differentiable loss functions. Basically decision trees are used for it and then generalize through optimization based on cost function. Thereby becomes a strong predictive model.

As this improves the strength of other learning algorithms, the idea is known as Probability Approximately Correct (PAC) learning. The hypothesis boosting tests identify the weak learner that was poorly classified and examples that were successfully classified to build a perfect model. As a whole gradient boosting involves three features, they are

- Optimizing the loss function
- Weak learner is used to make predictions
- Build an additive model to reduce loss function of weak learners.

Loss function for a classification problem can be logarithmic loss of the predictive model technique. Decision trees are used as weak learner. Trees are constructed using the best split point with scores of Gini index or Information Gain to minimize the loss. The error loss can be minimized while building trees. Modifying the parameters to reduce the residual loss is worked out as the last feature.

3.1.2.4   Random Forest

Random forest includes many individual decision trees that combine together as ensemble classification. The concept of training the ensemble decision trees is known as bagging. It's the idea of combining the learning models which increases the result. The merged prediction (as depicted in Figure 3.3) is more accurate and stable. Instead of identifying the best feature for splitting a node through parameter calculation, it can be random subset of features. The internal nodes in a decision tree represent the characteristics and the edges represent the prerequisite for rules to be formed.

Random forest algorithm proceeds in such a way that, random samples are selected from the dataset and using which decision tree is constructed. The process gets repeated for almost all samples. Voting is performed on the predicted results and the on most voted will be the final prediction class.

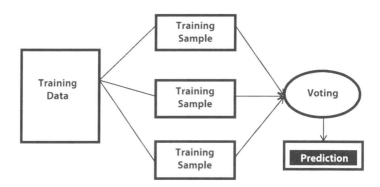

Figure 3.3 Working of random forest algorithm.

3.1.2.5   Ada Boost

Ada Boost is an adaptive boosting algorithm for binary classification. The algorithm proceeds like gradient boosting methods combining different decision trees. Weight is allocated for every instance in the training set. Weak classifier like decision trees performs classification on weighted samples. These kind of boosting algorithms normally combine the multiple low or weak classifier accuracy models to attain a strong highly accurate model. Thereby, Ada boost stands as an algorithm to boost the performance of weak learner in order to increase the accuracy of the decision stump built from training set.

3.2   Experimental Analysis

The data set for COVID-19 is obtained from Ref. [1]. Positive and negative data are used as two groups to predict COVID-19 disease based on the results of the input blood and urine test as a feature set. The results of the study were calculated based on the precision, accuracy, recall, and F1 score results.

3.3   Multi-Criteria Decision Making (MCDM) Procedure

This segment covers three different types of Multiple Criteria Decision Making (MCDM) and discusses how they are utilized in the sense of decision-making.

MCDM methods assist pronouncement manufacturer to make this greatest judgment in the presence of multiple (conflicting) criteria [2–7]. All the possible alternatives are assessed against the multiple criteria and the best of them is picked. The popular MCDM techniques available are SAW (Simple Additive Weighting), WPM (Weighted Product Model), TOPSIS (Similarity to the Ideal Solution Order Preference Technique), PROMETHEE (METHod for Enrichment Assessment Preference Ranking Organization), AHP (Analytical Hierarchy Process), SMART (The Simple Multi Attribute Rating Technique) and ANP (Analytic Network Process). In many real life applications, such as supplier selection, product selection, design selection, producer selection, and so on, MCDM methods play a vital role. The methods are chosen on the basis of the problem domain's demand and its applicability. Methods of MCDM help pick the most favored single alternative or help to classify a collection containing preferred alternatives.

In the decision making process, the following steps are carried out:

- Define the problem by identifying the set of alternatives,
- Identify the necessary requirements for determining the alternatives.
  - ➢ Criteria should be able to differentiate the substitute in terms of its performance.
  - ➢ Lesser number of criteria is preferred.
  - ➢ Criteria can be either of assistance type (positive) or of cost type (negative).
- Choose a form of conclusion production.
- Test substitutes alongside requirements.
  - ➢ Rating the choices or selecting the right alternatives.
- Validate solutions against statements of issues.
  - ➢ Make sure that the explanations produced are right.
  - ➢ Report the choices to stakeholders.

3.3.1   Simple Multi Attribute Rating Technique (SMART)

The SMART performance developed by Edwards in 1971 is a simple linear additive model. It calculates and assigns the overall utility assessment of a given substitute as product of the total sum of the routine achieve of both criterion and the weight of that criterion. The technique is more useful due to its simplicity.

The performance score of ith alternative is calculated as follows:

$$Utility_i = \sum_{j=1}^{m} w_j * U_{ij} \qquad (3.2)$$

Where, is the weight value assigned to jth criteria, is the performance score of the ith alternative on jth criterion. 'm' is the number of criteria. The best alternative is one which has the highest utility value. Alternatives are ranked based on their utility value.

3.3.1.1   COVID-19 Disease Classification Using SMART

Here, the classification algorithms (Stratified Classifier, SVM, Gradient Boosting, Random Forest, and Ada Boost) are alternatives and the performance metrics of the classification algorithm are considered as criteria (as it is given in Table 3.1); SMART decision making technique picks the right algorithm for classification based on the performance score of the

Table 3.1 Classification results for COVID-19 data set.

Classification algorithm	Precision	Recall	F1-score	Accuracy
Stratified Classifier	0.86	0.81	0.83	0.72
SVM	0.91	0.88	0.9	0.83
Gradient Boosting	0.91	0.92	0.91	0.85
Random Forest	0.92	0.89	0.9	0.83
Ada Boost	0.94	0.81	0.87	0.79

alternatives on different criteria: Precision, Recall, F1-score and Accuracy. All the chosen criteria are of benefit type and the performance score values are in the range between 0 and 1. Hence, there is no need of normalization. If the weight values for the parameters are assigned to as w1 = 0.15 (Precision), w2 = 0.25 (Recall), w3 = 0.1 (F1-score), and w4 = 0.5 (Accuracy) as given in Table 3.2. Then in Table 3.3, the SMART results for the selected weight factor are given.

We can infer from this SMART approach that Gradient Boosting and Random Forest are the two best classification algorithms for the classification of COVID-19 disease. Also, the Ada Boost algorithm is performing worse when compared to other algorithms taken into consideration.

Table 3.2 Weights of different criteria.

Criteria	Precision	Recall	F1-score	Accuracy
Weight Values	0.15	0.25	0.10	0.5

Table 3.3 Performance scores and rank by SMART.

Classification algorithm	Score	Rank
Stratified Classifier	0.7745	5
SVM	0.8615	3
Gradient Boosting	0.8825	1
Random Forest	0.8655	2
Ada Boost	0.8255	4

3.3.2   Weighted Product Model (WPM)

WPM was launched by Yoon and Hwang in the year 1995. Normalization is the primary step of any decision making method, but it is not needed in this WPM as the method is called as dimensionless method. Similar to SMART, in this method also, there are two types of parameters (benefit— higher value means improvement with lower cost assessment means improvement).

Weights become elements, positive power weight is utilized for gain criteria, and negative power weight is utilized for price criteria.

$$Utility_i = \prod_{j=1}^{j=m} (U_{ij})^{w_j} \tag{3.3}$$

We can sort the substitutes based on the output scores by following the calculation above.

3.3.2.1   *COVID-19 Disease Classification Using WPM*

This classification algorithms (Stratified Classifier, SVM, Gradient Boosting, Random Forest, and Ada Boost) are alternatives and the performance metrics of the classification algorithm are considered as criteria; WPM decision making technique selects the best classification algorithm on various parameters based on the output score of the alternatives: Precision, Recall, F1-score and Accuracy. All the chosen criteria are of benefit type and the performance score values are in the range between 0 and 1. The weight values are assigned to the different criteria as given in Table 3.2. Table 3.4 offers the WPM results for the selected weight factor.

Table 3.4 Presentation determined by WPM.

Classification algorithm	Score	Rank
Stratified Classifier	0.772449	5
SVM	0.860875	3
Gradient Boosting	0.881895	1
Random Forest	0.864727	2
Ada Boost	0.823865	4

From this WPM approach, we can infer that the two best classification algorithms for COVID-19 disease classification are Gradient Boosting and Random Forest. Here also, the Ada Boost algorithm is performing worse when compared to other algorithms taken into consideration.

3.3.3   Method for Order Preference by Similarity to the Ideal Solution (TOPSIS)

TOPSIS, originally developed by Ching-Lai Hwang and Yoon in 1981, is a common MCDM method and has undergone further improvements. It operates on the basis of the assumption that the best alternative should be the shortest path to the positive ideal explanation and the longest detachment to the negative ideal explanation [8, 9]. For all of the parameters considered, the optimal positive explanation is the one with the greatest assessment. The negative optimal explanation is the one that has the worst assessment for all the parameters believed. If we have 'n' alternatives and 'm' parameters then U_{ij} denotes for jth criterion the success value of ith substitute.

The steps involved in TOPSIS method for COVID-19 disease classification are as follows:

1. Build a normalized weighted decision matrix.

This step involves multiplying by its associated weight each column of the matrix's output score. The normalized weighted decision matrix is determined as follows:

$$V_{ij} = w_j * U_{ij} \tag{3.4}$$

2. Conclude the perfect positive and ideal negative explanations.

The following equations can be used to conclude the positive ideal explanation and the negative ideal explanation.

Positive ideal explanation:

$$V^+ = \{(\max V_{ij} \mid j = J), \}\forall\, i = 1, 2,..,n \tag{3.5}$$

$$V^+ = \{V_1^+, V_2^+, \ldots, V_n^+\} \tag{3.6}$$

Negative ideal solution:

$$V^- = \{(\min V_{ij} \mid j = J), \}\forall\, i = 1, 2,\ldots,n \tag{3.7}$$

$$V^- = \{V_1^-, V_2^-, \ldots, V_n^-\} \tag{3.8}$$

3. For each alternative, determine the separation measure.

The separation determines of an alternative from the positive ideal explanation and also from the negative ideal explanation is measured in this step.

The computation of separation from the constructive superlative explanation is calculated as follows:

$$S_i^+ = \sqrt{\sum_{j=1}^{j=m} (V_j^+ - V_{ij})^2} \quad \forall I = 1, 2, \ldots, n \tag{3.9}$$

Separation measure from negative ideal explanation is calculated as follows:

$$S_i^- = \sqrt{\sum_{j=1}^{j=m} (V_j^- - V_{ij})^2} \quad \forall I = 1, 2, \ldots, n \tag{3.10}$$

4. Calculate each alternative's relative coefficient of closeness.

By considering the positive ideal resolution and the negative ideal explanation, this step measures with similarity for alternatives. The coefficient value of relative closeness is determined as follows:

$$C_i^* = S_i^- / (S_i^+ + S_i^-) \tag{3.11}$$

Choose the High Relative Closeness Coefficient alternative C_i^* value.

3.3.3.1 COVID-19 Disease Classification Using TOPSIS

This classification algorithms (Stratified Classifier, SVM, Gradient Boosting, Random Forest, and Ada Boost) are alternatives and the performance metrics of the classification algorithm are considered as criteria; TOPSIS decision making technique picks the right algorithm for classification based on the performance score of the alternatives on different criteria: Precision, Recall, F1-score and Accuracy. All the chosen criteria are of benefit type and the performance score values are in the range between 0 and 1. Hence, there is no need of normalization. If researchers allocate the weight assessments with this criteria as w1 = 0.15 (Precision), w2 = 0.25 (Recall),

Table 3.5 Presentation determines by TOPSIS.

Classification algorithm	Relative closeness coefficient	Rank
Stratified Classifier	0.132	4
SVM	0.792	5
Gradient Boosting	0.914	1
Random Forest	0.8	2
Ada Boost	0.462	3

w3 = 0.1 (F1-score), and w4 = 0.5 (Accuracy) as given in the Table 3.2, then in Table 3.5, the products of the TOPSIS algorithm for the chosen weight factor are prearranged.

We can infer from this TOPSIS approach that Gradient Boosting and Random Forest are the two best classification algorithms in the COVID-19 disease classification. Here, the SVM algorithm is performing worse when compared to all the other algorithms taken into consideration.

3.4   Conclusion

This chapter proposes a decision making method that helps in making better decisions for patient affected with COVID-19. Due to lack of medical resources, many people are not prone to proper treatments in hospital and based on the vacancy only they are admitted. By making proper decision, the people with high impact, can be given preference in hospitals when compared with patients with low impact. It is concluded that the conventional classification algorithms and MCDM methods can be applied in healthcare domain for the betterment of public [10, 11].

References

1. Dong, E., Du, H., Gardner, L., An interactive web-based dashboard to track COVID-19 in real time. *Lancet Inf. Dis.*, 20, 5, 533–534, 2020.
2. Saroja, S., Revathi, T., Nitin, A., Multi-Criteria Decision-Making for Heterogeneous Multiprocessor Scheduling. *Int. J. Inf. Technol. Decis. Making*, 17, 5, 1399–1427, 2018.
3. Velasquez, M. and Hester, P.T., An Analysis of Multi-Criteria Decision Making Methods. *Int. J. Oper. Res.*, 10, 2, 56–66, 2013.

4. Patel, M., Bhatt, B., Vashi, M., *SMART-Multi-criteria decision-making technique for use in planning activities*, New Horizons in Civil Engineering (NHCE-2017) At: Surat, Gujarat, 2017.

5. Mulliner, E., Malys, N., Maliene, V., Comparative analysis of MCDM methods for the assessment of sustainable housing affordability. *Omega*, 59, Part B, 2016.

6. Triantaphyllou, E., Fuzzy Multi-Criteria Decision Making, in: *Multi-criteria Decision Making Methods: A Comparative Study. Applied Optimization*, vol. 44, 2000.

7. Madavan, R. and SujathaBalaraman, Saroja, S., Multi-Criteria Decision Making Methods for Grading High-Performance Transformer Oil with Antioxidants Under Accelerated Ageing Conditions. *IET Gener. Transm. Distrib.*, 11, 4051–4058, 2017.

8. Opricovic, S. and Tzeng, G.H., Compromise solution by MCDM methods: A comparative analysis of VIKOR and TOPSIS. *Eur. J. Oper. Res.*, 156, 445–455, 2004.

9. Malekpoor, H., Mishra, N., Kumar, S., A novel TOPSIS–CBR goal programming approach to sustainable healthcare treatment. *Ann. Oper. Res.*, 1–24, 2018.

10. Rouyendegh, B.D., Performance evaluation of healthcare: A pilot case study. *J. Perioperative Crit. Intensive Care Nurs.*, 21, 2019.

11. Chatterjee, S., Dey, N., Shi, F., Ashour, A.S., Fong, S.J., Sen, S., Clinical application of modified bag-of-features coupled with hybrid neural-based classifier in dengue fever classification using gene expression data. *Med. Biol. Eng. Comput.*, 56, 4, 709–720, 2018.

4

Touch and Voice-Assisted Multilingual Communication Prototype for ICU Patients Specific to COVID-19

B. Rajesh Kanna[1] and C. Vijayalakshmi[2*]

[1]School of Computer Science and Engineering, Vellore Institute of Technology, Chennai, India
[2]Department of Statistics and Applied Mathematics, Central University of Tamil Nadu, Thiruvarur, India

Abstract

The proposed work deals with the design and development of touch and native voice-assisted prototype to enable the intuitive communication & interaction between health professionals and patients who are affected with Severe Acute Respiratory Infection (SARI), Ventilator-dependent and admitted in Quarantine care. It also ensures the development of the multilingual capability to communicate effectively in most speaking ten Indian languages, so that the patients will be relieved from pains etc., as their queries are being addressed by health professionals. In this prototype, touch based gesture patterns can be effectively used as an interactive module and helps the doctors to monitor and answer to the queries of ICU patients regularly by updating it to the caretakers such that the patients are at ease to express their emotions or pains. The proposed prototype will be made available and accessible in an open software repository. As per the existing methods patients express their needs through non-verbal communication methods and they could be missed out or misinterpreted resulting in symptoms that are poorly understood and the clinicians overestimate their ability to understand their communication feelings. These situations are eradicated by employing the use of "Touch Voice of SARI" Application. Hence this can be considered as an assistive communication tool which replaces the nonverbal communication to a meaningful communication for ventilator patients and healthcare professionals.

Corresponding author: vijayalakshmi@cutn.ac.in

SK Hafizul Islam and Debabrata Samanta (eds.) Smart Healthcare System Design: Security and Privacy Aspects, (71–86) © 2021 Scrivener Publishing LLC

Keywords: Ventilator dependent, multilingual, communication, prototype, health professionals, ICU patients, intubation

4.1   Introduction and Motivation

To understand the patient's emotional feelings or pain, communication between health professionals and patients plays a vital role in identifying, understanding the patients problems and providing clinical solutions. Ventilator dependent, Severe Acute respiratory and quarantine care ICU patients frequently face difficulties for their most basic human interactions, namely communication due to either respiratory illness, language problem or intubated. ICU patients have serious implications with respect to physical and psychological due to non communication problems. Researchers have developed different types of services like Speech language Pathologist so that Augmentative and alternative communication assistance can be given to all health professionals and caretakers. Though the vital body parameters of patients are being monitored well, their intuitive feelings and their respective symptoms could not be effectively conveyed or understood by doctors/nurses during intensive caring because of being multilingual. It is the most distressing and stressful aspect of critical illness, more than one in four ICU survivors suffer from depression, anxiety or post-traumatic stress disorders. Although various assistive communication tools exist in one premier language those were infrequently used when the patient and doctor haven't found/known a common communication language. ICU patients express their needs by non verbal communication methods and it could be a little bit difficult to understand their complete requirements by the health professionals. In turn, a patient's emotions result in apprehension, anger etc. Based on the interviews and suggestions given by the patients it reveals to the fact that both do not have common communication language. Frequently, health professionals did not understand the gestures clearly. Similarly, interviews were conducted with health-professionals who have rich experience in handling and treating intensive care patients. Finally, under patients' interaction, comfort based questions were identified and those questions were considered for interaction. Based on the outcome of the interview with recovered patients and health professionals the communication lapses are identified, with an emphasis of interactive learning through touch gestures for effective multilingual communication.

Due to the rapid increase of COVID-19 spread, there is a substantial increase in the capacity of ICU beds, health professionals and ICU staff nurses. The Government and policy makers have been focusing on deploying manpower and mobilizing the infrastructure with respect to the infection affected localities. However, they should also analyze in a broad way on focusing the development of new mechanisms to improve effective communication between doctors and patients. Rather than doctors understanding the patient's health history they should also understand their pains, intuitive, emotional feelings via communication which will lead to speedy recovery in addition to medication. Hence, it plays a vital role as it helps doctors to achieve better outcomes, patient recovery and to understand patient's non-verbal communication [2–4] because of being multilingual or intubated. In order to eliminate the barriers involved in patient–doctor communication including fear, stress in work burden, patient's apprehension, non-viable expectations, a survey has been conducted to understand the needs of patients in order to design a multilingual prototype for effective communication. Carruthers *et al.* [5] have analyzed about the importance of alternative communication methods for voiceless patients in intensive care units [5]. Frequently, health professionals did not understand the gestures clearly. Similarly, interviews were conducted with health-professionals who have rich experience in handling and treating intensive care patients [9]. The information referred from the research article [1] which discusses that 81 nurses and 34 physicians and participated in the data collection, with 2,240 questions recorded. Finally, under patients' interaction, comfort based questions were identified. Those questions are being considered for interaction.

4.1.1 Existing Interaction Approaches and Technology

Existing applications such as Electrolarynx (EL), SmallTalk Intensive Care, Patient Communicator App, myICUvoice and High-tech communication intervention are being discussed below:

- *Electrolarynx (EL)*

This mainly consists of a battery powered handy device that could be pressed onto the skin of the neck. It will transmit the electronic sound in a vibrated way into the oropharyngeal cavity and the user can convert into speech using articulation.

- *High-Tech Communication Intervention*

All devices contain a database of prestored phrases or figures. Various control devices for navigation are being used by Miglietta and speech synthesizer with detector, touch sensitive screen. It's a kind of pain management system to know the needs of the patients.

- *SmallTalk Intensive Care*

Patients can express their needs and emotions to care takers using the picture based vocabulary of phrases as they are not in a position to speak. Device training for pathologists, individuals are provided by Lingraphica Company.

- *voICe*

In this app, when the picture icon is touched a voice will say about the patient's condition (in Dutch 2013 and now in English). Recent version has keyboard, clock, and notes to store the messages/video message given by the family members to the patients.

- *Patient Communicator App*

This app is designed by SCCM to improve the communication between health professionals and patients.

- *myICUvoice*

This is a tool for ICU patients, families, and staff members. Simple symptom selection tools combined to speak along with physiotherapy functions. It's a unique back end technology to monitor, evaluate in real time, their patients.

4.1.2   Challenges and Gaps

Although various assistive communication tools exist in one premier language, they were rarely used when the patients and doctors could not understand a common communication language in expressing their state of health. In this context an overview of the various challenges faced by ICU patients and the gap analysis is carried out to eliminate the complexities and it is summarized as follows:

- Severe Acute respiratory, ventilator-dependent and quarantine care patients frequently face difficulties for their most basic human interactions, namely communication due to either respiratory illness or intubated.
- Though the vital body parameters of patients are being monitored well, their intuitive feelings and its respective symptoms are poorly conveyed or understood by doctors/ nurses during intensive caring. This is the most distressing and stressful aspect of critical illness, where more than one in four ICU survivors suffer with depression, anxiety or post-traumatic stress disorders.

- Although various assistive communication tools exist in one premier language, those were infrequently used when the patient and doctor haven't found a common communication language.

Based on the above observations, questions below have been aroused to find out the gaps in the existing methods such that the communication barrier is analyzed for elimination and evaluation of new prototype design.

- ICU patients emotions that they are not able to communicate
- List the ways that the patients can express their needs to healthcare providers
- What are the communication needs?
- Severe Acute Respiratory Infection (SARI) ventilator dependent patients admitted in quarantine care would like to express their feelings to the health professionals? What are the methods?
- Feelings of ICU patients regarding their inability to communicate
- Ways of effective communication with the healthcare providers
- Who are the stakeholders and beneficiaries apart from ICU admitted patients and health professionals?

Based on the above questions, the patients prefer for a new mode which could offer less verbal, non-verbal and break the language barrier. By considering all these factors a touch-based modality is incorporated in the proposed system to resolve the aforementioned challenges encountered during patient–doctor communication in intensive care. Otuzoglu and Karahan [6] and Maringelli et al. [8] have determined the effectiveness of illustrated communication material for communication with intubated patients at an intensive care unit. Miglietta et al. [7] have briefly done a pilot study about the computer-assisted communication for critically ill patients. The prototype of touch and voice assisted multilingual communication is detailed in Section 4.2. A sample real-time handling and the way of interaction between doctor and patient is described with illustrations in Section 4.3. The conclusion section explains the significance of the proposed prototype.

4.2   Proposed Prototype of Touch and Voice-Assisted Multilingual Communication

Prototype is being designed as an interactive communication tool for Severe Acute Respiratory Infection (SARI) patients in intensive care who are ventilated and not in a position to speak due to breathing problems, making communication difficult for patients interacting with nurses, doctors and patient's relatives. Verbal sign is not effective between patients and doctors as they face so many problems and patients in ICU feel their symptoms are poorly understood. The clinicians overestimate the ability to understand their communication or emotional feelings as this is the most distressing and stressful aspect of clinical illness which leads to this depression, anxiety or post-traumatic stress disorders. The concept of multi lingual is not being addressed as they can choose the language in their own native language.

Figure 4.1 shows the user interface design of the home page of the proposed prototype featured with a separate touch interaction spot for doctor and patients for the selection of their native languages to facilitate the multilingual interaction through the proposed design. Figure 4.2 shows the list of few Indian languages such as Hindi, Bengali, Marathi, Telugu, Tamil, Gujarati, Urdu, Kannada, Odia, and Malayalam that are being used by a majority of populations. English is also considered.

The doctors–patient interface is being designed with respect to appetite, breathing, pain, cough, throat, body pain using the front and rear pose of bare human skeletons. Doctors can ask a question to the patient and patient in turn can reply by touching the icon of pictures using the touch gestures.

i)   APPETITE
   • Doctor: Are you comfortable with food intake?
   • Patient: Yes, No

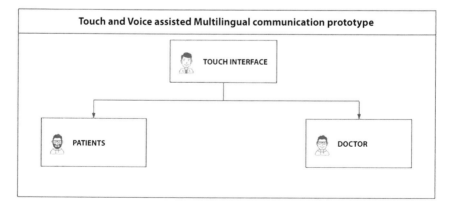

Figure 4.1 Home view of touch interaction.

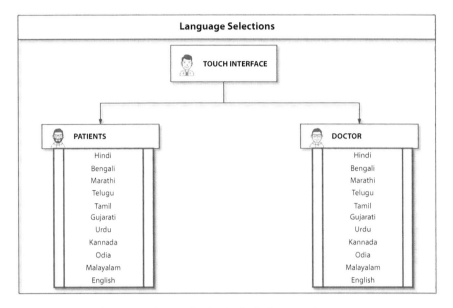

Figure 4.2 Cross language selection display for both doctor and patient.

ii) BREATH
- Doctor: Do you feel difficulty in breathing?
- Patient: Yes, No

iii) COUGH
- Doctor: Did you have a persistent moderate cough?
- Patient: Yes, No, Dry

iv) THROAT
- Doctor: Did you feel any sore in throat?
- Patient: Yes, No

v) COLD
- Doctor: Do you have a feel of start of the cold is?
- Patient: Runny nose, Sneezing, Fatigue

vi) SLEEP
- Doctor: Did you feel any disturbance during sleep?
- Patient: Moderate, Deep sleep, Distributed sleep

vii) BODY PAIN LOCATOR
- Doctor: Point out the location of your body pain in picture.

- Doctor: Still you have the pain?
- Patient: Yes, No

viii) GENERAL
- Doctor: Do you want to interact with Friend/Family/Relative/Psychologist?
- Patient: Friend/Family/Relative/Psychologist

In Figure 4.3, the Doctor–Patient interactions are being displayed which helps to have better understanding for further medical treatment by the doctor. The patient's interface is also framed based on the patient's basic requirements. It will be taken care as soon as the patient touches the icon such as clean the bed, dry mouth, mask off etc. The basic feelings or emotional feelings in terms of difficulties/discomfort, sleep disturbances due to the tube, swelling in any portion can be expressed in a clear way by touching the icon. Patient in turn wants to have a relaxation by having a talk with the family members, to know or drop down a message with respect to the health condition being dealt with. Patient and doctor responses are translated in their native way. Patients can ask a question to the doctor and the

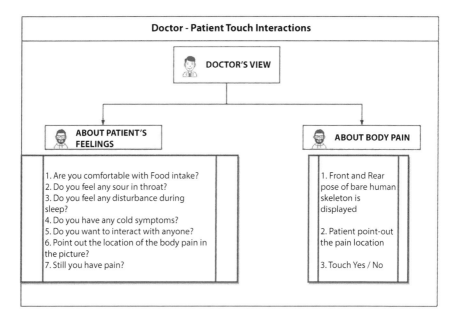

Figure 4.3 Categorical interactions initiated by doctor.

doctor in turn can reply by touching the icon of pictures using the touch gestures.

The patient interface includes their needs, feelings, about family, and requests to communicate with their well-wishers or other inmates.

i) PATIENT'S NEED
   - Patient: Dry mouth
   - Patient: Dry Tongue
   - Patient: Feeling Thirsty
   - Patient: Feeling Hungry
   - Patient: Mask off
   - Patient: Wash my mouth
   - Patient: Clean my bed

ii) PATIENT'S FEELINGS
   - Patient: Difficulties in respiration
   - Patient: Swelling
   - Patient: Difficulties due to pain
   - Patient: I am fatigued
   - Patient: Discomfort due to the endotracheal tube (ET),

iii) FAMILY/FRIEND
   - Patient: Can I meet my family?
   - Patient: How are my family members?
   - Patient: Want to drop a message to my family
   - Patient: Want to drop a message to my visitor
   - Patient: Want my family photos.

All the above interactions between doctor and patient are being depicted in Figure 4.4.

This helps both to use the Touch technology for effective interaction. Hence the main objective is to design a multilingual language using a technology through voice assistance or icons for intensive care unit patients. Doctor or patient can choose any language and this prototype will transform the language in a commendable way such that queries are being addressed in an effective way. As a result, doctors and patients can choose their own language and prototype will help them to have effective communication such that the language barrier is eliminated. Patients' health conditions will be improved and they will be out of stress. Both will feel the ease of operating the prototype and this will be extended to all languages in near future. Figures 4.5, 4.6, and 4.7 depict the single interaction event

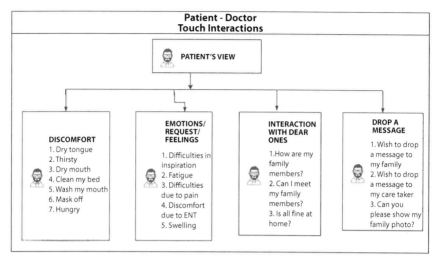

Figure 4.4 Categorical interactions initiated by patient.

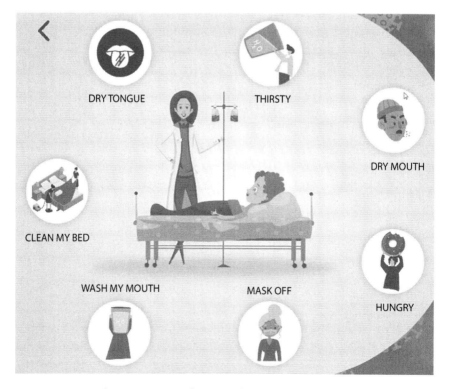

Figure 4.5 A sample interactive interface in English.

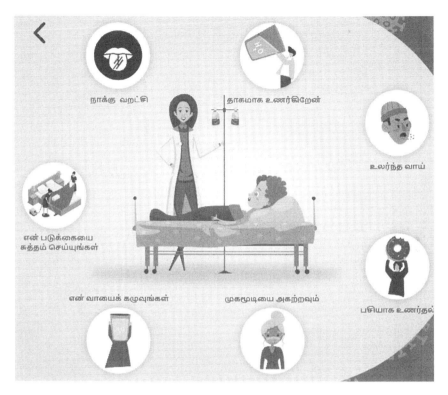

Figure 4.6   Figure 4.5's interactions in Tamil.

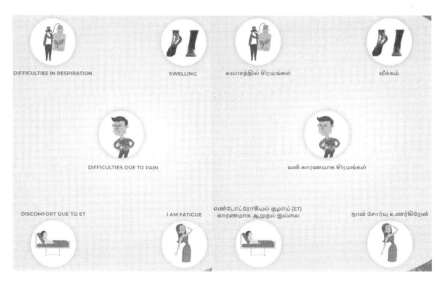

Figure 4.7   A sample interactive interface in English and Tamil.

in two different languages to facilitate the easy way of communication between patients and health professionals.

4.3   A Sample Case Study

An example case study is given to understand the proposal prototype wherein doctor has chosen his/her preferred language as English and patient has opted for Tamil as native language for communication. Figure 4.8 shows the sample interface of the aforementioned elections.

Then, the doctor tries to initiate the interaction in English by touching the icon which appears on the left side of the user interface as shown in Figure 4.9. Based on the doctor's interaction in English, the patient will receive the question raised by the doctor via audio in Tamil language. Also, the same UI initiated by the doctor will be displayed to patients in Tamil language. This facilitates the patient who gives a reply in Tamil language through a touch icon as depicted on the right side of Figure 4.10. This leads to the fact the communication barrier is eliminated between the doctors and patients. Thus, the prototype acts as an interface such that both are at easy phases.

4.4   Conclusion

The main significance for the doctors and patients is that they can choose their native language which enables the intuitive communication &

Figure 4.8 A sample case study for native language selection for patient and doctor.

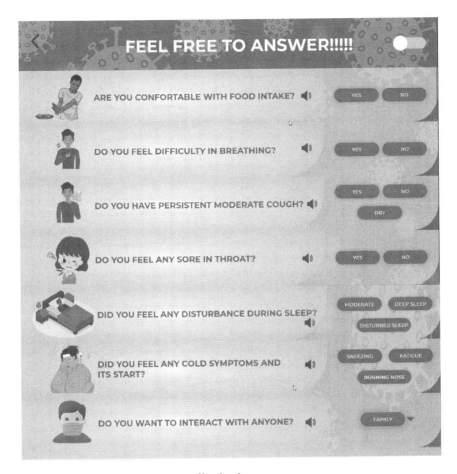

Figure 4.9 Doctor interaction view of his/her language.

interaction between stake-holder. The most distressing and stressful aspects of clinical illness lead to depression, anxiety, post-traumatic disorders are being reduced, and leads to possibilities of speedy recovery. Language barrier is eliminated among stake-holders. The Proposed Application will be made available and accessible in an open software repository. Application usages demo videos will be made available for easy operations. As per the existing methods patients express their needs through non-verbal communication methods and they could be missed out or misinterpreted resulting in symptoms that are poorly understood and the clinicians overestimate their ability to understand their communication feelings. These situations are eradicated by employing the use of "Touch Voice of SARI" Application.

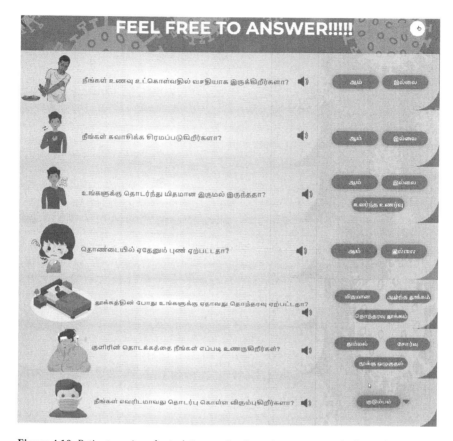

Figure 4.10 Patient receives doctor's interaction in native voice & reply through touch icon.

References

1. Zaytoun, T. *et al.*, Commonly asked questions by critically ill patients' relatives in Arabic countries. *Egypt. J. Crit. Care Med.*, 5, 1, 13–16, 2017.
2. Brinkman, W.B., Geraghty, S.R., Lanphear, B.P. *et al.*, Effect of multisource feedback on resident communication skills and professionalism: A randomized controlled trial. *Arch Pediatr Adolesc.*, 161, 1, 44–49, 2007.
3. Henrdon, J. and Pollick, K., Continuing concerns, new challenges, and next steps in physician–patient communication. *Joint Bone Joint Surg. Am.*, 84-A, 2, 309–315, 2002.
4. Leung, C.C.H., Pun, J., Lock, G. *et al.*, Exploring the scope of communication content of mechanically ventilated patients. *J. Crit. Care*, 44, 136–141, 2018.

5. Carruthers, H., Astin, F., Munro, W., Which alternative communication methods are effective for voiceless patients in intensive care units? A systematic review. *Intensive Crit. Care Nurs.*, 42, 88–96, 2017.

6. Otuzoğlu, M. and Karahan, A., Determining the effectiveness of illustrated communication material for communication with intubated patients at an intensive care unit. *Int. J. Nurs. Pract.*, 20, 5, 490–498, 2014 Oct.

7. Miglietta, M.A., Bochicchio, G., Scalea, T.M., Computer-assisted communication for critically ill patients: A pilot study. *J. Trauma*, 57, 488–493, 2004.

8. Maringelli, F., Brienza, N., Scorrano, F., Grasso, F., Gregoretti, C., Gaze-controlled, computer-assisted communication in intensive care unit: "Speaking through the eyes." *Minerva Anestesiol.*, 79, 165–175, 2013.

9. Otuzoglu, M. and Karahan, A., Determining the effectiveness of illustrated communication material for communication with intubated patients at an intensive care unit. *Int. J. Nurs. Pract.*, 20, 490–498, 2014.

5

Cloud-Assisted IoT System for Epidemic Disease Detection and Spread Monitoring

Himadri Nath Saha[1]*, Reek Roy[2] and Sumanta Chakraborty[3]

*[1]Department of Computer Science, Surendranath Evening College,
Calcutta University, Kolkata, India
[2]Department of Computer Science, Belda College, Vidyasagar University,
Paschim Medinipur, India
[3]Department of Computer Science and Engineering, Institute of Engineering
and Management, Kolkata, India*

Abstract

The advent of the Internet of Things (IoT) and large data analysis in the healthcare field has led to data obtained from areas where it was either performed manually or not at all before. The ability to detect an infectious disease and preventing it from spreading requires knowledge and monitoring in real-time. The IoT has been used to capture sensory data in real-time; by monitoring individuals, health systems, ecosystems, even in some of the globe's most remote areas. Based on a study, could recommend precautionary measures using data from the IoT network; further assess whether the suggested control measures are being implemented correctly. In scenarios like COVID 19 pandemic, it is important to get monitoring on the detection of the cause of the pandemic and on the spreading of the disease, especially in the developing countries. Our proposed framework includes a network model that uses wireless body sensors, wearable devices, and cloud computing to handle patient data in the form of text or pictures, or cloud voice. A mobile phone application and a website is built to keep track of the real-time data. Our system is robust and more efficient compared to other existing systems.

Keywords: Smart healthcare, wireless body sensors, cloud Server, Internet of Things (IoT), health monitoring, pervasive healthcare, epidemic outbreaks, epidemic detection

*Corresponding author: contactathimadri@gmail.com

SK Hafizul Islam and Debabrata Samanta (eds.) Smart Healthcare System Design: Security and Privacy Aspects, (87–114) © 2021 Scrivener Publishing LLC

5.1   Introduction

In today's cutting-edge time, the Internet of Things (IoT) has been the most revolutionary notion, providing support to all dimensions of the world. To minimize inefficiencies and maximize productivity in all domains, the Internet of Things (IoT) is starting to affect a wide variety of sectors and industries, ranging from engineering, health, agriculture, communications, and energy industries. Through linking the devices to the Internet, IoT executes data detection from the environment, actuating on the data, recording, and analyzing the data according to the latest scenario. Inside the IoT circuit, the actuator and networked intelligence are integrated to provide the customers with innovative and knowledgeable infrastructure. By introducing the current sensing and IoT technologies in healthcare practice, any component of conventional methods of healthcare can be radically altered. Seamless incorporation of wireless sensors and IoT in smart healthcare will potentially lift the healthcare sector to heights previously unthinkable. By adopting smart healthcare methods, IoT will help find solutions for many of the conventional health problems.

Cloud computing is rapidly becoming a technological need in the field of medicine. It could just be the solution to further evolve the healthcare sector to exchange patient details on acute cases in real-time among medical providers. Embracing technologies for cloud computing will make healthcare processes much more efficient and expense effective. Incorporating healthcare into the cloud is more than just delivering anywhere, anywhere, and on every mobile device, medical information from different computers. It is also about the benefits of linking medical centers and cloud users to share patient health information on the Internet. Hence, cloud computing provides sufficient tools for continuous storing and study of the vast majority of sensor-generated knowledge that can be used to simplify operations, predict situations, and enhance various healthcare facilities.

With the incorporation of many technological innovations such as Wireless Body Area Network (WBAN), Wireless Sensor Network (WSN), wearable, and embedded sensors, IoT is demonstrating its ability to overcome existing issues or challenges of healthcare monitoring systems. It can further enhance service efficiency, i.e. provide remote control, and phone applications while decreasing the expense of healthcare [1]. Healthcare is projected to have been one of the domains to be refashioned by IoT by raising its expansion and reducing the expenditure of operation. Due to its universal existence, IoT provides the opportunity for continuous and accurate remote control, thus allowing individuals freedom of movement. Wireless sensor devices (i.e. embedded or wearable detectors), which acquire bio-signals from a body of a human and transmit the transmissions wirelessly to a gateway, are commonly implemented to regulate the health of patients. These detector devices are compact and have restricted voltage regulation capacity [1]. The interoperability of diverse solutions currently available towards all holistic healthcare is essential and, at the very same moment, a necessary condition in IoT. This incorporation facilitates data synchronization with cloud-based services from wearable sensor devices. An effective technique is to link the embedded sensors straight to cloud services [2].

The use of Fog computing in IoT-based health surveillance coordination requires several unique healthcare features. Data collection and transmission are the principal functions of these gateways in conventional IoT-based systems. Platforms can be enhanced with Fog computing support to augment the productivity of healthcare infrastructure, which can be illustrated as a virtual portal that extends the cloud computing model to the network edge and reduces cloud pressures and burdens [1]. Initially, the design of the sensor devices (especially several portables or embedded devices) much more than other sectors need resource effectiveness. The form of interaction these devices provide is also the form of communication that streams. Then, due to the criticality of the device environment, it is imperative to respond immediately to crucial incidents that are collected by the sensor network. The aggregate framework needs a high degree of efficiency because physiological signal trends will have to be understood on a real-time basis. Besides, providing individuals with free mobility under clinical observation through smart technologies is also a critical prerequisite [2]. These features found in fog computing enable it to be quite famous use in the medical domain.

Increasing prospects for large-scale e-healthcare services have arisen from the express enlargement of smart devices and mobile cloud computing technology. In these technologies, the health information of individuals is remotely identified using wearable sensors and transmitted to a dedicated computer system for analysis and assessment using wireless devices where a range of professionals can handle control of such health information, including hospitals, medical institutions, and doctors. Recent advancements in wearable and embedded sensing systems, such as Wireless Body Area Networks (WBANs), have provided for a wide variety of sophisticated, real-time detection with tracking problems. That being said, WBANs are anticipated to suffer several challenges as stand-alone systems in terms of communications ability, information protection, storage, and distribution of the massive volumes of data acquired. WBANs are thus incorporated with cloud sensor-based architecture in many cases [3].

Smart monitoring devices are used by patients who need to capture personal health information such as heartbeat, blood pressure, and glucose stage using wearable technology sensors that are delivered to mobile phones. Mobile sensors that can be worn allow ongoing physiological and atmospheric observation over a prolonged period, which is essential for the behavior and diagnosis of many unremitting diseases, neurological disorders, and psychological problems. At about the same time the patient's medical status will also be tracked. For remote tracking of patients at residence, real-time as well as semi-real-time medical data is used. In a real sense, this encourages physicians and clinicians to provide urgent medical attention. Vast e-healthcare networks seek to broaden the coverage of person surveillance that includes a large community who live in families, in towns, maybe in a country.

Radio-Frequency Identification (RFID) and Wireless Sensor Network (WSN) equipments are used to transmit these data as communication and network infrastructure [4]. Farahani *et al.* [4] put forward a comprehensive review of the numerous published IoT e-Health papers and suggested a holistic e-Health ecosystem covering the multiple layers where different technologies can be connected to those levels, including assisted living, mobile health, e-medicine, and devices, detection systems and patient tracking. This patient-centered IoT e-Health environment has been demonstrated to require multi-layer architecture-computer, fog computing, and clouds to allow complicated data to be managed in forms of diversity, speed, and runtime.

During their lifespan, human beings suffer from numerous diseases, from mild to extremely somber. These diseases can be generally categorized as communicable (infectious diseases and non-communicable diseases into two groups. Infectious diseases are transmitted from one person to another by the direct movement of microorganisms causing diseases. It is recognized as an epidemic once a contagious (communicable) illness accelerates easily, touching a significant number of individuals in a given area within a brief episode [5]. Numerous epidemic outbreaks in human history have devastated humanity. To the current time, these epidemics have been fought by the International Health Organization (WHO), its managing doctors, and various administrative bodies around the world. A contagion can be characterized as the incidence of disease or health-related disorder that exceeds the normal prevalence in a given region or within a particular group of persons over a given period. The sustainability of universal healthcare services may rely on early diagnosis of such diseases instead of slow response and expensive medication. The most daunting area in the healthcare sector is not only constant surveillance of an eruption of any contagious diseases but also real-time interventions. The near range contacts between healthy and infected users ought to be eliminated to monitor the transmission of the disease.

A few of the pandemics that killed many people in the past are Dengue fever, Ebola, Zika virus outbreaks, Cholera, Influenza A (H1N1), Chikungunya virus, and Yellow fever. The inability to anticipate, track, and monitor them in time was the key explanation for their accelerated outbreak followed by high casualties. Traditional offline infection monitoring and forecasting strategies such as model-based strategies put lockdown and vaccinate individuals to manage outbreak spreads [5].

The COVID-19 global epidemic, widely known to be the coronavirus pandemic, is a recent 2019 epidemic of coronavirus disease worldwide and thus the term COVID-19. The disease was first identified in December 2019 in Wuhan, China; and soon subsequently, it became a global public health issue worldwide. COVID-19 is by far the most impactful occurrence since the last weapons went silent in 1945 during World War II. COVID-19 pandemic in India has had the greatest effect since the devastating partition events of 1947 until now. Since the time WHO declared it a global pandemic, the study of the coronavirus has been an emerging subject in the research world. This study has been dealt with in every area of science, from the field of medicine to the world of engineering. WHO scientists and medical industry experts are searching for innovative technologies to monitor infected patients at different levels to tackle this global new epidemic, identify the best clinical trials, control the spread of this virus, create an antibiotic to treat infected patients, track the experiences of the infectious individual.

All such conventional methods are influenced by many constraints, along with a lack of credible evidence and unreliable estimates resulting from erroneous assumptions used in models about the existence of social media networks. Therefore the need for active surveillance of healthcare to enhance health conditions and avoid infectious outbreaks has been recognized. Many researchers have thus established the IoT-based technology along with cloud computing to be able to solve problems with conventional approaches of constant tracking through the various types of devices and systems trying to predict and identifying pandemics along with alerting the public on these epidemics by raising awareness [5]. To overcome these challenges, such a system has been hence proposed in this book chapter.

Section 5.2 consists of a literature survey done on various existing systems mentioning the results, pros, and cons of these systems. In Section 5.3, the system proposes and the architecture of the suggested model has been elaborated. Section 5.4 has an explanation of the methodology of the proposed model. Section 5.5 has a short explanation of the performance analysis of the proposed model. In Sections 5.6, future research directions of the proposed model are explained. Section 5.7 has a short conclusion of this book chapter.

5.2   Background & Related Works

The healthcare system is projected to be one of the sectors to be remodeled by IoT that is supported by cloud computing by growing its adoption and reducing operating expenses. Owing to its pervasive existence, cloud-assisted IoT provides the opportunity for uninterrupted and efficient remote control, thus enabling users to move around freely. The ability to spot the activity of contagious diseases and to deter its dissemination demands real-time information and surveillance. In social and economic terms, responding rapidly with the right information will have a huge impact on the lives of people all over the world. The production of health surveillance services has been substantially improved in the recent several years. The main purpose of today's health monitoring structures is to provide an accurate evaluation of patients' critical symptoms in residential or mobile surroundings in order to achieve an up-to-date medical record. A range of wearable health-tracking devices have been produced.

Gia *et al.* [1] produced a minimum cost IoT-based remote medical surveillance system with the Fog layer. The developed device is capable of collecting data comprising of bio-signals and other relevant information and wirelessly exchanging information for real-time and remote tracking. The bio-signals include respiration and ECG, and humidity and ambient temperature are referred to in the other data. With the aid of the Fog layer, the system offers advanced facilities to enhance the efficacy of healthcare activities such as data collection, classification, push feedback and channel control. Owing to its high energy efficiency, the sensor node can run for a prolonged time that reaches up to 155 h. The proposed system can be further developed and data can be displayed to a patient using a mobile application.

Negash *et al.* [2] illustrated the significance of Fog computing, a range of utilities offered that enable IoT health services that are used in the development and deployment of a Fog computing smart gateway. The Fog layer in this framework has been generated by a geographically dispersed network of such smart gateways, individually managing a cluster of sensor nodes or patients. This gateway configuration maintains a constant means of patient tracking without restricting the patient's travel within the coverage range. Fog computing generates centralized patient observation capabilities and an immediate alert was sent. Fog computing offers remote patient control facilities by minimizing the latency in coordination and device performance improvement. To this extent, the vital signs of the patient have been recorded locally, and the recipient was issued with a local note. Besides, for even further evaluation, the sensory data was sent to the cloud server along with the findings collected. Descriptions of the Fog facilities and the advantages received were evaluated and metrics of success were provided. Any facilities, such as the Fog layer with the Cloud or the sensor layer with the Fog layer, may have been reproduced or subdivided into several ones. The details of the implementation depend on the relevant facilities and features. The sensor information including the observations collected was then again sent to the cloud server for further analysis. The specifics of the Fog systems have been assessed and the performance analysis was done. For instance, noise at nodes might be initially be eliminated before transmitting information from sensors to the fog layer. Fog computing can be used to enforce sophisticated and complicated techniques of noise reduction and signal analysis to increase the accuracy of data obtained. For the deployment of more specialized technologies, such as advanced machine learning techniques, the cloud layer can be included. Production and connectivity must also be taken into account in an attempt to produce a good degree of energy consumption at the sensor node. Finally, particular situations in medical usage can have external architecture restrictions that include adjusting of the Fog layer systems' behavior patterns. The disadvantage is that in case an incorrect position is applied, then the decisions may trigger power consumption, delay, and inefficient performance.

Berrahal *et al.* [3] have proposed a new healthcare infrastructure focused on a cloud sensor combined with Wireless Body Area Networks (WBANs) solution for the control of infectious diseases in remote regions. The developed framework aims to improve the identification and monitoring of infectious diseases by handling warnings created by individual people carried by WBANs and according to public and private clouds. It also attempts to suggest the progression of individual diseases and introduce a query management framework that enables coordinated responses from consolidated clouds. Three key layers are built into the framework, namely a private cloud, a core public cloud, and a cloud of WBANs. To calculate health status, and environmental conditions, motion parameters, the first stage describes circuits of sensor devices implanted on mobile people in the form of WBAN systems. Vital indicator variables such as electromyogram (EMG), the temperature of the body, electrocardiogram (ECG), blood pressure, breathing rate, oxygen saturation, and other parameters, are continuously obtained by each WBAN node. The purpose of environmental sensors is to quantify parameters that can be helpful for the spread of epidemic diseases, such as water contamination, atmospheric temperature and relative humidity, and the prevalence of unique fauna and flora types. In a given regulated region, the WBANs work together to make the diagnosis of the epidemic disease a shared target. In this instance, the various WBAN are considered as nodes in close proximity to each other that will form mobile cloudlets. The second level describes a single healthcare institution's private storage facility that is responsible for managing and recording the health status of patients as well as the evolution of epidemics. This cloud contains the cloudlet package of WBANs. The private cloud computing provides unified processing along with designated locations where data obtained by multiple mobile WBANs is preserved in order to be analyzed and compiled in real-time. Also, the private cloud holds confidential and valuable records, such as the identification of the patient, the background of medical procedures, the details of the incidence of special illnesses, the health-related details of the patient, and knowledge about the medical personnel. In addition to monitoring the health condition of patients and monitoring epidemic outbreaks, all this data is valuable. Towards this point, a national, unified, and public storage system is established by the third layer in the developed system, where anomalies and unusual measurements identified by private clouds are registered to be open to all entities involved in a specific form of statistics and for additional analysis. Real-time calculations must be transmitted within a set timeframe to the desired location; otherwise, the details obtained expire and are no further functional. To facilitate effective and real-time surveillance of infectious diseases and the efficiency of the proposed method, this study can be further tested for future work by simulations.

Sood *et al.* [6] proposed a healthcare system focused on IoT and fog computing to detect and monitor the Chikungunya virus (CHV) outbreaks. As we all know, Chikungunya is a contagious virus that spreads more easily, resulting in a new challenge to worldwide health security. With the evolution of IoT, fog computing, and cloud computing in information and communication systems, it has become feasible to improve the amount of information collection, processing, effective diagnosis, and global access to knowledge for consumers, physicians, and medical practitioners. The key characteristic of this method is the use of the exposure factor to assess the seriousness of health concerning the duration of different incidents. Health seriousness, on the grounds of disaster warnings, is created via the fog network to transmit event information on a timely basis to the user's smart phone. Fuzzy-C means (FCM) has been used to identify users who may have been infected and to automatically produce diagnostic and urgent warnings from the fog layer. Besides, Social Network Analysis (SNA) has been used on a cloud server to reflect the state of CHV spread. The outbreak function index is determined from the SNA graph that reflects every user's likelihood of having or spreading the infection. It also generates alarm warnings to monitor the occurrence of CHV in risk-prone or contaminated regions by government and healthcare agencies. The outbreak role index (ORI) is determined from the SNA graph that also reflects the risk of the infection being acquired or transmitted by some person. In due course, it also provides alarm warnings to non-infected people who visit or live in risk-prone or contaminated areas. Uninfected individuals would be helped to take urgent measures to avoid the spread of such viruses and to better monitor the concern by government health departments. Proposed device experimental findings are compared with cloud computing technology. The experiments demonstrated that the proposed architecture gains performance in bandwidth, minimal execution time, and minimal delay in producing real-time alerts. This system can be further developed to show in a mobile application the health conditions of the patient affected.

In their paper, Rahmani *et al.* [7] introduced the idea of fog computing and smart e-Health Gateways in the context of medical systems based on the Internet of Things. In smart homes or hospitals, advanced gateways near sensor nodes have been developed to take advantage of their unique pivotal approach to tackle many problems such as movement, energy usage, scalability, interoperability, and IoT-based health systems reliability. A number of high-level features that have also been offered in a geo-distributed format by smart gateways to detectors and end users at the edge of the network have been evaluated in detail by the system. This model, in which some of the higher-level functionalities are discussed, also incorporates the implementation of a smart e-Health Gateway called UT-GATE. The structure also integrates a health monitoring to efficiently show the efficiency and efficacy of the device in solving a specific medical case study, the IoT-based Early Warning Score (EWS). An IoT-based health surveillance system with improved overall system intelligence, energy consumption, agility, efficiency, interoperability, stability, and consistency is shown in this design model. All information flow processes from data collection on sensor networks to the cloud and end-users are included in the complete system demonstrated in this approach, which can be further developed for monitoring severe epidemics. This framework can be further developed using a mobile phone application to help users monitor their health conditions.

Sood *et al.* [8] proposed a cyber-physical device based on fog-cloud to effectively identify, diagnose, and track people contaminated with Mosquito-Borne Diseases (MBDs). A similarity factor has been used to distinguish between mosquito-borne diseases based on symptoms and the J48 decision tree has been used to define a group of consumers. The key aspect of this paper has been the use of the Temporal Network Analysis (TNA) on the TNA graph to depict any person infected with mosquito-borne illness. In the occurrence of any irregularity, the warnings are produced immediately and sent from the fog layer on the user's smartphone. Radio Frequency Identification (RFID) has been used to detect the close vicinity between people. It can help citizens who are not contaminated to take immediate measures to avoid the spread of these diseases. Experiment results of the proposed method produced high accuracy and low error rates to identify the diseases carried by the mosquito and also achieved 94% accuracy in classification. The findings also indicate that TNA is an effective instrument to use different parameters to determine the state of MBD outbreaks. Such a model can be used for other epidemic diseases in the future to control outbreaks.

Sareen *et al.* [9] suggested a novel system for the tracking and identifying of Ebola-infected patients based on wearable sensor technology, Radio Frequency Identification Device (RFID), and cloud technology network. The objective of this experiment has been to reduce the infection from spreading at the initial point of the eruption. To determine the extent of contamination in an individual user on his symptoms, the J48 decision tree has been used. Using RFID, proximity interactions (CPIs) among consumers have been automatically sensed. Temporal Network Analysis (TNA) is implemented using CPI data to identify and track the present scenario of the Ebola epidemic. A cloud-based infrastructure using TNA and wearable body sensor technology to anticipate and avoid EVD has been mentioned. Using WBAN and RFID respectively, critical body signs and social experiences are recorded. In comparison to conventional offline models, the strategy is focused on the capture of near proximity encounters and healthcare details in real-time to monitor the progression of the disease. To distinguish the consumers, the J48 decision tree is used in multiple groups. On the TNA graph, TNA has been used to describe each Ebola-infected person. In order to classify certain infected persons or regions that are heavily active, distinct temporal statistics are calculated about the distribution of outbreaks. The proposed model's performance and accuracy have been measured on the Amazon EC2 cloud incorporating simulated data from two million consumers. For the identification and 92% of the resource usages, the suggested framework achieved 94% precision. To increase the performance of the framework, the system can be used to concentrate on calculating the incomplete information of such users in future development.

Butca *et al.* [10] in their paper presented an experimental paradigm focused on wearable sensors that are designed to track patients' health conditions. The technology relies on a cloud platform-connected wearable sensor network that aggregates the data collected by sensors. The sensors calculate various parameters, including the body temperature and relative humidity or air moisture, which are sent to the cloud storage device by a microprocessor through a gateway. For more processing, the data obtained in the cloud system is accessible to researchers of certain associations between calculated parameters, environmental factors, and patients' medical conditions. For the duration of one month, the sensors are checked. Based on the overall scalability of storage, apps, and applications, a cloud approach was selected. In a Database-as-a-Service computing environment, the architecture presented uses the cloud to set up data obtained from detectors. Cloud computing optimizes architectural scalability and operating costs when responding flexibly to conditions of poor network efficiency. For more analysis, the information from the cloud infrastructure is usable. The knowledge obtained helps to establish certain associations between calculated parameters and the atmosphere, and the circumstances and health status of the citizens using the framework. The downside to this type of surveillance system is not sufficient for emergency circumstances, but this sort of system can help certain persons suffering from chronic illnesses and their families. Although developments in computer and communication technology have opened up new perspectives for healthcare services, there seems to be a range of issues that can be tackled by technical and medical practitioners working together.

Althebyan *et al.* [11] introduced a large-scale surveillance scheme for e-healthcare that aims to a multitude of people in a vast geographical region. Many new developments, such as mobile devices, edge computing technology, wearable sensors, and big data approaches, cloud computing, and decision making systems, are easily embedded into the structure. It will provide patients online control in a timely way at any moment and everywhere. There are also several special roles in the system which is of particular significance to the welfare of patients including communities, towns, and nations. These special characteristics are distinguished by long-term, cautious and insightful choices for anticipated dangers that may occur from the identification of adverse health behaviors after the examination. Massive volumes of data are obtained from patients. By capturing their vital indicators and biosignal details and uploading the data to a dedicated server, the proposed framework is designed to accommodate large numbers of patients concurrently. A series of cloudlets in such a cloud MEC server and mobile edge computing can manage big data for patients in a computational system that relies on Map-Reduce that ensures performance and scalability. Besides, it uses a collection of supporting evidence to maximize the impact of the recommendation system. There are two phases in this system: reactive and proactive. Decisions relying on the possibility of spreading an illness or a recognizable usual habit of people that may escalate to a medical problem will then be taken and forwarded to the health department to take necessary decisions and measures. Using the CloudExp simulation framework, a system has been developed as a simulation for our proposal system to evaluate our model. The research performed demonstrated that the model scheme is capable of reducing per user power consumption and latency. It also demonstrated that the device is flexible enough to accommodate vast numbers of users with a minimal expense suffered.

From the above literature review, we can conclude that there are some systems developed to detect epidemics with their drawbacks. Our system aims to overcome these drawbacks and establish a cloud-assisted IoT system for epidemic disease detection and monitoring of its spread in the community. We have aimed this system for the ongoing COVID-19 pandemic.

So, this book chapter proposes a model that will enable the healthcare system to detect and resist COVID-19. Using WBAN and RFID respectively, vital body symptoms and social interactions are recorded. In comparison to conventional offline models, our strategy is focused on collecting proximity contacts in real-time and health information to monitor the transmission of the COVID-19 epidemic. To classify users into two distinct categories, the J48 decision tree has been used.

5.3   Proposed Model

Fevers, dry cough, sore throats headaches are the most frequent symptoms that are associated with several other respiratory symptoms for COVID-19.

In COVID-19, rhinorrhea and gastrointestinal symptoms seem remarkably uncommon. Statistics from China indicate a large number of patients have minor side effects from COVID-19 (no pneumonia or moderate pneumonia). Patients with even more serious symptoms had extreme indications (dizziness, blood oxygen saturation 93%, respiratory rate 30/min, partial arterial oxygen pressure at a proportion of the inspired oxygen ratio <300, or lung penetration >50% within 24 to 48 h) and few were seriously ill (breathing arrest, septic shock, or numerous organ failure or damage) and ultimately leading to deaths [12].

The model that has been proposed here is a healthcare infrastructure focused on a cloud sensor combined with Wireless Body Area Networks (WBANs) solution for the control of COVID-19 in a region. The proposed framework aims to improve the identification and monitoring of the patients infected by the coronavirus by handling warnings created by individual people carried by WBANs using Radio-Frequency Identification (RFID) technology and according to clouds. The framework also aims to consist of a mobile application that will reflect the health condition details of the person wearing the portable health sensors and carrying the phone.

The model (in Figure 5.1) that has been proposed can keep a track of the sensor data and help the user to be identified as a positive or negative COVID-19 patient. Alerts are also sent to the phone application if an affected person is present in the vicinity of an unaffected person. These data are stored in the cloud server and are also reflected in the nearby hospitals via a website to ensure that a region affected by this epidemic can be managed and monitored efficiently. This website can be accessed by an individual patient to see his health details after logging into his or her

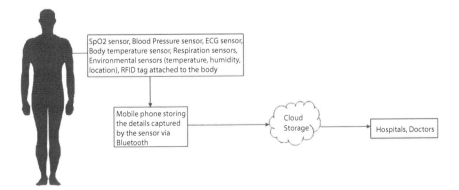

Figure 5.1 Framework of proposed system.

profile. The website also shows the test details if the patient is found to have symptoms of the disease.

5.3.1   ThinkSpeak

ThingSpeak is an open-source online cloud stage that enables the punter to store and analyze data as an electronic repository of memories. It allows the aggregation, visualization, and analysis of real cloud data sources. One can send the data to ThingSpeak as quickly as once per second. This data could be sent as one time per second which often enables the devices to be monitored almost in real-time, but also helps set up control loops from the cloud. ThingSpeak often records the data users send easily so that one can monitor their devices or equipment remotely from anywhere and even view the data from any mobile device or web browser, making it favorable for IoT ventures. It is integrated with many other open-source resources, such as MATLAB Visualizations, MATLAB Analysis, TimeControl, ThingTweet, and many more, and allows ThingSpeak to be connected to the hardware. These features also provide benefits when analyzing uploaded data. As a central server in our proposed model, ThingSpeak maintains all the meta-data. The sensor information is stored in a single location in the cloud, enabling us to easily access online or offline analysis information, making it easy for us to use it in our proposed model.

5.3.2   Blood Oxygen Saturation (SpO2)

Blood oxygen saturation (SpO2) is an incredibly useful critical stricture and is effortless to calculate using the concepts of pulse oximetry and photoplethysmography (PPG) technologies. The PPG approach allows the acquisition of waveform variance of the blood vessel, and it is feasible to approximate blood oxygen saturation when considered using two wavelengths (normally 660 nm and 905 nm). As an indicator associated with heart rate, sometimes, medical professionals recommend a pulse signal or pulse rate. Pulse signal or pulse rate can be calculated using the principles of pulse oximetry, a tool often used to calculate saturation of blood oxygen, and hence must not be regarded the same as heart rate. Pulse rate is characterized as the palpable harmonic development and contraction of an artery created by the elevation of blood volume forced into the vessel as a result of heart contraction and relaxation. This metric, like power, amplitude, and pulse regularity, presents detailed data than HR. This is related to the range of hemoglobin absorbance changes as it is bound by oxygen. The quantity of oxygen that is transported by blood cells can be measured (normally:

95–100%) using oximetry concepts. This measurement will assist in identifying variations in medical symptoms that would have otherwise been
ignored, such as a lowered level of oxygen (<95%), suggesting hypoxia and
causing the human body to have inadequate oxygen supply. One of the
difficulties with measuring blood oxygen saturation occurs whether the
patient is anemic. Many non-surgical techniques can be added to wearable devices for measuring blood oxygen saturation, but PPG is quite common in the medical industry. Mobile communications lead to a far simpler
autonomous and wearable system for such detectors.

5.3.3   Blood Pressure (BP)

The most important cardiopulmonary test, showing the blood pressure on
the wall of the artery, is considered to be blood pressure (BP). As the heart
contracts (systole) and relaxes (diastole), BP provides additional information on blood supply and can also indicate the distribution of cellular
oxygen. It is affected by various different physiological features: peripheral vascular resistance, cardiac production, blood flow, and viscosity;
and blood vessel elasticity. Using only a stethoscope on the patient's arm
and inflatable pressure belts, BP is usually measured. For autonomous BP
assessment, this method is well adapted, along with a fully computerized
inflatable cuff that measures BP by comparing peripheral pressure to the
degree of arterial volume pulsing. Prolonged monitoring of the cuff can
outcome in undesirable side effects, such as interrupted sleep with itchy
skin and increased levels of stress. To explain final issue, new BP monitoring technologies have been developed. One is to forecast BP, all calculated
on the chest or with the wrist-acquired PPG signal, depending on the transition time of the pulse signal between the photoplethysmography (PPG)
and ECG (R-peak) pulse wave.

5.3.4   Electrocardiogram (ECG)

Among the most widely used biosignals, electrocardiograms (ECGs) have
revealed information about the cardiac electrical cycle as a diagnostic
instrument in the medical setting. Five peaks and troughs (called P, Q, R,
S, T, and U) are known as the ECG waveform each of which reflects a difference in the heart's electrical potential, resulting in muscle activity and
as a consequence of heart movement. The ECG waveform is intended to
measure the heart rate, as well as to predict and diagnose serious myocardial and coronary events. The study of ECG waveform rhythms holds
an important role in diagnosing cardiovascular diseases (CVD), such as

congestive heart failure (CHF), coronary artery disease, heart attack, and other diseases. Ag/AgCl electrodes (wet electrodes) are the most commonly used electrodes for the transduction of ionic current from the core into electron current through metallic wires. Some other ECG sensor types are non-contact capacitive electrodes. Despite coming into direct contact with the skin, these electrodes can acquire ECG data, but they are far more sensitive to biomedical signals compared to traditional electrodes.

5.3.5   Body Temperature (BT)

Body temperature (BT) is the product of the equilibrium between heat manufacture and heat loss in the body and it is important to evaluate it in order to prevent the defunctionalization of many temperature-enhancing elements, such as protein deformity and decreased temperature-increased function. The core temperature (CT) and the skin temperature are divided by BT into two measurements. Skin temperature varies as the temperature regulation mechanisms of the body control core temperature across a broader temperature range than core temperature. Blood circulation controls skin temperature and is also associated with heart rate (HR) and metabolic activity. In the body temperature control system, environmental factors such as air circulation, atmospheric temperature and relative humidity also play a major role. To detect these temperature changes, numerous portable wearable systems have been developed, such as wearable adhesive devices and skin-like arrays of precise temperature sensors to closely monitor temperature. In our proposed method, a very recent reusable wireless epidermal temperature sensor, a battery-less RFID thermometer that appears to be a reliable CTT estimating system, has been used.

5.3.6   Respiration Rate (RR)

A basic physiological variable in the monitoring of patients is the respiration rate (RR). In some cases, this is reliable and authentic health information. This is among the most responsive markers for essential diseases, like those in cases of depression and possible hypoxia. In the diagnosis of signs of respiratory disorders such as sleep apnea syndrome, asthma, etc. control of the respiratory rate is essential, improving treatment administration where necessary. For people with pulmonary disorders, this continuous monitoring is especially necessary. There are three major strategies for gaining respiratory function: plethysmography of impedance (IP), elastomeric plethysmography (EP), and inductive plethysmography of respirations (RIP). Other technologies used include collected from the ECG signal, optical fibers, accelerometers, derived from polymer-based transducer sensors of pulse oximetry, etc.

5.3.7   Environmental Parameters

In each patient's region, ambient parameters are environmental parameters which have a strong significance in many testing areas of the human body. Temperature, light, humidity, and degree of sound are the most used sensors along with location sensors. Environmental parameters such as atmospheric temperature and humidity along with locations are composed for this proposed method. For this, temperature sensors, a location sensor, and humidity sensors are used.

5.4   Methodology

The above characteristics have been considered for the efficient management of our proposed COVID-19 epidemic disease control system: each WBAN node acts as a temporary storage system enabling rapid and efficient tracking and monitoring of appropriate patient-related data; the WBAN includes interdependent detectors responsible for producing priority-based data. The model has been constructed to track patients with COVID-19. In Figure 5.2, the flowchart of our proposed model is given.

The first level defines wearable sensor networks mounted on mobile devices in the WBAN structure format for the measurement of health, motion, and environmental parameters. Vital sign parameters such as electrocardiogram (ECG), body temperature, oxygen levels, blood pressure, respiration rate, pulse rate, and other specifications can be recorded by each WBAN node. The aim of the environmental sensors is to measure conditions, such as atmospheric temperature and humidity that may be favorable for the propagation of COVID-19 epidemic diseases. In addition, by monitoring climate conditions as well as using location data produced by the location sensor, the wearable health-tracking system can record the location and time of disease recognition and the associated geographic coverage.

The WBANs work together to establish a common diagnostic target for infectious disease in a given monitored area which has been affected by COVID-19. By providing his or her cell phone number and other

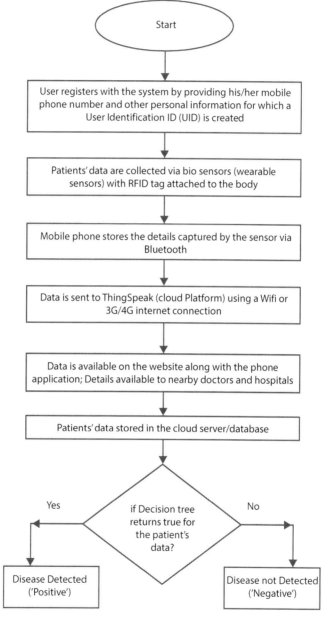

Figure 5.2 Flowchart of the proposed model.

personal details, each user is first registered with the arrangement. A User Identification ID (UID) is created for each person who registers, which will be used in future correspondence. The personal details of the users will also be stored in the cloud catalog.

The primary symptoms obtained by using the WBAN are transmitted via Bluetooth link to mobile phones. Data collected is sent to ThingSpeak (the cloud platform) from a router via a wireless network connection. The information is then collected on the mobile application and seen. This data and information is stored through a Wifi or 3G/4G internet link on the cloud server. In order to hoard and recover information from the WBAN, the cloud uses ThingSpeak.

Using MIT System Inventor 2, after the setup and continued functionality of the WBANs, a mobile application can be created. The mobile app opens, and the ThingSpeak results are shown to the user on the mobile screen. After that after a couple of minutes, the updated information reported in ThingSpeak is again shown to the user. Only when the user wants to exit the mobile application may users quit.

Health parameters such as an electrocardiogram (ECG), temperature of the body, respiration rate, blood pressure, oxygen levels, and pulse rate along with atmospheric temperature and moisture and location details are displayed in the phone application. The mobile application can be configured to show information about the user's health, environment details, and location details in real-time. The interactions in terms of physical and social between the users, who use this system, are captured using the RFID which is emotionally involved to the user's body.

The user carries a smartphone in which the android based phone application is installed and the phone also has an RFID reader sense which can read or sense the RFID tag attached to the user's body. These data and the information are transmitted to the cloud server in an aggregated form. These data are collected in real-time by the WBAN and the personal data and symptoms are accumulated in the cloud server.

A decision tree J48 is used to mark whether the user registered is a COVID-19 patient or not. So, two categories: 'Positive' (P) and 'Negative' (N) is established. If the person shows symptoms like fever with sore throat and cough along with a runny nose, low pulse rate, low oxygen level, unusual blood pressure levels, irregular respiration rate, then he or she will fall into the 'P' category; otherwise in the 'N' category.

These sensors keep updating the status of the body every 10 h. The server also keeps a track of the location and temperature and humidity of the region in which a person has been found affected. These data can be handled by the Governments to monitor those regions with special care. If a person is found in the 'P' category, he or she can directly go to the nearby hospital to get proper treatments and get better tests. This saves the people from getting unnecessary tests and also helps in saving the time in finding who and when has been affected.

The contaminated individuals are tracked and evaluated constantly until they are healed from COVID-19. The alerts and warning updates being created by the device and are sent to affected patients' smartphones. Alert notifications are even sent off to local hospitals or healthcare organizations based upon the GPS position of the patient's cell phone and often using the positioning sensor via the cloud. RFID has been used to detect if there is an affected person nearby. RFID tags attached to every person helps in identifying an infected person if an uninfected person comes in the vicinity of the affected person. The mobile phone has an RFID reader which can sense the RFID tag carried by another person. The sensor data are updated on the website for the doctors and the nearby hospitals to keep track and to take necessary actions.

The mobile application and the website are built to show the vital signs such as an electrocardiogram (ECG), temperature of the body, oxygen levels, blood pressure, respiration rate, pulse rate, and other specifications and surrounding environmental conditions. They also show details of the tests of the patients if the patient is found to be affected and has done tests. The registration page is present which takes each user's mobile phone number and other personal information with the system to provide a unique User Identification ID (UID). The phone application shows the different sensor readings (SpO2, Pulse Rate, BP Rate, Temperature) of a patient, along with a 'Details' button showing the patient details and a 'Quit' button to exit from the application. The website interface also works similarly to the phone application. These readings can be read from the cloud server by the doctors or nearby hospitals to treat the patients suffering or showing symptoms of COVID-19.

Figures 5.3, 5.4, 5.5, and 5.6 show snapshots of the home screen on the website, 'Registration Details' page on the website, 'Patient's Test Details' page on the website, and 'Sensor Readings' page of a patient in the website respectively. Figures 5.7 and 5.8 show snapshots of the screen of the phone application showing the different sensor readings (SpO2, Pulse Rate, BP Rate, Temperature) of a patient, along with a 'Details' button showing the patient details and a 'Quit' button to exit from the application, and phone application showing the Pulse Rate reading of the patient that is obtained using a sensor respectively.

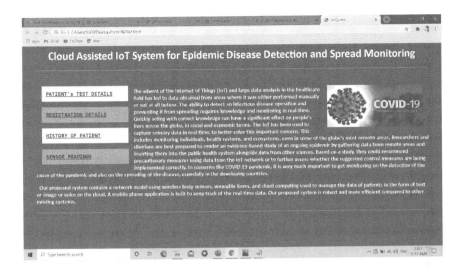

Figure 5.3 Snapshot of the home screen on the website.

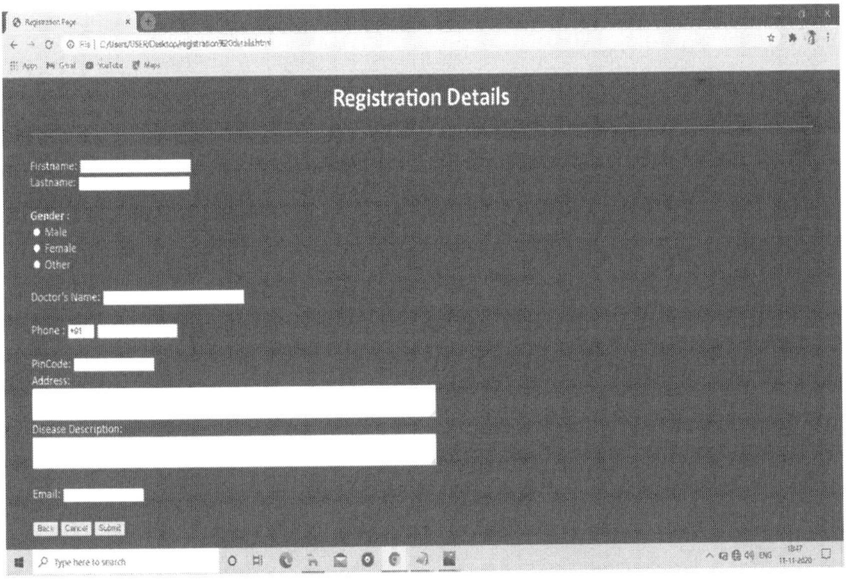

Figure 5.4 Snapshot of the 'Registration Details' page on the website.

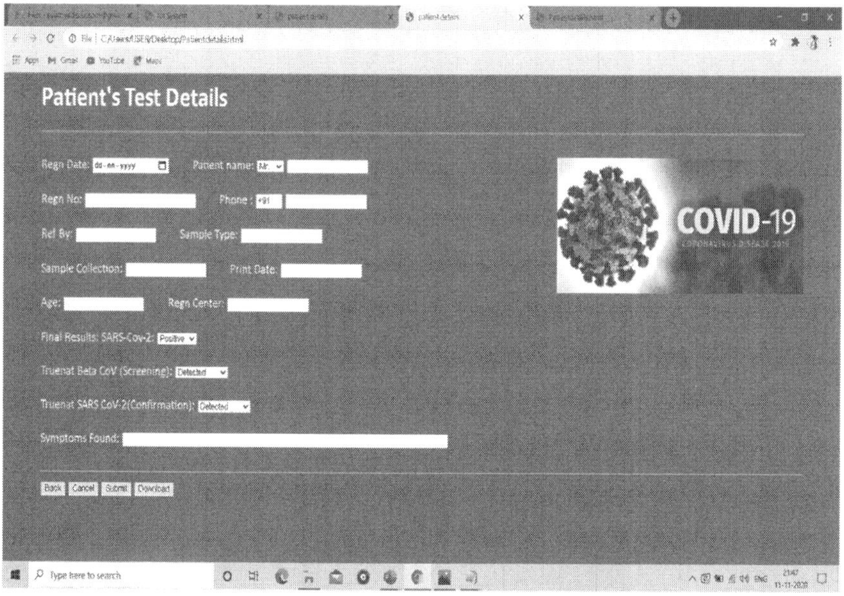

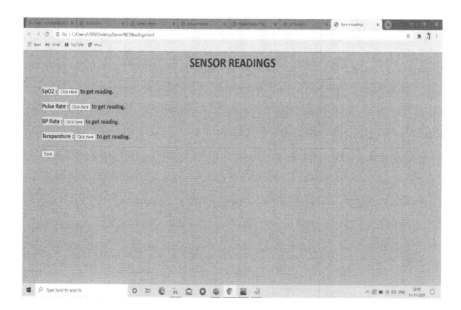

Figure 5.5 Snapshot of the 'Patient's Test Details' page on the website.

Figure 5.6 Snapshot of the 'Sensor Readings' page of a patient on the website.

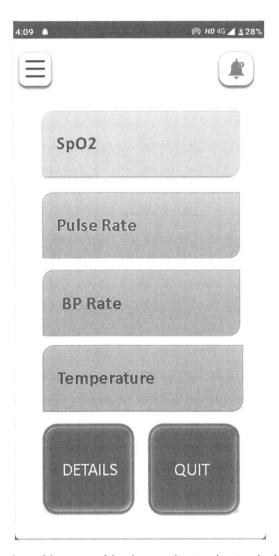

Figure 5.7 Snapshots of the screen of the phone application showing the different sensor readings (SpO2, Pulse Rate, BP Rate, Temperature) of a patient, along with a 'Details' button showing the patient details and a 'Quit' button to exit from the application.

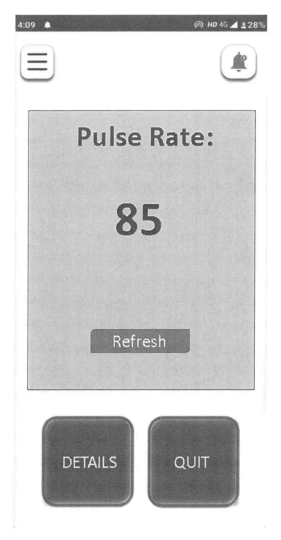

Figure 5.8 Snapshot from the phone application showing the Pulse Rate reading of the patient that is obtained using a sensor.

5.5   Performance Analysis

In our proposed model we have implemented a machine learning (ML)-based model to detect COVID-19 based on the currently known symptoms. However, we have not been able to practically detect COVID-19. But still, our model has been able to detect influenza with more than 80%

accuracies when applied to some local people having fever and or flu. So, our model can perform well to detect COVID-19, providing the known symptoms to the machine learning model. We have used highly accurate and low-cost bio-sensors. We have used ThingSpeak as the cloud platform, which is easy to be integrated with IoT devices and produces data visualization using MATLAB. Also, WBAN is used in the model in which the patients can be monitored while moving and even at home. The application can authenticate the users. Our model provides much faster services to rural areas than the other non-ML based models.

5.6   Future Research Direction

For future work, the system can be further developed to check other factors in real-time like electromyogram (EMG), heart rate (HR), blood glucose (BG) level, skin perspiration, capnography, and other health parameters. The model can be further developed to measure the physiological parameters like motion evaluation and integrate cardiac implantable devices with this model.

Additional sensors like the light and sound level can be further incorporated with this model. The sensors are also prone to attacks on the lateral channel. This can lead to misinformation caused by skewed values, which can affect agricultural production. Therefore, the data which can be specifically affected need to be masked before evaluating. For such protection, along with login authentication, and access control, the confidentiality of the information may be established.

Future research work can also include using lightweight cryptographic algorithms to protect personal information from across all sensors coming in. For this module, future research can be a middleware architecture that focuses on providing an end-to-end security system for the owners whose data are uploaded from sensor nodes [13].

We could incorporate the technology of Fog Computing into our future model. The Fog Computing Layer acts as a bridge between IoT sensors and the cloud computing layer. It can be used in real-time to process and interpret acquired data from IoT-based sensors. It can send immediate real-time alert or warning to the user as possible infected or uninfected about a specific category of user. Besides, this device can be linked to the cloud layer to store, interpret results, and compile each user's medical record. The analysis of the data collected can be performed based on this information and using machine learning algorithms. Based on this information and using machine learning algorithms, the analysis can also be carried out on the data collected. The intervention of fog computing would also minimize the use of the cloud platform, leading to a lower cost, more powerful, more reliable, and faster regulatory framework. Dealing with issues with big data in healthcare may also be an area of research for the future. The framework can be used further to focus on calculating the missing information of any of these users in future development to improve the efficiency of the model.

In the field of sensor systems, careful attention must be paid to 3 major components: long-term consistency; resilience; and biocompatibility. Water can cause chemical, mechanical, and thermal degradation in textile-based sensing devices; therefore an attempt must be taken to produce better resistant sensors to solve all these problems caused by prolonged durations of usability. Tinier sensors are also another absolute necessity for growing the flexibility and portability of this system, which is related to the advancement of technology. A significant feature that really should be critically examined is the sensitivity of wearable sensors. The utilization of nano-material based signal amplification can be one potential enhancement in the future. The biocompatibility of sensors with antimicrobial or protecting coating is important, avoiding any possible contamination of nano-materials which can be another future development for this system [14].

The model can be further developed in the future to use it to test metrics such as the efficacy of the implemented system to produce real-time warnings and they are forwarded immediately in the event of disease detection, the influence of the number of clouds and participants configured per cloud on service reliability, the effect of client mobility on reactions to real-time restricting requests, etc. for future scope.

At the very same time, for the future scope of the model, the customers may be able to enter their alternative and enhanced symptoms through the mobile software interface if needed. In 'YES' or 'NO', the values related to various symptoms can be entered. When the patient's response relevant to his health conditions is inserted, the data would be sent to the cloud.

5.7   Conclusion

The main objective of this chapter is to help doctors keep track of positive affected COVID-19 patients by keeping a track of sensor data collected from the various sensors like SpO2 sensor, blood pressure sensor,

ECG sensor, and body temperature sensor, respiration sensors, environmental sensors (temperature, humidity, location) and RFID tag attached to the body. These sensor data and information of the user are stored in a cloud server which can be accessed by a hospital and the doctors. The real-time data are updated every 10 h to monitor the health of the person who has the phone application. The data can also be seen on the website developed so that patients can check their details from a computer or tablet also. The data is stored in the cloud server, ThingSpeak. This is done to keep track of the patient is affected or not since COVID-19 is a contagious disease. This cloud-assisted IoT system will help to monitor the COVID-19 and help in the detection and excessive spreading of the disease. For every nation and healthcare organization today, COVID-19 is a national threat. In this book chapter, using smart wearable sensor systems, we suggested a cloud-assisted IoT framework to detect and resist COVID-19. Using WBAN and RFID respectively, vital body symptoms and social interactions are recorded. In comparison to conventional offline models, our strategy is focused on collecting proximity contacts in real-time and health information to monitor the transmission of the COVID-19 epidemic. To classify users into two distinct categories, the J48 decision tree has been used. Our proposed system aims to be robust and more efficient compared to other existing systems.

References

1. Gia, T., Jiang, M., Sarker, V.K., Rahmani, A.M., Westerlund, T., Liljeberg, P., Tenhunen, H., Low-cost fog-assisted healthcare IoT system with energy-efficient sensor nodes. *2017 13th international wireless communications and mobile computing conference (IWCMC)*, IEEE, pp. 1765–1770, 2017.

2. Negash, B., Gia, T.N., Anzanpour, A., Azimi, I., Jiang, M., Westerlund, T., Tenhunen, H., Leveraging fog computing for healthcare IoT, in: *Fog Computing in the Internet of Things*, pp. 145–169, Springer, Cham, 2018.

3. Berrahal, S., Boudriga, N., Bagula, A., Healthcare systems in rural areas: A cloud-sensor based approach for epidemic diseases management. *International Conference on e-Infrastructure and e-Services for Developing Countries*, Springer, Cham, pp. 167–177, 2015.

4. Farahani, B., Firouzi, F., Chang, V., Badaroglu, M., Constant, N., Mankodiya, K., Towards fog-driven IoT eHealth: Promises and challenges of IoT in medicine and healthcare. *Future Gener. Comput. Syst.*, 78, 659–676, 2018.

5. Kaushalya, S.A.D.S., Kulawansa, K.A.D.T., Firdhous, M.F.M., Internet of Things for Epidemic Detection: A Critical Review, in: *Advances in Computer*

Communication and Computational Sciences, pp. 485–495, Springer, Singapore, 2019.

6. Sood, S.K. and Mahajan, I., Wearable IoT sensor based healthcare system for identifying and controlling chikungunya virus. *Comput. Ind.*, 91, 33–44, 2017.

7. Rahmani, A.M., Gia, T.N., Negash, B., Anzanpour, A., Azimi, I., Jiang, M., Liljeberg, P., Exploiting smart e-Health gateways at the edge of healthcare Internet-of-Things: A fog computing approach. *Future Gener. Comput. Syst.*, 78, 641–658, 2018.

8. Sood, S.K. and Mahajan, I., Fog-cloud based cyber-physical system for distinguishing, detecting and preventing mosquito borne diseases. *Future Gener. Comput. Syst.*, 88, pp. 764-775, 2018.

9. Sareen, S., Sood, S.K., Gupta, S.K., IoT-based cloud framework to control Ebola virus outbreak. *J. Ambient Intell. Hum. Comput.*, 9, 3, 459–476, 2018.

10. Butca, C.G., Suciu, G., Ochian, A., Fratu, O., Halunga, S., Wearable sensors and cloud platform for monitoring environmental parameters in e-health applications. *2014 11th International Symposium on Electronics and Telecommunications (ISETC)*, IEEE, pp. 1–4, 2014.

11. Althebyan, Q., Yaseen, Q., Jararweh, Y., Al-Ayyoub, M., Cloud support for large scale e-healthcare systems. *Ann. Telecommun.*, 71, 9–10, 503–515, 2016.

12. Clerkin, K.J., Fried, J.A., Raikhelkar, J., Sayer, G., Griffin, J.M., Masoumi, A., & Schwartz, A., COVID-19 and cardiovascular disease. *Circulation*, 141, 20, 1648–1655, 2020.

13. Sadek, I., Rehman, S.U., Codjo, J., Abdulrazak, B., Privacy and Security of IoT Based Healthcare Systems: Concerns, Solutions, and Recommendations. *International Conference on Smart Homes and Health Telematics*, Springer, Cham, pp. 3–17, 2019.

14. Dias, D. and Paulo Silva Cunha, J., Wearable health devices—Vital sign monitoring, systems and technologies. *Sensors*, 18, 8, 2414, 2018.

6

Impact of Healthcare 4.0 Technologies for Future Capacity Building to Control Epidemic Diseases

Himadri Nath Saha[1]*, Sumanta Chakraborty[2], Sourav Paul[2], Rajdeep Ghosh[2], and Dipanwita Chakraborty Bhattacharya[3]

[1]*Department of Computer Science, Surendranath Evening College Calcutta University, Kolkata, India*
[2]*Department of Computer Science and Engineering, Institute of Engineering and Management, Kolkata, India*
[3]*Department of Computer Science, Bethune College, University of Calcutta, Kolkata, India*

Abstract

The term, "Healthcare 4.0" has been introduced from the Industry 4.0. The virtualization and automation in healthcare is included in Healthcare 4.0. The Industry 4.0 can provide the automation and data communication by using Cloud Computing, Internet of Things (IoT), Big Data, 4G and 5G technologies, cryptography, Content-Based Image Retrieval (CBIR), Augmented Reality (AR), etc. We can think of the Healthcare 4.0 as the application of the Industry 4.0. The health related processes include home care of patients, remote health diagnosis, personalized home treatments, etc. Healthcare 4.0 consists of computers, communicating interfaces, bio-sensors, bio-actuators, etc. In Healthcare 4.0 the surgical operations on the patients can be monitored remotely. The mobile gadgets use the bio-sensors. Our proposed system uses machine learning techniques on the collected data by the sensors for analyses. Our system collects the patients' medical histories for analyses. In the current COVID-19 pandemic situation getting a bed for the treatment is very much difficult, especially in the developing and highly populated countries. Our proposed healthcare system 4.0 is built for transfer of the treatments from the hospitals to the patients' home with a high accuracy rate of detection of the diseases and tests.

Corresponding author: contactathimadri@gmail.com

SK Hafizul Islam and Debabrata Samanta (eds.) Smart Healthcare System Design: Security and Privacy Aspects, (115–142) © 2021 Scrivener Publishing LLC

Keywords: Smart healthcare, Industry 4.0, RFID, cloud server, cyber-physical systems, COVID-19

6.1   Introduction

In Industry 4.0 or the Fourth Industry Revolution, researches are going on to automate the traditional manufacturing technologies by using smart technologies like Internet of Things (IoT), Cloud Computing, etc. so that human interventions will not be needed. Along with manufacturing sectors, Industry 4.0 will contribute to the other sectors like healthcare sectors. The Healthcare 4.0 is the applications of Industry 4.0 in healthcare sectors. The IoT can be described as a network of physical devices which are connected to transfer data among them. We have observed several technological improvements in healthcare sectors. In Healthcare 4.0 the doctors had to keep the records of the patients manually. After that in Healthcare 2.0 the patients' data are recorded using electronic devices. The patients' are collected using electronic wearable gadgets in Healthcare 3.0. Healthcare 4.0 is targeted to establish a system in which smart electronic devices can communicate to each other without the intervention of human beings.

If we recall in history we will be overwhelmed to see the overflowing modernized technology advancements. The influence of the pandemic malicious diseases over the human civilization is quite irresistible. Around 430 B.C. an epidemic was spread in Athens, Greece due to plague and in five years almost 1 million people died. Thucydides, a Greek historian wrote that even those healthy people got affected due to this disease with the symptoms like high temperature in the head, redness in the eyes, bloody tongue and unnatural breath. During 165–180 A.D. the Roman soldiers carried the Antonine plague (it might be a smallpox) while returning to the Roman Empire. It killed more than 5 million people in the Roman Empire. During 541–542 A.D. the Byzantine Empire was affected by the bubonic plague and the plague reappeared periodically even after. Due to this pandemic some estimates say that around 10% of the then world population died. The tragedy of demise continued with different influential diseases kept growing over the centuries. In the 14th century the Black Death came to Europe from Asia, causing half of Europe population's death. The 16th century observed another pandemic American plague which was brought by the Europeans to America and the Inca civilization was destroyed due to this pandemic. Some estimates say that due to this pandemic around 90% of the population in the Western hemisphere died. Hundred years back around 500 million people from the South Seas to the North Pole got infected due to the Spanish flu. Around one-fifth of the population covering the geographic regions from the South Seas to the North Pole died. However, the flu did not start spreading from Spain. It might be that the spread of this disease was first publicly known worldwide when it started spreading in Spain. In 2014–2016 the world observed the West African Ebola epidemic and according to the reports more than ten thousand people were killed. In current days from the beginning of 2020 we are fighting a battle with COVID-19 which have already cost over a million lives across all nations. The researchers, the authors and the medical community have been trying to develop a recovery from the demise. The anticipation of the smart health technology is still progressing with an influential rate. The COVID-19 virus was first observed in the food market of Wuhan, China in December, 2019. Still in November, 2020 there has been no licensed vaccine available to fight against the Corona Virus.

Cloud computing is rapidly becoming a technological need in the field of medicine. It could just be the solution to further evolve the healthcare sectors to transfer the patient details in real-time among medical providers. Embracing technologies for cloud computing will make healthcare processes much more efficient and expense effective. Incorporating healthcare through the cloud is more than just supplying medical details from various computers anywhere, anytime, and on any mobile device. It is also about the advantages of being capable of connecting medical centers and cloud users to share health information for the patients over the Internet. Hence, Cloud computing provides sufficient tools for continuously storing and studying the vast majority of sensor-generated knowledge that can be used to simplify operations, predict situations, and enhance various healthcare facilities.

The deep learning methodologies of the infected body and the applications of e-Health and m-Health are evolving with modern applications with IoT technologies to build a Smart healthcare system. The present medical care framework has likewise perceived the benefits of utilizing Information and Communication Technology (ICT) to make the nature of medical care better and improved, transforming the conventional care system into smart, intelligent one. As per Blue Stream Consultancy, "Savvy medical services is characterized by the innovation that prompts better demonstrative devices, better therapy for patients, and gadgets and innovation that improves the personal satisfaction for anybody and everybody." The key idea of keen well-being incorporates Smart HealthCare and Pandemic Health Management administrations, electronic record the executives, smart home administrations and associated clinical gadgets. With the advent of the data science technologies, the concept of the smart healthcare system has gradually developed. A smart healthcare system uses technologies, like the Internet of Things (IoT), Big Data, and Artificial Intelligence to rework the normal medical system in an all the directions, making the healthcare system more convenient, more efficient and more personalized.

Increasing prospects for large-scale e-healthcare services have arisen from the rapid growth of smart devices and mobile cloud computing technology. Using these technologies, the health information of individuals can be remotely identified using wearable sensors and transmitted to a dedicated computer system for analysis and assessment using wireless devices where a range of professionals can handle control of such health information, including hospitals, medical institutions, and doctors. Recent advancements in wearable and embedded sensing systems, such as Wireless Body Area Networks (WBANs), have provided for a wide variety of sophisticated, real-time detection and tracking problems. Smart monitoring devices are used by patients who need to capture personal health information such as heartbeat, blood pressure, and glucose level using wearable technology sensors that are delivered to mobile phones. Mobile sensors allow ongoing physiological and atmospheric observation over a prolonged period, which is essential for the treatment and diagnosis of many chronic diseases, neurological disorders, and psychological problems. At about the same time the patients' medical status will also be tracked. For remote tracking of patients at residence, real-time as well as semi-real-time medical data is used. In a real sense, this encourages physicians and clinicians to provide urgent medical attention. Vast e-healthcare networks seek to broaden the coverage of person surveillance that includes a large community who live in families, in towns, maybe in a country.

The word, 'Robot' was first coined in the play, "Rossuum's Universal Robots" by Karel Capek, a Czech writer in 1921. The term, "Robot" originated from the Czech word "Robota" means "forced labor" [26]. According to definition by the Robotic Institute of America, robot is a machine which is built in the form of a human being to perform the mechanical functions like a human being without having any sort of feelings. To work like the human beings was the motivation to invent the robots. So, we can say that a robot is a programmable machine that can do work. Since there have been lots of advancements in the field of artificial intelligence, we think a robot as a machine having intelligence. Robotics can be used in telepresence where the physicians can use the robots during examination of the patients' health conditions and supplying food and treatment to the patients. Also, the robots can also assist the doctors during surgeries. During the highly complicated surgeries the doctors can be benefitted by using 3D HD technologies with stereo visualization and Augmented Reality. Even the robots can operate the entire surgery where the doctors can guide the entire process, sitting at a remote place. In the pandemic situation the uses of robots will provide more safety to the support stuffs to sanitize and disinfect the hospitals.

Smart Healthcare was originated in 2009 from "Smart Planet" first coined by IBM (Armonk, NY, USA). Basically, Smart Planet is an astute framework which can utilize the sensors for data visualization, communicating the data via IoT, and analyzing the data utilizing Deep Learning methodologies. The shrewd medical care is an administration framework which can utilize innovation. Keen medical care can improve the coordination among all gatherings in the medical services framework. So, the shrewd medical service is a higher phase of data development in the clinical field. The Smart healthcare is about the union management product made with IoT and ML to outcast pandemic health problems. The smart and effective way is to propose a solution for the healthcare system to get the advantage of technologies during the pandemic situations in terms of the allotment of beds, home quarantine and the other health solutions. COVID-19 is great example which has led to losing lives due to lack of proper healthcare facilities.

In this proposed work, we have used various Machine Learning algorithms in connection with IoT to advance the sharing of real-time data of the patients and monitor their real time data and build a future approach for the doctors to detect the diseases. The doctors will be able to interact through the smart devices which can analyze and give the possible solutions through Deep Learning algorithms monitored by IoT leading to the possible prediction of diseases of the patients following their reports. Just in 2016, more than 100 organizations were offering AI calculations and prescient examinations.

It is not possible for the doctors to remember all the necessary and related information to diagnose fast and accurately. With the cutting edge plenitude, like, research papers, books and contextual analyses, no specialist can ace each part of clinical consideration and review everything about the comparable cases. However, it is conceivable to take care of an AI-based framework with significant information and let the PC move through the broad data set as opposed to depending on the substantially more restricted human information. Malady distinguishing proof was brought accordingly at the bleeding edge of ML research in medication. Central members available were among the first to join the mission for the exact analysis, especially in much-required fields like oncology. Boston-based BioPharma Company Berg applies AI to investigate and create diagnostics and restorative medicines in different regions, including measurements preliminaries for the intravenous tumor treatment.

Another significant model is Google's DeepMind Health with its various UK-based associations, incorporating with Moorfields Eye Hospital in London, in which they are creating innovation to address the macular degeneration in the eyes of the aged persons. The joint exertion expects to locate the early manifestations of visual issues brought about by diabetes and the sight degeneration for older persons—the most significant reasons for sight misfortune in the UK. Simulated intelligence innovations will dissect more than 1,000,000 eye sweeps and discover the main indications of visual degeneration which might be missed by most experienced specialists. Such a framework would of incredible assistance to the specialists during this COVID-19 multiple times. In Personalized Medicine, also known as Precision Medicine is extension to the traditional medication system. Personalized Medicine combines treatment, big data, cloud computing. Precision Medicine is an emerging practice to detect diseases, to provide treatment to the patients by studying several individual factors like gender, age, profession of the patients. The predominant exploration technique in this area is so far administered realizing, which permits the doctors to select from more restricted arrangements of findings and to measure the patient's danger depending on the side effects and the hereditary data.

Report arrangement utilizing support vector machines, just as optical character acknowledgment, for example changing penmanship into digitized characters, are both fundamental Machine Learning based advancements regarding the digitization and evaluation of the electronic wellbeing data.

Our proposed model can improve home care of the patients and remote healthcare up to 90% accuracies in detecting the common diseases. Our paper has been organized as follows. In Section 6.2 we have presented a literature survey of the related works. In Section 6.3 we have presented the architecture design of our proposed model. In Section 6.4 we have described the methodology of our system. Section 6.5 presents the performance analysis of our work. The future research directions are presented in Section 6.6. We have finally concluded our work in Section 6.7.

6.2   Background and Related Works

The machine learning techniques and IoT based technologies are playing the major roles in the healthcare systems. The term, 'e-health' is a broad term which indicates the uses of information and communication technologies and the applications of cognitive thinking in the healthcare system. The healthcare system refers to the organization of people, educational and training institutes and resources that can provide the healthcare services to people. Healthcare 4.0 not only provides more accurate, faster, cheaper (not always till now) health services, but allows also the doctors, nurses to get benefits from more powerful, automated, accurate services. The Healthcare 4.0 system requires a huge amount of investment for the maintenance purposes and a large number of skilled labors.

Chute and French [1] introduced a new paradigm in the digital healthcare service, named as 'Care 4.0'. It focuses on a trusted model of integrated networks of people, organizations and technologies. These networks of people and organizations help manage and use their own assets, within their own care community to build the personalized and more responsive services. In this model, the concept of IoT, Cyber physical systems are enabled, like health related devices (Smart Inhaler, etc.) can monitor the various dosage for different patients according to their problems as well as an overall report for the manufacturing organization regarding any product and can use these reports to predict the alarming situation for other people belonging to the care circle or the community of those already recorded patient, can manage their use with those devices. Many people are working on the challenges and opportunities of Industry 4.0. Industry 4.0 can be viewed as a network which is distributed in nature. In Healthcare 4.0 system there are six different principles which are Interoperability (people and machine can communicate with each other through a common infrastructure to share the data), Virtualization (with the communicating devices a virtual network can be established), Decentralization (customers and markets are also connected with the production body), Real-time capability (the model should be capable of being changed with real-time situation demands), Service Orientation (in place of products the use of data is practiced to provide more responses keeping in the mind the dynamic market needs) and Modularity (the loosely coupled models are rearranged by changing the configurations of the production capabilities in order to cope with the market needs). Also, a patient's safety and privacy is to be maintained abiding by the legal rules of different governments. Regarding Healthcare 4.0 system (Service Managed) to care for asthma, an intelligent inhaler can monitor the patients' conditions and produce digital records for the organizations by using a cyber-physical system. Also, the inhalers, the sleep monitoring devices and the activity monitoring devices can communicate with each other by transferring the data among them. There is an agent (virtual) that can help the doctors in reviewing the appointments, making personalized medicines. In Self-Managed Healthcare 4.0 system an intelligent inhaler can monitor the patients' conditions and produce digital records for the users or the patients by using a cyber-physical system so that the users or the patients can get medical advices. Also, like the Service Managed healthcare system, the inhalers, the sleep monitoring devices and the activity monitoring devices can communicate with each other. Hence the virtual agent can help the patients to make their own plans and to connect them with the doctors and the medical services.

In [1] it is mentioned that there can be three possible ways to meet the requirement in the Healthcare 4.0 system. The first one is the trust model which says that there should be a trust among the people and the organizations. In the context of the healthcare the trust can be defined in two different ways. The first definition says about the organization-oriented trust. Hence the service is to be built on a combination of quality of the services, safety of the shared information, security of the personal information and resilience to produce a stable service under the risks. There is a limited proof of a connection between the safety of the patients and improved patients' outcomes. Also the model is decentralized with improved sustainability. The second definition is person-oriented trust which is based on the relationships among the users. This type of trust is needed to deliver the community care to deliver the care for the community. The type-1 trust model, i.e., the organization-oriented trust model and the type-2 trust model, i.e., the person-oriented trust model are not mutually exclusive to each other. The second way to meet the requirement in the Healthcare 4.0 system is service and network care management, considering the autonomously managing by the individual devices. Hence the persons should develop themselves. So, they will need to build their own methodologies and tools, to build apps for monitoring the patients' bodies, monitoring the atmosphere. The third way to meet the requirement in the Healthcare 4.0 system is comparative context for Healthcare 4.0. The third way also deals with the qualities of the services provided. The qualities that can change the Healthcare 4.0 are person, community care in the context of community, the co-balancing care, building resilient workforce, individualization by building a self-learning system.

Cui *et al.* [2] proposed a Smart Nursing Home developed with the help of System Engineering. They use Vee Model for this purpose. Their proposed system contains two part one living place of patients specially aged, caregivers and sensors and actuators and another part depends on Cloud/IT where the actual analysis of the data has been done and remote care, electronic physician service given and further prediction took place. This solution can monitor each of the inhabitants of the Nursing home and if any abnormal condition identified by system, directly it alarms the care-giver and physician and they can either treat physically or remote care can be taken. The system engineering is expanded to the healthcare sectors. Several tools in system engineering are used in the healthcare sectors. The models used here are waterfall model, spiral model to develop an auto-mated nursing home. The authors used Vee model for developing an auto-mated nursing home. Hence, there is a need for defining verification plans, need for frequent risk measurements and the need for frequent validation. In the public nursing homes, many elderly people get admitted whereas in the private nursing homes the investors are more interested in gaining profits. The architecture need to be built up keeping in mind to produce solutions such that the requirements can be met. After analyzing the solu-tions, these are combined to automate the overall nursing system. Also, the staffs should be trained use the new AI-based IoT devices to provide the services to the users. The waste products should be destroyed in an eco-friendly way and the health records should be stored for further uses and analyses. Their model based on Vee model additionally includes the development of cyber-physical systems in an iterative fashion. This model is capable for being used where there are lots of different types of teams and contractors are present. Several analytical tools like Quality Function Development (QFD) are used to make the requirements easily figure out. They have introduced QFD to produce proper technical supports based on what a customer will demand. The house of quality (HOQ) is the matrix representation of QFD. HOQ represents the user requirements, considering what are specified in the requirements and how these can be implemented. To automate a nursing home the authors have chosen design facilities, catering facilities, AI-based systems, daily care facilities for nursing and medicines along with psychological treatments also. Then they have cal-culated some weighted values upon multiplying the array of importance with the correlation matrix. In the architecture the authors have identified the hardware components such as the workplace, home and the devices, the software components such as the cloud and AI-based models and the individual components such as the patients, the doctors, the nurses, the staffs and the managers. However, all the criteria should be traceable. For designing the layout traffic densities, noise levels can be measured. Also, the number of working hours for providing healthcare services is needed to be kept. Hence output several available solutions there is a need to select a solution which is nearly optimal. If there are two different architectures for emergency handling problems (i.e., if there are two different solu-tions), the selection between the two architectures will be made based on how well the architectures can meet the system requirements in terms of emergency handling. The metrics are the Measures of Performance (MOP) and the Technical Performance Measures (TPM). Every criterion should be traceable. In the verification process all the hardware, software and individual components meet the requirements in terms of performances. The simulation techniques are very much useful to optimize the performances in terms of operations and maintenance of the physical components. As specified, the agent-based approach in simulation is decentralized and bottom-up. There are three main functions of the simulation. The first one is static analysis and visual demonstration of the entire system. The second one describes the individual activities and the individual status monitoring. The third one help the model designers trace out the emergencies and how the system interacts during the emergency situations. The proposed model here an intelligent nursing home system can be established, rectified, and the produced solutions should be optimal in terms of the system requirements by the stakeholders. The QFD allocates all the requirements to the hardware components, software components, the individual components.

Donati *et al.* [3] highlighted the requirement of the patients having chronic diseases and tried to bring improvement on Chronic Care Model through Telemedicine. They discover that hospitalization is mostly required by chronic patients and those patients demand more care. In their model they have suggested to monitor these patients through regularly capturing their physical condition through Bluetooth sensors and smart devices as gateways and finally storing the information to the cloud architecture in order to get the service of caregivers. On the other end caregivers can access the information of patients from the cloud and guide them what to do when they are sitting at their home. The regular monitoring helps those patients especially elderly not to reach to an extent of their disease problems. The patients can get the treatment depending on their health conditions. The treatments differ based on the different situations. For a particular situation data collection approaches differ, keeping in mind what the patients need. Then the data are transferred to the healthcare team. Their presented solution is flexible and also configurable. The proposed system provides the user interface which is user specific in the sense that any user without much knowledge about the operations can use the system and also the professional users can operate the system. Their proposed system consists of several kits to monitor the patients at home and a centralized server with storage capabilities. The communication is bidirectional. The kit uses IoT sensors and BT/BLE (Bluetooth/Bluetooth Low Energy) for short-range communication. The system consists of wireless sensors, smart phones or tablets, local data storage and some parameter defined to measure lifestyle. The smart devices have software installed on it. The cloud software gives the resources to the users to communicate with each other. The server software gives the smart devices an access to collect the data and get the necessary update information at remote places. The model uses long-term data storage and a basic approach for authenticating the user information. One problem that can arise is interference due to the use of BT/BLE which operates in the same frequency of the WiFi. To resolve the problem the adaptive frequency hopping (AFH) technology is used. So, the overall structure of the proposed system can be thought as a combination of a data gathering module, a data storage module, a network module, a user interface4 module and a core module. The core module deals with scheduling the patient care plans and processing the data gathered and also it coordinates with the software applications. There are two types of monitoring kits. One is for patient monitoring and the other is used by the medical team. The authors have implemented their modules using Java Enterprise Edition (JEE), MySQL DBMS, Apache Tomcat.

In [4] there has been a study by Tortorella *et al.* who examine the effects of five contingency factors on incorporating Healthcare 4.0. The five internal contingencies to Healthcare 4.0 include the ownership information and the ages of the hospitals, the number of the employees, the number of the available beds and the functional operations. They have surveyed on 159 mid and senior-level managers from 16 hospitals from Brazil, India, Mexico and Argentina. According to the theory of the contingency, the optimal performance depends on the internal and the external factors of an organization and so there is no best possible procedure available to organize and manage the organization. The public hospitals are lack of resources like equipment, personnel and infrastructure, etc., compared to the private hospitals. Also, larger hospitals have a large number of personnel and equipment. In their survey, most of the respondents were from Brazil. The data analysis was done in two steps. They have performed first the cluster analysis and after that they have executed a MANOVA (Multivariate Analysis of Variance) with the help of Wilks' lambda test. The hierarchical cluster analysis indicates two clusters of the respondents. They used k-Means cluster analysis where k = 2. The first cluster is labeled as the high adopters and the second cluster is labeled as the low adopters.

In [5] Hamidi presented a new methodology to apply the biometric technology to build a smart healthcare system using IoT technology. The author claims that biometric provide more security and fast identity. Their proposed model includes four different levels which are the IoT device level, the Connectivity level, the analytical data management level; and access and application level. They have presented the basic features of IoT technologies in smart healthcare systems in a secured manner. They employed encryption Algorithms and developed the tunneling protocols like EOIP and SSL. They have used SSL and Active Directory (AD) to maintain the security of the session layer, the presentation layer and the application layer. They have used TCPView to detect the open ports, to display the remote and the local connections. They have used Portqry.exe to scan the open remote and local ports.

Alloghani *et al.* [6] presented that Industry 4.0 would have greater impacts in health sectors, education sectors and business sectors. The cyber physical systems have led to Medical Cyber-physical systems that can be applied in order to make the service provision more efficient. Natural Language Processing model can operate in the background to improve the diagnoses, treatments, etc. Although Industry 4.0 can be applied to the business sectors, education sectors, still there will be a lot of manpower and expertise required to the applications of Industry 4.0 in these sectors. In the educations sectors Industry 4.0 has contributed to a great extent in developing smart learning tools and devices. For example, the manufacturing prosthetic by using software has been effective to measure accurately the pressure distributions in the joints. Also, the audio learning platforms built by using deep learning and natural language based techniques, can be used to learn several languages. Also, a living room can also be used as a live classroom by using just very low cost resources like IoT devices, WAN and cloud services. In business sectors Industry 4.0 was not accepted earlier, but currently many industries are trying to build up smart factories by automating manufacturing or developing processes to provide improved performances in the factories and faster deliveries. The business sectors have been more developed, powerful and secured with the advent of cloud computing technologies. In this way the smart factories can reduce the total costs of operations up to 4% along with improving the efficiencies. The enterprise resources planning (ERP) systems are making significant impacts. The business sectors are utilizing the power of data collected from the customers and analyzed by machine learning algorithms. Another major application of Industry 4.0 is simplifying imports and exports for the product delivery systems by incorporating the concept of drop shipping. In this way the working days to deliver the products can be reduced even up to one-fourth of the previous working days. Also, business can be presented in an attractive way to the customers with the help of Augmented Reality techniques.

Pace *et al.* [7] proposed a novel architecture, Body Edge, for human centric application. This model has three layers—IoT Layer, Edge Layer and Cloud Layer. The two main components of this architecture are a tiny Body Edge Mobile Body Client (BE-MBC) that capture health related data of human beings and those data relayed to the Body Edge gateway (BE-GTW) supporting multi-radio and multi-technology communication. The edge gateway then processes those data and stores them to the cloud, by using both private and public platform facilities of Cloud. This work aims to reduce the traffic load through internet also tried to minimize the interaction time.

In [8] Elhoseny and his team proposed a new healthcare model to optimize the selection of the virtual machines (VMs) in Cloud-IoT based health services. Their motive is to suggest a model that can manage a huge amount of data in integrated Industry 4.0 efficiently. Industry 4.0 applications are used to process and analyze big data which are captured from different sources like sensors, etc. Their model targets to improve the performance of the healthcare systems by minimizing the time to minimize the stakeholders' requests and also optimizing the storage required by patients' data. The proposed hybrid cloud-IoT model consists of four main components: Stakeholders' devices, Stakeholders' requests, Cloud broker and Network administrator. In order to optimize the selection of the VMs, three different popular optimizer algorithms which are Genetic Algorithm (GA), Particle Swarm Optimizer (PSO) and Parallel Particle Swarm Optimization (PPSO), have been used to design the proposed model. These three algorithms are implemented using two different tools MATLAB and CloudSim package and a comparison among the results of these three algorithms has been observed to examine the performances regarding the time to execute the stakeholder's requests, the speed of live data processing and the overall system efficiencies.

Kumari et al. [9] emphasized the impacts of Internet of Things, cloud computing and fog computing in Healthcare to provide the context-aware and efficient services without any interruption to the users according to their needs. They propose a three-layer Healthcare model consisting of real-time gathering of the data, processing of the data and transmission of the data. In this model the three interoperable layers are namely medical device layer, Fog layer and Cloud layer. Medical device can be any bio-medical sensor or smart devices those can track the medical data of a user, the intermediate layer or the Fog layer consists of small processing units those can process the local devices' data with which the unit is connected and sometime make emergency decision for time critical medical situation and the highest layer i.e. Cloud layer stores huge amount of data of many Fog nodes and process them for future reference.

Alhussein et al. [10] proposed an intelligent healthcare monitoring architecture built by integrating IoT with the cloud. This framework is specifically built to detect and classify the epileptic seizure. The deep learning model

Convolutional Neural Network (CNN) and stacked autoencoders have been used for learning purpose. Under this system, the sensors help to record the psychological and physiological signals from a patient's body and transfer these to the cloud via the Internet. After studying these signals, the patients' states, i.e., movements, gestures, and facial expressions can be determined. Thereafter, the cognitive system takes the decision based on the state of the patient that, whether they require immediate medical assistance. Signal processing and seizure detection held in the cloud and the classification of the signal as seizure or non-seizure with a probability score. The outcome of the processing is transmitted to the medical practitioners or the other stakeholders to take care of the patients' health.

Hence, from the above discussion we can find out the advancement in the field of healthcare cannot be possible without the IoT, Cloud services in order to handle the huge amount of data. There is also a big role of Data Science and AI for such big medical data analysis and required high degree of precision as it is the matter of heath. Our model catches the later issue and tries to focus on the enforcement of Deep learning to the existing IoT-cloud based healthcare model to get fast and more accurate prediction for the patients suffering from different diseases. Our model tries to attend all types of patients rather a particular diseased and it is close to more generalization. The work [10] is close to our work, but it focuses on a particular disease and it is using only CNN for learning. Specifically in this pandemic situation when there is a huge lack of hospital beds, the more we can reach to different types of patients with the required treatments at their home, the proposed model become more efficient.

6.3   System Design and Architecture

In this section we present our proposed framework to build a smart healthcare system 4.0 using IoT technology to control epidemic diseases. Our model tries to win over four different challenges of the traditional healthcare systems by introducing Internet of Things and Machine learning techniques. The challenges include home care of patients, remote health diagnosis, personalized home treatments and controlling epidemic diseases. In our proposed model we have several different types of sensors to design the framework. The reason behind using the several different sensors is that there are several different physical quantities affecting the healthcare system and one particular type of sensor can measure one physical quantity. We have incorporated the RFID (Radio-Frequency Identification) technology along with the sensors. In our proposed model we have embedded the sensors into the RFID technology. Under the current COVID-19 pandemic it has become very much difficult to get admitted to the hospitals. Also, currently people are facing difficulties to get proper treatments for other diseases. Many people now prefer consulting to the doctors online to visiting directly at the chambers. Our model will collect the physical conditions from a patient's body and via the RFID and the cloud, then the data can be sent to the remote server for analysis.

In our proposed architecture we have used biosensors. The biosensors are actually biological sensors. A biosensor is composed of a biological element and a transducer. A biological element may be something like an antibody or an enzyme. The biological element reacts with the analyte to be tested. Then the transducer converts the biological response into an electric signal. The biosensors are so popular in medical diagnostics because they are simple in operation, higher in sensitivity, higher accuracy and precision, fast in operation. There are several biosensors like electrochemical sensors, optical sensors, piezo-electric sensors, thermal sensors and so on. The new generation nano-biosensors are quantum dots, grapheme based biosensors, micro-fluidic biosensors, etc. The biosensors are used mainly to collect the patients' physical data from remote places. In the rural areas where the medical facilities are not available profoundly, the biosensors are found very much useful. Also, during the rapid spread of epidemic diseases, people will not need to go to the clinics or hospitals to consult the doctors frequently if remote health diagnosis can be well-implemented.

As we know that the medical diagnoses determine the infections, the patients' health conditions and detect diseases, if any. The traditional medical diagnosis often takes a significant amount of time, which needs to be speeded up especially during pandemic situations. Our proposed model is designed to automate the traditional medical diagnoses using machine learning techniques so as to speed up the diagnoses processes and also to reduce the human errors. We have used AI-based chatbot in our model. The user will provide his or her symptoms via texts or speech. The chatbot will compare the symptoms available in the cloud database and reports the user accordingly. If the symptoms are detected critical, the user will be notified to immediately contact to the hospitals. While diagnosing critical diseases like cancers, we need to use deep learning techniques. Google's Convolutional Neural Network (CNN) performs almost the same as the diagnoses by the dermatologists. Using deep learning techniques the sizes of the tumors and the growth of the tumors can be measured and new metastases can be predicted more accurately. To achieve this purpose the deep neural model has been fed with a large amount of CT (computed tomography) scan reports and MRI (Magnetic resonance imaging) reports from the patients.

AI based automated personalized treatment can help the medical practitioners detect the diseases at the earlier stages with more accuracies. During the rapid spread of the epidemic diseases, it becomes mandatory to keep the social distancing. To deliver medicines to the patients in the hospitals, to sanitize the hospitals the robots are now being used.

All of the monitoring systems communicate with the RFID and vice versa. A RFID system has two components which are a RFID tag or label and a reader. The RFID tag again has two components which are a microchip and an antenna. The microchip is responsible for the storage and processing of information. The antenna receives and transmits the signals. The RFID reader or interrogator send a signal to the RFID tag using the antenna and receives the signal through the antenna from the tag about the data encoded in the tag. The reader then automatically sends the information to the mobile or the computer through a communication interface. The RFID data can be read from a distant location and even outside the direct line-of-sight of the reader.

The applications of the RFID include tracking objects, monitoring supply network between the producers and the suppliers, developing smart agriculture, etc. In our proposed architecture we have used the RFID system to collect and analyze the data about the patients' current health conditions, the patients' past medical reports, etc. by sending the data to the remote cloud server. We have implemented neural models on the cloud server platform. The server can analyze the collected data using the models and sends the reports to the users' mobiles. We have trained our model with a large amount of clinical data.

The sensors can send the data through the internet by using a networking protocol, LoRaWAN (Low Power, Wide Area Networking Protocol). LoRaWAN is designed to connect the battery powered devices to the regional, national, or global networks. LoRaWAN provides an end-to-end security in the bi-directional communication. It is a star-of-stars topology. There is a central network server. The gateways are there to relay the messages between the devices and the server. The gateways convert the RF (Radio-Frequency) packets to the IP (Internet Protocol) packets and vice versa. On receiving the packets each gateway forwards these from the devices to the cloud server through Ethernet or Wi-Fi. We have used the platform ThingSpeak for analyzing and visualizing the data in the cloud. LoRaWAN consumes the battery life during the long-range communication. For long-range communication the capacities of the gateways to receive the messages should be very high. LoRaWAN provides the security to the network and the application by using AES (Advanced Encryption Standard) encryption. The frequency band of LoRaWAN is 865–867 MHz in India.

6.4   Methodology

Since the most recent two-decade mechanical technology is one of the rising, testing, creating and imaginative fields of examination among analysts, enterprises colleges. The robots can be portrayed as the machines which are good for performing several computational tasks with more freedom and more levels of chances than the individuals. Nowadays clinical consideration organizations and structures become very stunning and encompass innumerable components that are depicted by shared and heterogeneous contraptions, sensors, information and correspondence advancement. With the presence of Internet of Things (IoT), each robot is connected as a 'thing' and develops a communication network with the various things over the Internet. This part clearly shows the drawn-out preferences of the individuals in clinical consideration division, well-being related emergencies, e-prosperity, etc. by using new mechanical innovations and IoT technologies [25]. A robot may have a direct physical appearance that grants it to definitely act and react as a general rule, yet it may moreover work in the virtual world using concealed information propels as a conductor for inescapable authentic coordinated effort (for instance confer sensible information to distant spectators) [25]. A robot has an ability to adapt real data sources, produce a 'sensible sentiment' out of them and go about according to its programming and what it has figured it out [11–13]. This viewpoint on acknowledgment, control and affiliation serves well though it misses one point that can consistently be found in the domain of science fiction, whether or not a robot can be truly mindful [26]. The overall approach of our proposed model is spoken to in Figure 6.1. In our proposed model the patients' data profile is sent over the cloud server and the information is analyzed using machine learning algorithms. After training our model, the model has been tested with unknown data. If the data match with any pattern in our database, the model can be able to detect the disease or the disorder.

It is the best way to analyze COVID-19 and finding out an objective to cure many patients in long run. To an ever increasing extent, government ventures, medical services and even the training areas are utilizing the Internet of Things (IoT) and artificial intelligence (AI) to automate the fight against the continuously spreading pandemic throughout the world.

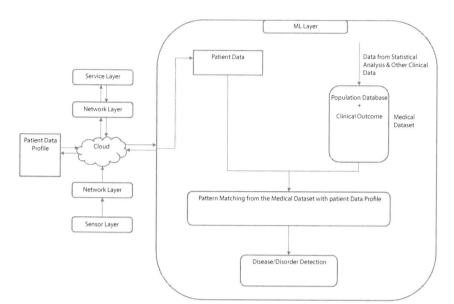

Figure 6.1 General methodology of our proposed model.

The best way is observed by social distancing and their IoT can make a huge impact on daily supervision on our need. The Robotics and IoT are relevant and similar powered and engineered to provide an environment about COVID-19 and other upcoming similar disease to be a curable a manhandled well with AI.

The relevant data of patients are focused with privacy features, the patients' reports via the cloud server are shared with the eHealthcare and doctors on-board. Attending service will be monitored by Robotic surveillance and powered by AI to arrange suitable similarities with the database in the Cloud reports. Doc's guidelines will be generated by AI system himself. The Robotics had a relevant approach in this edge of technology and it has greeted with upmost feeds in the health industry. The machines powered by AI are built in cutting edge technology with IoT, Robotics, Cloud computing, Deep learning will make the future happen a proficient eHealth facility organized with research technologies. The benefactors of the research will the commoners as the technology upgrades.

The wearable technology made with the aid of using IoT and AI is actually a not unusual in place of knowledge. Many offices use these of wearable gadgets for touch tracing and tracking the fitness of scientific employees and sufferers. A touch-tracing tool consists of passive GPS area monitoring and proximity sensors powered with the aid of using *Bluetooth*® and ultra-wideband connectivity, chargeable battery and integrated Long-Term Evolution (LTE). On wearing the smart devices the users can replace their fitness reputation to suggest whether there may be any possibilities of infection and the gadgets will notify human beings they have been in touch with the infected persons, primarily based totally on the history of the areas. A centralized device in the corporation can use this fact for a complete fitness dashboard in the workplace. A sensor implemented without delay to the wearer's frame video display unit's real-time temperature change. The tool transfers the data to the hospitals for non-stop tracking [27]. Through this capability the doctors or the practitioners can screen and advise the greater sufferers who are at home, maintaining health centered ability for the ones at better hazard.

In the extraordinary push to avoid human-to-human touch, drones are helping to save humans from the disease. Drones are most secure in this regard to supply scientific elements and groceries to places with excessive fees of infection, screen quarantine regions for motion and congregation of human beings and carry out thermal scans to screen the frame temperature of human beings in a selected area. Agricultural drones perform duties which include spraying sanitizers in the affected regions.

Integrated Facial Recognition, Temperature-Sensing Systems, and Contactless Access Control, reducing human touch points is critical to slowing the spread of the virus. For healthcare facilities and other major sectors hit hard by the pandemic, embracing IoT technologies is one way to improve the safety of patients, executives, and administrators [27]. A face recognition system along with a thermal imaging device for monitoring the body temperature and sending the data over cloud can be used to detect a person with a high temperature. If IoT-based sensors are enabled to the doors, the system can be able restrict the infected persons to enter the place. Using the smart contactless system the workplaces can avoid spreading of infection due to the uses of the finger-print detection sensors.

The COVID-19 pandemic has spread with nearly 18 million confirmed cases and close to 6 million active cases [20, 22]. The amount of data will grow exponentially. The exponentially large amount of data cannot be maintained by the traditional data base systems [35]. The traditional data base management system cannot be able to handle such exponentially growing data. Hence we need Big data concepts. The security of the private data is also a major concern. The side-channel information can also be retrieved from the lightweight devices like the sensors.

The COVID-19 outbreak has highlighted the revamping of health infrastructure across the world with cutting-edge technologies [14]. This helps in reducing the strain on the frontline COVID-19 warriors like doctors and nurses. Various IoT devices are getting used for quarantine tracking and IoT cloud platforms play a crucial role in completing the daily operations [15]. The growing impacts of smart hospitals with the IoT technologies, a combination of artificial intelligence and the Internet of Things technology invites extensive growth across the IoT-cloud platforms market. Microsoft lately brought a brand new platform, the Azure IoT Connector for Fast Healthcare Interoperability Resources (FHIR). This is designed mainly for the change of scientific records and assisting the healthcare specialists for securely dealing with records seeping in from diverse settings [21]. Such technology might also additionally increase the multipliers for the IoT-cloud platform market. IoT-cloud platform allows tracking of numerous operations and additionally tracks assets. This prevents thefts and fraud throughout an organization. The Oracle IoT cloud platforms have numerous tracking capabilities that allow the whole provision of solutions for an organization. It tracks employee motion and does environmental tracking via its Connected Worker Cloud Service. Many different tracking packages are found in several IoT-cloud structures that allow smooth functioning.

Personalized Medicine is a directed approach using various methods and algorithms that would help in guiding and aiding diagnosis and better treatments for the patients. We have applied an AI-based solution which has two steps. The first step involves detection of diseases like COVID-19. We will be using a set of parameters in the detection. We already have seen COVID-19 detection through Chest X-Ray images as seen in the paper [28]. But we felt that determining whether a patient has been declared positive only based on the above parameter according to the current scenario is not proper, not to mention how reflecting may the result be on a person's life [29–33]. We would like to add many parameters to the existing model. The first would be Polymerase chain reaction (PCR). In which that a small, well-defined DNA segment is replicated up to many hundreds of thousands of times in order to produce a huge dataset for data analysis. The second test sample we are going to use is from Antigen tests. This was just an example of our detection algorithm in case of COVID-19. In general, diseases and tests are computed on genomes and cell abnormalities or to put in simply changes.

We would be describing our detection algorithm through COVID-19 detection. It would not be feasible to obtain numerous amounts of sample data. We would obtain the initial data from Kaggle's Open Research Dataset. Owing to the limited availability of tests in the dataset, we would then generate our dataset using data augmentation [29]. Data augmentation is an AI method for increasing the size and the diversity of labelled training sets by generating different iterations of the samples in a dataset. To assess the reliability of the proposed deep learning-based COVID-19 detector, we adopt the same metrics as those used by Alazab *et al.* [16–19]. In our system, we would predict the required results, confirmations, recoveries and prescribing by using the following three well-known forecasting algorithms: i) PA [27], ii) ARIMA [28], and iii) LSTM [29]. These algorithms were trained to make predictions for the next 7 days from datasets that were collected from a statistics website [23]. Now we would implement our personalised home treatment along with precision medicine. Accurate prognosis is a milestone for the customized medication. DL structures are capable of combining heterogeneous records from the patients throughout the time, permitting better predictions and recommending remedy to every patient [25]. Now to enforce our personalized domestic remedy we might require a few AI algorithms. Those techniques encompass guide vector, random forest, neural community and an evolutionary set of rules (EA). We have visible in the recent years, each neural community pushed gadget studying and evolutionary set of rules have proven promising predictive capacity for issues which are not solvable in polynomial algorithms (referred to as NP-hard) [23, 24]. These fashions may be tailored via way of means of offering enter records in supervised, unsupervised or semi-supervised fashions. Ideally, we might like to have the entire information approximately all current phenotype or genotype categories, along with the disorders and for each category there is a populace of sufferers of limitless sizes. We have seen three important factors being described in [27]. The three important factors that we are going to improve upon are firstly phenotype categories which is basically the cell representation of various diseases or put it simply is the understanding of human diseases and its subtypes. For example inside the body of a COVID-19 patient the antibodies to SARS-CoV-2 is present which signifies that the person is tested positive. Reaching for an improved model we would also be using the model from [28]. Second factor is the population size. We may obtain data from a dataset to build our model. But we consider it a separate feature because in that case obtaining the selective data from an arbitrarily large sample size would be very much difficult. For example, for ribose-5-phosphate isomerase deficiency [27], only one diagnosis has been made for a single patient [28]. However, there are many such disorders. According to [29], there are more than 5,000 rare disorders. We now come to our third feature which is statistical analysis. It is an interference mechanism to classify, predict, or diagnose a patient, using statistical analyses. We use pattern recognition to build a statistical model from a dataset to realize the entire outcomes. In reality there is small error owing to various factors [34–37].

We use an error function to work on our error which is indicative of a false positive probability and understand it better for a better model. The error we talk about is due to various external factors like sample size, effect size, etc. This model is not ideal as it assumes we have complete knowledge and database of all kinds of disorders, diseases and also their subtypes. But we still haven't reached to that stage yet. However with the current resulting database we have been able to successfully identify majority of the diseases [38, 39].

Using the factors we have to evaluate our model. We made some advances to enhance our model for better real life approach to personalized Medicine. In population size if we can enrol more patients, it will in turn improve facilitation of more test data and also large clinical trials. Second on phenotype categories we need to perform more research for a better understanding of the phenotype categories. A lack in the identification of new and rare diseases will lead to a lack in our clinical side, ultimately hampering diagnosis and concurrently treatment. Third we come to statistical analysis. This depends on proper investigation, the quality, quantity and type of the data and finally the algorithmic approach itself. If we come across missing data that can lower the result of model even though a large sample of data is present.

Keeping in mind all these factors as well as shortcomings our basic Machine Learning model structure would be first using individual patient data. We would also have what we call our Master Database which contains patient population database along with the clinical outcomes. We would match and compute the Database data with the individual patient data and we run it through a pattern recognition algorithm that pattern matches the patient profile with the database with reference profiles. Now formulating with this model, we can infer with working on these features or components of characterization. They are as follows

a) Patient Data
b) Population Database
c) Clinical Outcome
d) Pattern recognition.

We can consider the Population Database as the prior statistical data and each data in that database of discrete variables quantified as vectors. We even have worked more on the syntactic pattern recognition hence we may have to compromise on the time and complexity but we have a much deeper working of the attributes/patterns. It also allows for better representation of the different types of data used in the analysis. Now for the disease/disorder, the Clinical Outcome is the different disease information and cause prediction tests and every other relevant information about the various human diseases, body related information. We combine both the data from the population database and the clinical outcomes to get a proper representation of the various diseases/disorder, etc. Finally, the Pattern Recognition is the root algorithm that will be completing our model. It is a Machine Learning algorithm that allows us to recognise and classify patterns based on statistical information. We use the feature vectors to recognize patterns by running it against the Master Database (Population Database + Clinical Outcome) and now the Patient Data is matched along with the database. The most important part of our model, pattern matching or recognition part can be thought of as a combination of two types of algorithm, one is the basic machine learning algorithm like classification, regression for simple diseases like fever, cold and cough or may be the chronic diseases and another one is the deep learning algorithm like CNN (Convolution Neural Network) for critical diseases like tumour detection, cancer cell detection

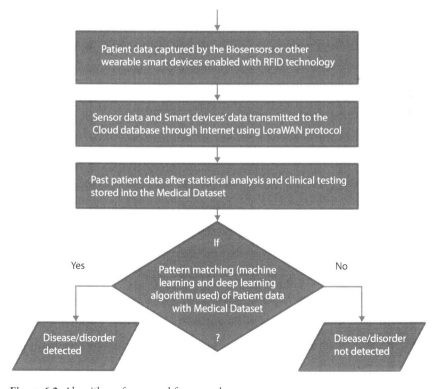

Figure 6.2 Algorithm of proposed framework.

or pandemic diseases like COVID-19 where high precision of accuracy is required. In Figure 6.2 the workflow of the whole system is shown.

This is the first step towards our detection algorithm. Secondly we also know about various health devices that continuously keep track of our heartbeat, blood oxygen levels and many more. They also play a key role in detection and in detail analysis. A continuous monitoring helps us getting more accurate data and more in-depth knowledge of the underlying problems. Figure 6.2 demonstrates our model with a flowchart. The patients' data collected by the biosensors or wearable devices are sent over the cloud using LoRaWAN protocol. Also the patients' past data are stored for statistical analyses. When any data are captured, the data are stored in the local storage. Now the data are fed to the machine learning based module to detect the disease or the disorder.

6.5   Performance Analysis

Our proposed model improves home care of the patients and remote healthcare up to 90% accuracies in detecting the common diseases. Our model is able to disrupt the exponential spread of the COVID-19 disease. In our model we have used biosensors. The accuracy levels of the biosensors are very high. We have Jelastic as a cloud service. The cloud server can analyze the patients' data using machine learning and deep learning techniques with high accuracies. We have used LoRaWAN networking protocol that can provide security with AES encryption.

6.6   Future Research Direction

There are lots of future research scopes in the field of Healthcare 4.0. Our model shows low accuracies in detecting cancer. As a future research work we are currently working to implement a model where small bots can work to deliver medicines to the patients. The Sawai Man Singh (SMS) Government Hospital in Jaipur, India is conducting a series of trials to find the way to appoint a humanoid robot for delivering medicines and food to the patients in the hospitals so that the doctors and the staff can maintain safe distances to reduce the chances of contracting infections. Though LoRaWAN provides a secured long-range communication, the long-range communication is generally unreliable, costly and also prone to the side-channel attacks. So, implementing fog technology can be another future work where the data collected using the sensors can be first sent to the nearby servers in the rural areas. Lots of patients' data need to be stored in the cloud databases. The traditional central database cannot be work well where there is a large amount of data to be handled. So, incorporating the Big Data technology in Healthcare 4.0 can be a promising future research area.

6.7   Conclusion

Our proposed model has been able to improve home care of the patients and remote healthcare up to 90% accuracies in detecting the common diseases. Our model can also disrupt the exponential growth of the COVID-19 disease. In our model we have used biosensors. The accuracy levels of the biosensors are very high. We have Jelastic as a cloud service. The cloud server can analyze the patients' data using machine learning and deep learning techniques with high accuracies. Incorporating automation and robotics will not leave negative impact on the job market. That is, people will not lose their jobs, rather automation and robotics will increate a huge job opportunities because a lot of skillful persons will be required.

References

1. Chute, C. and French, T., Introducing Care 4.0: An Integrated Care Paradigm Built on Industry 4.0 Capabilities. *Int. J. Environ. Res. Public Health*, 16, 12, 8–10, 2019.
2. Cui, F., Ma, L., Hou, G., Pang, Z., Hou, Y., Li, L., Development of Smart Nursing Homes Using Systems Engineering Methodologies in Industry 4.0. *Enterprise Inf. Syst.*, 14, 3, 1–17, 2018.
3. Donati, M., Celli, A., Ruiu, A., Saponara, S., Fanucci, L., A Telemedicine Service System Exploiting Bt/Ble Wireless Sensors for Remote Management of Chronic Patients. *Technologies*, 7, 1, 2–5, 2019.
4. Tortorella, G.L., Fogliatto, F.S., Esposto, K.F., Vergara, A.M.C., Vassolo, R., Mendoza, D.P., Narayanamurthy, G., *Effects of contingencies on healthcare 4.0 technologies adoption and barriers in emerging economies*, vol. 156, March 31, 2020, Technological Forecasting and Social Change, Elsevier, 2020.
5. Hamidi, H., An approach to develop the smart health using Internet of Things and authentication based on biometric technology. *Future Gener. Comput. Syst.*, 91, 434–449, 2019.
6. Alloghani, M., Al-Jumeily, D., Hussain, A., Aljaaf, A., Mustafina, J., Petrov, E., Healthcare services innovations based on the state of the art technology trend industry 4.0. *2018 11th International Conference on Developments in Esystems Engineering (DeSE)*, IEEE, pp. 64–70, 2018, September.

7. Pace, P., Aloi, G., Gravina, R., Caliciuri, G., Fortino, G., Liotta, A., An Edge-Based Architecture to Support Efficient Applications for Healthcare Industry 4.0. *IEEE Trans. Ind. Inf.*, 15, 1, 481–489, 2019.

8. Elhoseny, M., Abdelaziz, A., Salama, A.S., Riad, A.M., Muhammad, K., Sangaiah, A.K., A hybrid model of the Internet of Things and cloud computing to manage big data in health services applications. *Future Generat. Comput. Syst.*, 86, 1383–1394, 2018.

9. Kumari, A., Tanwar, S., Tyagi, S., Kumar, N., Fog Computing for Healthcare 4.0 Environment: Opportunities and Challenges. *Comput. Electr. Eng.*, 72, 1–13, 2018.

10. Alhussein, M., Muhammad, G., Hossain, M., Amin, S., Cognitive IOT-Cloud integration for smart healthcare: case study for epileptic seizure detection and monitoring. *Mob. Netw. Appl.*, 23, 6, 1624–1635, 2018.

11. ATOS White Paper connected Robots. https://atos.net/wp-content/uploads/2016/06/atos-white-paper-connected-robots.pdf, accessed date: 15.09.2020.

12. The art, science of robots. https://daily-dose-of-art.com/2012/07/15/the-art-science-of-robotics-1-a-brief-history/, accessed date: 15.09.2020.

13. IoT Health Evolutions. https://www.iotevolutionhealth.com, accessed date: 20.08.2020.

14. Alazab, M., Shalaginov, A., Mesleh, A., Awajan, A., COVID-19 Prediction and Detection Using Deep Learning. *Int. J. Comput. Inf. Syst. Ind. Manage. Appl.*, 168–181, 2020.

15. Buslaev, A., Iglovikov, V.I., Khvedchenya, E., Parinov, A., Druzhinin, M., Kalinin, A.A., Albumentations: Fast and flexible image augmentations. *Information*, 11, 125, 2020.

16. Alazab, M., Shalaginov, A., Mesleh, A., Awajan, A., Intelligent mobile malware detection using permission requests and API calls. *Future Gener. Comput. Syst.*, 107, 509–521, 2020.

17. Alazab, M., Automated Malware Detection in Mobile App Stores Based on Robust Feature Generation. *Electronics*, 9, 435, 2020.

18. Alazab, M., Analysis on Smartphone Devices for Detection and Prevention of Malware. *Eng. Built Environ.*, Deakin University, 2014.

19. Alazab, M., Venkatraman, S., Watters, P., Alazab, M., Zero-day malware detection based on supervised learning algorithms of API call signatures. *Ninth Australasian Data Mining Conference: AusDM 2011, Ballarat, Australia*, pp. 171–181, 2011.

20. Taylor, S.J. and Letham, B., Forecasting at scale. *Am. Statistician*, 72, 37–45, 2018.

21. BazilaBanu, A., Priyadarshini, R., Thirumalaikolundusubramanian, P., Prediction of Children Diabetes by Autoregressive Integrated Moving Averages Model Using Big Data and Not Only SQL. *J. Comput. Theor. Nanosci.*, 16, 3510–3513, 2019.

22. Worldometers Coronavirus Cases. https://www.worldometers.info/coronavirus/, accessed date: 20.09.2020.

23. Rizzi, R., Cairo, M., Makinen, V., Tomescu, A., II, Valenzuela, D., Hardness of covering alignment: phase transition in post-sequence genomics. *IEEE/ACM Trans. Comput. Biol. Bioinform.*, 16, 23–30, 2019.

24. Kapun, E., Tsarev, F., De Bruijn, Superwalk with multiplicities problem is NP-hard. *BMC Bioinforma.*, 14, Suppl 5, S7, 2013.

25. Chen, J.H. and Asch, S.M., Machine Learning and Prediction in Medicine—Beyond the Peak of Inflated Expectations. *N. Engl. J. Med.*, 376, 2507–2509, 2017.

26. Uddin, M., Wang, Y., Woodbury-Smith, M., Artificial intelligence for precision medicine in neurodevelopmental disorders. *NPJ Digit. Med.*, 2, 112, 2019.

27. Huck, J.H., Verhoeven, N.M., Struys, E.A., Salomons, G.S., Jakobs, C., van der Knaap, M.S., Ribose-5-phosphate isomerase deficiency: New inborn error in the pentose phosphate pathway associated with a slowly progressive leukoencephalopathy. *Am. J. Hum. Genet.*, 74, 745–751, 2004.

28. Wamelink, M.M., Grüning, N.M., Jansen, E.E., Bluemlein, K., Lehrach, H., Jakobs, C., Ralser, M., The difference between rare and exceptionally rare: Molecular characterization of ribose 5-phosphate isomerase deficiency. *J. Mol. Med.*, 88, 931–939, 2010.

29. Schieppati, A., Henter, J.I., Daina, E., Aperia, A., Why rare diseases are an important medical and social issue. *Lancet*, 371, 2039–2041, 2008.

30. Gia, T.N., Jiang, M., Sarker, V.K., Rahmani, A.M., Westerlund, T., Liljeberg, P., Tenhunen, H., Low-cost fog-assisted healthcare IoT system with energy-efficient sensor nodes. *2017 13th International Wireless Communications and Mobile Computing Conference (IWCMC)*, IEEE, pp. 1765–1770, 2017.

31. Negash, B., Gia, T.N., Anzanpour, A., Azimi, I., Jiang, M., Westerlund, T., Tenhunen, H., Leveraging fog computing for healthcare IoT, in: *Fog Computing in the Internet of Things*, pp. 145–169, Springer, Cham, 2018.

32. Berrahal, S., Boudriga, N., Bagula, A., Healthcare systems in rural areas: A cloud-sensor based approach for epidemic diseases management. *International Conference on e-Infrastructure and e-Services for Developing Countries*, Springer, Cham, pp. 167–177, 2015.

33. Farahani, B., Firouzi, F., Chang, V., Badaroglu, M., Constant, N., Mankodiya, K., Towards fog-driven IoT eHealth: Promises and challenges of IoT in medicine and healthcare. *Future Gener. Comput. Syst.*, 78, 659–676, 2018.

34. Kaushalya, S.A.D.S., Kulawansa, K.A.D.T., Firdhous, M.F.M., Internet of Things for Epidemic Detection: A Critical Review, in: *Advances in Computer Communication and Computational Sciences*, pp. 485–495, Springer, Singapore, 2019.

35. Sood, S.K. and Mahajan, I., Wearable IoT sensor based healthcare system for identifying and controlling chikungunya virus. *Comput. Ind.*, 91, 33–44, 2017.

36. Rahmani, A.M., Gia, T.N., Negash, B., Anzanpour, A., Azimi, I., Jiang, M., & Liljeberg, P., Exploiting smart e-Health gateways at the edge of healthcare Internet-of-Things: A fog computing approach. *Future Gener. Comput. Syst.*, 78, 641–658, 2018.

37. Sood, S.K. and Mahajan, I., Fog-cloud based cyber-physical system for distinguishing, detecting and preventing mosquito borne diseases. *Future Gener. Comput. Syst.*, 88, 13–16, 2018.

38. Sareen, S., Sood, S.K., Gupta, S.K., IoT-based cloud framework to control Ebola virus outbreak. *J. Ambient Intell. Hum. Comput.*, 9, 3, 459–476, 2018.

39. Butca, C.G., Suciu, G., Ochian, A., Fratu, O., Halunga, S., Wearable sensors and cloud platform for monitoring environmental parameters in e-health applications. *2014 11th International Symposium on Electronics and Telecommunications (ISETC)*, IEEE, pp. 1–4, 2014.

40. Althebyan, Q., Yaseen, Q., Jararweh, Y., Al-Ayyoub, M., Cloud support for large scale e-healthcare systems. *Ann. Telecommun.*, 71, 9–10, 503–515, 2016.

41. Clerkin, K.J., Fried, J.A., Raikhelkar, J., Sayer, G., Griffin, J.M., Masoumi, A., Schwartz, A., COVID-19 and cardiovascular disease. *Circulation*, 141, 20, 1648–1655, 2020.

7

Security and Privacy of IoT Devices in Healthcare Systems

Himadri Nath Saha[1]* and Subhradip Debnath[2]

[1]Department of Computer Science, Surendranath Evening College, Calcutta University, Kolkata, India
[2]Department of Computer Science, Institute of Engineering and Management, Maulana Abul Kalam Azad University of Technology, Kolkata, India

Abstract

Evolving Internet of Things (IoT) paradigms contribute significantly to the enhancement of current healthcare systems. It would be a universal fact to claim that the IoT provides many advantages in healthcare, including that of the opportunity to better track patients. Focusing on the patient's end helps healthcare providers to quickly collect details and make data-based recommendations to enable quicker medical intervention. Healthcare firms, however, sometimes don't consider the safety risks of linking such devices to the internet. There are many privacy and security issues that end-users must acknowledge. End-users can be prone to malware activity when permission is granted to any potentially insecure or any leaky third-party applications. Smart technologies offer many advantages in healthcare, but the same devices pose higher incidence to both confidentiality and protection. Some possible threats include hacks on frameworks, threats to privacy, data eavesdropping, etc. Our proposed system uses Wireless Body Area Network (WBAN) along with a cloud server to keep a patient's record to make it accessible to the only concerned people by developing a role based assigning and least access privilege system. It collects the patients' medical histories for future reference. This system is efficient and robust as compared to similar existing systems.

Keywords: Centralized network coordinator, Internet of Things, healthcare systems, patient monitoring, centralized ledger, database, smart sensors, cloud application

---

*Corresponding author: contactathimadri@gmail.com

SK Hafizul Islam and Debabrata Samanta (eds.) Smart Healthcare System Design: Security and Privacy Aspects, (143–166) © 2021 Scrivener Publishing LLC

7.1   Introduction

There are around two billion customers around the globe who check and browse contents, access the multimedia resources, email and engage in social networking. But with time, the objective of the Internet kept changing. It started with it being a network serving to share data between devices. As the number of devices began to grow exponentially over the years it is now expected to serve as a platform over the world to interconnect devices. These devices do not necessarily mean smart devices but the traditionally dumbest objects lying around, which are made to be smart with some modifications to be referred to as 'Things' later on. This enabled a new way for those objects or Things to work, communicate, interact through the internet to operate simultaneously automating tasks and reducing manual workloads in different sectors. This internetworking of smart object or Things embedded with sensors, softwares, technologies with the intent to exchange or share data with other devices and collect the data is well known as the Internet of Things (IoT).

The cost of the IoT Devices, sensors, mobile devices and the network connectivity are decreasing and will continue to drop. Also the networking has gradually been changed from wired network to wireless network. Communication technology has become faster, cheaper and changes the way people access information. Adoption of RFID-based technology has gradually changed the course of usage of the Internet of Things. The IoT uses hyperlinking technology aiming to connect the real physical world to the virtual internet [1].

Healthcare is one of the top challenges that every developing and developed country faces in the present day. The healthcare industry invests massively in information technology but still the promised improvement in patient data safety and productivity has not been up to the standards. Even standing in the year of 2020 almost all organizations still rely on the conventional paper medical records and handwritten notes to inform and make decisions. The digital information is concealed and stored in between the departments and the applications, thus the effective sharing of the patients data is very rare and complex. The answer to this issue is the introduction of IoT Technology with the integration of Cloud. This enables the healthcare organizations to direct them towards the clinically relevant services that are needed or required by the patient in arriving with required outcomes making health monitoring, diagnostics and treatment in less time, in an organized and low expense manner.

The security and privacy in IoT-based Healthcare systems is of a very high priority. There are hundreds and thousands of patients who are registering to the healthcare services at a time where the patients need to disclose personal information which may be relevant to the diagnostics and treatments they would need. Thus after the information is received by the Institutional Entity a trust based mutual agreement is formed, popularly known as the "Doctor–Patient Confidentiality". Now in order to respect this mutual agreement the Institutional Entity also needs to implement steps and measures to make sure that there is no breach in the information received from the patients. In order to enforce these measures our proposed model serves as an efficient alternative to the already existing systems.

The model proposed in the chapter uses Wireless Body Area Network (WBAN) [2–4] along with a cloud server to keep a patient's record to make it accessible to the only concerned people by developing a role based assigning and least access privilege system. It collects the patients' medical histories for future references. The application encrypts the data received from the devices and hides it under a cover image to send it over to the local server which after decrypting, redirects and appends the data over into the cloud based databases, Quantum Ledger and object based storage systems, a website and a phone application to display the records of the patients. This system is efficient and robust as compared to similar existing systems.

The chapter spans over several sections where the general architecture is described over in the Section 7.3 and the implementation methodology is mentioned over in Section 7.4. The model designs of the proposed system have been given in the Section 7.3.1 for the reference.

7.2   Background and Related Works

Security and Privacy in the IoT in the Healthcare system is very important in the stage where the world is in the Information Age. Healthcare systems have been trying to adopt and use Internet of Things to automate several of their processes because in this industry response time is very much crucial. Many research works have been carried out regarding the IoT usage in the healthcare industry. Research on securing IoT Devices using Wireless Body Area Network for Health Monitoring proposing a secure wireless small network in which health information can be shared or monitored has been worked upon. But the information flow was constrained to the Network Coordinator.

Gong *et al.* have proposed a lightweight private homomorphism algorithm and encryption algorithm improved from DES Algorithm considering the privacy protection of IoT Devices [5].

Yeh in a paper has proposed that there also have been work upon constructing communication mechanisms for ensuring transmission confidentiality proving the entity authentication among the smart objects, the local processing units and the backend servers [6]. Access control systems devise and employ policies and roles and capabilities. There has been a basic model of granting least access and privileges which is also being followed in our proposed model.

There have also been works upon suggesting the use of multiple cloud servers to ensure that the privacy of the patients' personal data be protected and to ensure the availability of the data. The attack modules that are considered in there are patients' data leakage and destruction, collusion attacks, insider attacks, the amount of big data handling and the amount of data storage. In case of the insider attack the system administrator of the patients' health databases may disclose the patients' sensitive confidential data [7].

Kumar *et al.* [8] presented a paper which has presented a very secure and efficient method for the RGB Images based on gray level modified and multi-level encryption (MLE). The private key and the data are encrypted using the MLE algorithms before mapping to secret gray levels of cover image to be used as a stego image.

There are also existing IoT based health monitoring systems like KHealth to illustrate the existing IoT Based Health Monitoring Systems [9, 10]. It senses both personal and physiological devices to aggregate data.

Maheau *et al.* [11] write that there are a range of PDA's, Smartphones, Smart Devices which a range of healthcare apps compatible with devices with 165,000 apps. There has been researches on capability based access control approaches and distributed capability-based access control systems to be used for providing a finely grained access control for being used in IoT Systems [12, 13].

These are existing systems which are still being implemented and research lack some or the other methodologies. Existing implemented systems are either unsecure or cannot protect the privacy of the user data that has been gathered over. Or if the architecture is secure enough still the system is not elastic and cannot be scaled up and down fast whenever required. Resulting in high latency and packet loss or overloading of servers. In our proposed model we have tried to eliminate these problems with some added functionalities of data processing and keeping the elasticity of the system in mind.

Some works have also been done on the securing the information flow from the IoT Devices and looking into the privacy of the model using hardware based Ciphers which have tried to mitigate collusion attacks, eavesdropping, impersonation and patient's data leakage and destruction. In many of the research works the data is tried to be stored in Blockchains to feature in the hashing of the data i.e. to avail verifiability of the data. Also the immutability of the blockchain has made the data more and more secure averting any kind of update of records. But in order to achieve this Distributed Immutable Ledger advantages there is a massive computation involved in the process. Even the smallest Querying of Data can result in a huge computation that can produce significant lag. In the healthcare industry time is not compromisable so blockchain or the distributed architecture is not a viable option for practical implementation.

7.3   Proposed System Design and Architecture

IoT Devices and sensors measuring, tracking and recording the patient data are transferred to a Raspberry Pi which would be unique to every bed in an institution. The Raspberry Pi collects the data provided by the sensors in close proximity, encrypts it over and sends it to the private server setup locally within the compound of the institution. This procedure ensures that the data is secure when in transit (Figure 7.1). After the data is received and decrypted in the server end the text based data are parsed and saved in an

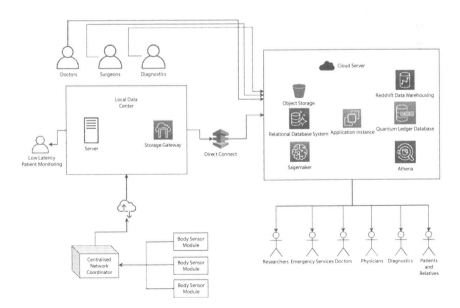

Figure 7.1 Proposed system design and architecture model.

SQL based database against the patient bed and patient id. The object based data such as the images, scanned documents etc. will be saved as objects in buckets in the public cloud infrastructure. Thus featuring a Hybrid Cloud System which shall ensure a high availability of information. The local private servers and the public cloud infrastructure will be in connection with AWS Direct Connect ensuring smooth and secure flow of information.

By this the doctors, medical health professionals and the nurses inside the local network of the institutions hold the capability to edit, write, and update the health records of the patients.

The body sensors which will be connected to any patient for diagnostic, treatment or health monitoring will be readily using a wireless area body network to send the data over to the nearest Raspberry Pi to which they are assigned to update and append the data tracked into the private dataserver present within the compound in sync with the cloud. The doctor, physicians or the emergency response teams can access patient's data directly from the local data server itself. Even if the stakeholders are not present within the compound they are able to login in to the cloud server to keep track of the medical record of the respective patient.

To ensure the security and privacy of the data that has been received from the body sensors on the patient, data transferred from the Raspberry Pi to the local server is encrypted. The encryption key is automatically managed by the local server itself which stores the ids for every Raspberry Pi for every specific bed. The data stored in the local servers are encrypted at rest. The data is analyzed using the cloud data lakes analytics using services like Amazon Redshift for a highly scalable data warehousing.

Further the stakeholders in the systems i.e. the medical health professionals, doctors, diagnostic centers, emergency health services such as ambulances and also authorized medical researchers can have access into the system.

7.3.1   Modules

7.3.1.1   Wireless Body Area Network

The wireless body area network is being proposed where the sensors are to be implemented in a hop star topology in the beacon modes where the network coordinator gets triggered up when the sensor nodes transmits any data. The standalone sensors such as the body temperature measuring and the ECG and respiration signal in real time sense the data and transmit it to the centralized network coordinator. The sensors are in a very close vicinity to the centralized network coordinator.

The sensors are not standalone but in small modules. They have their own micro processors modules which control and transmit the data to the Centralized Network Coordinators.

7.3.1.2   Centralized Network Coordinator

Raspberry Pi 4 Module's are used as Centralized Network Coordinator. Raspberry Pi 4 has a 2.4 Ghz and 5.0 Ghz IEEE 802.11ac wireless and Bluetooth 5.0 BLE. The Raspberry Pi 4 uses the UART Protocol to accept the string commands being sent by the Body sensor modules accepting the SPP profile requests through PDA connection for the remote data transmission.

The task of the Centralized Network Coordinator is to coordinate the body sensor nodes sending periodic data requests for efficiency in the network operations. It then receives the patient's physiological data from the sensor nodes in the real time. It further encrypts that data and sends it over to the Local Server.

7.3.1.3   Local Server

The local server hosted in the institution mainly acts as the data parser and router for the data to get securely routed to secure cloud servers. It mainly consists of an application instance used by the stakeholders in the institution i.e. the doctors, physicians, nurse and other health officials to allow and add their notes and observations and reports and diagnostics using registered institute devices and authentic credentials. The data received from the Centralized Network Coordinator's or the CNC's are decrypted based on the private keys pre-assigned to the CNC's stored in the database of the server. After data decryption is done the data is sorted and forwarded over to the SQL based Relational Database System hosted over by the Public Cloud Server.

If the reports and observations generated against the patients are object based like image or pdf based reports, observations, or diagnostics, the data is stored over to Object Based Storage Buckets in the Public Cloud Server.

Local Servers and the Cloud Servers will be connected through secure Virtual Private Networking services like AWS Direct Connect to facilitate secure smooth flow of information through private institutional networks directly to the Cloud network.

7.3.1.4   Cloud Server

In the public cloud server there are four components:

- An Application Instance housing the application through which every prospective stakeholder with authentic identities will be able to check on through the data of the patients they are granted the access privileges to view. The Application Instance here is an AWS EC2 instance running Linux Based Web Server hosting a web application which can lead the stakeholders to access the real time data just over from their devices.
- A Relational Database System—This is an SQL-based relational database housing several tables which institutional staff, doctors, access control lists and the patient details. Using of a cloud based Relational Database System makes the system easy to be administered and integrate with the application using API to access capabilities without infrastructure provisioning or the need of maintenance of a versatile big database. It is very much scalable. Availability of the database is also very high due to the Multi Availability Zone deployment. It is fast, secure and inexpensive so that the variable cost of deployment stays low even after the gathering of petabytes of data.
- A Quantum Ledger Database—Immutable Database Hosting the health records of the patients. The Quantum Ledger Database also keeps a track of who logs in to the system to view the records of which patients alongside the timestamps. The quantum ledger databases stores the records and hashes them in a chain to achieve immutability. The records can also be verified upon by just matching the hashes of the records using SHA-256 to generate a secure output file of the change of the data through its history to validate the integrity of the data. The availability of the data is quite high as the data is spin up over and deployed over Multiple Availability Zones.
- Data Analysis Warehouse such as Redshift which facilitates arranging of patients data across the RDS and the Object Storage Data Lakes allowing the users to perform extensive queries on to analyze patient data more effectively. This enables the structured data over in the Relational Databases and the unstructured Data's over in the S3 buckets to be queried simultaneously and be brought in to the operational insights of the applications and the systems that are being deployed.

- Amazon Athena will be used for fast query facilitating searching data effectively over the mass of the data over in the S3 buckets. It is an Extract, Transform and Load the Data service which loads the S3 Data over to be queried using standard SQL Statements.
- Amazon SageMaker is Machine Learning can be used upon the patient's data to be monitored and analyzed to detect diseases by learning and tracking symptoms. Here the researchers in accordance with the health institutions would be able to build, train and deploy machine learning models quickly. This will facilitate datasets to be trained and configured for analysis on patient's data.

7.3.1.5   Dedicated Network Connection

The local servers/data centers are connected to the cloud servers with Dedicated Network Connections i.e. private connection which would facilitate a secure smooth transfer of data from the local server. Many public cloud service providers come up with support for the service such as of AWS providing Direct Connect, Azure providing ExpressRoute, Google Providing with Dedicated Interconnect. This is also a cost effective alternative than to buy more bandwidth over the public internet.

7.4   Methodology

The sensor modules generating data takes the data and sends it over to the Centralized Network Coordinator through a small wireless body network spanning over from 2 to 3 m. The Wireless Body Network is a Bluetooth [15] network in a hop star topology where the Centralized Network Coordinator is in the middle and coordinates the other Sensor Modules wirelessly and fetches the information. After the information is transferred to the Centralized Network Coordinator it determines if the information received is text-based or object-based and accordingly encrypts that information.

The encryption methodology proposed in here follows a hybrid RSA AES algorithm. In this methodology the plain text is divided up into odd text and even text. AES is used to encrypt the odd text using a secret public key *Saes* assigned to each of the Centralized Network Coordinator. The even text is encrypted using RSA with a secret public key *Srsa*.

The encrypted data is encoded and concealed within a cover image using 2D-DWT-1L or 2D-DWT-2L and transferred over to the local server as a stego-image. Which after Further the encrypted data is then being tried to be concealed with a The private key X with which the contents will be decrypted in the local server will be saved over in the SQL Based Database housing the private key for all of the Centralized Network Coordinators.

Now after the data is decrypted in the local server's application instance the decrypted data is categorized and after authenticating its origin with reference to the validity of the registered Centralized Network Coordinator a json file is created cross referencing the CNC No., Bed No., Patient ID, Patient details alongside the data received.

The json file is then transmitted and then the data is transferred over through the secure channel using TLS/SSL with Encryption in Transit over to the public cloud through a dedicated private connection from the local datacenter to the public cloud datacenter (in here AWS). AWS Direct connect is used to connect the local data center and the public cloud datacenter.

The data will be received through an application instance and the patient data would be appended in a Quantum Ledger Database. QLDB or the Quantum Ledger database having immutability will withhold the information transferred. The immutability feature of the QLDB will facilitate the data appended cannot be modified or changed or deleted. After the data gets inserted into the QLDB, it can be queried into the application using the web interfaces provided the users need to log in and authenticate their credentials. But in here comes another privacy feature of the proposed model.

The privacy models have been designed specific to that the patient and relatives will be able to see the diagnostics and reports with transparency but will not be able to append the data in there. The patients will be able to edit their preferences and their personal information but the updation will remain recorded for future references.

Emergency services also include the (Figures 7.2–7.5) emergency ambulance services, pharmacy services, diagnostic centers (Figures 7.6, 7.7). These services will be able to access a screened relevant patient record and patient details and would also be able to add comments. But every activity including their viewing of any specific patient record is recorded for keeping track of unnecessary privacy infringements and accountability. Also in case of the services like that of a pharmacy the pharmacist is in no need of viewing patient details. In that case if the patient tells the report id where the drugs needed are mentioned and show him the report the pharmacist will be able to verify the report just by typing over the report id. Automatically the hash key of the report id would be matched over to the health records and the basic details of the patient would be revealed for the

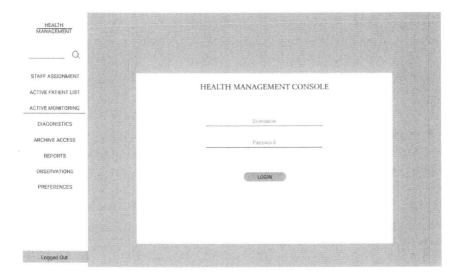

Figure 7.2 Login window for Doctor/Nurse/Health official login from computer terminal.

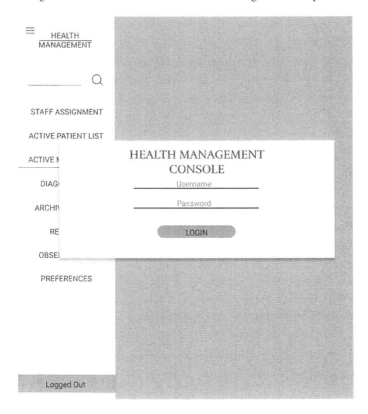

Figure 7.3 Login window for Doctor/Nurse/Health official login from Android device.

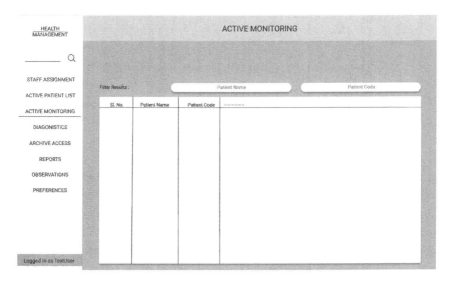

Figure 7.4 Patient monitoring window from computer terminal.

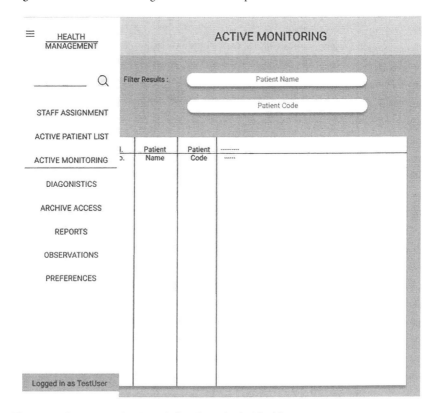

Figure 7.5 Patient monitoring window from Android tablet.

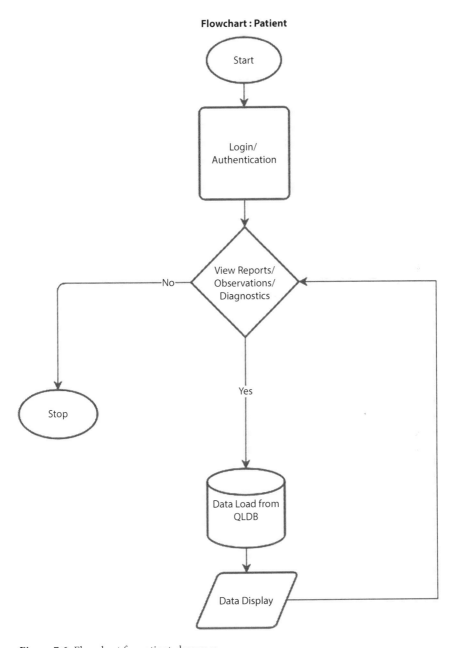

Figure 7.6 Flowchart for patient clearance.

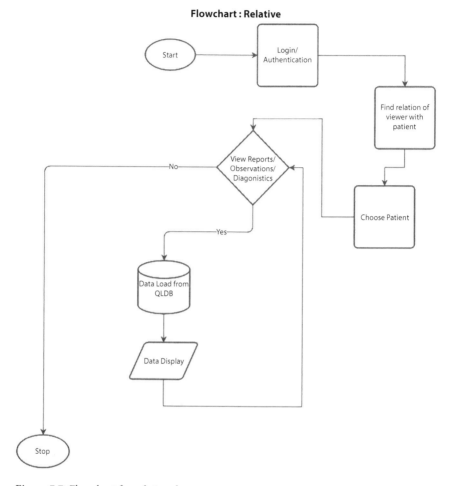

Figure 7.7 Flowchart for relative clearance.

pharmacist to verify patients identity and the drugs assigned to the patient if valid or not (Figure 7.8).

Similarly any 3rd diagnostic service center just needs to verify the patient credential just by typing in the patient id and the patient details along with the relatable information will be cryptographically verified and all the required tests asked to be performed by the doctors will be listed and can be uploaded in there easily.

Researchers, doctors and health officials would be able to access medical records without any filter but they will be able to access the relevant records of the patients under their care and would be able to write reports (Figures 7.9–7.11) and observations into the patients records and would have every

Flowchart : Pharmacy Services

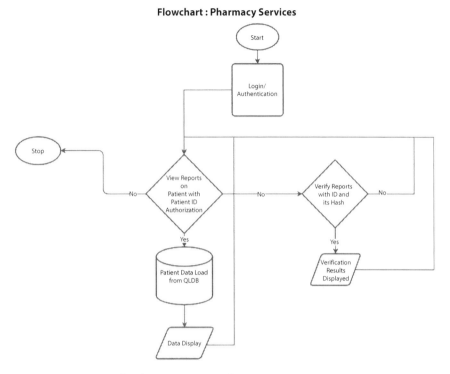

Figure 7.8 Flowchart for pharmacy services clearance.

records of the patient apart from the personal details of the patient at their disposal for observation. But every detail including writing of reports or viewing patient data is recorded for keeping track of unnecessary privacy infringements and accountability. Similarly nurses who are assigned to any particular wards will only be able to access and monitor the standard sensor readings of the patients in those wards and not any other. Credential specific roles could also be created like "Cardiologist" which would give him access to the data of all the heart rate monitors along with the basic patient details associated with it. Also temporary patient specific roles can also be created "Cardiologist for 'Patient X101'", "Nurse for 'Patient X101'" which would give them temporary access to the monitors for the patients they are assigned to temporarily.

All stakeholders would only be able to perform the activities they have logged in to the system and have necessary clearance. Any change of clearance would needs to be cleared by institutional authority and vetted. Also these changes will also be recorded.

These micro level trackings of every activity will be recorded in a Relational Database System hosted in the cloud. Also the Relational

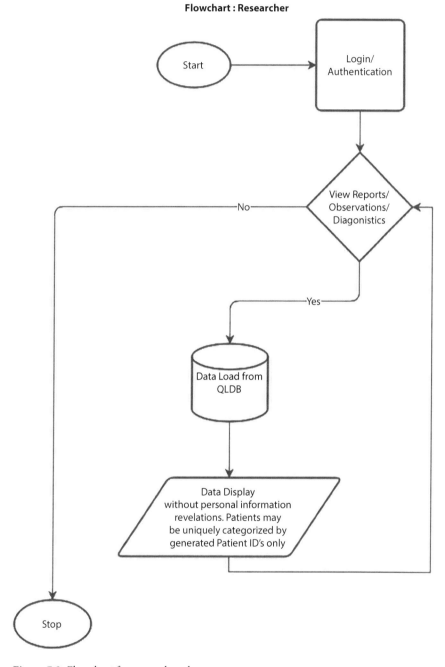

Figure 7.9 Flowchart for researcher clearance.

Flowchart : Emergency Services

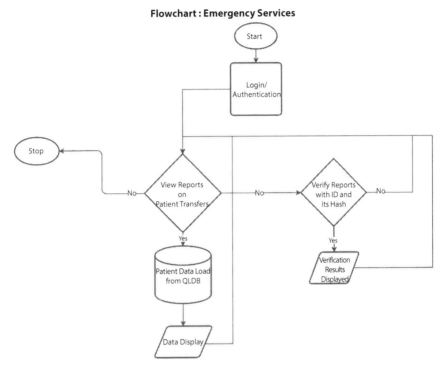

Figure 7.10 Flowchart for emergency services clearance.

Database System will hold the patient details, and the details of all the stakeholders.

All the object based files such as pictures or reports/diagnostic observations in pdf or any such format will be saved as objects in folders within a bucket named to individual to patient ID unique to every patient.

Every such document can also be accessed by every stakeholder with above mentioned above through the same application with the transparency varying with the clearance they have. The local data centers are also linked with the public cloud servers hosting the buckets using storage gateways so that the files are easily accessible to the institutional servers when required with low latency networks apart from going over through the public internet.

Now, when all the data is over on the public cloud server the data needs to be aggregated using data warehousing services such as Redshift. This makes the data available booth object based and present in the relation databases easily available to be queried substantially in much less time. Amazon Athena also provides with analytics tool to analyze patterns of stakeholders accessing data of patients and check and alert if there is

Flowchart : Doctor

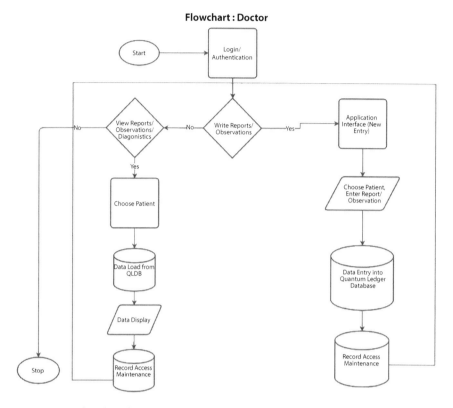

Figure 7.11 Flowchart for Doctor clearance.

any pattern of unnecessary information checking violating the privacy/ confidentiality of the patient's information.

Artificial Intelligence Services like Amazon SageMaker used with the patient's data trained with approved pre recorded datasets of diseases to track patient records to find and detect diseases and warn the patients ahead of time.

The same application can also be used in from portable devices such as tablets and phones. Only condition is the application has to be in connection with public internet. The data will be streamed from over the public cloud.

7.5   Performance Analysis

We have observed the latency to be minimal and within 500 ms in total at an average. The upload latency is minimized to a great extent by using load balancers into the local network system.

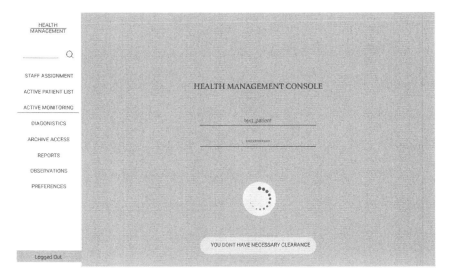

Figure 7.12 UI of unsuccessful login authentication.

Also the Role Backed Access System maintains a constant record of people accessing the system and data with authentication. The record can be kept downloaded by the System Administrator and malpractices can be tracked down to specific users.

The authentication systems work perfectly for different roles (Figure 7.12). Patients and relatives cannot use the observation application endpoint developed for the health officials, doctors, nurses, emergency service provider and pharmacists.

This is also same for each of the other roles where they cannot access other roles other than the application in their local devices. The Web Interface is however universal and does not limit this feature. The feature is limited over in the application to make it lightweight and more responsive in low specification devices.

Also multi factor authentication based login systems check for correct entries within 30 s entry time. If the login window expires after every 30-second interval the One Time Password gets reset and needs to be re-entered to verify user. The OTP can be send through Email and also through the telephone (Figure 7.13).

7.6   Future Research Direction

Next our research will be focused upon to reduce the latency in the systems when the load of the multiple centralized network coordinators increases.

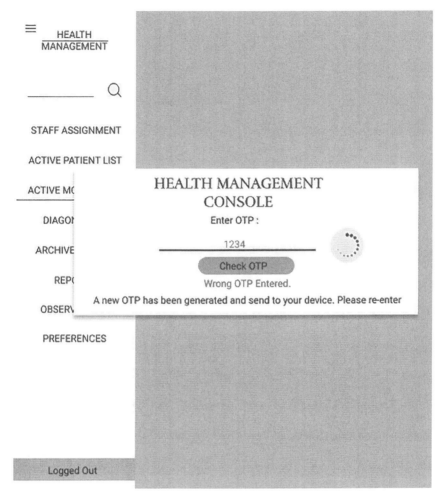

Figure 7.13 UI of unsuccessful OTP/MFA authentication.

Also the research will focus on machine learning algorithms to detect network attacks if originating from within the network and mitigating them accordingly. With machine learning and deep learning techniques the threat originating from inside the closed network within the institution can be traced out. Techniques like RNN's and XgBoost can be implemented with pre-trained datasets to track vulnerabilities.

Through the system we would also like to further focus on the interconnectivity of institutions/entities where multiple hospitals would be able to link through secure networks transfer data and also if a patient is transferred can access his/her medical records thoroughly. Also it would feature where hospitals, diagnostics centers and medical colleges will be able to interact and share their research data's and cooperate in the diagnosis. A patient even if opting to have a checkup in a diagnostics centre the report will be shared within the network where the doctor who is overlooking the patient can access the report seamlessly. This will also help doctors having much specialty in a field living far away diagnosing a patient from their nearest hospitals without any travels involved in the whole process.

Also in the full scale deployment there also have been reports of experimental implementations like that of using patients biometric signatures into the systems for high levels of authentication and also to identify patients who are asleep using nothing but their accelerometer data [13]. To track this workflow the Kyoto University used a real time locationing system by employing hand held barcode scanners, bluetooth transmitters and a beacon relay system and some barcode tags on patients, nurses and the supplies [14].

7.7 Conclusion

In our proposed model we have designed a system through which sensor data can be easily be transferred from the premises to a cloud storage securely step by step. We have also discussed a system in which the privacy of the patient data can be maintained and using a least access policy the patient data can be analyzed, viewed, observed by the health officials accordingly in a smooth transition. Further the system can also help facilitate the patient and his/her relatives to track her progress and view periodic reports sitting from their homes itself and also go to diagnostic centers or pharmacists and perform tests and buy drugs and keep all those in record for future references. Also through the system the pharmacist who is selling the drugs can verify the patient's identity and check if the patient is allowed to/has been prescribed to buy that drug by a certified doctor or not. The system also allows emergency response systems to track the patients basic info i.e. name, age which is relevant, his/her illness during patient transfers making it more safer for the patient to adjust as the medical staff would be prepared accordingly. In this due process many of the crises in the present situation can be overcome and met. Rising shortages in healthcare systems, delivery costs, information sharing between entities and the shortage of healthcare professionals for better treatment can be easily overcame and enhanced services can be provided. Our proposed system aims to be robust and more efficient compared to other existing systems and provides a more secure approach to utilizing IoT in healthcare systems.

References

1. Darwish, A., Hassanien, A.E., Elhoseny, M., Sangaiah, A.K., Muhammad, K., The impact of the hybrid platform of Internet of Things and cloud computing on healthcare systems: Opportunities, challenges, and open problems. *J. Ambient Intell. Hum. Comput.*, to be published, 12652, 659, 2017, https://doi.org/10.1007/s12652-017-0659-1.

2. Yuce, M.R., Implementation of wireless body area networks for healthcare systems. *Sens. Actuators A, Physical*, 162, 1, 116–129, 2010. https://doi.org/10.1016/j.sna.2010.06.004.

3. Wu, T., Wu, F., Redouté, J., Yuce, M.R., An Autonomous Wireless Body Area Network Implementation Towards IoT Connected Healthcare Applications. *IEEE Access*, 5, 11413–11422, 2017.

4. Khan, J.Y., Yuce, M.R., Bulger, G. *et al.*, Wireless Body Area Network (WBAN) Design Techniques and Performance Evaluation. *J. Med. Syst.*, 36, 1441–1457, 2012. https://doi.org/10.1007/s10916-010-9605-x.

5. Gong, T., Huang, H., Li, P., Zhang, K., Jiang, H., A Medical Healthcare System for Privacy Protection Based on IoT. *2015 Seventh International Symposium on Parallel Architectures, Algorithms and Programming (PAAP)*, Nanjing, 2015, pp. 217–222.

6. Yeh, K., A Secure IoT-Based Healthcare System With Body Sensor Networks. *IEEE Access*, 4, 10288–10299, 2016.

7. Luo, E., Bhuiyan, M.Z.A., Wang, G., Rahman, M.A., Wu, J., Atiquzzaman, M., Privacy Protector: Privacy-Protected Patient Data Collection in IoT-Based Healthcare Systems. *IEEE Commun. Mag.*, 56, 2, 163–168, Feb. 2018.

8. Kumar, P. and Lee, H.-J., Security issues in healthcare applications using wireless medical sensor networks: A survey. *Sensors*, 12, 1, 55–91, 2012.

9. Anantharam, P., Banerjee, T., Sheth, A., Thirunarayan, K., Marupudi, S., Sridharan, V., Forbis, S.G., Knowledge-driven personalized contextual mhealth service for asthma management in children. *2015 IEEE International Conference on Mobile Services*, 2015.

10. Muhammad, K., Sajjad, M., Mehmood, I. *et al.*, A novel magic LSB substitution method (M-LSB-SM) using multi-level encryption and achromatic component of an image. *Multimed. Tools. Appl.*, 75, 14867–14893, 2016. https://doi.org/10.1007/s11042-015-2671-9.

11. Maheu, M.M., Nicolucci, V., Pulier, M.L. *et al.* The Interactive Mobile App Review Toolkit (IMART): a Clinical Practice-Oriented System. *J. Technol. Behav. Sci.*, 1, 3–15, 2016. https://doi.org/10.1007/s41347-016-0005-z

12. Gong, Li. A Secure Identity-Based Capability System., In *IEEE symposium on security and privacy*, pp. 56–63, 1989.

13. Hernández-Ramos, J., Jara, A., Marín, L., Skarmeta Gómez, A., DCapBAC: Embedding authorization logic into smart things through ECC optimizations. *Int. J. Comput. Math.*, 93, 2, 345–366, 2016.

14. Catarinucci, L. *et al.*, An IoT-Aware Architecture for Smart Healthcare Systems. *IEEE Internet Things J.*, 2, 6, 515–526, Dec. 2015.
15. Sato, K. *et al.*, Feasibility Assessment of Bluetooth-Based Location System for Workflow Analysis of Nursing Staff. *Trans. Jpn. Soc. Med. Biol. Eng.*, 51, supplement, R–314, 2013.

8

An IoT-Based Diet Monitoring Healthcare System for Women

Suganyadevi S.[1]*, Shamia D.[2] and Balasamy K.[3]

[1]*KPR Institute of Engineering and Technology, Coimbatore, India*
[2]*VSB College of Engineering and Technical Campus, Coimbatore, India*
[3]*Dr. Mahalingam College of Engineering and Technology, Coimbatore, India*

Abstract

One of the significant elements of smart healthcare and the smart home is diet tracking. With an injective monitoring system to track one's eating frequency, researchers have addressed this issue. Using a weighing sensor and radio-frequency-identification (RFID) to measure the weight of food intake, a smart dining table was installed. To detect food portion size and intake, hybrid eating behaviour monitoring device involving a camera and microphone has been suggested. The proposed system is a fully automated diet tracking solution consisting of Wi-Fi powered sensors for food nutrition assessment and a smartphone application that collects food ingredient nutrition information. A food weighing sensor is included in the monitoring device, which calculates the weight of the food product and is transmitted via wireless to the cloud over the Internet via a microcontroller integrated with a wireless module synchronisation. Two different methods are used in order to obtain the appropriate nutrient values. Then the result, food is classified on the basis of the highest nutritional content, the relationship between the food eaten and the lack of nutrients. The method also describes the deficient nutrient, obesity, and it means that the consumer has the food dependent on the maximum nutrient content and low calories.

Keywords: IoT, healthcare system, nutrition monitoring, microcontroller

*Corresponding author: suganya3223@gmail.com

SK Hafizul Islam and Debabrata Samanta (eds.) Smart Healthcare System Design: Security and Privacy Aspects, (167–202) © 2021 Scrivener Publishing LLC

8.1   Introduction

Food is fundamental for endurance; however to carry on with a top notch way of life, smart dieting [1] is imperative. Great quality food consumption can possibly straightforwardly forestall metabolic unsettling influences bringing about reduced mankind work [2], and forestall food consuming related sicknesses, for example, diabetes [3], weight [4] and cardiovascular sickness [5]. Eating-related illnesses, for example, corpulence not just influence physical wellbeing yet additionally bring about huge monetary (finding, treatment of illnesses, and so on) and cultural (loss of efficiency, handicap annuities, and so on.) costs [5]. As per Ref. [6], for a person having a BMI (Body Mass Index) of 39 kg/m², and a weight reduction of 6 percent [%] is relied upon to bring about a 401-dollar ($) decrease in yearly doctor prescribed medication amounts, an 11% weight reduction spares $679, a 16% weight reducing spares $870, and a 19 percent [%] of weight misfortune spares $998. Additionally, amount lost efficiency because of heftiness is $12,989.51 every year [7].

A few methodologies were reviewed since before the early 2000s to resolve this problem of preserving solid food admission. Handbook procedures [8], including deciphered diet confirmation self-reports, are one of the critically recognized scopes in nutrition-use documentation. Starting late, with the popular use of gadgets, approaches were advanced. A few eating routine journal applications have been created [9]. Notwithstanding, these note-put together methodologies depend intensely with respect to client memory and review, which isn't viable for some, particularly incapacitated clients with memory problems. Hence, it is important to build up a more compelling methodology with the assistance of innovation for programmed food admission checking. In earlier days, a large extent of methodologies has been investigated in various examinations using different devices. These devices include fluctuating identifying modalities, for instance, visual, Electro Myo Graphy (EMG), acoustic, inertial, Electro Glotto Graph (EGG), capacitive moreover, piezoelectric sensors. A few methodologies utilize a consolidated combination of sensors. Since each detecting innovation has its preferred position and constraint for food-admission observing relying upon its application, we lead this top to bottom audit zeroing in on the latest and promising wearable advances.

Health is described as a full condition of physical, mental, and social prosperity and not just an absence of sickness. Health is a principal component of individuals' requirement for a superior life. Shockingly, the worldwide health issue has made a problem as a result of specific variables, for example, chronic weakness benefits, the presence of enormous holes among provincial and metropolitan regions, doctors, and medical caretakers inaccessibility during the hardest time.

A fourth of ladies of conceptive age in India are starving, with a BMI of under 19 kg/m (Source: NFHS 4 2015-16). It is notable that a weak mother unavoidably brings forth an undernourished child, sustaining an intergenerational pattern of under-nutrition. Undernourished young ladies have a more prominent probability of turning out to be undernourished moms who thus have a more noteworthy possibility of bringing infants with low weight, propagating an intergenerational cycle of malnutrition. This flow of cycle could be intensified further in youthful moms, particularly young adult young ladies who start childbearing before they have developed and grown enough. At the point when moms take just short stretches among pregnancies and have numerous youngsters, this can fuel sustenance deficiencies, which are then given to their kids. Fetal hindering is commonly achieved by the mother's lacking food before beginning and in the essential trimester. The significant purpose behind stale degrees of under-nutrition among Indian youngsters is a result of a disappointment so far to enough forestalls under-nutrition when it happens most—in the belly, which is brought about by helpless sustenance of ladies previously and during pregnancy. Given this current, ladies' sustenance—previously, during and after pregnancy—has now been incorporated as an uncommon center zone in UNICEF India's nourishment programming. The association presently means to give added center to universalize the inclusion of the five fundamental nourishment intercessions for ladies that have been shown up at dependent on worldwide and public agreement.

There was an unexpected focus on widespread health inclusion (or all inclusive healthcare) (UHC) at the 2019 United Nations General Assembly. This General Assembly reaffirmed that 'wellness becomes a precondition, also a consequence or marker and each of the 3 components of the economic turn of events' and unambiguously committed to 'achieving universal inclusion of wellness before 2030, for the ultimate objective of scaling up the global initiative to create a safe environment for all'. A popular independence and not the profit of only the people who can stand to pay are ideally health and prosperity.

The United Nations affirmation on United Healthcare (UHC) perceives essential healthy environment as a greatest comprehensive, successful, productive entire of the public way to deal with guaranteeing individuals' physical and emotional wellness and social prosperity. In addition to quality instruction, sex uniformity and women's reinforcement, admission to safe drinking water and sterilization, and social security programs, the announcement also features the key role of healthy weight management plans and healthy, equitable and sustainable food structures in creating healthier social orders.

The argument for incorporating sustenance as a fundamental segment of critical healthcare is convincing: for a long time, health frameworks and physicians centered mostly on model of psychological, alcohol-treatment-based disorder that lacks main factors, including such diet, lifestyle, for example. The results of this limited scope are apparent: the international pandemic of ailing health that cleans the world. In the modern society's biggest wellbeing and cultural problems, less than stellar eating routines are causing incapacity, passing, developing inequalities, shocking healthcare costs and ecological repercussions.

They are constrained to behave because policy makers and regulators increasingly perceive its scope and depth concerning hunger problems. It will produce generous health benefits and be remarkably cost-effective to integrate sustenance practices into health frameworks to encourage healthy eating [2], and forestall and manage constant diseases associated with under-nutrition and diet.

The key partners are responsible for healthier and fairer food and health frameworks, including governments and the private sector. This shift represents a move away towards setting the maximum responsibility and blame on people to settle on healthy options, which has become a rising population that brings food practices together on a worldwide scale. Mediations based on communities can cover greater parts of society, very little personal action and perhaps less exorbitant, contrasting and personal methodologies may be involved. Everybody could benefit from such 'upstream' techniques, particularly to someone less advantageous as well as of lower financial situation, especially when coordinated within a widespread framework of health inclusion. While arrangements and projects were made over a very long period of time to address yearning and food weakness, abundant fewer was thought concentrating on the class improvement of diets and also report non-transferable sickness interrelated to diet. Continuing developments and initiatives in dietary arrangements to forestall NCDs will advise territories requiring ebb and flow and also subsidize with the improvement in general well-being inclusion strategy towards counter chronic nutrition-associated disorders.

Guaranteeing unbiased admission to viable diet intercessions within health frameworks will play an urgent role in improving weight management strategies, preventing and managing illness, lowering healthcare costs, and finally improving the health of everyone. Nonetheless, in terms of equal arrangement, funding, control and evaluation, these aids are not yet organized by a strong methodology that blends sustenance and health-care. In public healthcare planning and funding discussions, nutrition is much of the time under-organized. The new Total Nourishment Explosion recognizes the essential and to coordinate nourishment for all inclusive fitness attention by way of an imperative aimed at enhancing weight loss plans, redeemable survives and dropping dietcare expenditure however safeguarding that nobody is abandoned [3].

WHO and UNICEF's vision for the general inclusion of essential diet-care in this modern society stays: a societies-focused way of dealing with health that expects to expand the level and dispersion of health and pros-perity evenly by zeroing in on the needs and inclinations of individuals (as individuals and networks) as well as on time as conceivable along the continuum of health advancement and disease [4].

Essential healthcare is essential to achieving all inclusive health inclu-sion and prompts a variety of health [5] and financial welfares. By itself, this is the main techniques through which nourishment attention can remain smoothed out and transmitted in that levels of the network, thus ensuring optimum inclusion and dissemination of top-notch administrations. In any case, nourishment administrations ought to be presented at numer-ous degrees in diet attention conveyance, together with optional and in third consideration. Absence in admittance towards essential diet attention through fittingly incorporated nourishment activities can imply that qual-ity sustenance administrations don't arrive at everybody. It is frequently the most helpless and impeded individuals who have least admittance to administrations. There is a possibility that they are not of a reliably high caliber or ideal inclusion at the point where subsistence administrations are distributed across various components, and those were not remains methodically tested and assessed.

In order to coordinate sustenance hooked on critical diet attention custom-made into various settings and necessities, scope of a better admin-istration, organizational switches are required. This contains arrangement schemes, even-handed portion of properties, interaction with network partners and secretive zone [6], adequate health staff, and also in phys-ical environment. Definition of an accessible critical wellbeing adminis-tration, and hence the degree and form of food mediations that can and should be implemented, changes from nation to nation, as set out in the explanation. For instance, essential healthcare frameworks in delicate states are custom-made to manage expanded degrees of hindering, squan-dering, and micronutrient insufficiencies, while additionally confronting different other cultural difficulties, for example, limited populace access, frameworks interruption, flexibly breaks and high staff turnover. Urgently, essential healthcare frameworks should be touchy and receptive into variance populace requirements and public factors, for example, this impacted through area, time of life, sex, riches, nationality, movement status, and handicap, so as to target and tailor mediations as per need. Strikingly, around the world, just 5 million of the 17 million youngsters under 6 years old with extreme intense unhealthiness right now approach therapy [7], featuring the critical must to report this unsuitable problem.

Foremost universal effects in nourishment uncertainty and also under-nutrition had for quite some time been perceived, prompting a conventional spotlight on activities focused on under-nutrition. Neglecting to perceive and focus on the amazing eating routine related NCD loads—that can exist together with under-nutrition—through our health frameworks, will exasperate sustenance disparities and the hunger troubles. The basic sustenance activities set forward by WHO feature [8] a base arrangement of nourishment mediations over the existence course that ought to be all around accessible, pointed principally at under-nutrition. Micronutrient items for example iodine, iron, nutrient and additional action taken of extreme unhealthiness, and also in advancing and promoting acceptable baby and small child care are key basic maintenance practices related to critical healthcare. Of the thirty specific sustenance practices suggested, however, only one emphasis on broad eating regimes and diet-related NCDs by methods for developing a more systematic environment that advances regular safe eating propensities (mostly based on soil goods, absolute fats, soaked fats and trans fats) that have expansions to critical healthcare arrangements. Intercessions focusing on different territories of the health area (e.g., irresistible infection control and conceptive health) additionally can possibly on the whole improve dietary status.

Starting late, a couple of another key nutritive factors and also methodology had been recognized for dealing with all around [9] under-nourishment and nutrition-associated NCDs those can be measured aimed at compromise mad about far and wide wellbeing coverage. Examples fuse clinical answers [10] to no end or restricted sound foods, coordination of standardized clinical examinations for qualifying the nutrition and food vulnerability [11] hooked on automated wellbeing archives, besides restoratively redid suppers aimed at great-peril [12], sustenance-unpredictable patients by intricate steady situations. This is necessary intended for wellbeing structures towards stretch out theirs organizations towards board nutrition, nutrition-associated NCDs, to report wretchedness completely and also broadly.

IoT is making any items inside associated in the ongoing decade and it has been considered as the following innovative transformation. Keen health checking component [1, 2], shrewd stopping [3], brilliant home [4], savvy city [5], keen atmosphere [6], modern locales [7], and farming fields [8] are a portion of the uses of IoT. The most enormous utilization of IoT is in healthcare the board which gives health and climate condition following offices. IoT is only connecting PCs to the web using sensors and organizations [9, 10]. These associated parts can be utilized on gadgets for health observing. The pre-owned sensors at that point forward the data to removed areas like M2M, which are hardware for PCs, machines for individuals, handheld gadgets, or cell phones [11]. It is a straightforward, energy-effective, a lot more intelligent, adaptable, and interoperable method of following and improving consideration to any health issue. These days, present day frameworks are giving an adaptable interface [12], collaborator gadgets [13], and emotional well-being the board [14] to have a savvy existence for the individual.

Pulse and internal heat level are the two hugest pointers for human health. Pulse is the per-minute measure of pulses, generally known as the beat rate. To gauge the beat rate, an expansion in the blood stream volume can be utilized by figuring the beats. Typical pulse ranges somewhere in the range of 60 and 100 beats for every moment for healthy individuals. The regular tranquil heart for grown-up guys is around 70 bpm and for grown-up females 75 bpm [15]. Female with 12 years old or more, ordinarily have higher paces of heart interestingly with guys. The temperature of human body is basically the warmth of body and the total of warmth emanated by the body is logically decided. The normal individual's internal heat level depends on various factors, for example, encompassing temperature, the individual's sex, and his dietary patterns. In healthy grown-ups, it is probably going to extend between 97.8 °F (36.5 °C) and 99 °F (37.2 °C). Various factors, for example, influenza, low-temperature hypothermia, or some other ailment may prompt an adjustment in internal heat level. In practically all ailments, fever is an ordinary marker [16]. Different techniques exist to intrusively and noninvasively evaluate the pulse and internal heat level. For the shopper, noninvasive methodologies over some time have demonstrated precise and helpful [17]. It is recommended that a healthcare ought to give great room conditions to encourage the patients [18]. A few estimates like room dampness, level of all gases like CO, and CO2 can decide the nature of room climate. The poisonous gases and certain degrees of moistness are exceptionally hurtful to patients. For ideal solace, the room mugginess ought to be somewhere in the range of 30 and 65%. A few investigations [19, 20] are done uniquely for a brilliant home, not for devoted healthcare.

There are a few lethal illnesses like coronary illness [21], diabetes [22], bosom malignancy [23, 24], liver issue [25], and so on in clinical area however the primary worry of our created framework is to screen the principal indications of a wide range of patients and the patient's room climate. This paper proposes a redid healthcare framework that screens the beat and internal heat level of patients just as room moistness, CO, and CO2 gas level of patient's room by means of sensors and communicates the information through Wi-Fi that empowers the clinical staffs to get information from the worker. The created framework additionally gives an answer for the issue of keeping up a solitary information base of patients in clinics utilizing a web worker, aside from the personalization of basic health-related measures. In this framework, the gas sensor is utilized to recognize an unforeseen event that stands out the exhibition from the edge and creates a PPM signal if the yield esteem crosses the edge.

Induction to trustworthy and ground breaking sustenance statistics are vital towards an extent in an accomplices, comprising policymakers and regulators, medical care workers and also analysts. In this way it is essential that the standard arrangement of phenomenal sustenance information (data) transforms into a fundamental bit of, and finished, government wellbeing information systems. Wellbeing information structures fill various customers and needs and are planned to help orchestrating, the board and dynamic happening in this wellbeing system [72], together proceeding a standard reason and also throughout difficulties.

Respectable wellbeing evidence scheme guarantees variety, assessment, dissipating, usage of strong, ideal wellbeing evidence concluded 3 main restrictions: period of specific, office and people glassy statistics; limit, in sensible period, to perceive, examine, pass on and comprise actions that the speak to the peril into general wellbeing; and ability of assembling [73], scatter, advance the utilization of that understanding.

The mix of nourishment inside these capacities is fundamental for gathering and using top notch sustenance information to: survey individual and populace healthful status/needs; give sound individual sustenance care; and configuration, screen and assess focused on nourishment approaches and interventions [74]. Yet, there are a few holes and difficulties, yet additionally openings, in accomplishing this.

Wellbeing evidence structures use various types of data, or sources [75], each of which serves unmistakable purposes. These forms include: detailed data information on the profile, requirements, and care of a patient (i.e., well-being documents), filling in with the reason behind rational individualized thinking; wellbeing office level (public and private) data to report and moreover regulate regular assignments for example, HR, booking, hardware/supplies, charging/financing, and inclusion and execution of administrations and projects; populace level information for general health dynamic, for the most part through public health and segment studies; and nourishment reconnaissance office and network data, primarily to cover critical administrations, for example, for pandemic maladies or crisis help.

The underlying stage in passing on extraordinary support organizations, from screening, looking at, diagnosing intervening and tracking, to providing preparation, should be enhancing (electronic) well-being records [76] for food care. The two key segments to accomplish this consolidate using a conscious structure and language to energize food care transport documentation [78], such as the Nutritrit NCP has been applied logically across the globe over the previous decade. Clinical evaluations of diet consistency and food precariousness, similar to acceptable screening methods, however, are typically not completely structured or standardized in well-being documents [79]. Similarly, data from the well-being office is inconsistently enhanced to report the introduction and implementation of preventive or remedial food services and is not certainly illustrative of organizations open to the general public as a whole [80]. This limits the ability supply tailored equipped sustenance treatment, especially for the people who need it most [81], and makes the load the opportunity to provide tailored equipped sustenance treatment Fusing such evaluations into a traditional record of prosperity (in a perfect world electronic) and routine idea would smooth out the mix of food into clinical consideration, and could incite diminished prosperity Fusing such assessments into standard prosperity records (in a perfect world electronic) and routine idea would smooth out the mix of food into clinical consideration, and could incite diminished prosperity [83] and budgetary burdens.

Information on population level sustenance is important for the study, identification, organization, evaluation and verification of population level issues. Enormous scope broadly delegates reviews of health and nutrition, that the health and sustenance status of the population is a primary source of such knowledge in all surveys. Preferably, information ought to be gathered at the individual level, utilizing normalized evaluation apparatuses and strategies, and in a precise, predictable [84] and tantamount manner. Moreover, the information ought to permit disaggregation and investigation by key segment qualities, for example, sex, age, identity, riches, relocation status, inability, geographic area, and others as applicable to public settings. Granular information is basic to recognize imbalances in healthful status across various populace gatherings and advise the plan and execution regarding evenhanded nourishment intercessions.

Less-salary nations are either deficient with regards to sustenance information or depending on restricted information. In these settings, populace level nourishment information is essentially gotten from: public family unit utilization and [88] use reviews (HCESs), that don't gather singular level dietary admissions, consequently blocking evaluation of socio-demographic contrasts; Demographic [89] and Health Surveys or Multiple Predictor Cluster Surveys [90], which are moderately uncommon (usually for every 3 years) inconsistent narrow scope overviews on population subsamples with minimal generalizability; and information on network and office maintenance that addresses enormous general health issues (e.g. micronutrient deficiencies and supplementation, baby taking care of practices [91], and anthropometry/development status), or advise dynamic [92] during emergencies.

These sources inconsistently assemble data on other critical sustenance markers, for instance, solitary level dietary confirmations, biomarkers, distinctive other anthropometric pointers, related wellbeing results, supplement supplementation during pregnancy, clean water straightforwardness, sanitization and orderliness rehearses, or different markers to follow the consolidation and nature of preventive or medicinal food actions [93]. A ceaseless organizing of food parts inside prosperity data structures in 58 nations of the Scaling Up Nutrition (SUN) improvement demonstrated that frameworks most ordinarily track supplement. A supplementation [49], trailed by breastfeeding planning in antenatal idea [34] and the main gathering of genuine needing [33, 93]. Only 19 nations reliably amass information on iron and folic dangerous supplementation during pregnancy.

We need instruments to streamline and improve the typical grouping, use and blend of first class food data in lower-compensation settings. It is basic to utilize existing structures and resources for construction, restriction and overhaul food assessment framework and gadgets. At the same time, this is similarly an open entryway for progression, given the rapidly developing openness and utilization of convenient stages and various advances in more significant compensation countries [96]. The International Dietary Data Expansion (INDDEX) Project attempts to address phenomenal dietary data collection checks and broaden limit in low-pay countries, by making and endorsing standardized and streamlined developments for the variety and treatment of individual dietary data [96, 97]. The National Information Platforms for Nutrition (NIPN) action reinforces low-pay countries in strengthening their information structures for sustenance and improving data examination to even more viably hinder malnutrition [97, 98]. Data for Decisions to Expand Nutrition Transformation (DataDENT) expects to change the availability and use of food data by tending to gaps in food assessment and supporting for more grounded food data systems [97, 98].

A significant improvement and an important resource for general health would be to advance the variety, quality, accessibility and availability of population-level sustenance information around the world, and to incorporate this into health data frameworks. Peru and Guatemala are 2 examples of center-wage nations that have figured out how to create and update health data frameworks with coordinated nutrition information every year [99, 100]. Several low-pay nations are currently structuring their own data systems for sustenance [99, 100].

It is vital, presently like never before, to put resources into the exhaustive joining of nourishment into health data frameworks. This will guarantee the sound arrangement of focused sustenance care, opportune distinguishing proof of those at expanded wholesome danger, quickest conceivable reaction to crises, more prominent responsibility, educated strategy plan and anticipation activities, and proficient and compelling administration of monetary, human and different assets. Exhaustive data frameworks for health and sustenance are a complicated, yet achievable, undertaking. Whenever achieved, these frameworks will have multiple benefits for general health.

8.2   Background

8.2.1   Food Consumption

Food consumption and dietary habits directly impact one's health. In the energy balance referred to by calories [18], food admission is fundamental. Besides, the significance of nourishment admission on energy homeostasis was emphasized by Schwartz *et al.* [19]. Food intake regulating vitality homeostasis, the combination of energy intake and energy usage, seemed to have an effect on the heaviness of rodents, with its importance for human health [19]. Remember that energy consumption is also a critical variable in preserving optimum health. Energy consumption observation using detached sensors has been widely studied, such as action screen-based [20], accelerometer-based [21], and armband-based multi-sensor [22], for example. Because this paper focuses on observing food consumption, the verification of energy use will not be studied top to bottom. Food consumption has a corresponding relationship with levels of liver strength other than energy control, affecting liver disappointment and persistent liver sickness. In particular, liver solidity increases rapidly for up to 1 h after food consumption (p = 0.02). After 3 h, the liver firmness level got back to a consistent state. Food admission was also shown to improve the firmness of the liver in patients with Hepatitis C infection and with safe controls [23]. The action of rumination, including bolus size and biting rates, also has a major impact on food assimilation [24]. Poor execution of the masticatory framework causes ulcers and gastric carcinoma [25]. Otherwise, valid propensities for rumination promote the cycles associated with the stomach. Blisset [26] notes that characteristic chomp figures (the size of food that constitutes a typical piece) have been accounted for to weigh between 5.6 and 7.5 g for guys and somewhere in the range of 3.5 and 5.5 g for females when devouring peanuts and doughnuts, separately. Chomp sizes greater than these have an extraordinary effect on masticatory proficiency [27]. The biting rate affects both the stomach-related structure and the masticatory muscle. Karibe [28] demonstrated that patients with persistent masticatory muscle torment benefit from a moderate rate of biting. In addition, biting rate is a stress point with its effects on the levels of salivary cortisol [29]; subsequently, biting rates and bolus size/weight during food consumption are essentially critical to control.

8.2.2   Food Consumption Monitoring

The monitoring of food intake plays an important part in safeguarding natural, substantial development. This ordinary [30] production is dominated by AA (amino acids), which are used for the union of protein and various other low-sub-atomic weight mixes. In addition, trivial amino acids (NEAA), integration done with the human body, are in charge for a significant number of our physical capacities, as discussed in Figure 8.1. For ideal growth, progress, lactation, multiplication, and fitness, people must have NEAA in their eating regimen [1]. In any event, due to inappropriate

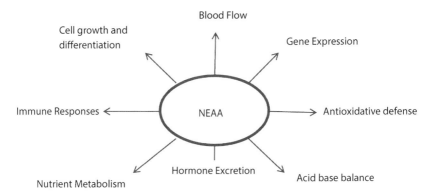

Figure 8.1 Important physiologic roles of non-essential amino acids (NEAA) in human cells.

eating routine and food admission [31], amino corrosive union is defenseless against restriction. Similarly, valid food admission observation guarantees the regulation of amino corrosive digestion to meet the needs of full human growth and ideal health. Monitoring of food consumption impacts the main physiological capacities referenced in Figure 8.1.

8.2.3   Health Monitoring Methods Using Physical Methodology

8.2.3.1   Traditional Form of Self-Report

The endorsement correlations with set up discoveries and closures as to self-announcing procedures were altogether analyzed by Square [34], for example, the assortment of involvement strategies, the 24-h dietary examination approach and the seven-day strategy. Bingham [35] discussed a superior examination of procedures composed by showing the paces of mistakes in every methodology among people who inevitably finished the investigation. As mentioned in the investigation, the pace of misclassification of results into quartiles of food affirmation transmission is around 10%, and just 15% of members have finished the method. Besides, self-revealing strategies keep individuals from participating in food affirmation tests attributable to the inaccessibility of accommodation [35].

8.2.3.2   Self-Reporting Methodology Through Smart Phones

With the reputation of PDAs, self-report draws close to enhancing accommodation and time to complete self-checking. The skill of the company on a PDA also makes this way to deal with more highlights, such as a rapid response from specialists and continuous self-observation. On the Motorola Q9h advanced cell, Wohler [36] set up a food intake overview structure. The structure allows members to record long dinner stretches and to send the details out of sight to a SQLite data set for investigation.

8.2.3.3   Food Frequency Questionnaire

The manual dietary assessment tactic includes utilizing food recurrence surveys (FFQ), utilizing poll frameworks (e.g., applications, sites, and so forth.) to gather food utilization recurrence of nourishments and drinks over some stretch of time, yet not for each and every dinner. Generally speaking, the manual methodologies depend on emotional instinct and review, as they rely on reports as opposed to obvious data on target food intake. It is agreed that self-revealing or manual technique is uncertain and very one-sided [40]. For example, the predisposition is too strong in heavy individuals to even care of receiving a valid evaluation of nutritional energy expenditure.

8.2.4   Methods for Health Tracking Using Automated Approach

8.2.4.1   Pressure Process

Pressure sensors mounted in a decorative liner or under a table exploit the weight strategy. In food admission control, this strategy isn't wearable, however is novel. Chang *et al.* [41] distributed the soonest research on the weight approach. A weight sensor encased under the table endeavors the examination. When there are changes in the plates' weight, this estimating surface will ascertain the measure of food moved between segments of the table and the measure of food devoured by every person at the table. Considering weight minor departure from various plates, a weight coordinating calculation is intended to identify and separate how people eat. This present technique's precision is around 80%, showing a promising beginning for a novel methodology. This gadget is basically a weight sensor with both security and an eating surface going about as the upper layer. At the point when somebody feasts on this decorative spread, specific eating acts (e.g., cutting, scooping and shipping food) are watched. There is less strain on the sensor than the one in Chang *et al.* [41]. Notwithstanding, without either weight estimation or food characterization, it is fit for recognizing just taking care of developments.

8.2.4.2   Surveillance-Video Method

The surveillance-video approach uses an external camera for automatic food intake detection in comparison to wearable camera approaches. A functioning appearance model framework for biting recognition dependent on caught pictures of the human face from an outer camera during the eating cycle was made by Cadavid *et al.* [43]. The detection of chewing is defined by the quasi periodic existence of chewing found in the accurate parameters of the model.

8.2.4.3   Method of Doppler Sensing

Utilizing microwave Doppler movement sensors is another current robotized way to deal with food admission following. Tanigawa *et al.* [45] investigated the utilization in their technique for the Doppler impact to detect the

Doppler biting sign made by vertical jaw developments. From the condition of the connection between Doppler recurrence and moving pace, the particular moving pace of the jaw during biting is resolved. In identifying dietary patterns by estimating and recognizing strong nourishments that require jaw development, strain, observation video and Doppler detecting approaches are restricted. Current accomplishments using these three methods have not made it possible for them to detect particular food or food structure types. In addition, the non-wearable limitation of these methods limits the versatility of the food intake monitoring sensor system, thus reducing their effectiveness in detecting the activities in living communities.

8.3   Necessity of Wearable Approach?

As long as physical methodologies have shown to be unreliable and one-sided [46], we need a more targeted, more effective dietary evaluation framework. Wearable sensors are likely arrangements because they do not rely on the abstract choices of individuals; moreover, wearable sensors provide ongoing food admission screening. For helpful feedback, information collected can be easily synchronized with a data entryway, such as a PDA program. Another fundamental piece of leeway for wearable sensors is knowing free-living people's behavior. It provides customers with accommodation, eliminating weight of own-explosion, which can be useful in clinical uses particularly when patients are customers. There are broad applications for wearable food consumption control frameworks, which will be surveyed in a subsequent section of this paper. The accuracy of the computerized wearable sensor approach can also be enhanced by minimizing the undesirable effects of outside variables, such as climate commotions, for example. The sensor-based approach, for instance, involves denoising the symbol, which can also fully destroy the commotions inserted in the information gathered. Scientists had the choice to build satisfying denoising signal handling techniques with the propulsion of creativity. In terms of designing a technique to denoise double hub gulping accelerometry signals with crucial improvements to past methodologies, Ervin *et al.* [47] prevailed.

8.4   Different Approaches for Wearable Sensing

In this section, with their associated food admission applications and huge exams, we include a nitty gritty survey of various sensors. Applications for food admission include food type arrangement, eating behavior and measurement of volume/weight. Various types of sensors will concentrate on applications that understand explicit food consumption.

8.4.1   Approach of Acoustics

8.4.1.1   Detection of Chewing

Determination and measurement of chewing sound by acoustic means would become one of the important enticing topics in tracking food intake. It attracts more and more day-by-day research in this area. Overall, current methods rely on the use of wearable devices to accumulate sound waves, such as microphones, using a certain technique to identify and interpret chewing events. For food classification, Amft [49] defined its vibration-based detection method using a condenser microphone embedded in an ear pad, further expanding the food classification to chewing and bite weight recognition. Chewing sequences, waveforms of sounds suggesting chewing recorded by ear pad sensors, are used in the chewing recognition technique. The chewing sequences are defined by the recognition algorithm of the feature similarity search case. Later on, this chewing identification contributes to the recognition of bite weight from micro-structure variables. Their sound-based bite weight recognition system shows high precision results with just 19% error on one food type: apple. However, only three food types (apple, potato chips and lettuce) are included in the report, which is inadequate to draw comprehensive conclusions as to the efficacy of this strategy. Another research by Amft *et al.* [78] explores in-depth chewing sound analysis and determines the technique protocol and the most suitable location of the microphone (inner ear, directed towards the eardrum). There are a variety of other scientific articles on the automatic detection of chewing. One of them is from Yatani and Truong [79], who are proficient in separating chewing events from the softness of the food from the sounds obtained. Furthermore, using a template-matching system, Olubanjo *et al.* [80] focused on differentiating chewing acoustic events from noisy conditions. In order to confirm the validity of the outcome, the analysis shows a positive result of up to 83.3% on reasonably large data samples (13 separate tasks, including five solid, four liquid foods and four tracheal and non-tracheal events). Also capable of detecting chewing sounds is a related method developed by Pabler and Fischer [81]. This approach was further used by Pabler and Fischer [82] through the development of a low computational cost algorithm for food intake sound detection. Similarly, in the breakdown phase observed in the outer ear canal by the sensor system, Pabler *et al.* [83] took advantage of chewing sound. Other experiments are suggested in Refs. [84, 85] that are also capable of detecting chewing events with chewing count numbers and food texture classification. The microphone for this approach is not a singular sensor. For the detection of vibration in chewing events, a strain sensor is also possible.

8.4.1.2 Detection of Swallowing

Detection of swallowing is essentially equal to the discovery of chewing since swallowing is the following mechanical absorption chewing phase. In addition, the acoustic technique for this discovery is feasible. Swallowing consists of opening/closing the upper esophageal sphincter and moving the bolus through peristaltic waves, which are immense vibration wellsprings, as alluded to in Section 8.4. On this form of food consumption location, a few important reviews on wearable sensors have been proposed. A device containing a throat mouthpiece set over the laryngopharynx in the throat was designed by Sazonov *et al.* [87]. In this position, the sign is solid, as it is near the birthplace of the swallowing sound. In addition, the system also contains the equipment/programming sections for catching, scoring information for sounds. Sazonov *et al.* [64] studied the approaches to acoustic identification of swallowing occasions in more prominent detail. The proposed position strategies depend on the following time-recurrence deteriorations: msFS (Fourier range of mel-scale) and WPD (decay of wavelet bundle) with aid vector machine (SVM) characterization. Generally speaking, with a test size of 81 participants, the procedure demonstrates satisfactory after-effects of about 87%.

8.4.1.3 Shared Chewing/Swallowing Discovery

Here chewing, swallowing steps are matching with one another, it is possible to use combination methods to continuously distinguish their occasions. Lopez-Meyer *et al.* [88] suggested a model-based SVM way of distinguishing the time of food intake from data derived from the momentary [89] swallowing recurrence (ISF) signal and the double chewing markers. In another study, Kalantarian *et al.* developed sound cutting spectrograms for four forms of swallowing and chewing occasions (sandwich bites/swallows, water swallows and no activity) and subsequently applied highlight pulling out to distinguish with that occasions. On chewing and swallowing occasions, distinct techniques do not zero in, but on food order. A vital model is AutoDietary from Bi *et al.* [90]. In identifying strong food and fluid food with the consequences of 99.7 and 97.8% precision, individually, it appears to have positive execution.

8.5   Description of the Methodology

For all people, proper nutrition is an essential part of a balanced lifestyle. For nutritional counseling practitioners all over the world, eating habits and the nutritional value of consumed foods are becoming highly important fields of study. Knowledge of the nutrients found in foods in relation to their roles in human body maintenance, development, reproduction, health and disease prevention must therefore be promoted. The goal of this research was to investigate the knowledge among women in different age categories of food nutritional value and eating practices. This can be done by monitoring the daily food intake among women by using automated monitoring system. To address this challenge we have proposed an IoT-based system which monitors the nutrients value intake, BMI and the amount of calories burnt of the user and also suggests the future meals to be consumed by the user to fulfill their target nutritional value to lead a healthy life.

The proposed system is a fully automated diet monitoring solution which consists of Wi-Fi enabled sensors in order to evaluate the nutrition of food, and also a smart phone application that helps in collecting nutritional facts of all the ingredients in the foodstuff. The overall block diagram of IoT-based health monitoring system is described in following Figure 8.2. The system for monitoring includes a food weighing sensor which estimates the

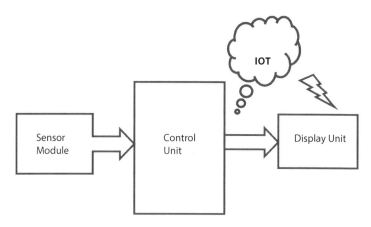

Figure 8.2 Overall block diagram of IOT-based health monitoring system.

weight of the foodstuff and sends it through a wireless network that uses internet to the cloud by synchronizing a microcontroller that is integrated with again a wireless module. In order to acquire the appropriate values of nutrient, two different methods are being used. The first method deals with Optical Character Recognition, where nutrient value is calculated through FDA-mandated Nutritional Facts Label. The second method uses the barcode of the foodstuff which is scanned, and using the APIs from the Internet, the nutritional information is retrieved. As a result, the food is categorized on the basis of the highest nutrient value along with the relationship between the food consumed and the deficient nutrition. Also, deficient nutrient and obesity are identified by the system and it gives suggestion for the user about the food that delivers the highest nutrient value as well as low calories. If deficiency is encountered, the system will suggest the meal for healthy life style. As a result, there will be low obesity and high nutritious life. Future Meal Predictions is done by classification algorithms. The results can be viewed by the user in their smart phone application.

8.6   Description of Various Components Used

8.6.1   Sensors

8.6.1.1   Sensors for Cardio-Vascular Monitoring

The Electrocardiograms (ECG) is a non-obtrusive methodology used for computing and for storing the variances of the potential of heart. It can be noticed that this is the most broadly utilized and successful symptomatic apparatus that doctors have been utilized for quite a long time to distinguish issues related to heart, say for example, the various types of arrhythmias.

It is well known that albeit numerous arrhythmias are not dangerous, a few upshots from frail or harmed heart, say, myocardial localized necrosis (MI) that indicates a heart failure, which if not taken care immediately [24–26]. After a cardiovascular failure, patients are needed to get quick clinical consideration, which, in any case, may turn lethal. These inconveniences can be maintained a strategic distance if any irregularities in the cardiovascular movement is being identified and is treated in the initial phase which calls for the outpatient drift monitoring of the ECG. Certain uncommon, genuine arrhythmias (say for example, the Brugada Syndrome, the Arrhythmogenic Right Ventricular Cardiomyopathy, Long QT condition and the hypertrophic Cardiomyopathy) are considered to be inconsistent while it is identified on delayed monitoring. Using an ECG system with 12 leads, the heart's electrical activities along 12 explicit spatial bearings are assessed using around 10 Ag–AgCl terminals (the hydrogel method or the wet ECG), that are added to some specific bits of the body. Anodes that contain a leading gel in the cushion act as a medium of conduction between the cathode and the skin. The gel is considered to have poisonous and aggravating impacts over the skin, so these lines are not best reasonable to use for long haul framework using mobile monitoring however as of now, it is the main framework accessible [10, 27]. Be that as it may, just a couple of quantities of terminals are utilized in walking, monitoring of ECG framework by the expense of the restricted data. A persistent gadget for monitoring the walking pattern requires the use of wearable and versatile framework that can be utilized easily by not influencing a person's every day exercises.

Numerous scientists have created and utilized piezoelectric sensors for weight measurement that estimates the HR by detecting the blood vessel beat waves produced due to the occasional withdrawal and also the heart's relaxation. Remote gadget for HR monitoring was introduced in [32] which can appraise HR that can be obtained from the variations in the surface of the ear's trench. A Piezoelectric pressure film is utilized to detect the in-ear beat waves (EPW) and also to convert them to electric flow. Information centered calculation has been executed in a microcontroller which can distinguish the beat top continuously from the sign in the wake of playing out a morphological transformation. Notwithstanding, the weight fluctuation, and consequently the highest weight waves are influenced by the developments that in the body that presents blunder in HR assessment. Also an ear-mounted gadget is considered to be badly arranged for long haul use. A comparative framework is mentioned in Ref. [33] which mentions about the authors who built up a polymer-based adaptable piezoresistive weight sensor which could detect pressure from the skin brought about by the blood vessels. It can also be read about the utilization of carbon dark or silicon elastic nanocomposite that is used as an adaptable piezoresistive stuff. Increase in affectability and the linearity shown in the weight sensor was attained by shaping the microstructures along the contact surfaces of the two layers of the piezoresistive stuff [34–36]. Also a minimal effort simple sign handling (ASP) framework that could perform denoising, information preparing, and HR estimation was proposed.

8.6.1.2   Sensors for Activity Monitoring

Monitoring a person's physical exercises and movement can be considered worthy in the field of sports and identify location of musculoskeletal or may be intellectual illnesses [37, 38]. Compensating a person's strolling designs are emphatically connected with their health condition [39]. It is to be noted that Strolling may include a few joints like the spine, the hip, the knee, the lower leg, the tarsal and the metatarsal joints. It also includes some muscles, like the muscles of the back and around the hip joints, the thigh, the lower leg muscles and a few tiny muscles of the foot. walking, particularly turning occasion requires great parity and also the coordination among various parts of the body.

Examples of strolling of feeble individuals will in general vary from that of ordinary healthy individuals. For instance, individuals at the beginning stage of neurodegenerative problems, for example, Alzheimer's or Parkinson's will in general show distinctive strolling designs [40, 41]. Possibility of conceivable prior detections of Parkinson's ailment is little and rearranged strolling steps. An individual at the beginning phase of the Parkinson's might encounter troubles at the beginning, halting and turning occasions during strolling. A loss of related developments may be identified. Old individuals, inferable from their declining engine control and also the muscle quality are generally comparatively more helpless against fall, and if it happens, may cause joint wounds, breaking of hip and bone and awful cerebrum damage. They may require a long recuperation period, confine development and influence the day to day exercises of the person. There is also a solid connection with the transience and the related cracks [41]. The examination of walk can be quantitatively considered worthy for early recognition of a few illnesses, expectation of fall just as the restoration time frame.

Another method called as the fixed position monitoring, which uses camera-based frameworks for action monitoring [42, 43] is being used. The strategies are equipped for perceiving complicated walk exercises. In any case, such frameworks confine the development of the client inside a certain range. Also, these frameworks are mind boggling and costly [44]. Utilization of wearable movement sensors, like the accelerometers, the whirligigs, and the magnetometers are picking up in prevalence for computing human stride exercises [6, 11] progressively. The sensors are used to measure straight and rakish movement of the body where various key highlights are separated.

8.6.1.3   Sensors for Body Temperature Monitoring

It is a well-known fact that body temperature is the important sign that can reflect health conditions. The temperature of body can increase variably in contaminations, and other numerous incendiary conditions [48]. Temperature estimations over an extensive stretch of time may incite the conclusion as opposed to spot checks. Center internal heat level (CBT) has solid impact on different physiologic conditions too [50–59]. Interruptions in the internal heat level cadence are e related to various sorts of sleep deprivation [60]. Say for example, patients experiencing rest stage during a sleeping disorder may have a ~2 h of postponement in the arrival at their base CBT against the gathering of good sleep samples [60]. A variety of internal heat level cadence with period cycle was additionally seen in certain examinations [61, 62].

8.6.1.4 Sensor for Galvanic Skin Response (GSR) Monitoring

Autonomic Sensory System (ANS) is used to control and direct body's reaction to the inner or the outer improvements just by considering the exercises into two categories: (i) thoughtful and (ii) parasympathetic sensory systems [80]. The latter, named as "the rest and overview" framework monitors and reestablishes energy of the body [63]. This thoughtful framework triggers all that is frequently alluded to as a battle or a flight reaction by just expanding metabolic yield to bring about all the outer boosts. Extending the action of the thoughtful framework quickens pulse, builds circulatory strain, and sweat emission, just as readies the body for engine activity by siphoning more blood to muscles, lungs, and mind.

Albeit right now, this data is of no noteworthy clinical use, there is developing enthusiasm for certain conditions that include dysautonomia, the postural orthostatic tachycardia disorder (POTS), as well as the inappropriate tachycardia disorder. Expanded perspiration discharge from eccrine organs fills the perspiration pipes. Being a feeble electrolyte, sweat, expands the skin's conductance with expanded emission. Thusly, all varieties skin conductance, which is moreover referred to as the Electro-Dermal Movement (EDA) or the Galvanic Skin Reaction (GSR), that reflects the activity of tactile framework and gives a direct, delicate and strong limit for assessing the anxious activities that are related with weight and feeling [81, 82].

GSR mandatorily estimates the aspect of skin having sweat organs in an enormous count, for example, the palm, the fingers, or the bottoms of the feet. Talking about dynamic estimation, a constant DC voltage is considered to be applied across the two significant on-body cathodes and also is used to acquire the skin conductance from the Ohm's law simply by calculating the current passed through it. Researchers generally centered across the time-restricted GSR estimation frameworks that are being used in labs and healthcare centers [65, 66]. Developments in low-force and wearables open up another window that is subtle GSR precise monitoring that allows to be worn for a more drawn out timeframe [83]. Haul monitoring of GSR allows evaluating the reaction of the thoughtful sensory system that is allocated for a more drawn out timeframe and can possibly unfurl significant physiological data that can't be acquired by restricted time monitoring. The wearable GSR monitoring framework also permits patients to screen GSR to give a superior appraisal of their psycho-physiological nature more than the assessment that is made at research facilities or may be medical clinics from momentary estimation [83, 84].

8.6.1.5 *Sensor for Monitoring the Blood Oxygen Saturation (SpO_2)*

The Peripheral Capillary Oxygen Immersion (SpO_2) is the measure of oxygenated hemoglobin in the blood. This level can be diminished because of various health conditions like the cardiovascular maladies, the pneumonic illnesses, frailty and rest apnea. It can likewise be decreased after exorbitant physical exercises. Moreover, it is important to have a record of satisfactory oxygen measure (i.e., >94%) content in the blood to guarantee legitimate working of cells and the tissues [95, 96]. It is also essential to look into screening SpO_2 ceaselessly, particularly in people who have issues in their respiratory organs and heart.

The broad utilization of Heartbeat Oximeters as a quick, non-obtrusive agent intends in quantifying the level of oxygen in blood. The ingestion qualities of blood because of the red (660 nm) and the infrared (940 nm) light represent the scale of SpO_2. When hemoglobin is said to be oxygenated, it changes shades from dim red to brilliant red that represents decrease of the ingestion of red light [67–70]. Light assimilation in blood also shifts showing differences in blood vessel and the volume of blood during the systolic and the diastolic period of the heart, thus by bringing about a cyclic change sign called as the photograph plethysmograph (PPG).

8.7   Strategy of Communication for Wearable Systems

A short-extend communications convention is used in the main stage to transmit the intentional information to a nearest door hub, such as a PDA, mobile phone, PC, specially designed FPGA, or a handling board based on a microcontroller [71]. The passage is responsible for the handling, display, and the following long-range communication stage of cutting-edge information, where the prepared sign is sent to a far-off worker in a healthcare office.

It is possible to submit the data through the web or cell correspondence organization. As of now, by General Packet Radio Service (GPRS),

Enhanced Data GSM Environment (EDGE), 3 G, High Speed Packet Access (HSPA), Long-Term Evolution (LTE) administrations, most cell networks give clear admission to the web [77–79]. For ensuring a secure transmission channel over the long-range correspondence vehicle for the shielding of individual clinical data [80–82], it is necessary to conduct solid encryption and validation innovations.

On account of short-extend correspondence, the respective sensors shall convey up to the door legitimately over a remote middle. The sensors, on the other hand, will frame the geography of a body sensor organization (BSN), star network and submit information to the focal BSN center. In the aftermath of some planning, the BSN hub can send data to the entry-way. By using wired or remote media, the on-body sensors and the BSN hub might transmit. Wired associations can frustrate the versatility of the customers as it can, and can trigger continuous bombed associations. It is also found that they are also not capable for frameworks of wearable as well as long haul tracking. The use of conductive texture yarns as the optional conductive medium is a decent alternative. In order to speak with material-inserted sensors [83–85], these textures can be easily coordinated into dress. The conductive texture can be produced using customary material developments, such as spinning, sewing, spinning, and printing, as described before. In any event, due to their low solidity and launderability, conductive filaments have a problem that may prompt bad or bombed accessibility after a significant amount of usage. Remote innovation can hence be adopted as one of the most appropriate as well as solid alternative for a short-run correspondence.

Bluetooth is considered as a prominent advancement in low-force RF correspondence are widely used in gadgets, like workstations, mobile phones, as well as short-range information correspondence wellness trackers [86, 87]. In the mechanical, logical and clinical (ISM) radio range, it utilizes the 2.4 GHz recurrence band and transmits signal using the Frequency Hopping Spread Spectrum (FHSS) technique to more than 79 allocated channels. The FHSS system is less prone to commotion and obstruction and also provides deeply insured information transmission. Along these lines, one ace gadget can speak with seven slave gadgets, framing a network structure of the star type depending on Bluetooth availability (Piconet). The clock and bouncing group for the entire Piconet are defined by the ace. In spite of the fact that the greatest throughput can only achieve ~2.1 Mbps, the Bluetooth breakthrough can sustain an information rate of about ~3 Mbps liable on the balance plans. Transmission isolation usually has a range from about 1 to 10 m for general applications. For convenient and wearable gadgets with minimal battery limit [15, 87], an ultra-low-power rendition of Bluetooth technology, the Bluetooth low energy (BLE) or the Bluetooth V4, was also later introduced. BLE utilizes a similar recurrence band to the old Bluetooth invention style, it hops over 40 channels. As the name suggests, BLE provides remote availability of low force (~10 mW) and is therefore a strong possibility for a short-range correspondence in the prominent long-term monitoring frameworks.

ZigBee [18, 21] is another famous and open distant norm for low power and insignificant exertion correspondence inside a short reach. It works in the unlicensed ISM scope of 2.4 GHz (around the globe), 915 MHz (Americas and Australia) and 868 MHz (Europe) repeat gatherings and communicates data independently to more than sixteen, ten and one organizations. The double stage move keying (BPSK) balance is used by the 868 and 915 MHz classes, while the 2.4 GHz band uses equilibrium quadrature stage move keying (OQPSK). Unlike Bluetooth and BLE spread by lone backups (P2P) and star geographies, P2P, star, tree and work network geographies can be correlated with ZigBee devices. The ZigBee show at first tests the correspondence connection before sending a group by utilizing the CSMA/CA (carrier sense numerous passage with impact avoidance) show or by sending advisers for the association's different center points. Because of its low yield power and furthermore the presence of high dielectric materials, the transmission extent of the ZigBee standard is restricted to inside 10–20 m for indoor applications by and large. Regardless, with no obstacle of view, the reach will increment up to 1,500 m. In contrast with the Bluetooth advancement, the data rate is a lot of lower and can accomplish a constraint of 250 kbps for the 2.4 GHz band. Regardless, the low power prerequisite of the ZigBee standard causes an improved battery life that is significant for long stretch wellbeing observing applications, notwithstanding the way that the lower data rate can put limitations on the measure of sensors, the quantity of synchronous assessments and the buffering of data is different.

Subterranean insect is very much a convention stack in sensor organizations designed for super low-power, short-go remote correspondences, particularly for health and wellness monitoring frameworks [19, 88]. To connect with various hubs over a solitary 1 MHz channel, it uses TDMA (time division separate admittance). When any impedance occurs, it can switch channels. By its remarkable aspect in which it goes around as an ace for one channel while at the same time filling in as a slave for another channel, subterranean insect can be identified from various remote conventions. Like ZigBee, ANT bolsters different organization geographies and furthermore guarantees conjunction with neighboring ANT hubs utilizing versatile isochronous organization innovation. The best information rate accomplished by ANT structures differs from 20–60 kbps and there is a harmony between the pace of data and the utilization of low power. A constant movement in the ANT show, ANT+, utilizes express application 'device profiles' to cooperate between two contraptions.

Implementation of clinical embed correspondence (MICS), is a short-run, super-low-force remote invention created to interact with embedded clinical devices, like the cardiovascular pacemakers, defibrillators, and neuro-triggers [89, 90]. This works with 300 kHz channels within the 402–405 MHz recurrence band. This recurrence band provides the human body with great sign distribution characteristics that make it appropriate for implantable gadgets. Before starting transmission, the MICS makes use of the tune in before-talk (LBT) convention to survey the link [94]. MICS turns to an alternative radio channel on account of some impedance and listens once more. The MICS structure has a ~2 m run of the mill transmission range and devours as little as 25 µW of intensity. Be that as it may, because of restricted accessibility of business MICS gadgets alongside some systems administration requirements [191], this innovation has not been utilized much in wearable frameworks.

8.8   Conclusion

This chapter gives a best in class study on physiological boundaries and movement observing frameworks created in a wearable device that is used to monitor the health condition of a woman. Highlights of the basic role of a wearable wellbeing observing framework is noted to permit individuals in leading autonomous as well as dynamic lives as in their recognizable home-based climate while guaranteeing constant, consistent observation of their wellbeing and physical prosperity. The colossal improvement of innovation in the previous scarcely any many year's prompts assembling and the utilization of usually smaller, low-power, ease sensors, actuators, electronic segments, and amazing PCs that makes ready to non-obtrusive, non-meddling, and persistent checking of a person's ailment easily.

Consistent checking of wellbeing status can give extensive data about people's wellbeing status over some stretch of spell. The described wearable sensors as well as actuators, combined with a serious data and corresponding advancements that have opened the concerned window to also another period of medical care administrations. All the frameworks can incorporate information investigation just as revelatory calculations, which can possibly make the forecast of specific ailments with a further extent of certainty, thus prompting early determination and treatment. Consolidation of shrewd material advances, say for example, interconnections for sensors in especially wearable medical services frameworks could prompt further stages for monitoring one's health.

The bio-potential (ECG, EDA) estimation frameworks regularly experiences the ill effects of low sign to-commotion proportion (SNR) that fundamentally develops from the clamor incited by the development of the client. Movement antique (MA) can be restricted by using versatile terminals. It is moreover possible to improve the SNR by abusing signal dealing with techniques, for instance, flexible filtering, observational mode breaking down (EMD), free portion examination (ICA) or time-repeat assessment. Next, the hardware and figuring resource for the on-body central center point of a multi-sensor BSN system can be a confining component for reliable accessibility and data dealing with. The central taking care of center point of the BSN network exchanges data with the on-body sensors similarly as the home entryway, and to a great extent performs limited planning. In this way, a powerful and proficient calculation is required for the focal BSN hub to advance its exhibition. Notwithstanding that, a proficient information pressure calculation should be executed in the focal hub so as to manage a huge volume of information and send them to the closest passage. To follow next, a key worry for the wearable medical services framework is related with the protection and security of the delicate clinical data of the client. More accomplishments are required so as to create calculations to guarantee profoundly made sure about correspondence directs in existing low force, short reach remote stages. Low force utilization and high energy effectiveness are basic for long haul checking frameworks. Power need of the structure can be satisfied by using low power fragments, more capable batteries or by using energy gathering strategies. Battery lifetime can moreover be improved by ensuring 'rest and wake up' of the sensors in a fortunate way without upsetting the ideal assessment repeat.

Examinations at different remote advances and evaluations of their possibility in wearable wellbeing checking frameworks have been effectively carried out. Most importantly, the frameworks measure a few physiological boundaries from the human body and send them to a focal hub or primary passage. The passage hub measures and sends the information to medical care work force at a distant office. More examinations and innovation advancements are expected to guarantee data protection and information security, along with strong information pressure calculations, dependable correspondence connections, and energy productivities.

References

1. Centers for Disease Control and Prevention, *The State of Aging and Health in America 2013*, Centers for Disease Control and Prevention, US Department of Health and Human Services, Atlanta, GA, USA, 2013.
2. Global Age Watch Index, 2015. Available online: http://www.helpage.org/global-agewatch/.
3. World Health Organization Family Planning/Contraception, 2015. [(accessed on 20 June 2016)]. Available online: http://www.who.int/mediacentre/factsheets/fs351/en/.
4. World Health Organization Are You Ready? What You Need to Know about Ageing, in: *World Health Day*, 2012, [(accessed on 20 June 2016)]. Available online: http://www.who.int/world-health-day/2012/toolkit/background/en/.
5. U.S. Healthcare Costs Rise Faster Than Inflation, [(accessed on 20 June 2016)]. Available online: http://www.forbes.com/sites/mikepatton/2015/06/29/u-s-health-care-costs-rise-faster-than-inflation/#1384765c6ad2, 2017(1), 130.
6. Deen, M.J., Information and communications technologies for elderly ubiquitous healthcare in a smart home. *Pers. Ubiquitous Comput.*, 19, 573–599, 2015.
7. Agoulmine, N., Deen, M., Lee, J.-S., Meyyappan, M., U-Health Smart Home. *IEEE Nanotechnol. Mag.*, 5, 6–11, 2011.
8. Wang, H., Choi, H.-S., Agoulmine, N., Deen, M.J., Hong, J.W.-K., Information-based sensor tasking wireless body area networks in U-health systems. *Proceedings of the 2010 International Conference on Network and Service Management*, Niagara Falls, ON, Canada, pp. 517–522, 25–29 October 2010.
9. Pantelopoulos, A. and Bourbakis, N., A Survey on Wearable Sensor-Based Systems for Health Monitoring and Prognosis. *IEEE Trans. Syst. Man Cybern. C*, 40, 1–12, 2010.
10. Nemati, E., Deen, M., Mondal, T., A wireless wearable ECG sensor for long-term applications. *IEEE Commun. Mag.*, 50, 36–43, 2012.
11. Hong, Y., Kim, I., Ahn, S., Kim, H., Mobile health monitoring system based on activity recognition using accelerometer. *Simul. Model. Pract. Theory*, 18, 446–455, 2010.
12. Ullah, S., Higgins, H., Braem, B., Latre, B., Blondia, C., Moerman, I., Saleem, S., Rahman, Z., Kwak, K., A Comprehensive Survey of Wireless Body Area Networks. *J. Med. Syst.*, 36, 1065–1094, 2012.
13. Al Ameen, M., Liu, J., Kwak, K., Security and Privacy Issues in Wireless Sensor Networks for Healthcare Applications. *J. Med. Syst.*, 36, 93–101, 2012.
14. Castillejo, P., Martinez, J., Rodriguez-Molina, J., Cuerva, A., Integration of wearable devices in a wireless sensor network for an E-health application. *IEEE Wirel. Commun.*, 20, 38–49, 2013.

15. Dementyev, A., Hodges, S., Taylor, S., Smith, J., Power consumption analysis of Bluetooth Low Energy, ZigBee and ANT sensor nodes in a cyclic sleep scenario. *Proceedings of the 2013 IEEE International Wireless Symposium (IWS)*, Beijing, China, pp. 1–4, 14–18 April 2013.

16. Suzuki, T., Tanaka, H., Minami, S., Yamada, H., Miyata, T., Wearable wireless vital monitoring technology for smart healthcare. *Proceedings of the 2013 7th International Symposium on Medical Information and Communication Technology (ISMICT)*, Tokyo, Japan, pp. 1–4, 6–8 March 2013.

17. Malhi, K., Mukhopadhyay, S., Schnepper, J., Haefke, M., Ewald, H., A Zigbee-Based Wearable Physiological Parameters Monitoring System. *IEEE Sens. J.*, 12, 423–430, 2012.

18. Valchinov, E., Antoniou, A., Rotas, K., Pallikarakis, N., Wearable ECG System for Health and Sports Monitoring. *Proceedings of the 4th International Conference on Wireless Mobile Communication and Healthcare— "Transforming Healthcare through Innovations in Mobile and Wireless Technologies"*, Athens, Greece, pp. 63–66, 3–5 November 2014.

19. Mehmood, N.Q. and Culmone, R., An ANT Protocol Based Healthcare System. *Proceedings of the 2015 IEEE 29th International Conference on Advanced Information Networking and Applications Workshops*, Guwangiu, Korea, pp. 193–198, 24–27 March 2015.

20. Coskun, V., Ozdenizci, B., Ok, K., A Survey on Near Field Communication (NFC) Technology. *Wirel. Pers. Commun.*, 71, 2259–2294, 2013.

21. Pang, Z., Zheng, L., Tian, J., Kao-Walter, S., Dubrova, E., Chen, Q., Design of a terminal solution for integration of in-home healthcare devices and services towards the Internet-of-Things. *Enterp. Inf. Syst.*, 9, 86–116, 2013.

22. Corchado, J., Bajo, J., Abraham, A., GerAmi: Improving Healthcare Delivery in Geriatric Residences. *IEEE Intell. Syst.*, 23, 19–25, 2008.

23. Stav, E., Walderhaug, S., Mikalsen, M., Hanke, S., Benc, I., Development and evaluation of SOA-based AAL services in real-life environments: A case study and lessons learned. *Int. J. Med. Inform.*, 82, e269–e293, 2013.

24. Vaishnav, S., Stevenson, R., Marchant, B., Lagi, K., Ranjadayalan, K., Timmis, A.D., Relation between heart rate variability early after acute myocardial infarction and long-term mortality. *Am. J. Cardiol.*, 73, 653–657, 1994.

25. Bigger, J.T., Fleiss, J.L., Kleiger, R., Miller, J.P., Rolnitzky, L.M., The relationships among ventricular arrhythmias, left ventricular dysfunction, and mortality in the 2 years after myocardial infarction. *Circulation*, 69, 250–258, 1984.

26. Kleiger, R.E., Miller, J., Bigger, J., Moss, A.J., Decreased heart rate variability and its association with increased mortality after acute myocardial infarction. *Am. J. Cardiol.*, 59, 256–262, 1987.

27. Hadjem, M., Salem, O., Nait-Abdesselam, F., An ECG monitoring system for prediction of cardiac anomalies using WBAN. *Proceedings of the 2014 IEEE 16th International Conference on e-Health Networking, Applications and Services (Healthcom)*, Natal, Brazil, 15–18 October 2014.

28. Andreoni, G., Perego, P., Standoli, C., Wearable monitoring of elderly in an ecologic setting: The SMARTA project. [(accessed on 5 January 2017)]. Available online: https://sciforum.net/conference/ecsa-2/paper/3192/download/pdf, pp. 15-30, 2015.

29. Tseng, K.C., Lin, B.-S., Liao, L.-D., Wang, Y.-T., Wang, Y.-L., Development of a Wearable Mobile Electrocardiogram Monitoring System by Using Novel Dry Foam Electrodes. *IEEE Syst. J.*, 8, 900–906, 2014.

30. Lee, J., Heo, J., Lee, W., Lim, Y., Kim, Y., Park, K., Flexible Capacitive Electrodes for Minimizing Motion Artifacts in Ambulatory Electrocardiograms. *Sensors*, 14, 14732–14743, 2014.

31. Komensky, T., Jurcisin, M., Ruman, K., Kovac, O., Laqua, D., Husar, P., Ultra-wearable capacitive coupled and common electrode-free ECG monitoring system. *Proceedings of the 2012 Annual International Conference of the IEEE Engineering in Medicine and Biology Society*, San Diego, CA, USA, pp. 1594–1597, 28 August–1 September 2012.

32. Park, J.-H., Jang, D.-G., Park, J., Youm, S.-K., Wearable Sensing of In-Ear Pressure for Heart Rate Monitoring with a Piezoelectric Sensor. *Sensors*, 15, 23402–23417, 2015.

33. Shu, Y., Li, C., Wang, Z., Mi, W., Li, Y., Ren, T.-L., A Pressure sensing system for heart rate monitoring with polymer-based pressure sensors and an anti-interference post processing circuit. *Sensors*, 15, 3224–3235, 2015.

34. Yoon, S. and Cho, Y.-H., A Skin-attachable Flexible Piezoelectric Pulse Wave Energy Harvester. *J. Phys. Conf. Ser.*, 557, 012026, 2014.

35. Tajitsu, Y., Piezoelectret sensor made from an electro-spun fluoropolymer and its use in a wristband for detecting heart-beat signals. *IEEE Trans. Dielect. Electr. Insul.*, 22, 1355–1359, 2015.

36. Izumi, S., Yamashita, K., Nakano, M., Kawaguchi, H., Kimura, H., Marumoto, K., Fuchikami, T., Fujimori, Y., Nakajima, H., Shiga, T. *et al.*, A Wearable Healthcare System With a 13.7 µA Noise Tolerant ECG Processor. *IEEE Trans. Biomed. Circuits Syst.*, 9, 733–742, 2015.

37. He, D.D. and Sodini, C.G., A 58 nW ECG ASIC With Motion-Tolerant Heartbeat Timing Extraction for Wearable Cardiovascular Monitoring. *IEEE Trans. Biomed. Circuits Syst.*, 9, 370–376, 2015.

38. Helleputte, N.V., Kim, S., Kim, H., Kim, J.P., Hoof, C.V., Yazicioglu, R.F., A 160 µA biopotential acquisition ASIC with fully integrated IA and motion-artifact suppression. *Proceedings of the 2012 IEEE International Solid-State Circuits Conference*, San Francisco, CA, USA, pp. 552–561, 19–23 February 2012.

39. Mulroy, S., Gronley, J., Weiss, W., Newsam, C., Perry, J., Use of cluster analysis for gait pattern classification of patients in the early and late recovery phases following stroke. *Gait Posture*, 18, 114–125, 2003.

40. Snijders, A.H., Warrenburg, B.P.V.D., Giladi, N., Bloem, B.R., Neurological gait disorders in elderly people: Clinical approach and classification. *Lancet Neurol.*, 6, 63–74, 2007.

41. Coutinho, E.S.F., Bloch, K.V., Coeli, C.M., One-year mortality among elderly people after hospitalization due to fall-related fractures: Comparison with a control group of matched elderly. *Cadernos de Saúde Pública*, 28, 801–805, 2012.

42. Zhou, Z., Dai, W., Eggert, J., Giger, J., Keller, J., Rantz, M., He, Z., A real-time system for in-home activity monitoring of elders. *Proceedings of the 2009 Annual International Conference of the IEEE Engineering in Medicine and Biology Society*, Minneapolis, MN, USA, pp. 6115–6118, 3–6 September 2009.

43. Ni, B., Wang, G., Moulin, P., RGBD-HuDaAct: A Color-Depth Video Database for Human Daily Activity Recognition, in: *Consumer Depth Cameras for Computer Vision*, pp. 193–208, Springer, London, UK, 2013.

44. Derawi, M. and Bours, P., Gait and activity recognition using commercial phones. *Comput. Secur.*, 39, 137–144, 2013.

45. De, D., Bharti, P., Das, S.K., Chellappan, S., Multimodal Wearable Sensing for Fine-Grained Activity Recognition in Healthcare. *IEEE Internet Comput.*, 19, 26–35, 2015.

46. Bertolotti, G.M., Cristiani, A.M., Colagiorgio, P., Romano, F., Bassani, E., Caramia, N., Ramat, S., Wearable, A., and Modular Inertial Unit for Measuring Limb Movements and Balance Control Abilities. *IEEE Sens. J.*, 16, 790–797, 2016.

47. Panahandeh, G., Mohammadiha, N., Leijon, A., Handel, P., Continuous Hidden Markov Model for Pedestrian Activity Classification and Gait Analysis. *IEEE Trans. Instrum. Meas.*, 62, 1073–1083, 2013.

48. Bejarano, N.C., Ambrosini, E., Pedrocchi, A., Ferrigno, G., Monticone, M., Ferrante, S., A Novel Adaptive Real-Time Algorithm to Detect Gait Events from Wearable Sensors. *IEEE Trans. Neural Syst. Rehabil. Eng.*, 23, 413–422, 2015.

49. Ngo, T.T., Makihara, Y., Nagahara, H., Mukaigawa, Y., Yagi, Y., Similar gait action recognition using an inertial sensor. *Pattern Recognit.*, 48, 1289–1301, 2015.

50. Alshurafa, N., Xu, W., Liu, J.J., Huang, M.-C., Mortazavi, B., Roberts, C.K., Sarrafzadeh, M., Designing a Robust Activity Recognition Framework for Health and Exergaming Using Wearable Sensors. *IEEE J. Biomed. Health Inform.*, 18, 1636–1646, 2014.

51. Ghasemzadeh, H., Amini, N., Saeedi, R., Sarrafzadeh, M., Power-Aware Computing in Wearable Sensor Networks: An Optimal Feature Selection. *IEEE Trans. Mob. Comput.*, 14, 800–812, 2015.

52. Chen, B., Zheng, E., Wang, Q., Wang, L., A new strategy for parameter optimization to improve phase-dependent locomotion mode recognition. *Neurocomputing.*, 149, 585–593, 2015.

53. Cristiani, A.M., Bertolotti, G.M., Marenzi, E., Ramat, S., An Instrumented Insole for Long Term Monitoring Movement, Comfort, and Ergonomics. *IEEE Sens. J.*, 14, 1564–1572, 2014.

54. Tang, W. and Sazonov, E.S., Highly Accurate Recognition of Human Postures and Activities through Classification with Rejection. *IEEE J. Biomed. Health Inform.*, 18, 309–315, 2014.

55. Friedman, N., Rowe, J.B., Reinkensmeyer, D.J., Bachman, M., The Manumeter: A Wearable Device for Monitoring Daily Use of the Wrist and Fingers. *IEEE J. Biomed. Health Inform.*, 18, 1804–1812, 2014.

56. El-Gohary, M. and Mcnames, J., Human Joint Angle Estimation with Inertial Sensors and Validation with a Robot Arm. *IEEE Trans. Biomed. Eng.*, 62, 1759–1767, 2015.

57. Wan, E. and Merwe, R.V.D., The unscented Kalman filter for nonlinear estimation. *Proceedings of the IEEE 2000 Adaptive Systems for Signal Processing, Communications, and Control Symposium (Cat. No. 00EX373), Lake Louise, AB, Canada*, pp. 153–158, 1–4 October 2000.

58. Hsu, Y.-L., Chung, P.-C., Wang, W.-H., Pai, M.-C., Wang, C.-Y., Lin, C.-W., Wu, H.-L., Wang, J.-S., Gait and Balance Analysis for Patients with Alzheimer's Disease Using an Inertial-Sensor-Based Wearable Instrument. *IEEE J. Biomed. Health Inform.*, 18, 1822–1830, 2014.

59. Pierleoni, P., Belli, A., Palma, L., Pellegrini, M., Pernini, L., Valenti, S., A High Reliability Wearable Device for Elderly Fall Detection. *IEEE Sens. J*, 15, 4544–4553, 2015.

60. Lack, L.C., Gradisar, M., Someren, E.J.V., Wright, H.R., Lushington, K., The relationship between insomnia and body temperatures. *Sleep Med. Rev.*, 12, 307–317, 2008.

61. Kräuchi, K., Konieczka, K., Roescheisen-Weich, C., Gompper, B., Hauenstein, D., Schoetzau, A., Fraenkl, S., Flammer, J., Diurnal and menstrual cycles in body temperature are regulated differently: A 28-day ambulatory study in healthy women with thermal discomfort of cold extremities and controls. *Chronobiol. Int.*, 31, 102–113, 2013.

62. Coyne, M.D., Kesick, C.M., Doherty, T.J., Kolka, M.A., Stephenson, L.A., Circadian rhythm changes in core temperature over the menstrual cycle: Method for noninvasive monitoring. *Am. J. Physiol. Regul. Integr. Comp. Physiol.*, 279, R1316–R1320, 2000.

63. Reith, J., Jorgensen, H.S., Pedersen, P.M., Nakamaya, H., Jeppesen, L.L., Olsen, T.S., Raaschou, H.O., Body temperature in acute stroke: Relation to stroke severity, infarct size, mortality, and outcome. *Lancet.*, 347, 422–425, 1996.

64. Wright, K.P., Hull, J.T., Czeisler, C.A., Relationship between alertness, performance, and body temperature in humans. *Am. J. Physiol. Regul. Integr. Comp. Physiol.*, 283, R1370–R1377, 2002.

65. Shibasaki, K., Suzuki, M., Mizuno, A., Tominaga, M., Effects of Body Temperature on Neural Activity in the Hippocampus: Regulation of Resting Membrane Potentials by Transient Receptor Potential Vanilloid 4. *J. Neurosci.*, 27, 1566–1575, 2007.

66. Buller, M.J., Tharion, W.J., Cheuvront, S.N., Montain, S.J., Kenefick, R.W., Castellani, J., Latzka, W.A., Roberts, W.S., Richter, M., Jenkins, O.C. *et al.*, Estimation of human core temperature from sequential heart rate observations. *Physiol. Meas.*, 34, 781–798, 2013.

67. Buller, M.J., Tharion, W.J., Hoyt, R.W., Jenkins, O.C., Estimation of human internal temperature from wearable physiological sensors. *Proceedings of the 22nd Conference on Innovative Applications of Artificial Intelligence (IAAI)*, Atlanta, GA, USA, pp. 1763–1768, 11–15 July 2010.

68. Oguz, P. and Ertas, G., Wireless dual channel human body temperature measurement device. *Proceedings of the 2013 International Conference on Electronics, Computer and Computation (ICECCO)*, Ankara, Turkey, pp. 52–55, 7–9 November 2013.

69. Boano, C.A., Lasagni, M., Romer, K., Lange, T., Accurate Temperature Measurements for Medical Research Using Body Sensor Networks. *Proceedings of the 2011 14th IEEE International Symposium on Object/Component/Service-Oriented Real-Time Distributed Computing Workshops*, Newport Beach, CA, USA, pp. 189–198, 28–31 March 2011.

70. Boano, C.A., Lasagni, M., Romer, K., Non-invasive measurement of core body temperature in Marathon runners. *Proceedings of the 2013 IEEE International Conference on Body Sensor Networks*, Cambridge, MA, USA, pp. 1–6, 6–9 May 2013.

71. Chen, W., Dols, S., Oetomo, S.B., Feijs, L., Monitoring body temperature of newborn infants at neonatal intensive care units using wearable sensors. *Proceedings of the Fifth International Conference on Body Area Networks— BodyNets '10*, Corfu, Greece, pp. 188–194, 10–12 September 2010.

72. Mansor, H., Shukor, M.H.A., Meskam, S.S., Rusli, N.Q.A.M., Zamery, N.S., Body temperature measurement for remote health monitoring system. *Proceedings of the 2013 IEEE International Conference on Smart Instrumentation, Measurement and Applications (ICSIMA)*, Kuala Lumpur, Malaysia, pp. 1–5, 25–27 November 2013.

73. Rahman, M.A., Barai, A., Islam, M.A., Hashem, M.A., Development of a device for remote monitoring of heart rate and body temperature. *Proceedings of the 2012 15th International Conference on Computer and Information Technology (ICCIT)*, Chittagong, Bangladesh, pp. 411–416, 22–24 December 2012.

74. Miah, M.A., Kabir, M.H., Tanveer, M.S.R., Akhand, M.A.H., Continuous heart rate and body temperature monitoring system using Arduino UNO and Android device. *Proceedings of the 2015 2nd International Conference on Electrical Information and Communication Technologies (EICT), Khulna, Bangladesh*, pp. 183–188, 10–12 December 2015.

75. Vaz, A., Ubarretxena, A., Zalbide, I., Pardo, D., Solar, H., Garcia-Alonso, A., Berenguer, R., Full Passive UHF Tag With a Temperature Sensor Suitable for Human Body Temperature Monitoring. *IEEE Trans. Circuits Syst. II*, 57, 95–99, 2010.

76. Milici, S., Amendola, S., Bianco, A., Marrocco, G., Epidermal RFID passive sensor for body temperature measurements. *Proceedings of the 2014 IEEE RFID Technology and Applications Conference (RFID-TA)*, Tampere, Finland, pp. 140–144, 8–9 September 2014.

77. Sim, S.Y., Lee, W.K., Baek, H.J., Park, K.S., A nonintrusive temperature measuring system for estimating deep body temperature in bed. *Proceedings of the 2012 Annual International Conference of the IEEE Engineering in Medicine and Biology Society*, San Diego, CA, USA, pp. 3460–3463, 28 August–1 September 2012.

78. Kimberger, O., Thell, R., Schuh, M., Koch, J., Sessler, D.I., Kurz, A., Accuracy and precision of a novel non-invasive core thermometer. *Br. J. Anaesth.*, 103, 226–231, 2009.

79. Kitamura, K.-I., Zhu, X., Chen, W., Nemoto, T., Development of a new method for the noninvasive measurement of deep body temperature without a heater. *Med. Eng. Phys.*, 32, 1–6, 2010.

80. Jänig, W., *Integrative Action of the Autonomic Nervous System: Neurobiology of Homeostasis*, Cambridge University Press, Cambridge, UK, 2008.

81. Critchley, H.D., Book Review: Electrodermal Responses: What Happens in the Brain? *Neuroscientist*, 8, 132–142, 2002.

82. Bakker, J., Pechenizkiy, M., Sidorova, N., What's your current stress level? Detection of stress patterns from GSR sensor data. *2011 IEEE 11th International Conference on Data Mining Workshops*, Vancouver, BC, Canada, pp. 573–580, 11–14 December 2011.

83. Bonato, P., Wearable sensors/systems and their impact on biomedical engineering. *IEEE Eng. Med. Biol. Mag.*, 22, 18–20, 2003.

84. Sano, A. and Picard, R.W., Stress Recognition Using Wearable Sensors and Mobile Phones. *Proceedings of the 2013 Humaine Association Conference on Affective Computing and Intelligent Interaction*, Geneva, Switzerland, pp. 671–676, 2–5 September 2013.

85. Poh, M.-Z., Swenson, N.C., Picard, R.W., A Wearable Sensor for Unobtrusive, Long-Term Assessment of Electrodermal Activity. *IEEE Trans. Biomed. Eng.*, 57, 1243–1252, 2010.

86. Sugathan, A., Roy, G.G., Kirthyvijay, G.J., Thomson, J., Application of Arduino based platform for wearable health monitoring system. *Proceedings of the 2013 IEEE 1st International Conference on Condition Assessment Techniques in Electrical Systems (CATCON)*, Kolkata, India, pp. 1–5, 6–8 December 2013.

87. Kim, J., Kwon, S., Seo, S., Park, K., Highly wearable galvanic skin response sensor using flexible and conductive polymer foam. *Proceedings of the 2014 36th Annual International Conference of the IEEE Engineering in Medicine and Biology Society*, Chicago, IL, USA, pp. 6631–6634, 26–30 August 2014.

88. Garbarino, M., Lai, M., Tognetti, S., Picard, R., Bender, D., Empatica E3—A wearable wireless multi-sensor device for real-time computerized biofeedback

and data acquisition. *Proceedings of the 4th International Conference on Wireless Mobile Communication and Healthcare—Transforming healthcare through innovations in mobile and wireless technologies*, Athens, Greece, pp. 39–42, 3–5 November 2014.

89. Guo, R., Li, S., He, L., Gao, W., Qi, H., Owens, G., Pervasive and Unobtrusive Emotion Sensing for Human Mental Health. *Proceedings of the 7th International Conference on Pervasive Computing Technologies for Healthcare*, Venice, Italy, pp. 436–439, 5–8 May 2013.

90. Setz, C., Arnrich, B., Schumm, J., Marca, R.L., Troster, G., Ehlert, U., Discriminating Stress From Cognitive Load Using a Wearable EDA Device. *IEEE Trans. Inform. Technol. Biomed.*, 14, 410–417, 2010.

91. Crifaci, G., Billeci, L., Tartarisco, G., Balocchi, R., Pioggia, G., Brunori, E., Maestro, S., Morales, M.A., ECG and GSR measure and analysis using wearable systems: Application in anorexia nervosa adolescents. *Proceedings of the 2013 8th International Symposium on Image and Signal Processing and Analysis (ISPA)*, Trieste, Italy, pp. 499–504, 4–6 September 2013.

92. Subramanya, K., Bhat, V.V., Kamath, S., A wearable device for monitoring galvanic skin response to accurately predict changes in blood pressure indexes and cardiovascular dynamics. *Proceedings of the 2013 Annual IEEE India Conference (INDICON)*, Mumbai, India, pp. 1–4, 13–15 December 2013.

93. Yoon, Y., Cho, J.H., Yoon, G., Non-constrained Blood Pressure Monitoring Using ECG and PPG for Personal Healthcare. *J. Med. Syst.*, 33, 261–266, 2008.

94. Blacher, J., Staessen, J.A., Girerd, X., Gasowski, J., Thijs, L., Liu, L., Wang, J.G., Fagard, R.H., Safar, M.E., Pulse Pressure Not Mean Pressure Determines Cardiovascular Risk in Older Hypertensive Patients. *Arch. Intern. Med.*, 160, 1085–1089, 2000.

95. Baker, C., Method and System for Controlled Maintenance of Hypoxia for Therapeutic or Diagnostic Purposes. No. US 11/241,062. U.S. Patent. International Application No. PCT/US2006/038123, 2005 Sep 30.

96. O'driscoll, B.R., Howard, L.S., Davison, A.G., BTS guideline for emergency oxygen use in adult patients. *Thorax.*, 63, vi1–vi68, 2008.

97. Duun, S.B., Haahr, R.G., Birkelund, K., Thomsen, E.V., A Ring-Shaped Photodiode Designed for Use in a Reflectance Pulse Oximetry Sensor in Wireless Health Monitoring Applications. *IEEE Sens. J.*, 10, 261–268, 2010.

98. Chen, W., Ayoola, I., Oetomo, S.B., Feijs, L., Non-invasive blood oxygen saturation monitoring for neonates using reflectance pulse oximeter. *Proceedings of the 2010 Design, Automation & Test in Europe Conference & Exhibition (DATE 2010)*, Dresden, Germany, pp. 1530–1535, 8–12 March 2010.

99. Li, K. and Warren, S., A Wireless Reflectance Pulse Oximeter with Digital Baseline Control for Unfiltered Photoplethysmograms. *IEEE Trans. Biomed. Circuits Syst.*, 6, 269–278, 2012.

100. Guo, D., Tay, F.E., Xu, L., Yu, L., Nyan, M., Chong, F., Yap, K., Xu, B., A Long-term Wearable Vital Signs Monitoring System using BSN. *Proceedings of the 2008 11th EUROMICRO Conference on Digital System Design Architectures, Methods and Tools*, Parma, Italy, pp. 825–830, 3–5 September 2008.

9

A Secure Framework for Protecting Clinical Data in Medical IoT Environment

Balasamy K.*, Krishnaraj N., Ramprasath J. and Ramprakash P.

Department of Information Technology, Dr. Mahalingam College of Engineering and Technology, Pollachi, India

Abstract

The Internet of Things (IoT) is a booming research area in recent world, which has many potential problems to solve. It grants anyone to interface anything with the web. Then again, secure association, correspondence and sharing of data are additionally under investigation in IoT condition. Communication and storage of information on any IoT device makes genuine security issues. As the use of the smart devices have steadily increased across different applications, this chapter concentrates on fusing IoT in medicinal domain to upgrade the patient focused clinical consideration. In any case, guaranteeing the security of the information produced and gathered by the IoT devices is the most testing issue in medicinal services administrations. The primary objective of this chapter is to design a framework for securing the IoT information produced in the medicinal services. Thus, security mechanisms utilized in the IoT environment must be capable of making communications from end to end and must be embraced in low cost IoT devices. The proposed framework achieves high throughput with less latency, which results in better efficiency.

Keywords: Internet of Things, healthcare, security, encryption, medical data

9.1 Introduction

The digital world is rapidly moving to a model where billions of electronic devices will be interconnected by computer networks, especially the

---

Corresponding author: balasamyk@gmail.com

SK Hafizul Islam and Debabrata Samanta (eds.) Smart Healthcare System Design: Security and Privacy Aspects, (203–234) © 2021 Scrivener Publishing LLC

Internet. This technologies can interact with the human space, carry their knowledge to the electronic content and make the digital and physical realms inseparable. The Internet of Things (IoT) concept in which devices are uniquely identified and accessible via the network is represented in this scenario. An immediate result is the implementation of creative resources and knowledge on the Internet [1]. There are extensive possibilities for IoT applications, such as agriculture, distribution of electricity, healthcare, and [2] Transportation.

IoT systems interact directly with the cloud in the conventional method [3]. For certain applications, the volume of data from sensors to the cloud to connect is however, prohibitive. Connected cars, for instance, can produce voluminous data even in megabytes (MB) for every second [4]. In addition, few applications need rapid reaction, such as face recognition need dedicated artificial intelligence (AI) based hardware for processing in devices like smartphones. The fog and edge layer paradigm has therefore been applied to the IoT [4] architecture. Data processing and local decisions can be performed by fog and edge systems, eliminating additional cloud communication [5]. The implementation of this modern model, however, is trailed by important side special effects that need to be properly handled, such as cost and security [6], for example.

IoT has been given a considerable concern as it has vast opening potentials for a huge number of cutting-edge application domains. IoT is a network of physical devices that interface and transfer information with computers, which includes mobile phone, home appliances, automobiles and some more, from a more substantial point of view. Most multinational businesses and start-up attempts have hooked up with IoT innovation in the hope of profiting from whatever business opportunities it can offer. IoT has a major impact on the financial sector, farming, supply chain management, management of business processes, remote monitoring, and so on. The present situation allows us to spend millions of dollars on business as a result of the improvements in the IoT. Since there are more opportunities available for IoT business, there are security problems where all devices are connected via the internet.

9.1.1   Medical IoT Background & Perspective

9.1.1.1   Medical IoT Communication Network

Real-time data communication between devices in medical network took place across four major key communications infrastructure. They are Body-Area Networks (BAN), Home-Area Networks (HAN), and Neighbor-hood Area Networks (NAN).

A BAN is a communication platform which is analyzed by either a tracker or a lightweight sensor for the communication of patient vital signals as shown in Figure 9.1. In Ref. [17], biomedical signals can be used to secure contact between medical devices. Therefore, a low-power bio-identification mechanism was proposed in Ref. [12], via an Inter-Pulse Interval (IPI) to protect contact between sensors in the Body Area Network. A physical sign that approves with a hidden code of the symmetric key crypto-system for BAN sensor communications was used in Ref. [11].

Finally, the medical information obtained is submitted in two separate ways to the controller:

- *Smart-Phone:* transmits the data collected from the base station (BS) via a mobile network that directs it before it enters the medical information centre.
- *Cordless Medical Device:* transmits information through one of many protocols for wireless communication, such as Wi-Fi, Bluetooth or Zig-Bee.

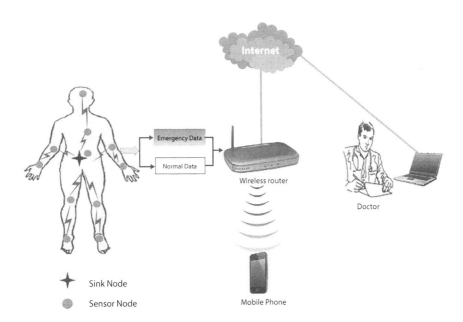

Figure 9.1 Body area network [18].

A *HAN* practices a controller that manages connectivity to transfer the data collected from the access point (AP) located at the home of the patient.

A *NAN* helps operators to associate with the internet quickly [14]. The major role is to create cordless communication within neighbouring regions, such as home communities. It can be centred on an omnidirectional antenna that enables a range of at least half a mile to be protected by a single access point. In addition, NAN depends on a directional antenna to boost the frequency of the signal as shown in Figure 9.2. The communication device also transmits the information to a base station, enabling the data to be transmitted to residential house and immediately collects from the source device.

They differentiate pharmaceutical products and according to their needs. In reality, many of them are available on the healthcare market as a gadget, or were used for monitoring real-time medical information shared by hospitals. Such Intelligent Medical Equipment (IME) can expand from exercise devices to sugar-level devices, to blood pressure devices. A far more sophisticated and suitable healthcare system is required, given that the ageing population in developing countries is rising. The new medical IoT technology is regarded as one of the most significant solutions that have been implemented to meet the rising needs and requirements. Medical

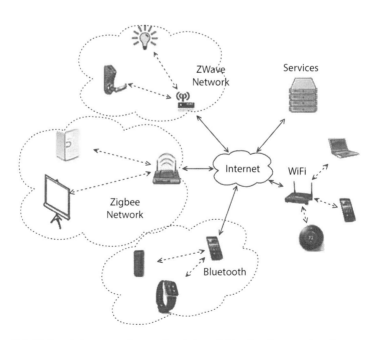

Figure 9.2 Various interconnection protocols in neighborhood area network.

IoT provides physical independence for patients, which, as reported by the World Health Organization (WHO), leads to a drop in the rate of hospital patients conducting blood pressure or cardiovascular disease investigations, which account for 30% of world-wide deaths. Furthermore, diabetic patients can now be managed from hospitals remotely.

Smart medical devices can be manufactured by incorporating biomedical instruments and pharmaceutical products. In addition, some in-home systems can be used and others are advanced and can be used in hospitals and clinics. In Table 9.1, different protocols that contains the collections of all devices that supports are listed.

Wearable Devices: Intelligent and digital medical devices are included in wearable devices to record, track and enhance the patient's health condition in real-time at low cost [6]. Fitness apps, smart health watches, wearable Blood Pressure Monitors (BPM), ring-type heart rate sensor and biosensors are included in the wearable device [7, 8]. There is a greater need for online-home healthcare due to the growth in the proportion of elderly populations and the spread of diseases. Below listed are the few of those devices.

Table 9.1 Protocols used for interconnection in medical IoT.

Protocol	Range	Classification	Description
LTE/4G	Mid-Range	Wireless	Cordless equipment that link wearable and medical equipment
Zigbee	Mid-Range	Wireless	Health communications with minimal latency & power usage used for short wavelengths
Bluetooth	Short Range	Wireless	Used to attach a medical system with short distances like intelligent medical sensors.
802.1x, Wi-Fi	Mid-Range	Wireless	Reliable patient link, particularly high power and long range.
Internet Protocol (IP)	High Range	Wireless	Patient IoT and E-Health services related communications

Intelligent Fitness Systems: Intelligent Fitness Systems helps in promoting healthy patient lifestyles and strengthening health outcomes. This is done by following a daily exercise regimen that varies based on age, gender and their health condition, which relies on the physical status of the patients. In Ref. [9], several additional smart fitness equipment have been identified, including "TomTom Spark 3" which helps in tracking the fitness and "on-wrist navigator".

Smart Blood-Pressure Systems: In several medical IoT areas and domains, Smart Blood-Pressure Systems are deployed. They are also used to monitor monitoring of blood pressure remotely and continuously. These devices search for blood pressure variations from the standard to detect any disturbance quickly and relay on the real-time data. The range of such smart systems includes "Omron EVOLV" [2], "iHealth Feel & View BPM" [3] and "Philips Upper Arm BPM" [4].

Smart Glucose-Level system is able to identify and track the sugar level in patients with type 1 and type 2 diabetes in real-time. To ensure the safety of patients, these devices helps in retaining the exact amount of insulin. This decreases the consequences and complicationsallied with low or high insulin levels that are unforeseen. GlucoWise device is a kind of such devices [5] and the iBGStar Blood Glucose Meter [7], besides turning a given IoT system into a blood sugar meters monitor, primarily smartphones [6]. The insulin pump actuators are transmitted with signals to administer the required insulin prescribed amount in the event of an insulin drop. The spinal cord stimulator is an example of an actuator that is inserted into the patient's body to confirmlong-standing pain relief.

Medical devices at Home: This include devices that are mostly supplied by a nurse practitioner that rely on common hospital connectivity technologies like email, Telephone, smart medicines and dialysis devices that are actually in use outside a hospital or clinical facility [2]. The more products are classified as test sets, first aid equipment, secure medical instruments, feeding devices, vacuum equipment, breathing equipment, childcare and other devices, which are further classified in Ref. [4].

Clinical Medical Devices: Hospitals, whether they are life-threatening or not, must always be prepared for any emergency or incident. As such, to provide the best care for patients, a high degree of preparation for both medical equipment and personnel is a must. Health donations play a key role in this sense [10]. Defibrillators, anaesthesia machines, patient monitors, electrocardiogram (EKG) machines [11], surgical tables, blanket and fluid heaters, electro-surgical systems, surgical tables and lights are classified among these medical devices, as further mentioned in Ref. [12].

9.2   Medical IoT Application Domains

This Medical IoT provides many benefits through healthcare apps, considering the difficulties surrounding this domain [5]. First, because a patient's vital signs can be tracked in real diagnosis, whichallows patients and healthcare personnel to interact immediately. This declines the budget of hospital treatment by lowering the number of visits. Another advantage of Medical IoT is to improve the health and lifestyle of patients. The direct access to vital patient signs enables early diagnosis, drug prescription, and medication injection through a wearable device.

In the positions of physicians, medical practitioners, healthcare devices and receptionists, the future of Medical IoT aims to further include devices and applications. The general public, however, also has security and privacy concerns, privacy, confidence and accuracy of certain medical IoT systems that are required.

9.2.1   Smart Doctor

In order to fulfil the function and duties of a real physician, the notion of autonomous robotics is one of the future goals. Some patients have raised doubts about this issue, while others have felt more comfortable talking about their private medical problems with a robot doctor than with a real surgeon. In spite of the contrary viewpoints, the word smart-doctor that is used in the near future can constantly be heard.

9.2.2   Smart Medical Practitioner

Smart-healthcare robots may also carry out minor medical duties, like the task of a nurse. In certain circumstances, in order to facilitate the tasks of the nurse, they can execute the role of a smart helper to a nurse. Depending on the medical conditions and requirements, the aim is to focus on the medical robotics to perform a minor or/and supporting healthcare role.

9.2.3   Smart Technology

It includes intelligent medical equipment and kits which paramedics now use to provide emergency assistance to patients who are desperately in need of medical treatment and assistance. One example is the use of these medical drones to accomplish such a mission. Medical drones have originally been equipped in response to heart arrest emergencies, as they are the fastest drones to reach the medical scene. The drones are programmed to travel to their targets, save time and save lives as a result, so paramedics can get stuck and not respond as quickly as possible. It encourages a focus on intelligent medical robots [13] in hospital surgery. Medical technology focused on Virtual/Augmented Reality and Artificial-Intelligence (AI) has also been used for numerous clinical purposes. Medical technologies based on AI are therefore relies to guarantee a greater rate of accuracy [17]. This involves exploring biochemical interactions [8], such as IBM Watson and Gene Network Sciences (GNS) AI systems for healthcare used to find the best treatment for cancer.

9.2.4   Smart Receptionist

Another trend in the Medical IoT sector is a smart receptionist; a medical robot is able to act like a regular receptionist, possessing the capacity to "think" and "understand" a specific Medical or trauma situation until the patient is referred to the proper department of healthcare. Such robots will also respond to telephone calls and book patient appointments, thus classifying urgent and regular appointments. Such a grouping may even be based on mathematical or machine-learning algorithms.

9.2.5   Disaster Response Systems (DRS)

These mechanisms rely on the concept of alerting clinicians and patients where high emergency medical occurrence of any patient (e.g. seizure, stroke, heart arrest, etc.) by transmitting critical indications to the hospital remotely [8] on the basis of a proactive risk evaluation method [2]. For a greater precision and quick response time, DRS are now being updated to become location-based [3]. The Active-Protective intelligent band that can be mounted on the wrist of a patient and uses Bluetooth and AI to communicate data during real scenario.

9.3   Medical IoT Concerns

Medical IoT-related issues can be categorized into three key categories, each being presented by the common public and that relates to issues in the security, privacy and trust areas.

9.3.1 Security Concerns

These devices are vulnerable to different wireless/security threats because of the dependency of medical IoT devices around the practicein the unsecured cordless communications. In fact, because of the lack of safety measures in which most clinical IoT devices as shown in Figure 9.3 the perpetrator will eavesdrop and decrypt received data and information, either because of nature, or due to inadequate security authentication mechanisms that could easily be prevented by a competent assailant. Another problem with protection is the potential to get unauthorized access even without detection, so such attacks cannot be known and stopped. This will result in higher rights, malicious codes being injected, or malware devices being infected. Medical IoT computers, on the other hand, may be hacked and used to initiate attacks against Distributed Denial of Service (DDoS). In Ref. [7] how medical equipment is vulnerable to botnet attacks may lead to physical attacks on individuals. For instance, an attack can potentially control a drug dose that kills a single patient or has serious health consequences. In addition, when seized by terrorists, medical IoT systems may be used as a form of targeted assassination. In addition, as stated in Ref. [7], medical IoT devices may have a detrimental impact on patients'

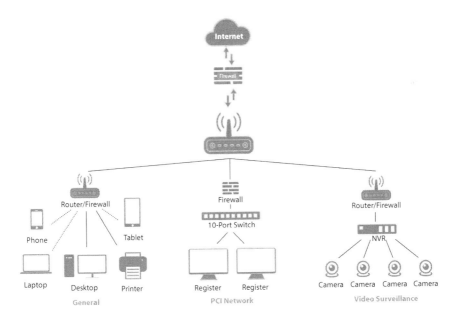

Figure 9.3 Various IoT networking devices.

psychological status, as patients may actually be frightened when they are rounded by robots instead of humans, which leads them to have a heart attack.

9.3.2   Privacy Concerns

Passive threats including certain traffic monitoring contribute to privacy concerns as information about the identities of patients may be gathered and revealedalong with patient clinical confidential information. As an intruder is able to recognize his/her clinical history and health conditions, this is a very dangerous threat to patients that leads to dramatic serious impacts on patients. Another justification for compromising patients' privacy, by targeting hospitals, is identity fraud. Several of these actual attacks lead either to leaks or to the publication of confidential data compromising the confidentiality and privacy of the patients.

9.3.3   Trust Concerns

The violation of the privacy of patients transforms into significant lack of identity. The idea of automation takes over the duties of physicians, nurses, and receptionists is becoming sceptical among patients. As a result, customers are more worried about having their health conditions monitored and controlled by a smart medical robot or a healthcare device.

9.4   Need for Security in Medical IoT

IoT applications in real time gather vast quantities of personal data from Company firms in hospitals, household and financial transactions. In order to access user data, heterogeneous real time IoT presents a need for proper protection algorithms. While several security algorithms exist, they do not provide the IoT environment with higher order security. It is difficult to perform complicated data encryption techniques in IoT devices due to the energy limited nature of IoT devices. There is therefore a need for lightweight security algorithms that provide IoT data with a higher degree of security with minimal transmission and overhead computation on those kind of IoT devices.

IoT systems are a favored target for attackers because of the existence of particular applications, such as the storage of confidential data and connected to large number of network devices. Additional vulnerabilities are emerging with IoT [6] beyond the real internet security problems. Specific

applications can pose a serious life or business risk [15–17]. Imagine a scenario in which an intruder takes control of a car. Other threats include
private information theft (privacy/confidentiality), information alteration
(authenticity), and system malfunctioning (availability and resilience).
Furthermore, an affected device can pose potential threats to entire secure
connections, such as when a hacked device, along with web camera, that
is connected in the secure home network. So it is needed to create a secure
network with IoT in healthcare as shown in Figure 9.4.

Unauthorized access to data and equipment raises concerns regarding patient safety in the healthcare system. Data confidentiality is one of
the key aspects of protection that must be taken into consideration when
sharing data. In addition, it is important to minimise high computation
overhead caused by existing cryptographic security algorithms and to
withstand different attacks such as Brute Force, Eavesdropping, Man-
in-the-Middle, etc. This creates a need for reliable, effective and lightweight
security algorithms to be created. It is therefore important to build lightweight algorithms to monitor and manage data protection across different
layers of the IoT architecture.

Figure 9.4 Smart medical network.

9.5   Components for Enhancing Data Security in Medical IoT

There are five different components that are associated with enhancing data security in IoT domain as shown in Figure 9.5.

9.5.1   Confidentiality

In the IoT environment, confidentiality needs to meet two essential necessities. A controlling access mechanism and a device authentication method with a related identity management system must be specified. Another necessity related to data confidentiality in the IoT scenario is the specification of a query language to allow applications to recover information from a data stream.

9.5.2   Integrity

Environmental risks, such as fire, dust, and electrical surges, can also endanger data integrity. Practices adopted to maintain physical environment data integrity include: making servers available to network administrators only, holding shielded and secured media for the transmitting (for example, wires and connectors) to guarantee that power interventions, electrostatic leakage, and hardware and storage media magnetism cannot be tapped. Network security steps to ensure data integrity include: preserving current levels of authorization for all users, recording processes, requirements, and maintenance activities of system administration, and implementing disaster retrieval strategies for events include power cuts, server crashes or assaults by viruses.

Figure 9.5 Level of data security.

9.5.3 Authentication

The mechanism of ensuring authenticity between computers, objects and people is authentication. Therefore, preparing a mechanism or architecture that can manage the scalability of entities in the IoT ecosystem reliably is important. In an IoT-based hospital environment comprise of thin/fat sensors, detecting tags or labeled objects, it needs adequate authentication structures for use as the key security technique. The authentication mechanism also offers vigorous object validation and protected information for IoT network services during data communication.

9.5.4 Non-Repudiation

This provides with indisputable evidence of the authenticity and source of the transmission of all data. Digitally signed the document and hardware security system transactions might provide some clear non-repudiation of the date of the transaction and origin.

9.5.5 Privacy

All devices transmit personal information to the user without encryption, such as credit card details, person name, residential address, healthcare information and much more. Although IoT has privacy and security issues, it adds values to our lives by permitting us to remotely and automatically handle our daily routine tasks and, more importantly, it is a game-changer for industries.

9.6 Vulnerabilities in Medical IoT Environment

9.6.1 Patient Privacy Protection

Smart phones containing user's personal healthcare details are connected to the IoT devices to promote users convenience of services. IoT devices based on android with outstanding usability and transparency are rapidly developing. However it has also a detrimental effect, i.e. exposure to certain vulners. By using reverse engineering to achieve access to the original file, hackers can retrieve code from an insecurehealth app in smart phones, thus using the program to steal or steal private patient data. Apples IOS has a closed official software deployment policy concerning the store, while Android has an open policy that requires third-party stores and also allows for the installation of apps via Android application package (APK) files. This open source architecture structurally weakens the software and encourages malicious behavior on smartphones since the android platform is straightforward.

9.6.2   Patient Safety

The level of threat of malicious hackers approaching organisations through IoT devices, such as smart watches, VR headsets, etc., is classified higher than average, as per the ISACA IT Risk/Reward Barometer report. Hackers can interfere with programs that interact with smart wearable devices. In many ways that can cause physical damage. The biometric data gathered from Wearable devices provide hackers with opportunity to share private information and cause its need for social engineering to target ransom-ware attacks. Actually, Using Bluetooth network, wearable transmission of data sources to smart phones and these systems can be attacked for security breaches and exposed to further attacks. The FDA, for example, released a Class I recall in 2014 for a variety of ventilators and infusions. Such appliances are used by patients who are unable to breathe on their own. While using these devices, the patients both virtual and physical lives are at risk and then it requires the successful method of ensuring the protection of such instruments during usage without failure becomes important for medical practitioners.

9.6.3   Unauthorized Access

Medical Devices (MDs) could even be subjected to malicious attacks or other unintended software or firmware design generated by external opponents. These devices consist of an efficient computing programmer's radio transceiver for better communication. To customize MD configurations and to retrieve medical data, an MD programmer issues commands. The patient's health caregivers track and operate MDs remotely through networks or the internet. MDs are greatly exposed to security threats through wireless networking and communication technologies. The packets transmitted can be eavesdropped and patient privacy can also be exposed, such as forging, tampering and replaying the messages. Cyber assaults on patient records or user accounts are also at risk, because patient data is accessed remotely. There are two types of opponents that can strike an MD. First, the messages can be tampered with by an active adversary and give unauthorised orders. Secondly, passive opponents can listen to the communication that takes place. Two standardhacking models are the subject of existing

MD access control schemes. The clinical data stored in the MD is retrieved in the first form of attack by an unauthorized systems analyst who directs mischievous instructions or alters computer patterns. An unauthorized user fraudulently encrypts MD in the second form of attack and thus activates the persistent performance of authorization computations to drain the power.

9.6.4   Medical IoT Security Constraints

As soon as the introduction of medical devices into IoT networks began, medical IoT problems arose. The lack of standardization is one big obstacle. The key Medical IoT problems were addressed in depth in Ref. [1]. To have various medical devices working together the problem of standardization is important and for vendors to take the right security measures to prevent them from being hacked. This will lead to greater security, performance, scalability, consistency, and productivity. In fact, many of these challenges are primarily related to but not limited to, different security constraints of Medical IoT are listed in Figure 9.6.

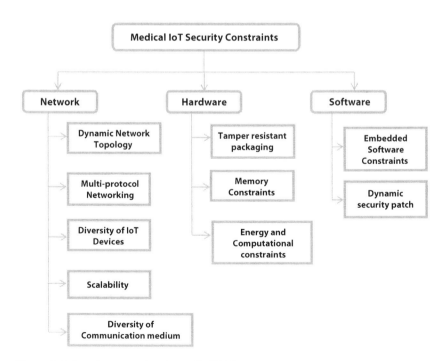

Figure 9.6 Security constraints in medical IoT.

9.7   Solutions for IoT Healthcare Cyber-Security

Although the development of IoT architecture is seen as the model of fog/edge computing is considered as the protection solutions research is still at the beginning era [9]. This chapter therefore concentrates on delivering new approaches aimed at enhancing safety in medical IoT devices are light enough for coexistence and complementary at a reasonable overhead and footprint cost in the same facilities. Such methods are as follows:

9.7.1   Architecture of the Smart Healthcare System

The amount of IoT healthcare-connected medical users and devices are on the rise. There is a significant development in the relation of the room of patients, including medical equipment, room lighting, air conditioners, beds of patients, etc. The healthcare IoT system's physical and cyber world interconnections are in four distinct layers as shown in Figure 9.7.

 (i) Data Perception layer
 (ii) Data Communication layer
 (iii) Data Storage layer and
 (iv) Data Application layer.

9.7.1.1   Data Perception Layer

The main task of this layer is to deal with personal clinical information that is collect data from the user in real time. Medical information's are

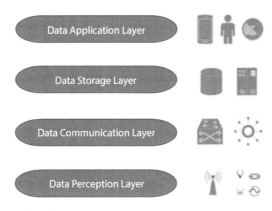

Figure 9.7 Layers of healthcare security.

collected through various short-range communication technologies such as Radio Frequency (RF) Waves, Z-wave, Near Field Communication (NFC), ZigBee, Bluetooth etc., and to transfer it to the upper layer for processing this data. Sensors such as RFID tags are incorporated into the Medical IoT devices and contain all the information that can be scanned to receive all the related data. Once the scanned data is transferred to the upper layer in the hierarchy, i.e. the networking layer, the data is processed accordingly.

Medical devices such as pulse oximeters, surgical lights, blood pressure monitors, glucose monitors and other devices in the patient room can be connected to the IoT gateway using the above-mentioned short-range communication technologies. The medical information gathered in the perception layer is encrypted using different techniques.

9.7.1.2   Data Communication Layer

It is the main channel between the other layers in IoT architecture and the different IoT operating activities. The whole physical structure has a lot of patient evidence and knowledge to communicate with other nodes. It is therefore necessary to establish an appropriate network of connections between these nodes through a communication protocol. On the basis of the designer's protocol, the interaction could be wired or wireless. In addition, networks are highly critical IoT elements that bind the external world of the internet. Intelligent network infrastructure is required for IoT.

9.7.1.3   Data Storage Layer

The patient data contained in the Cloud Medical Server (CMS) is managed in the storage layer. Remote user authentication for accessing IoT data is handled by the Cloud Authentication Server (CAS) and the Central Cloud Server (CCS) stores the other metadata. The obligations of this layer are also the identification and management of IoT user data.

9.7.1.4   Data Application Layer

Another end of an IoT system is formed by applications. Applications are vitally important for all the collected data to be properly used. These cloud-based applications are responsible for giving the collected data an effective meaning. Applications are controlled by users and are the point of delivery for specific services. Examples of apps are: apps for home automation, security systems, industrial control centers, etc.

9.8   Execution of Trusted Environment

Since many products for a variety are placed by unauthorised personnel in outdoor areas with easy access, it is important to ensure that the executing software environment has not been maliciously modified or transformed. A root-of-trust (RoT) environment and, finally, a chain of trust (CoT) with authentication and encryption [6] can be generated using strong authentication system protocols and its use of dedicated hardware and cryptographic techniques.

9.8.1   Root of Trust Security Services

GlobalPlatform has identified nine services that could be provided by Roots of Trust, based on its experience with the devices and markets addressed by GlobalPlatform through its members: authentication, confidentiality, identification, integrity, measurement, authorization, reporting, updating, and verification.

With one or more security services, one can create a Root of Trust. However, unless it reveals the interface to the service in any way, the Source of Confidence cannot claim to deliver the service. For instance, consider the deployment of many Protection Services by a Root of Trust where the Verification Service can preserve the public key shielded position and be able to check the legitimacy of the next item in the Chain of Trust without revealing the Integrity Service and Measurement Service's protected capability. In this scenario, the RoT is just verification RoT and thus cannot pretend to be a secrecy or calculation RoT, because such facilities are exclusively customised to and reserved for using the verification RoT.

To securely store and protect sensitive information, a Root of Trust can retain one or more protected areas used. A protected area should be assisted by an interface that offers an acceptable degree of security in order to control access to sensitive information and discourage unwanted dissemination, usage and use (for example, sensitive data stored in a protected area should only be accessed by an API when the API verifies the right of access to this sensitive information in an implementation). Certification policies, or the willingness of a vendor to provide value-added features for their goods, can determine the level of physical and logical security of the shielded site.

These resources can be used in the first boot code for safety-related operations, for instance, to check the credibility of others before the control is turned over, or to document potential comparison and monitoring network characteristics. Each part in the sequence can easily implement additional RoT Protection Services and use them to conduct security-related tasks, such as approving access to protected resources, upgrading essential system firmware, or reporting platform functionality, as the device boots its way through initialization. Certain protection services may use RoT Security Services to secure the keys, information stored on computers, and data in transit (e.g. Trusted Service Manager) to and from back-end services. Developers of applications can either specifically or indirectly use RoT Security Services via the use of these other security services.

For the purposes of protected storing and maintains the privacy of at least one certificate, the RoT for authentication retains one or more shielded locations. One or more access controls are stored here by a service user for later use to help authenticate compliance with a protocol, such as performing access control over the use and/or release of keys, or authorising access to data. An app is also included in the Root of Trust for Authentication to preserve permitted access to and use of shielded location information, as well as protect it from unauthorised use and disclosure. Registered usage in this case is for authentication purposes only.

A RoT factor is necessary for the stable boot phase to conduct code verification in a trustworthy manner at the boot stage of the first unit.

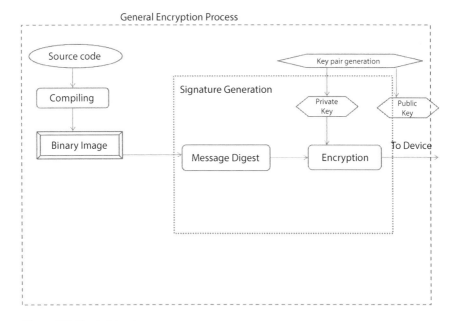

Figure 9.8 Root of trust.

Figure 9.8 explains the phases of general creation and application testing. First, as with any development environment, the developer compiles the source code that produces the binary image or firmware of a computer. Second, the binary image's hash digest (a number code that can identify it uniquely) is determined. Thirdly, public key pair that comes from a private key, encrypts the hash digest. The effect is a signature that, along with the firmware, must be put on the computer. The developer must also write a public key to the computer's writing-once memory. The bootstrap programme performs on-storage hash digest recalculation firmware during initialization. The final stage is to use the public key to decode the signature and equate it to the firmware digest.

9.8.2   Chain of Trust Security Services

There are two kinds of confidence relationships in the Chain of Trust: Internal Chain of Trust and the External Chain of Trust. An Internal Chain of Trust is instantiated by a platform as it executes a set of code modules in an environment in which the effect of any inspection of code or data integrity that might take place is difficult to log. In the other hand, as it intentionally extends a security service in such a manner that you can check the links in the chain generated by the extensions at any time and validate their validity, a platform instantiates a Clear Chain of Confidence, thus verifying the legitimacy of the security service it extends from end to end. The External Chain of Confidence exists through a set of code modules in which a RoT tests the next code module for authentication and authorization. If it passes such tests, it can be executed and becomes an eRoT in an external Chain of Trust.

Currently, an External Chain of Trust expands a service to other modules from a RoT (either a Main or a Secondary RoT) or module. The Chain of Trust for Authentication, under which the RoT requires a verification service, is a clear example of this, and it uses that service to validate a module providing a verification service close to that of the parent verification service. In a RoT, an explicit chain of confidence will always start. Explicit Chains of Trust, including Roots of Trust, must contain a minimum of one security service. The approach of expanding the Root of Trust service to subsequent modules is strongly dependent on implementation.

This method is a multi-layered framework, which includes a hypervisor. Next, the boot loader is validated by the hardware. If efficient, it is treated as a trustworthy part and the next boot step can be checked. In this case, the next move to trust is the hypervisor. The hypervisor begins and tests its fields until they are booted until confirmed as shown in Figure 9.9.

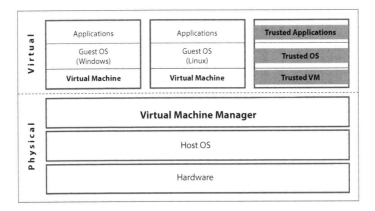

Figure 9.9 Chain of trust.

The coexistence of trustworthy and unverified realms, using the hypervisor to implement the distinction, is feasible in this case.

9.9   Patient Registration Using Medical IoT Devices

The architecture of smart healthcare system is represented in Figure 9.10, which contains security phases starting from patient registration till he leaves the hospital. The process for registration is a one-time process. It is running after the installation of the medical devices and devices for users. Three types of registration processes exist. Since various methods and inputs are used for medical and user device registration, registrations based on text, token and image are performed. The parameters used in the registration process are Patient ID, Password and Device Product Code.

Patient ID (PID): For every person, it is a proposed unique identification number. It is similar to the Aadhaar number in India and Social Security Number (SSN) in the USA. Every patient should have Unique ID that is registered in Medical IoT environment.

Passcode (PC): A passcode, also referred to as a password, is a memorised secret, normally a character string, commonly used to validate a user's identity. The patient and user can select the password based on their circumstance and wish, with the conditions specified in the portal.

Device Product Code (DPC): This is a number of 96 bits, built as a global identifier. It gives any physical object a unique identity. It is a format that is open and can be encoded on RFID tags. Tracking all sorts of objects, including fixed properties, records, business goods or recycled transport items, can be done using device product code.

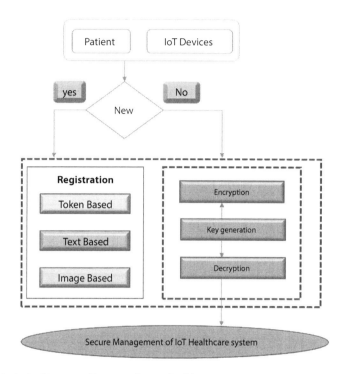

Figure 9.10 Architecture diagram of smart healthcare.

Text Based Registration: During the induction process, every patient outside the hospital sector must be registered. Of the patients, the PID and a PC are collected. A hash function to produce a hidden Patient Unique Number (PUN) is added to them. These data are preserved for further reference in the archive of the cloud application. After a patient's satisfactory registration, an acknowledgment will be submitted to the patient stating that the registration has been done successfully.

9.9.1 Encryption

Encryption is a process that encodes a text or file such that certain users can read it only. Encryption means encrypting, using data and a key to convert it into secret message and at the receiver side decrypt, or decode, the received data. The message is referred to as plaintext in a hidden text. In its encrypted, unreadable form, it is called cipher text. A sequence of numbers used to encrypt and decrypt data is an encryption key. Algorithms are used to construct encryption keys. It's random and special to each key.

There are two types of encryption systems: symmetric encryption and asymmetric encryption. Symmetric encryption is used to encrypt and decrypt data with a single password. For encryption and decryption, asymmetric encryption uses two keys. A public key, which is exchanged between users, encrypts the secret. Data is decrypted by a private key, which is not exchanged.

9.9.2   Key Generation

Using the symmetrical key cryptography, key control triggered nightmare for the parties. They were concerned about how to safely and reliably relay the keys to all users so that the message could be decrypted, which offered the opportunity to intercept the keys in transit for third parties to decipher the top-secret communications. Thus, the entire coding scheme was corrupted if the key was compromised and a "Secret" would no longer remain a "Secret." So there exists a concept called key generation, where the required key for encryption is generated using random number permutation.

9.9.3   Security by Isolation

Security by isolation is a conventional security strategy that has proven to be effective over time [8]. It may be applied using multiple physical equipment or technically, implementing policies of usage, with the intention of reducing the supply and access to services. Separation of separate physical devices involves duplication of energy, which means higher costs. Maintaining two machine working models in separate processors and memory, for example. Virtualization could achieve logic isolation, and is able to simulate a network to access the underlying domains or application hardware, while preventing replication of resources. In addition, any form of connection, such as data dependencies or synchronization, may be necessary for the functionality of a given programme, meaning the entities concerned cannot be entirely segregated. Many IoT implementations would involve coordination with sensors and network transmission, making it less desirable to complete isolated systems.

9.9.4   Virtualization

The ability to separate programmes (code and data) in order to share the similar memory is spatial isolation. A feasible approach to minimize costs is to make easy during the deployment of applications is memory sharing. Through the address bus, data bus and control buses, the memory is linked to a processor, and applications that shares the common physical address space. It is thus possible to enforce correspondence through shared memory than transferring messages. A running program, however, may have access to the address space of all processors without sufficient isolation, i.e. a malicious or malfunctioning code may enter any memory location. For memory provision the processor has to be fitted with a hardware block separating it, which provides the device with virtual memory abstractions, called a Memory Management Unit (MMU). Initially, in bothprocessors (desktop and server), the MMU was available, being essential for the installation of complex and reliable operating systems.

The generated memory addresses are referred to as virtual in these processors addresses (VAs) and physical addresses (PAs) need to be translated by the MMU, handled by the host OS or virtualization layer. The OS holds a table to perform the operation, called a page table, which maps VAs to PAs. For each virtual address, the MMU makesinterpretations with a Translation Lookaside Buffer (TLB), transforming VAs to PAs. The most regular translations are preserved by TLB entries, preventing memory access from the page table intrusion. A trap is provided to the OS when there is no efficient translation (the event of a page fault). Mischievous or flopping memory access is thereby established, and it is possible to terminate the liable operation.

The distinction between VMs or domains must be maintained while the virtualization layer is present, while the guest OS (virtualized OS operating on a VM) should capable of preserving the separation between processes. By establishing a new level of abstraction in the interpretation of the memory location, this is possible. VAs are converted to hypervisor-managed Intermediate Physical Addresses (IPAs). However, additional MMU hardware features may be required for the efficient management of IPAs. The IPA management must be emulated by the hypervisor without sufficient hardware assistance, through shadow paging method, which preserves the IPA and PA relationship in an in-between page. Without proper support, virtualization on processors gives the resulting hypervisor extra complexity, and often prohibitive overhead.

The need to maintain an equal time allocation between programs based on the execution priorities of the processor is temporalparting. Temporal parting is achieved by software, unlike spatial separation, which doesn't need any specific hardware configurations, regardless of the addition of functionalities by some processors to boost the system performance. This technique originated as a method for enhanced processor use with the first

OSs and to permit several programs and operators for resource sharing of the device concurrently. For two separate factors, in ES, temporal differentiation is a problem. First, many ES have extreme time limitations, and this must be properly resolved by temporal separation. Second, by hogging the CPU, a mischievous or flopping program may decline or even hinder the other software execution.

A program block named the scheduler, which is deployed for both the OSs kernel and the hypervisor, is used to enforce temporal separation for virtualized systems. Hypervisors create a virtual CPU (VCPU) abstraction, which is connected to virtual machines. The Virtual CPU is a physical processor machine illustration that permits multiplexing the time. The scheduler then executes an algorithm which must pick the next one to run from the available VCPUs.

Operating networks have examined and manufactured virtual equipment developers, programmers of languages, developers of compilers and hardware. While any virtual machine implementation has its own specific characteristics, there are also fundamental principles and technology similar to all virtual machines. Since the numerous systems and technology of the virtual machines have been created by different parties, this set of information and the core technologies of the various types of virtual machinery are particularly important to unify. The fidelity whereby a structural interface is applied by a virtual machine is also connected to architectural boundaries and is a major factor in designing a virtual machine. Consequently, device architecture is useful to describe and to sum up. A whole system is supported from the viewpoint of the operating system by the machine underneath. A method is a total execution systemcan endorse a variety of potentially important processes at the same time various users. A file system and other I/O resources are common to all processes. With the processes coming and going, system environment persists over time (with reboots occasionally). The framework allows processes to communicate with their resources with an OS which is part of the system and assigns physical memory and I/O resources. Therefore, the computer is only controlled by the underlying hardware from the system's viewpoint, as well as the ISA offers the communication between the device and the system.

Hypervisor based system isolation methods have the benefit of greater risk security, such as root phones, since a user who roots his personal OS device instance does not jeopardize the corporate OS instance. However, these hypervisor methods usually have better efficiency or battery impacts and can often be more cost effective since a corporate OS picture has to be created and secured. Container approaches often benefit from seamless user experience because certain aspects of personal and business use can interact in ways that are never possible for separate OS instances. The compromise is usually the need to manage the underlying OS instance to prevent root attacks on the device from protecting the application layer container.

There are three major hypervisor deployment approaches are adopted: (1) Full virtualization (FV), (2) para-virtualization, and (3) virtualization hardware supported. This technique may be used independently or by integrating two or more techniques with a composite approach.

Full Virtualization includes a processor that facilitates the installation of a hypervisor capable of offering virtualization on the guest OS without any alteration. This helps unmodified visitors to virtualize and carry out more tech activities. But the hypervisor must obey preferential instructions which can lead to performance penalties, since the time taken for emulating trap mechanism instructions are thousands of times longer than executing the intrinsic instructions.

Different methods that do not include processor architectures in hypervisors should not match the specified ISA. A workaround is to change and reexecute the guest OS, resulting in para-virtualization, prior to its launch in a VM. These modifications replace hypercalls for critical instructions (instructions that alter the actions of the processor) or other OS modules, such as the I/O subsystem. Hypercalls are utilities that the hypervisor provides that are invoked by the guest OS. They are similar in an OS to machine calls (syscalls). In addition, hypervisor functionality can be expanded by using PV, for maximizing the inter-VM communication implementation. Additionally, PV is also used to boost performance in environments where performance problems are faced by completely virtualized hypervisors.

In history, ARM architecture is not virtualizable, because when executed in unprivileged mode, some sensitive instructions do not trap. However, as an ARMv7 architectural expansion, the most current 32-bit ARM processors, including the Cortex-A15, have virtualization hardware support. There have been a variety of research ventures aiming to while they need different degrees of para-virtualization and have not been stabilised, they allow virtualization on ARM processors without hardware virtualization support. KVM/ARM is primarily designed to work with the virtualization extensions allowed to run unmodified guest OS on ARM processors. The need of stronger and easier hypervisors led to hardware support for processor vendors, which culminated in hardware-assisted virtualization. A variety of methods may be used to support hardware. Various rights permitting hypervisor, application and operating system kernel with multiple authorizations; and intrude virtualization for enhanced device hypervisor power. Therefore the vendor of the processor decides the hardware-assisted support standard, the functionality required and the costs depending on the market niche.

9.10   Trusted Communication Using Block Chain

The center of IoT creativity and, at the same time, the biggest danger of its acceptance is communication skills. The block-chain [10] is a promising technology aim of supporting integrity of data and reliable communications. As a level of protection, it is focused upon decentralisation. In order to carry out verifiable, safe and it operates by keeping a list of documents linked by digital signature via time-stamped collaboration with external parties. This technology has some appealing features that make it suitable, despite all threats and vulnerabilities involved in the IoT, for potential developments.

Blockchain is an IT mechanism that requires a community of untrustworthy actors to validate transactions. It offers a distributed ledger that is immutable, open, secure and auditable [1]. This is essentially a distributed archive of all transactions or digital activities carried out and exchanged by the parties concerned. When information is entered into the blockchain, it can never be changed or erased. A certain and verifiable record of any single transaction ever made is included in the blockchain [2]. On a blockchain network, a new block is automatically formed when the next transaction is formed. A new block is immediately connected to the previous block, the original block, using Hash in the previous block. Once a new block is created, they are sent to all connected computers involved in the blockchain network in real time.

9.10.1   Record Creation Using IoT Gateways

Blockchain multi-layer can merge the features of blockchain and IoT, providing solutions to all issues which cannot be addressed by using only one technology. By integrating these two innovations, blockchain offers a next-generation IoT platform based on blockchain technology. The key benefits of this architecture are the solving of the existing blockchains, particularly in the absence of scalability. The IoT devices may be the private blockchains nodes, some of them even belong to the next existing blockchain layer. The whole network will be involved in this case. The sensors and their gateways are now the nodes in the private BC (BlockChain), therefore the miner is the gateway since it is the most important node in its private blockchain. Before transmitting data using public and private keys, each system needs to authenticate with the network. Both keys are unique to each one. The gateway stores all keys in the local storage so that any system authenticating with it is quickly recognized. There may be a local storage for each private blockchain. Notice that only filtered data that represent essential conditions can be stored in the cloud, processed and irregular data. The computer begins constructing a new block after the registration is complete. The patient's private BC will be attached to this block until checked by the gateway (Figure 9.2). All captured data is stored in the blockchain (local storage portal) database. The portal processes the medical data and regularly generates diagnostic knowledge.

9.10.2   Accessibility to Patient Medical History

The documents containing patient data have already been deposited in the patient's cloud service in this case. A record that has already been preserved must be accessed by the gateway/authorities that have authorisation. The core work, using public blockchain, is concentrated in layer 3 where all cloud services are linked. The access and authorization management is achieved by the use of the cloud contract. By using his account, the patient has full access to the data in the cloud; he is simply the owner of the data. The cloud gives back the ID of this record as it holds the record. The patient can access this record by means of this ID. The cloud then produces a transaction to remember that on this day, the patient has accessed the record of that ID. The authority sends its ID to the cloud that is acceptable and waits for the ACK. In this case, the ACK is the result of learning that the ID of the authority is one of the authorised IDs in the contract of the cloud list.

9.10.3   Patient Enquiry With Hospital Authority

When a patient visits an agency, a new block is added to second level of blockchain. As a result, both officials will add a certain block and a similar block will also be added to the blockchain supplier of the cloud. When the patient ends his visit, the authority attaches to the public blockchain, a new block that contains the authority's ID, the patient's ID and any information about the data contained in the authority's blockchain storage. The visited authority creates a block in the blockchain of the cloud to remember that the patient of this ID has visited the proper authority. It also mentions the location where the data was stored.

9.10.4 Block Chain Based IoT System Architecture

The architecture is composed of three layers as shown in Figure 9.11.

9.10.4.1 First Layer

This is the "patient" layer; it contains all the IoT nodes that obtain information about a single patient; medical information or some other form of information that explains his environment. A strong device that will serve as a key to the higher layer blockchain is a primary node in this blockchain. Notice that there would be a proper blockchain for each patient.

9.10.4.2 Second Layer

"This is the central layer" or "authority" layer; it includes representative nodes for all medical stakeholders that are involved in patient-related data, such as hospitals, medical facilities, laboratories, etc. Members of this blockchain are also the gateways in the first layer.

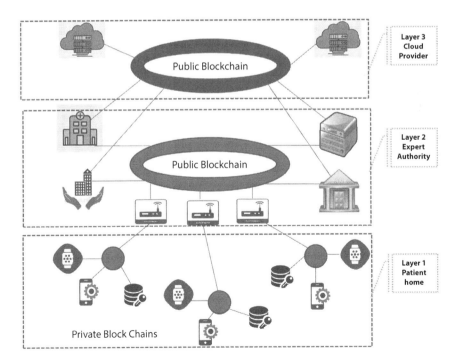

Figure 9.11 Blockchain based IoT smart healtcare.

9.10.4.3 *Third Layer*

"This is the upper layer or the foundation of the" cloud supplier. IoT machines, in fact, are in typically completed by cloud computing and storage capabilities. A domain-level blockchain is important to monitor the relationship between cloud services in order to allow each other access to patient data wherever it is stored.

9.11 Conclusion

The purpose of this research is to discover new IoT-driven healthcare technologies, sensors, or systems to provide healthcare practitioners with improved knowledge, helping them to take action to prevent and diagnose diseases. In addition, our research opens a forum for data protection experts to do further research to mitigate IoT healthcare sensor and system vulnerabilities. Healthcare is a major industry in the country, and since the IoT revolution, healthcare systems have become more effective and secure. Health experts and scientists have improved the diagnosis and prevention of diseases with the exponential development of IoT products. As a consequence, multiple sensors and systems powered by IoT have been launched and some are now being used successfully in hospitals and for personal healthcare. In a relatively short time span, these instruments gather a vast volume of data. Therefore, during the use of such instruments, data breaches may occur.

We found that the most important advantage of using smart healthcare technologies and systems was performance. Around the same time, we have found that the protection and privacy of personal data were the most critical problem when using IoT healthcare devices. Researchers interested in biomedical science may focus their studies and experiments on advanced IoT sensors to detect health problems and diseases by measuring various body parameters. In order to ensure the secrecy and credibility of the information, information management professionals and IoT-driven healthcare manufacturers are advised to concentrate further on establishing users' protection and privacy. Future researchers may pay further attention to the development of IoT-based devices or sensors that help other body systems-related medical conditions that have not been described in this segment.

References

1. Balandina, E., Balandin, S., Koucheryavy, Y., Mouromtsev, D., IoT use cases in healthcare and tourism. *Business Informatics, CBI, 2015 IEEE 17th Conference on*, vol. 2, IEEE, pp. 37–44, 2015.

2. Pang, Z., Yang, G., Khedri, R., Zhang, Y.-T., Introduction to the special section: convergence of automation technology, biomedical engineering, and health informatics toward the healthcare 4.0. *IEEE Rev, Biomed. Eng.*, 11, 249–259, 2018.

3. Bogaz Zarpelão, B., Sanches Miani, R., Kawakani, C.T., de Alvarenga, S.C., A survey of intrusion detection in Internet of Things. *J. Netw. Comput. Appl.*, 84, 25–37, 2017.

4. Trnka, M., Cerny, T., Stickney, N., Survey of authentication and authorization for the Internet of Things. *Secur. Commun. Netw.*, 2018, https://doi.org/10.1155/2018/4351603.

5. Kuila, S., Dhanda, N., Joardar, S., Neogy, S., Kuila, J., A generic survey on medical big data analysis using internet of things. *First International Conference on Artificial Intelligence and Cognitive Computing*, Springer, pp. 265–276, 2019.

6. Challoner, A. and Popescu, G.H., Intelligent sensing technology, smart healthcare services, and internet of medical things-based diagnosis. *Am. J. Med. Res.*, 6, 1, 13–18, 2019.

7. Kang, S., Baek, H., Jung, E., Hwang, H., Yoo, S., Survey on the demand for adoption of Internet of Things (IoT)-based services in hospitals: Investigation of nurses' perception in a tertiary university hospital. *Appl. Nurs. Res.*, 47, 18–23, 2019.

8. Adhikary, T., Jana, A.D., Chakrabarty, A., Kumar, J.S., The Internet of Things (IoT) augmentation in healthcare: An application analytics. *International Conference on Intelligent Computing and Communication Technologies*, Springer, pp. 576–583, 2019.

9. Kocabas, O., Soyata, T., Aktas, M.K., Emerging security mechanisms for medical cyber physical systems. *IEEE/ACM Trans. Comput. Biol. Bioinform.*, 13, 3, 401–416, 2016.

10. Venkatasubramanian, K.K., Banerjee, A., Gupta, S., Kumar, S., PSKA: Usable and secure key agreement scheme for body area networks. *IEEE Trans. Inf. Technol. Biomed.*, 14, 1, 60–68, 2010.

11. Ye, F., Qian, Y., Hu, R.Q., Energy efficient self-sustaining wireless neighborhood area network design for smart grid. *IEEE Trans. Smart Grid*, 6, 1, 220–229, 2015.

12. Koydemir, H.C. and Ozcan, A., Wearable and implantable sensors for biomedical applications. *Annu. Rev. Anal. Chem.*, 11, 127–146, 2018.

13. Hiremath, S., Yang, G., Mankodiya, K., Wearable Internet of Things: Concept, architectural components and promises for person centered healthcare. *2014 4th International Conference on WirelessMobile Communication and Healthcare-Transforming Healthcare Through Innovations in Mobile and Wireless Technologies*, MOBIHEALTH, IEEE, pp. 304–307, 2014.

14. Yuen, S.G.J., Park, J., Ghoreyshi, A., Wu, A., *User identification via motion and heartbeat waveform data*, Google Patents, US Patent 9, Fitbit, Inc., San Francisco, CA (US), 851, 808, 2017.

15. Pinto, M.B. and Yagnik, A., Fit for life: A content analysis of fitnesstracker brands use of Facebook in social media marketing. *J. Brand Manag.*, 24, 1, 49–67, 2017.

16. Asmar, R., Validation of the automatic blood pressure measurements device, the OMRON evolv (hem-7600 T-E)®. *Pregnancy according to the modified European Society of Hypertension International Protocol* (ESH-IP), 2017.

17. Wang, R., Blackburn, G., Desai, M., Phelan, D., Gillinov, L., Houghtaling, Penny, Gillinov, Marc, Accuracy of wrist-worn heartrate monitors. *Jam. Cardiol.*, 2, 1, 104–106, 2017.

18. Awan, K.M. *et al.*, A priority-based congestion-avoidance routing protocol using IoT-based heterogeneous medical sensors for energy efficiency in healthcare wireless body area networks. *Int. J. Distrib. Sens. Netw.*, 15, 6, 2019.

10

Efficient Data Transmission and Remote Monitoring System for IoT Applications

Laith Farhan[1*], Firas MaanAbdulsattar[2], Laith Alzubaidi[3],
Mohammed A. Fadhel[4], Banu ÇalışUslu[5] and Muthana Al-Amidie[6]

[1]*College of Engineering, University of Diyala, Diyala, Iraq,
Manchester Metropolitan University, Manchester, UK
[2]*Refrigeration and Air Conditioning Engineering,
Dijlah University Collage, Baghdad, Iraq
[3]*School of Computer Science, Queensland University of Technology, Brisbane, Australia
[4]*College of Computer Science and Information Technology,
University of Sumer, Dhi-Qar, Iraq
[5]*Department of Industrial Engineering, Marmara University, Istanbul, Turkey
[6]*Faculty of Electrical Engineering, University of Babylon, Babylon, Iraq

Abstract

The Internet of Things (IoT) has a huge influence on the modern world and how the Internet communicates with it. In order to allow IoT networks, the wireless sensor network (WSN) is a promising wireless communication system. These networks, however, have limited energy (battery) resources and energy savings in these networks have become a pressing need and growing efforts have been made to reduce energy consumption by efficient routing, transmission methods, aggregation techniques, etc. Aggregation and transmission of data are considered as the main reasons for energy consumption by WSNs and IoT devices. These devices waste some of their energy in processing and transmitting redundant and unnecessary data. Therefore, this chapter presents means to eliminate redundant data and consequently reduce the number of data transmissions. Consequently, energy consumption of the IoT device is reduced. The chapter also includes a remote monitoring system for the end-user that can track and check the performance of these smart objects during the real-time communication.

Keywords: Internet of Things (IoT), wireless sensor networks (WSN), remote monitoring system, energy efficiency, data management

Corresponding author: l.al-bayati@mmu.ac.uk

SK Hafizul Islam and Debabrata Samanta (eds.) Smart Healthcare System Design: Security and Privacy Aspects, (235–264) © 2021 Scrivener Publishing LLC

10.1   Introduction

In daily life, the Internet of Things (IoT) is becoming increasingly ubiquitous, linked to an ever-greater range of diverse physical objects [1]. Wireless sensor networks (WSNs) are at the heart of the IoT [2]. For allowing IoT apps, it is one of the most promising wireless communication systems. The IoT and WSNs' main vision is to link a large number of smart devices together in numerous interconnected and automated networks, making the Internet much more useful [3]. It is a futuristic model where all possible devices can communicate with each other regardless of their scale, processing power and network connectivity, in a seamless environment [3]. Via sensing, data harnessing and decision-making, applications are smart, often without human interference.

The uses of IoT and WSNs often require a dense deployment of sensor nodes over the area to be monitored [4]. Dense deployment will often produce highly related and redundant data which need to be processed for redundancy checks and routed appropriately in a single or multi-hop manner to the ultimate receiver [5]. Sensor nodes normally rely on limited battery power and each sensor is contained three main parts, sensing unit, computing unit and communication unit [6]. All three units require power for operation. According to an investigation by Ref. [7], the communication unit uses 60% of the energy available, and the sensing unit consumes 30%. As a result, transmitting multiple copies of the same packet consumes proportionally more energy and leads to reduce the network lifetime. Thus, adopting a suitable aggregation method that allows the connected devices to sense useful data and share only these data when required is highly recommended.

In this chapter, as an example of the many industries that use real-time networks to promote the operation of manufacturing processes is discussed [8]. We choose a gas turbine engine blade as an application of the IoT to sense, forward and monitor data over the internet, based on the cloud infrastructure. The objective of this chapter is to filter and eliminate redundant data, decrease the data transmitted, and reduce the amount of data transmitted over the network. This should improve energy efficiency and performance of the entire system. It also proposes a real-time monitoring system that allows the end-user to interrogate the transmitted data and quickly check the machine's condition in real-time.

10.2   Network Configuration

This section provides a description of a suitable aggregation technique to reduce the data redundancy of a typical IoT monitoring system. A distributed software and hardware system are developed that can sense the analog data via sensors from the blade of the gas turbine engine and forward it to a Raspberry Pi (RasPi) through a Custard Pi (CPi). The RasPi is one of the key learning platforms for IoT. It provides a complete operating system (i.e., Raspbian Linux, Windows, Android, IoT Core, etc.) in a tiny platform for a very low cost [9] and was used as an IoT device for this study.

However, RasPi does not have any analog input to read the data from sensors [4] and the CPi was used to convert the data from analog to digital. After that, the RasPi processed and filtered data redundancy and then forwarded digital information to the end-user via a cloud infrastructure over an IP network. The use of the RasPi should, in effect, reduce the overall resources usage and improve the efficiency of the overall network. The functions of the various components and software are explained below and shown in Figure 10.1.

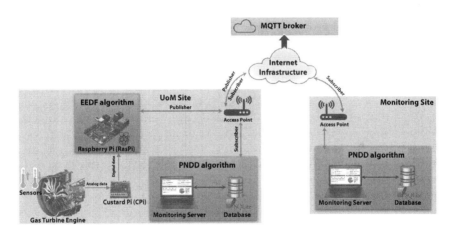

Figure 10.1 Overview of system architecture.

The overall system is contained in two main parts. The first part is located at the University of Manchester (UoM). It includes the test section (water rig) which simulates the blade of a gas turbine engine. The reason for using water as the working fluid is that due to the lower kinematic viscosity of water compared to air, high Reynolds and rotation numbers can be achieved at lower velocities [10]. The test section had six sensors positioned randomly in different locations of the test section to detect the flowrate of the water and provide data to the publisher device (RasPi) through the CPi board. The RasPi collects and processes these data based on the energy-efficient data forward (EEDF) policy and then transmits to the hosted message broker (MQTT) over the internet.

The second part of the system is located at the monitoring site and contains the subscriber device (monitoring server) and database to receive the data that comes from the MQTT broker, and to store it on the monitoring server database using the predictive non-dispatch data (PNDD) algorithm. The PNDD protocol also provides a real-time plotting system to the end-user on the monitoring server.

Figure 10.2 shows the data flow direction in each part of the system. The system includes several subsystems and protocols that manipulate the data to share and communicate with each other, each will be explained in detail below.

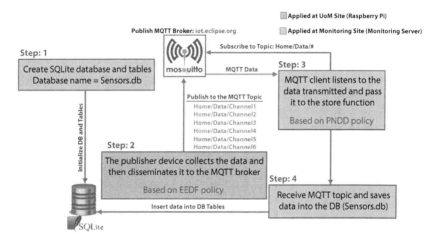

Figure 10.2 Schematic diagram of the proposed system.

10.2.1   Message Queuing Telemetry Transport (MQTT) Protocol

MQTT is one of the most commonly used protocols in IoT applications [4]. It was originally created and developed by the IBM company. It is an ISO standard based on the publish/subscribe (pub/sub) communication pattern. MQTT works on the top of the TCP/IP protocol which can carry a sequence of nearly 256 MB of data, usually adding a fixed header of 2 B to most payloads [11, 12]. The main purpose of MQTT is to reduce the burden of IoT constrained devices for sending/receiving messages. These devices usually have limited memory, power, bandwidth and processing unit. Figure 10.3 express an example of MQTT protocol u Q1 se-case with different topics and clients.

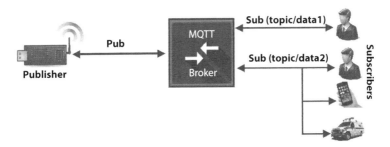

Figure 10.3 An example of MQTT protocol use-case with different topics and clients.

There are three kinds of actors in the pub/sub architecture system; publisher, broker and subscriber [4]. A publisher device sends the messages identified by a specific topic to the broker. Then, the broker forwards these messages to every subscriber device interested in that topic. A broker handles all messages passing from the publisher to subscriber devices. There are no standard topics for the MQTT protocol. The publisher can define any topic with one or more subscribers.

MQTT protocol supports a hierarchical topic name-space [13]. The subscription topics consist of one or more topic levels. Each level is separated by a forward slash "/" as shown below:

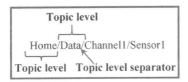

Two wild cards characters are supported for subscriptions to hierarchical topics as described below [14]:

- Single Level Wild-card (+): presents one topic level of the hierarchy and uses the character "+" between delimiters, for instance:

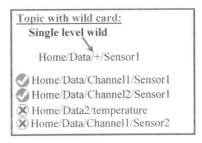

- Multi-Level Wild-card (#): covers many topic levels. The character # shows the multi-level wild card in the topic. It must be placed as the last character in the topic and is preceded by the character "/".

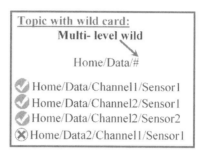

The MQTT protocol supports three possible quality of service (QoS) values concerning the guarantee of delivering a packet between publisher and subscriber devices. The QoS level implementations for the MQTT protocol are [4, 14]:

- QoS (0), at most once: is the simplest, fastest mode method of transfer with lowest overhead. The sender simply publishes the message to the broker; there are no acknowledgement packets between the publisher and the broker. Therefore, there is no guarantee of message delivery. Figure 10.4 shows Quality of service (0) of MQTT.

Figure 10.4 Quality of service (0) of MQTT.

- QoS (1), at least once: delivers the messages at least once to the receiver. The sender forwards the message and waits for an acknowledgement (PUBACK) packet from the broker. This level guarantees that the data will be forwarded successfully to the broker. However, the message may reach the broker more than once. Figure 10.5 represents Quality of service (1) of MQTT.

Figure 10.5 Quality of service (1) of MQTT.

- QoS (2), exactly once: is the highest and safest level of MQTT services. This level guarantees that the message will be received once by the broker. There is a sequence of four messages (a four-part handshake) between the sender and MQTT broker. When the handshake messages have been completed, both the sender and receiver have confirmed that the data was sent exactly once. Figure 10.6 projects Quality of service (2) of MQTT.

Figure 10.6 Quality of service (2) of MQTT.

Because the MQTT protocol consumes less power and is faster than the HTTP, many systems use the MQTT instead of the HTTP protocol as the core of data transportation [4]. Therefore, in this study, the MQTT protocol has been selected to control the IoT device (RasPi) through the internet. Furthermore, the experiment results in Ref. [15] revealed that the QoS (2) has less packets loss rate than QoS (0) and QoS (1). Therefore, the QoS (2) was selected for this study in order to receive the data exactly once.

Most MQTT brokers do not have any built-in technique to store MQTT client data permanently into the database. If the connection between sender and broker is QoS (0) then the data does not need to be stored, and the messages are delivered to only the currently active and connected subscribers [16]. When the connection is QoS (1), the messages often have to be stored temporarily on the broker if the subscriber is online. However, the message is stored for longer if the subscriber is offline or the retain flag is on the message [16]. However, if QoS (2) is selected then the messages are stored in the broker for a period of time until the transaction is fully committed [16]. For these reasons, a database must be installed on the monitoring server to store the data sent by the publisher device.

10.2.2   Embedded Database SQLite

SQLite is an open source and extremely lightweight relational database considered the most widely used of all database engines [17]. It was written by D. Richard in 2000 using C-language. SQLite is used by several web browsers in common use (e.g., Safari), operating systems (e.g., Windows 8, Windows 10), and in embedded systems (e.g., mobile phones). It is faster than other popular client/server SQL database engines such as MySQL, Oracle, etc. for most common operations [4]. SQLite is a zero-configuration which means no complex setup is needed and it supports terabyte-size databases. Therefore, it was selected as an embedded database for monitoring server storage.

10.2.3   Eclipse Paho Library

"Paho project was created to provide scalable opensource client implementations of open and standard message protocols aimed at new, existing, and emerging applications for IoT" [18]. Paho initially began publishing/subscribing client implementations for use on embedded platforms with MQTT. On various platforms and programming languages, such as Python, Java, C, C++, etc. [18], Paho client libraries are available. Paho client programming is being done in Python for this analysis.

10.2.4   Raspberry Pi Single Board Computer

RasPi is a tiny and affordable microcomputer based on the Raspbian Linux operating system [4]. It comes in different models ranging from RasPi1 A (first produced in 2013) to RasPi4 B (first produced in 2019). This study used model RasPi3 B because it is cheaper than other models and still suitable for our purpose. It includes 512 MB of RAM and an ARM1176JZF-S 700 MHz processor [9].

Figure 10.7 shows the RasPi board. The board does not support with a built-in hard disk and so relies on a micro secure digital (SD) card for running the operating system and long-term storage. It also uses a 5-Volt power supply with recommended input current of 700 mA. The unit offers less complexity and better solutions than other IoT platforms for monitoring IoT devices. In this research, the RasPi is used as an example of an

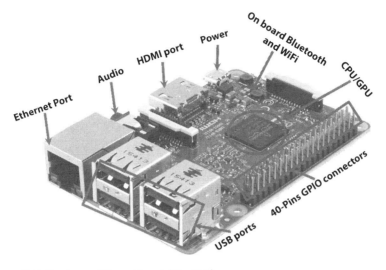

Figure 10.7 Raspberry Pi board (model RasPi B).

IoT device to collect the data from six sensors deployed in the test section, then to process information, and send this information to the end-user (monitoring server).

The output of these sensors is voltages, and the RasPi converts the output data into pressure using the digital manometer and Equation (10.1). For a given voltage (V, milli-volts), the pressure (p, mbar) is given by:

$$\text{Pressure (P)} = (261.95 * V) - 129.96 \qquad (10.1)$$

Where V is the aggregated data from a single sensor. The RasPi was integrated with Wi-Fi, ethernet port and Adafruit IO as an IoT platform. It also included USB ports, general purpose input/output (GPIO) pins to interface with LEDs, high definition multimedia interface (HDMI) port, and others. The digital manometer device includes calibration facilities and can be used to measure low-pressures [4].

10.2.5 Custard Pi Add-On Board

The CPi board is a range of cards that connect to the GPIO pins of the RasPi to provide a variety of options [19]. The RasPi GPIO does not support any analog inputs and thus, CPi was added. The CPi has 8 analog channels with 12-bit analog-to-digital (ADC). The CPi 1 and 2 use non-stackable connectors. Hence, once the board is fitted into the RasPi, nothing else can be plugged into the GPIO connectors. However, the CPi3, 4 and 5 does use stackable connectors which means that other boards can access the GPIO pins if required. CPi 6 uses a ribbon cable to transfer the data and is too large to plug into the RasPi [19]. The current study used CPi 3A. The board simply plugs into the 26-way (RasPi B) GPIO connector. The LED is fitted on the board and supplied with the 3.3 V to confirm correct plug-in. The RasPi is protected from accidental connection of a high voltage by the use of an analog to digital chip connected to the SPI bus using MCP3208 IC. Each analog input is 2.5 V per channel in single-ended mode. Easy to connect crew terminals are supplied for the 8 channels for the external sensors. The CPi3A unit is shown in Figure 10.8.

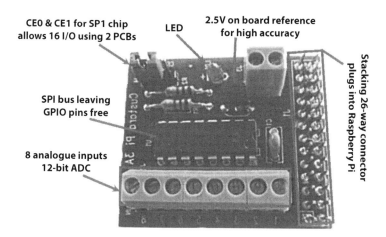

Figure 10.8 Custard Pi 3A.

10.2.6   Pressure Transmitter (Type 663)

The Huba Control Type 663 pressure level transmitter, see Figure 10.9, has calibrated and temperature compensated sensor signals output as a voltage [20]. Sensor sensitivity/accuracy is largely unaffected by temperature, because each sensor automatically compensates for surrounding temperatures in range −20 to 70 °C [20]. You can directly link the pre-amplified linear voltage output signal to an electronic control system. This study used six pressure transmitter sensors to collect data from the test section. Each sensor is positioned in a different place in the test section and connected to an individual channel via the CPi board. The pressure transmitters read the pressure values and forwards them to the RasPi via the CPi.

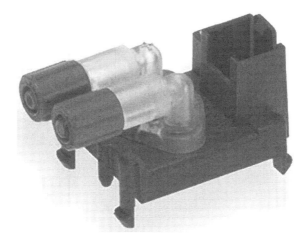

Figure 10.9 Huba type 663 differential pressure transmitter.

10.3 Data Filtering and Predicting Processes

This study aims to reduce redundant data transmissions and thus help minimize energy consumption of the IoT device (RasPi), to help minimize transmission delay, amount of data and bandwidth used over the entire network (i.e., from publisher to the subscriber device) [21]. The proposed work also provides a real-time remote monitoring system to the end-user that allows checking and tracking of the status of the IoT-device. In such a study, the data aggregation is generally divided into two stages. The first stage is called the energy-efficient data forward (EEDF) algorithm. While the second stage is called the predicted non-dispatch data (PNDD) algorithm. The EEDF protocol senses, filters and forwards the data by RasPi to the MQTT broker. However, the PNDD protocol predicts and receives the data from the MQTT broker and then stores and plots these data on the monitoring server. The EEDF and PNDD algorithms were written in Python and implemented in the RasPi and monitoring server, respectively.

In the following sub-sections, further details about the proposed algorithms are described by highlighting their techniques and strategies.

10.3.1 Filtering Process

The first purpose of the EEDF algorithm is to sense the analog data from the six sensors connected to the RasPi via the CPi. The RasPi is required to establish a connection with the MQTT broker before the actual data communication begins. Any device that is linked to the network and establishes the connection with the MQTT broker requires an MQTT client. Therefore, an MQTT client is installed on both publisher (RasPi) and subscriber devices (monitoring server) to connect, disconnect, publish and subscribe data. The RasPi must specify a topic to publish data to the MQTT broker, and only the device that is subscribing to the same specified topic can receive that data from the MQTT broker. By establishing connections between the RasPi and the MQTT broker based on MQTT QoS (2), the important decisions taken are based on the EEDF algorithm.

Each sensor senses 7 B of data, obtained by sensing events from the test section. Thus, the total data gathered by all sensors is 42 B. It is now proposed that the EEDF algorithm also checks and compares simultaneously collected data with the previous record for each sensor individually. If the collected data in each sensor is not equal to the previous record, then it is sent to the broker via the internet. Otherwise, the EEDF protocol detects no change in the data and then filters the duplicated data out and thus this data is not sent to the broker. As a result, the RasPi antenna goes into sleep mode. Of course, in the first round, all the collected data is sent to the broker because there is no previous data record for comparison. As a result, the proposed scheme minimizes the processing and transmission time for the RasPi. This, in turn, helps minimize the energy consumption of the RasPi. It also reduces the delay time and bandwidth used over the entire path of the network and improves the performance of the end-to-end system. The flowchart of the proposed algorithm to sense and forward the data is presented in Figure 10.10.

10.3.2   Predicting Process

The first concern of the PNDD protocol is to establish the connection between the monitoring server and MQTT broker based on MQTT QoS (2). When the QoS (2) process is complete, the connection is created and the monitoring server can communicate with the MQTT broker and receive messages. However, the PNDD algorithm requires a database to store the data that comes from the MQTT broker. Therefore, SQLite was installed on the monitoring server to store, analyze and plot the data.

After that, the PNDD protocol listens to the MQTT broker and gets a copy of the data forwarded by RasPi. The transmitted data could be a number of bytes or an empty row based on the EEDF publisher policy. The PNDD algorithm receives and stores the empty row of data when there is a connection between monitoring server and RasPi through the MQTT broker, but no data is received (data filtered by EEDF algorithm). Otherwise,

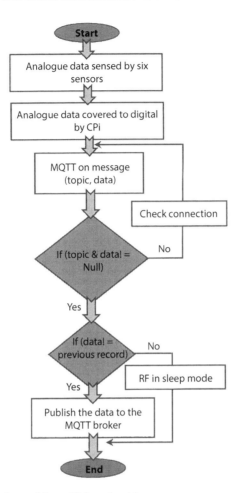

Figure 10.10 Flow chart of the publisher algorithm.

the PNDD algorithm stores the transmitted data (payload) in the monitoring server database.

Real-time plotting plays a significant role in the diagnostics of any remote monitoring system. Thus, the PNDD protocol provides the end-user with a real-time plotting system for further processing and diagnosing the information. The PNDD algorithm predicts and retrieves data when it is required. If the collected data in the database is not equal to the empty row data, then it plots the current data. Otherwise, it plots the previous record as the new data. As a result, the PNDD protocol reduces the capacity required to store information. The flowchart of the PNDD protocol is shown in Figure 10.11.

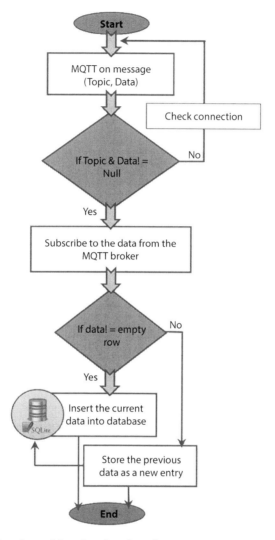

Figure 10.11 Flow chart of the subscriber algorithm.

10.3.3   Remote Monitoring Systems

IoT has gained considerable popularity and is widely applied in many fields, but different devices using various sensors are utilized for monitoring activities [22]. These sensors collect data and use that data to trigger automatic alerts and actions such as maintenance requests, remote diagnostics and other optional processes [23, 24].

Thus, this chapter, in addition to a filtering mechanism also proposes a remote monitoring system for a gas turbine engine in an IoT environment.

The system aims to monitor and diagnose the condition of the gas turbine engine, sensors and IoT device (RasPi). Here, the RasPi acts as the gateway, connecting the sensors to the internet. The data is gathered by the six sensors and forwarded to the RasPi which uses its WiFi connectivity to establish the connection and disseminate the data to the monitoring server (end-user) based on the MQTT broker.

On the monitoring side, each item of data that is sent by each sensor requires the plotting of an individual sub-figure. Therefore, the end-user has a dashboard for displaying and analyzing the data for each sensor (see Figures 10.14 to 10.19). Based on these figures, the end-user can check the system status, sensors or RasPi for errors during real-time communication. For instance, the end-user checks the engine condition based on the x- and y-axes of the sub-figures. Should the RasPi experience connectivity issues or sensor stop sending data to the end-user, the sub-figure stops plotting the data. Thus, the end-user can see which sensor is faulty. Figure 10.12 presents the architecture of the proposed work which includes four main parts: engine, sensors, gateway (RasPi) and end-user.

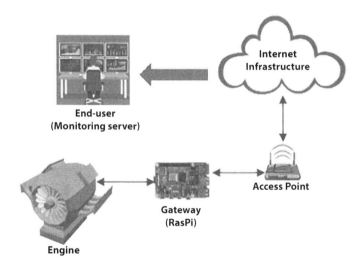

Figure 10.12 Remote monitoring system for gas turbine engine using IoT.

10.4 Experimental Setup

The experimental set-up to test the performance of the proposed algorithms for an IoT application is defined in this section. In Figure 10.13, the hardware is deployed. As the working medium, water is used and pumped from the tank into the test section. Six transmitter sensors measure the

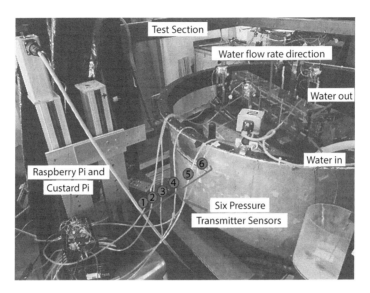

Figure 10.13 The experimental setup.

volume of the water flow rate. The sensors are interfaced and powered by the CPi. They are placed in different positions in the test section to sense and forward the data to the RasPi via the CPi. The CPi is linked to and powered by the RasPi. The RasPi is used to process and forward the data to the monitoring server via the cloud. The data is dispatched by the RasPi every 15 s. The network was tested for 25 min. The parameters and protocols used in the setup are shown in Table 10.1.

Here the RasPi is mains powered, but in a real situation, it will most certainly be battery powered, i.e., resource-limited. To validate the reduced energy consumption, the measurements were made using a USB 3.0 LCD voltmeter ammeter voltage multimeter tester.

Table 10.1 A list of all parameters used in this study.

Parameter	Value
Type of IP	IPv4
Header Size + Payload	27 bytes
Type of MQTT-QoS used	2
RasPi B power	5-volt, 700 mA
RasPi to access point link	Wireless
Monitoring server to access point link	Wireless
Monitoring server operating system	Windows 8.1
RasPi B operating System	Raspbian

10.4.1   Implementation Using Python

After the hardware was connected and seen to be working correctly, the Python script file was constructed on the RasPi and monitoring server to read and receive the sensor values, respectively. The collected data was then forwarded to the MQTT broker via the internet. On the other hand, the monitoring server received and saved the transmitted data into the database table. In order to implement the proposed system, there are several requirements to be met:

10.4.1.1   Prerequisites

The inherent requirements of the proposed protocol are listed below [4]:

- *Python 2.7:* is installed in both devices; RasPi and the monitoring server which helps to read the sensor values, process and forward the data to the monitoring server. It also assisted in receiving, plotting and storing these data sets on the monitoring server database.
- *SQLite3 database:* is installed in the monitoring server and used to save the data on it. SQLite3 is integrated with Python using a Sqlite3 module. Thus, it did not require any further installation.
- *Python pip:* is a package management system which was used to install and manage software packages that were written in Python.
- *Paho MQTT Client:* is a lightweight publish and subscribe system that allows sending and receiving data as a client. It was installed in both RasPi and the monitoring server.
- *MQTT Broker:* helps to establish the connection and exchange information between the publisher and subscriber devices. The open service MQTT broker (iot.eclipse.org) was used in this study.
- *Python matplotlib:* is a Python library that draws graphs and plots the data during real-time communication. It was installed on the monitoring server.

10.4.2   Monitoring Data

Matplotlib is a plotting library for the Python programming language and was used to plot the collected data during the real-time communication on the monitoring server. The Python script ran for 25 min on the monitoring server to plot figures in real-time.

Figures 10.14 to 10.19 show the graphic display of the data received from the six sensors.

Each figure presents the data from a particular sensor, and each has three panels. In each case, the uppermost panel, labeled (a), presents the actual data gathered by the sensor. Because the sensors were deployed in different locations in the test section, each sensor measured a slightly different pressure than the other sensors. The middle panel, labeled (b), presents the data published, transmitted from the RasPi to the monitoring server based on EEDF policy. The EEDF protocol eliminated the continuous reading of similar data and drops these data before published it to the MQTT broker. The bottom panel, labeled (c), shows typical data collected from the MQTT broker and retrieved to the original data collected, based on the PNDD algorithm.

To assess how accurately, reliably and economically the PNDD algorithm reproduced the original date we compare, for each sensor, panels (a) and (c) in Figures 10.14 to 10.19.

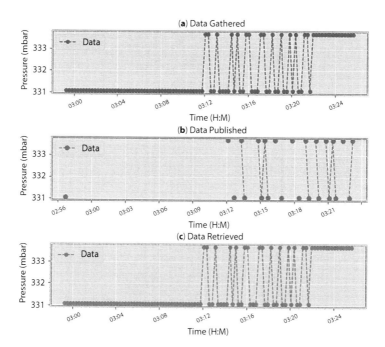

Figure 10.14 Data from sensor 1.

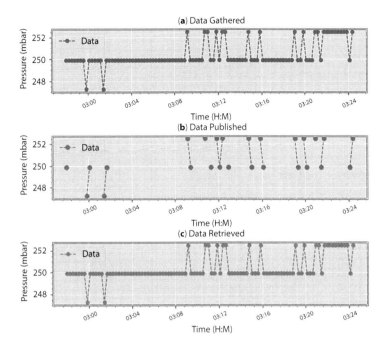

Figure 10.15 Data from sensor 2.

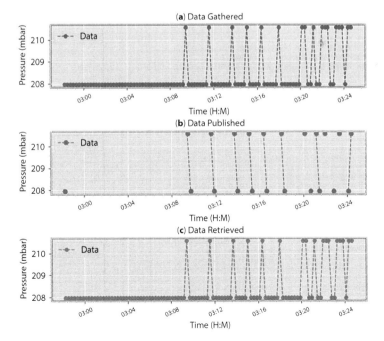

Figure 10.16 Data from sensor 3.

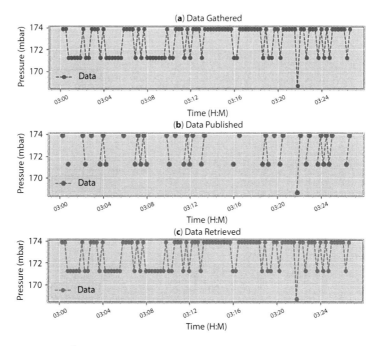

Figure 10.17 Data from sensor 4.

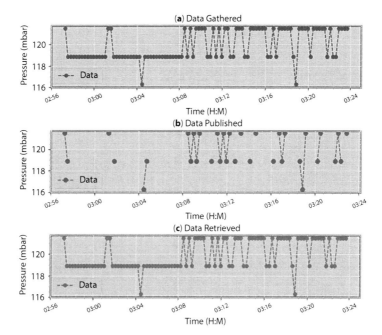

Figure 10.18 Data from sensor 5.

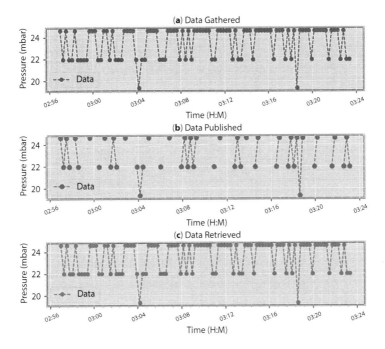

Figure 10.19 Data from sensor 6.

10.4.3   Experimental Results

This section introduces the experimental results obtained by using the proposed algorithms. This section is divided into two sub-sections. In the first, we explain the outcomes of the proposed scheme for IoT device, and in the second, we introduce the outcomes for a traditional network.

10.4.3.1   IoT Device Results

It is clear from Figures 10.14 to 10.19 that use of the energy-efficient data forward (EEDF) and the predicted non-dispatch data (PNDD) algorithms reduced data redundancy which reduced the number of data transmissions. This had a positive impact on the overall energy consumption of the publisher device, (RasPi) as shown in Figure 10.20. It is obvious from this figure, when the proposed EEDF algorithm is implemented, that the energy consumed by each sensor is far less than without algorithm. However, with the algorithm in use we see that each sensor consumes a different amount energy. This is because of the data

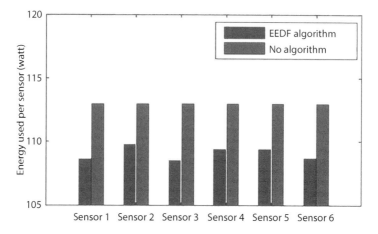

Figure 10.20 Total energy consumed by each sensor with and without the proposed algorithm.

redundancy is different for each node. It is also shown, without the algorithm that not only was the energy usage higher, but it was higher for every sensor node. This was because the RasPi sent all the data gathered without any filtering.

The total network energy is the total energy used by each sensor for each transmission, see Figure 10.21. This figure presents a comparison between using the EEDF protocol and no-protocol scenario in terms of overall energy wasting. We see a 3.5% reduction in total energy exhaustion with the addition of the proposed algorithm which would lead to prolong network lifetime.

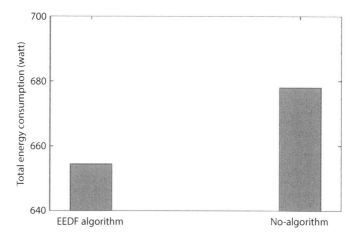

Figure 10.21 The overall energy consumption in the system with and without the proposed algorithm.

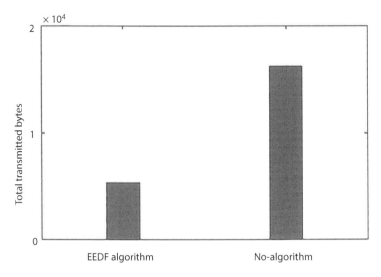

Figure 10.22 Total bytes transmitted by RasPi with and without the proposed algorithms.

In Figure 10.22, the no-algorithm scenario, the transmitted packets by RasPi require 27 B. This includes the IPv4 header which is 20 B plus the payload of each sensor (7 B). By calculating the overall value for six sensors for 25 min, the RasPi transmitted 16,200 B of data. However, when the proposed algorithm was implemented the number of bytes sent by the RasPi could be calculated based on the redundant data gathered by each sensor that would be removed by the proposed algorithm. The proposed technique significantly reduces the total data transmitted by up to 76%, and correspondingly reduces the volume of data traffic on the network. Furthermore, Figure 10.23 shows that the proposed scheme also reduces data storage in both the cloud and monitoring server. It is seen from this figure that the data storage is reduced by 80% when the proposed new forms of the EEDF and PNDD algorithms are implemented.

10.4.3.2   Traditional Network Results

The literature review revealed that IoT devices substantially increase the volume of data transmitted over the internet [25]. These data are routed via the existing traditional network infrastructure, and it is important to minimize network traffic load, bandwidth and storage on the traditional networks to meet the requirements for the expected growth in IoT devices.

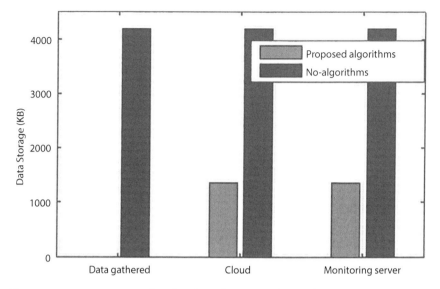

Figure 10.23 Data storage with and without the proposed algorithm.

This study proposes reducing data transmissions which could lead to significantly reducing the processing time and bandwidth used in the overall network (i.e., from publisher to subscriber device via MQTT broker). In this chapter, the traceroute command is applied in the RasPi and monitoring server using traceroute and tracert commands, respectively (see Figures 10.24 and 10.25). This command is used to determine the number of intermediate routers which are required in the transmission process from the source to the ultimate receiver.

Figure 10.26 shows the difference between the total number of transmitted bytes with and without implementing the proposed algorithms. The calculation of the number of devices was achieved in two stages: the first stage was from the RasPi to the MQTT broker, and the second stage was from the monitoring server to the MQTT broker, and was based on Figures 10.24 and 10.25. The summation of both stages gives the total number of devices which took part in the communication between the RasPi and the monitoring server. The total transmitted bytes were calculated as the total number of devices x total number of transmitted bytes of

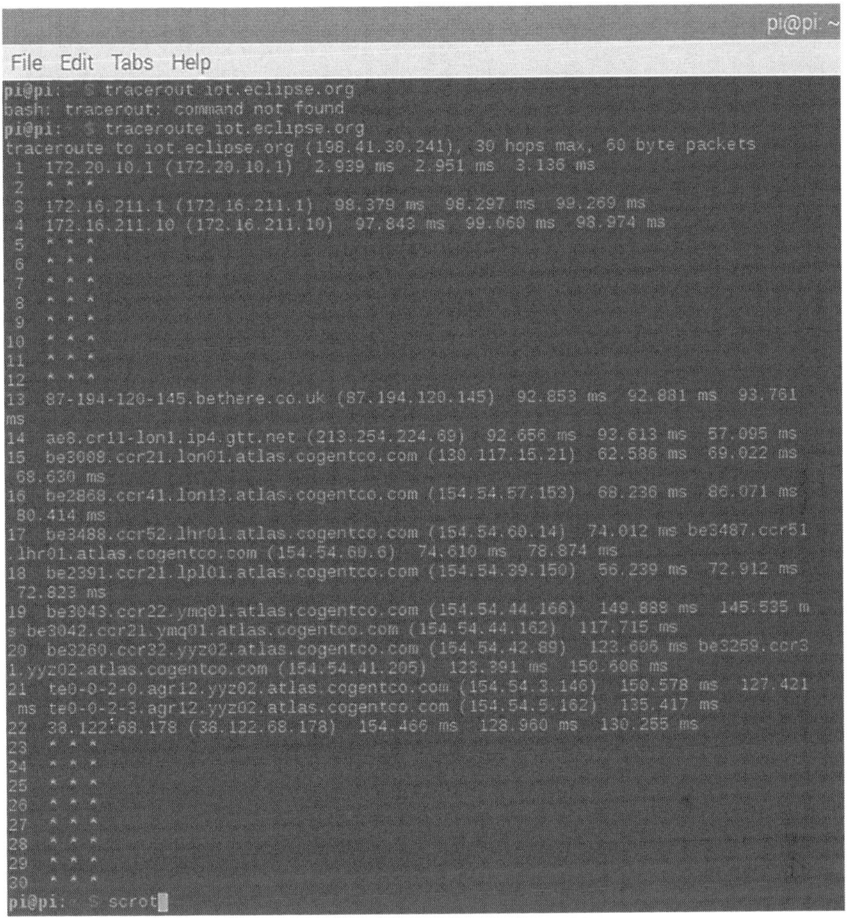

Figure 10.24 Traceroute command in Linux.

each sensor. Figure 10.26 presents the overall number of transmitted bytes falls by approximately two-third with the implementation of the proposed EEDF and PNDD algorithms. This would be a means that using the proposed development would substantially reduce the amount of data, bandwidth used, processing time in each device on the transmission path over the entire network.

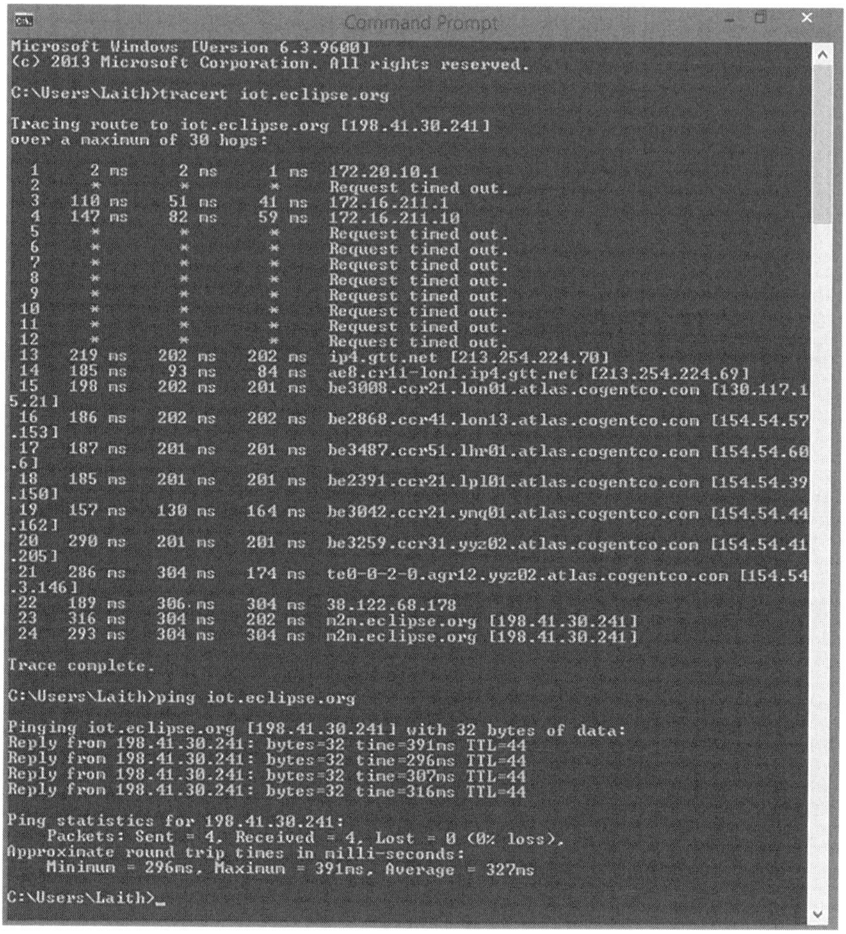

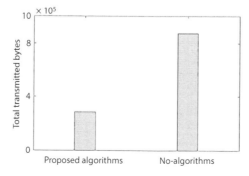

Figure 10.25 Traceroute command in Windows.

Figure 10.26 Total number of transmitted bytes from the RasPi to the monitoring server with and without the proposed algorithms.

10.5   Conclusion

Redundant data increases the unwanted/unnecessary communication and processing of data which consumes energy and reduces network lifetime. Here a proposed method for more efficient data transmission has been presented for IoT-based real-time monitoring and communication networks. The proposed method reduces the communication costs sending/receiving unnecessary data and removes redundant data transmission.

The test system was divided into two phases: Phase 1 involves six sensors to gather the data from the test section and forward it to the RasPi B. The RasPi filtered and performed data redundancy checks before sending the data to the end-user via the MQTT broker. It only sends data acquired from the sensors after removing redundant data. Phase 2 listens to the data that comes from the RasPi via the MQTT broker and predicts the data which was eliminated by the RasPi. Simulation results confirmed that the proposed scheme outperformed the no-algorithm protocol, minimizing the energy consumption, database storage, and total bytes transmitted by approximately 3.5, 80 and 76%, respectively. The proposed system also provided the end-user with a remote monitoring system that can periodically track and check the performance of the smart objects based on published and subscribed data.

The EEDF and PNDD protocols developed here have been successfully demonstrated using RasPi B device in a controlled environment. It is judged that the proposed technique would be valuable if implemented in a remote monitoring scenario for mission-critical applications with a huge number of battery-powered nodes with limited network connectivity.

References

1. Hammoudeh, M., Al-Fayez, F., Lloyd, H., Newman, R., Adebisi, B., Bounceur, A., and Abuarqoub, A., A wireless sensor network border monitoring system: Deployment issues and routing protocols. *IEEE Sens. J.*, 17, 8, 2572–2582, 2017.
2. Farhan, L. and Kharel, R., Internet of things: Vision, future directions and opportunities, in: *Modern Sensing Technologies*, pp. 331–347, Springer, Cham, 2019.
3. Stallings, W., *Foundations of modern networking: SDN, NFV, QoE, IoT, and Cloud*, Addison-Wesley Professional, New Jersey, US, 2015.
4. Farhan, L.K., *Energy Efficiency in Green Internet of Things (IoT) Networks*, Doctoral dissertation, Manchester Metropolitan University, Manchester Metropolitan University, UK, 2020.

5. Abuarqoub, A., Hammoudeh, M., Adebisi, B., Jabbar, S., Bounceur, A., Al-Bashar, H., Dynamic clustering and management of mobile wireless sensor networks. *Comput. Networks*, 117, 62–75, 2017.

6. Brohi, A.M., Malkani, Y.A., Chandio, M.S., Data provenance in Wireless Sensor Networks (WSNs): A review. *2018 International Conference on Computing, Mathematics and Engineering Technologies (iCoMET)*, pp. 1–5, 2018.

7. Shabna, V.C., Jamshid, K., Kumar, S.M., Energy minimization by removing data redundancy in wireless sensor networks. *2014 International Conference on Communication and Signal Processing*, pp. 1658–1663, 2014.

8. Hammoudeh, M., Newman, R., Dennett, C., Mount, S., Aldabbas, O., Map as a service: A framework for visualising and maximising information return from multi-modal wireless sensor networks. *Sensors*, 15, 9, 22970–23003, 2015.

9. Deshmukh, A.D. and Shinde, U.B., A low cost environment monitoring system using raspberry Pi and arduino with Zigbee. *2016 International Conference on Inventive Computation Technologies (ICICT)*, vol. 3, pp. 1–6, 2016.

10. Abdulsattar, F., Cooper, D., Iacovides, H., Zhang, S., Turbulent Flow Development inside a Rotating Two-Pass Square Duct with Porous Blocks. *23rd ISABE Conference*, Manchester, United Kingdom, 2017.

11. Atmoko, R.A. and Yang, D., Online Monitoring & Controlling Industrial Arm Robot Using MQTT Protocol. *2018 IEEE International Conference on Robotics, Biomimetics, and Intelligent Computational Systems (Robionetics)*, pp. 12–16, 2018.

12. Farhan, L., Kharel, R., Kaiwartya, O., Quiroz-Castellanos, M., Raza, U., Teay, S.H., LQOR: Link quality-oriented route selection on Internet of Things networks for green computing. *2018 11th International Symposium on Communication Systems, Networks & Digital Signal Processing (CSNDSP)*, pp. 1–6, 2018.

13. Dizdarević, J., Carpio, F., Jukan, A., Masip-Bruin, X., A survey of communication protocols for internet of things and related challenges of fog and cloud computing integration. *ACM Comput. Surv. (CSUR)*, 51, 6, 1–29, 2019.

14. Quality of Service 0,1 & 2—MQTT Essentials. https://www.hivemq.com/blog/mqtt-essentials-part-6-mqtt-quality-of-service-levels, 2019.

15. Lee, S., Kim, H., Hong, D.K., Ju, H., Correlation analysis of MQTT loss and delay according to QoS level. *The International Conference on Information Networking 2013 (ICOIN)*, pp. 714–717, 2013.

16. Al-Joboury, I.M. and Al-Hemiary, E.H., F2CDM: Internet of Things for Healthcare Network Based Fog-to-Cloud and Data-in-Motion Using MQTT Protocol. *International Symposium on Ubiquitous Networking*, Springer, Cham, pp. 368–379, 2017.

17. Qinlong, G., Xingmei, C., Weiwei, T., Minghai, Y., Study and application of SQLite embedded database system based on windows CE. *The 2nd*

International Conference on Information Science and Engineering, pp. 6920–6923, 2010.

18. Sinha, A., Sharma, S., Mahboob, M.R., An Internet of Things based prototype for smart appliance control. *2017 International Conference on Computing, Communication and Automation (ICCCA)*, pp. 1358–1363, 2017.

19. Custard Pi 3A. http://www.sf-innovations.co.uk/custard-pi-3.html, 2019.

20. Relative, absolute and differential pressure transmitter 663. http://www.sts-italia.it/2011/pdf/663.pdf, 2019.

21. Farhan, L. and Kharel, R., Internet of things scalability: communications and data management. *Mod. Sens. Technol.*, 311–329, 2019.

22. Farhan, L., Alzubaidi, L., Abdulsalam, M., Abboud, A.J., Hammoudeh, M., Kharel, R., An efficient data packet scheduling scheme for Internet of Things networks. *2018 1st International Scientific Conference of Engineering Sciences-3rd Scientific Conference of Engineering Science (ISCES)*, pp. 1–6, 2018.

23. Raju, H.S. and Shenoy, S., Real-time remote monitoring and operation of industrial devices using IoT and cloud. *2016 2nd International Conference on Contemporary Computing and Informatics (IC3I)*, pp. 324–329, 2016.

24. Farhan, L., Alissa, A.E., Shukur, S.T., Hammoudeh, M., Kharel, R., An energy efficient long hop (LH) first scheduling algorithm for scalable Internet of Things (IoT) networks. *2017 Eleventh International Conference on Sensing Technology (ICST)*, pp. 1–6, 2017.

25. Beecks, C., Grass, A., Devasya, S., Metric indexing for efficient data access in the Internet of Things. *2018 IEEE International Conference on Big Data (Big Data)*, pp. 5132–5136, 2018.

11

IoT in the Current Times and its Prospective Advancements

T. Venkat Narayana Rao[1], Abhishek Duggirala[1], Muralidhar Kurni[2]*
and Syed Tabassum Sultana[3]

*[1]Department of Computer Science and Engineering, Sreenidhi Institute of Science
and Technology, Hyderabad, India
[2]Department of CSE, Anantha Lakshmi Institute of Technology & Sciences,
Ananthapuram, India
[3]Matrusri Institute of Post Graduate Studies, Hyderabad, India*

Abstract

IoT has opened a huge portal of possibilities where every gadget or thing can be connected on the internet to participate in data exchange. Presently, it is used across a wide spectrum of applications like irrigation and other agricultural activities, retail, healthcare, smart vehicles, and so on. IoT has encountered several drawbacks in terms of security, data storage, and efficiency, which led to several companies thinking twice before incorporating IoT into their projects. Data on the cloud is more often than not compromised, and with the increasing number of users and devices on the internet, data management is inefficient. However, these drawbacks are being rectified as new ways of using IoT are taking shape. In the coming decades, the world awaits several advancements that will gracefully improve the existing systems; for instance, the introduction of edge computing will transubstantiate cloud computing by minimizing the technicalities, hence maintaining data privacy rightful usage of bandwidth. The future of IoT is quite promising, what with its growing popularity and consistent improvement, it's destined to pave a new way of technological development. This chapter focuses on the current trends in IoT, its limitations, and the scope for future advancements.

Keywords: Internet of Things (IoT), Industrial IoT (IIoT), Industry 4.0, applications of IIoT, challenges, advancements

Corresponding author: muralidhar.kurni@gmail.com

SK Hafizul Islam and Debabrata Samanta (eds.) Smart Healthcare System Design: Security and Privacy Aspects, (265–280) © 2021 Scrivener Publishing LLC

11.1   Introduction

11.1.1   Introduction to Industry 4.0

The evolution of technology and industrialization through industrial revolutions has changed how the various industries function [1]. First, the first industrial revolution was introduced to water and steam power, revolutionizing hydropower. Later in the second industrial revolution, electric energy took shape. The third revolution witnessed electronics and information technology. With the advent of the fourth industrial revolution termed Industry 4.0, cyber-physical systems are taking shape [2], aiming for an advanced manufacturing and production process through reliable and efficient communication of raw materials and machines. Taking automation to the next level through intelligent factories is a vision of this industrial revolution [3]. In an attempt to converge both real and virtual worlds and make manufacturing and overall functioning of the various supply chains more productive, a fusion of IoT with the concepts of industry 4.0 is foreseen [4, 5].

11.1.2   Introduction to IoT

Today we live in a world where living beings are not the only ones to communicate with each other. When enabled with sensors and connected on the internet, things and devices communicate effortlessly to accomplish tasks together. A term coined to explain this technology is the internet of things. The essential part of communication is to have a network that enables data exchange from one device to another. IoT connects them in a network called the Internet.

There are countless applications of IoT [6], be it smart homes, smart cities, smart cars, etc. These applications are an implementation of a series of actions generated through effective data transfer between the nodes. For instance, when the temperature gets extremely hot, our brain sends a signal, which leads to a voluntary action of switching on a fan. The imitation of the same actions by a series of computational devices results in a smart application. With IoT, all of our activities can now be imitated efficiently. A technology like IoT can automate tasks and help make smart decisions, and with its exceeding usage and popularity, it is bound to transform how the world runs [7].

Numerous industries have incorporated it into their products and services. There have been disadvantages, as nodes connected on the internet could be vulnerable to cyber-attacks, compromising data security in the system [8]. However, it has been a constantly improving technology, opening doors to endless possibilities. This chapter reflects the current trends of IoT in various industries and explains its issues, and prospectively throws light on the scope of improvement that could multiply the applications of IoT in the future.

11.1.3   Introduction to IIoT

An interrelated automated network of machines that collaboratively function efficiently and carry out the production process, thereby reducing human effort and a human's involvement in the process, is called IIoT [9]. The IIoT fuses several concepts like big data, machine learning, etc., to collect data in the manufacturing process to enable communication between the machines, sensors, and products and hence automate the entire process [10]. The machines and computers work together with the IoT to give rise to tomorrow's intelligent factories [11].

11.2   How IIoT Advances Industrial Engineering in Industry 4.0 Era

Industrial engineering has gone through 4 phases so far [12]. The first phase being the first industrial revolution. It happened after the 1700s. This revolution brought in a change where manual labor, which included humans and animals, can be enhanced if people used the power-driven by steam and water and other tools driven by the hydropower.

In the early 20th century, the world witnessed the second industrial revolution wherein electricity was introduced, and so was steel. The advent of electricity greatly improved the mobility of the various machines, and this revolution was when mass production began. Assembly lines were also an invention from 2.0.

During the end of the 1950s, the third industrial revolution began [13]. Computers and electronic devices were used along with the manufacturing processes, which changed the dependence of factories on analog machinery and gave rise to the digital era.

Today, With the advent of Industry 4.0, a shift in manufacturing operations is bound to take place. With the inclusion of new technologies in industrial engineering like IIoT, Big Data, Machine learning, etc., smoother workflows across various industries are promised [14].

Industries have always seen it as a promising way to advance their operations like manufacturing and transportation. With IoT enabled systems, industries have incorporated effective ways of keeping track of their goods and monitoring them while being transported with efficient tracking mechanisms that it has made possible [15]. Over the years, several industrial enterprises have shifted their attention towards IoT enabled operations to reduce delivery time, maintain quality services, maintain a standard in production processes, and most importantly to cut down unnecessary costs. Remote production monitoring, logistic management, predictive repairing, and systematic asset management are just some of the many wonders contributing to the industries [16].

11.3 IoT and its Current Applications

The Internet of things has touched every industry that one can think of [17]. It has transformed the digital world's very functioning, welcoming the most inanimate objects into the digital realm. IoT has been trending since the beginning of the 21st century, and today, it is said that more than 120 new IoT gadgets are joining the internet per second. 2020 has seen more than 30 billion devices in use, and the numbers are only aimed to reach greater heights [18]. Initially, it was claimed to have been majorly focused on reducing human effort, but it has made way to some extremely essential advancements that played a crucial role in the most important industry, which is healthcare, with a count of almost 40% of the devices solely dedicated for healthcare [19]. Among the countless applications of this booming technology, there are some applications in current times that are worth knowing.

11.3.1 Home Automation

Today the world is witnessing an era of smart homes with overall control over various appliances that work together in creating a home that runs on automation. IoT has several applications, but the most popular of them all is Home automation. Controlling the climate, entertainment devices, and maintaining an economically viable home is briefly what it offers. Home security can also be ensured with various alarm and security cameras [5, 20].

The devices, when enabled with sensors, are connected to the internet. This network can be remotely controlled through a mobile phone; in other words, a user can now access all the applications at home even if he is away. To make the system smarter, these devices automatically set themselves by taking into account the data sensors collect [21]. For example, the room temperature is valuable data for automatically controlling air conditioners and fans in the room.

Some serious domestic disasters could occur in the absence of people at home. One such disaster could be a gas leak. Through IoT-enabled home automation, our homes can be protected from disastrous gas leaks. Using a GSM module, Arduino, and a sensor, detecting any leakage, sending instant notification via an SMS to the user can prevent a potential disaster.

11.3.2   Wearables

Smart bands, Smartwatches, Smart glasses, etc., have become an integral part of every individual today [22]. Although fulfilling fashionable purposes, these wearables are vital for sensing body data like pulse, body heat, and other important data that can provide instant biofeedback to the user. The sensors or microprocessors which are embedded in these wearables have the ability to send and receive data via the internet. Wearable technology has been booming for several years now, improving the health and fitness of people. These systems can be worn, or tattooed to the body, or embedded into clothing [23]. The wearables era began with fitness tracking watches called Fitbits, which further evolved to smarter applications over the years.

Although these wearables positively impacted the fashion industry, their focus has lately been on more practical uses. Pet tracking and child tracking devices, air quality and pollution hotspot detection wearables, heart and brain activity monitoring tattoos are just some of the many examples of wearable technology [24].

11.3.3   Connected Cars

Cars have been a revolutionary invention in the world. Today we observe two kinds of communication in cars. Car to infrastructure communication is one where all the sensors and controllers communicate data to the system to control the vehicle's brakes and speed [25].

Another interesting communication is a vehicle-to-vehicle communication, wherein all the sensors and other devices of a car are connected in a network to the neighboring car; this helps control the speed, avoid accidents and improve traffic conditions [26].

11.3.4   Smart Grid

With the advent of urbanization, power is always increasingly in demand. Power production, distribution, consumption, and overall analysis is made easy today through smart grids. Several European countries have implemented these techniques and have seen a massive improvement in controlling power consumption. The smart grids are an application of IoT because the data required for the system comes from IoT enabled sensors and devices that people use at home [27]. This data reflects on consumption, overall cost and helps understand which areas use more power. By evaluating this data, power supply chains can control and coordinate accordingly, involving the public as an active part of the process, utilizing the data extracted and distributing power efficiently.

Smart power meters are an example of IoT-enabled devices used in smart grids. These meters maintain communication between power suppliers and users and automate fault detection, collection of cost data, and other activities, making the power supply process more effective [28].

11.4   Application Areas of IIoT

11.4.1   IIoT in Healthcare

It has the potential to connect remote devices in a network for effective communication and data exchange, and this very aspect of it is why it can be of huge importance in advancing healthcare facilities of today. It can be a flexible alternative for several medical applications, including examining and keeping track of patients remotely, incorporating several devices like sensors and other medical equipment into the IoT networks to accomplish tasks gracefully, carry out fitness programs, and identify intensities illnesses, and many more. Using IoT as an alternative in medical care reduces doctors' effort and cost by simultaneously maintaining the quality of treatment [29].

For instance, let's take the example of one of the healthcare applications of IoT, M-health. M-health stands for mobile health, wherein data from patients is collected regularly and made available to a range of clients and doctors through a network. This will not only help keep track of a patient's health every day by obtaining data from various sensors and wearables, like heart rate data from smartwatches but could also help identify potential health anomalies that might arise [30].

11.4.2   IIoT in Mining

Besides the obvious benefits, it regulates operations in such a way as to ensure safety and carry out disaster forecasting for selective industries. One such example is the mining industry, which needs an effective communication system to ensure safety and predict any foreseen disasters underground. Sensors in the mine could provide data on the conditions inside, and body sensors can help monitor the miners' condition, thereby ensuring their safety throughout the mining process [31]. Although the right way of carrying out this process has not been figured out yet, given that the devices require power and protection from gases underground, research on the idea continues.

11.4.3   IIoT in Agriculture

Today agriculture is no more the traditional practice that people believe it is. Technologies like IoT have transformed the agricultural industry into a more precise, efficient, and data-driven industry. Preparing the soil to detect pests has opened endless opportunities for advancements with or without humans' involvement. The IoT-enabled systems assist farmers through all the stages of farming like sowing, harvesting, and even transporting the crop [32]. Unmanned surveillance of crops and the state-of-the-art optimizing techniques for crop yields are a reality today [33].

With the increasing population and an overall improvement of human life expectancy, the demand for food is bound to be higher every year, and it is now that we need efficient technologies the most to meet the demand [34]. Hence many countries have started using IoT-based techniques in crop production, foreseeing the crucial times ahead.

One of the most intriguing uses of IoT in agriculture is for pest monitoring and disease forecasting [35]. Generally, farmers spray pesticides beforehand to prevent pests, but this is a huge compromise on the crop's quality and the consumer's health. Therefore IoT-based systems have been introduced that proctor the crop through sensors, drones, and other equipment to detect pests. Through techniques like image processing coupled with IoT, these pests' images are uploaded on the cloud to gain a deeper knowledge about them and precisely activate the field robot to spray only to the specific plant [36]. This is just one of the many advantages these systems offer in the field of agriculture.

11.4.4   IIoT in Aerospace

IoT has entered the realm of aviation too. It promises faster arrival times, better passenger comfort, and overall efficiency. Through industrial, IoT airplanes are connected to detect the possible collisions in their paths beforehand and calculate better routes for each of them [37]. On land, IoT can ensure tracking and monitoring of operations that are carried out at the airport. Also, IoT is foreseen to help improve navigation with more accuracy in location tracking.

11.4.5   IIoT in Smart Cities

With the heavy increase in the urban resident population comes an increasing need to have systematic ways of maintaining the cities. Recently a couple of cities have incorporated IoT-based systems, and their progress has been an encouragement to the others. IoT-enabled cities aim at the safety and well-being of residents and maintain a clean environment and optimize electricity [38].

Smart road traffic management and smart traffic lights are a step towards helping people reach their destinations safely and on-time. They take the vehicles' GPS data to prevent accidents and manage the traffic lights by turning on green when there is congestion. Smart parking is also an efficient application in smart-cities that manages the parking space more effectively [39]. Apart from safety, cost-cutting is another advantage of smart cities. With features like smart-lighting that control the street lamps through people's or vehicles' movement on the road, the lighting is adjusted accordingly, adapting to certain schedules based on the patterns.

11.4.6   IIoT in Supply Chain Management

Today, we see factories turning to intelligent factories, with machinery driven by Big Data, machine learning, and artificial intelligence. The machinery is now highly suitable to be connected to a smart network through IoT [40]. Thus, both operational and informational systems of a factory go hand in hand, and the data produced is put to effective use to run the factories with maximum efficiency. With continuous monitoring of machines and improved visibility, factories are bound to get intelligent through the years.

11.5   Challenges of Existing Systems

Indeed, IoT is widely being implemented across a wide range of industries. However, there is an underlying cost that these industries have to deal with in terms of security, data availability, and other issues. Given the opportunities that IoT is creating, companies make a tough decision to choose it. This section focuses on the issues that are restricting it from being used to its full potential by the enterprises [28, 41].

11.5.1   Security

With the increasing number of devices on the cloud, the scope of unauthorized devices hacking into the network is huge. The various IoT driven gadgets that participate in the networks may or may not be polished enough not to compromise their data. The data required for systems to function is openly shared across the network, increasing data vulnerability.

The RFID (Radio-frequency identification) tag has data of any sort, and if it gets into the hands of any unauthorized user, it is not a tough job if he gets hold of front-end devices to alter and pave the way to further threats. Data on the cloud may not only be altered but can be lost permanently or even flooded across the network by a hacker. Interception, also popularly called the man in the middle attack, is another security issue.

Hence many companies that work on sensitive and private data are not taking a step towards IoT-driven technologies and are looking for safer options elsewhere. Research and work are still in progress, and with all the new ideas being discussed on the table, there could be a promising future for IoT soon.

11.5.2   Integration

When manufacturing processes incorporate IIoT, they face a challenge to merge the information technology components and operational technology components. To ensure there is no loss of data and integrate effectively is the real challenge that factories face. Issues in synchronization and overall connectivity arise. Financially and practically, IIoT seems impossible for now in being integrated into businesses.

11.5.3   Connectivity Issues

Ensuring that the machines are working without producing errors is vital for better production. Without proper visibility over the machines' condition, defects may arise in the machines, which could affect the overall production cycle. Synchronization could become more problematic without proper visibility of the various machines. On a global scale, this will be a crucial challenge with IIoT.

11.6   Future Advancements

IoT has hit several milestones on its path to success. The future is bound to be limitless with its increasing scope of advancement [42]. Limitations are on the verge of being diminished with new promising technologies taking shape to make IoT sustainable and the most sought-after technology for enterprises. Some of the advancements that the future holds are discussed below.

11.6.1   Data Analytics in IoT

With more and more devices being associated with IoT, data being exchanged is huge. Efficient data management is most necessary to carry out the IoT operations. Hence researchers have been discussing incorporating data analytics to manage better, analyze, and retrieve valuable insights [43]. This will open doors to machine learning and artificial intelligence, which have the capability to make it more convenient and help provide better data insights.

11.6.2   Edge Computing

Imagine that an autonomous car has come across a hazard; the time it takes to actually send the information detected by the sensors through the network all the way to the data center where a decision is made, which again travels back, is huge. Imagine your enterprise sharing its most important information on a cloud that other enterprises can so easily view? We would rather prefer a local network.

When utilizing a cloud for data exchange, the cost that the bandwidth takes up is not effective, and one would rather switch to a more cost-effective way. All of the above factors, i.e., time, privacy, and cost, are the underlying issues of existing cloud computing systems driven by IoT [44].

Hence a more advanced approach to address these issues has taken shape, which is edge computing. Here, the intelligence is done right at the edge of the node (local network), and decisions are made right at the data source. This way, the enterprise data is restricted to the enterprise only, the time taken is comparatively reduced, and the cost is under control.

11.6.3   Secured IoT Through Blockchain

Among the numerous enterprises using IoT today, there are financial and government enterprises that work on exchanging transactions and other private data. These enterprises initially found it challenging to trust IoT based systems with security. However, through blockchain technologies, the infrastructure of IoT systems is altered so that the network is no more centralized, and a peer to peer secure communication is made possible to ensure security and privacy of data [45]. This advancement is one of the most anticipated among other trends as it will see more and more enterprises opting for IoT without having to compromise the security of data.

11.6.4   A Fusion of AR and IoT

IoT has the capacity to get any inanimate entity to the digital network and make it function. AR makes any digital entity feel like a real-life entity. When going hand in hand, these two technologies can make way to a whole new realm of technological possibility [46]. Especially in healthcare fields, complex procedures can be simplified if surgeons can recreate any body organ in 3D to understand better and efficiently diagnose.

11.6.5   Accelerating IoT Through 5G

IoT contains a network of various home, computer, car appliances, exchanging data efficiently. 5G, which is new to the technological world, is appreciated for its lightning-fast data transfer speed, reduction in interruptions, and efficient use of bandwidth.

If these factors are coupled with IoT, the data exchange will attain high speed, ultimately reducing the delivery time, thereby attracting more enterprises. The future will see operations merge the two technologies creating more sophisticated IoT networks [47].

11.7   Case Study of DeWalt

Problem: A manufacturing company called DeWalt manufactures tools like screwdrivers, jigsaws, floodlights, and other common tools. They have a huge factory with tons of people assigned for a series of operations, right from designing to packaging. With loads of labor and thousands of machines working together, it is quite challenging to monitor and keep these machines' connectivity effective. Due to untimely technical or manual errors, product delivery is being delayed. This not only increases delays but also affects the company and its customers [48].

Solution: The issue reflects the importance of monitoring the machinery and labor of a factory. Hence DeWalt incorporated Cisco wireless infrastructure and AeroScout real-time location solutions. By mounting an aero scout tag over every cisco Wi-Fi point across each factory's production line, any minor fault at any line is effectively monitored and tracked through the servers that connect the monitored data to the management. This helped improve visibility and motivated the labor to work better, ensuring synchronizing all the production lines effectively without much loss [48].

11.8   Conclusion

The Internet of Things has played a vital role in technological evolution, introducing state-of-the-art systems that have transformed various operations today. Besides all the development it has made possible, there are underlying issues that pertain. Security has been a constant question in these networks' working, as data is extensively visible and susceptible to threats. Other issues like complexity, lack of interoperability have surfaced too. With the ongoing research, the future definitely foresees IoT in the prospective projects as technologies like 5G, edge computing is entering the IoT field and fortunately solving its issues. Data analysis will also add more meaning to the data by providing valuable insights that are only possible through data science techniques like machine learning and artificial intelligence. Like augmented reality, some independent technologies can also merge well to give rise to networks beyond our imagination. Overall, it is a very flexible technology that will soon be seen collaborating with many technologies to create innovative projects. The future looks promising for IoT, with every inanimate object participating in a network as the world looks towards automation.

References

1. Zhou, K., Liu, T., Zhou, L., Industry 4.0: Towards future industrial opportunities and challenges. *2015 12th International Conference on Fuzzy Systems and Knowledge Discovery, FSKD 2015*, pp. 2147–2152, 2016, https://doi.org/10.1109/FSKD.2015.7382284.

2. Jazdi, N., Cyber physical systems in the context of Industry 4.0. *Proceedings of 2014 IEEE International Conference on Automation, Quality and Testing, Robotics, AQTR 2014*, pp. 2–4, 2014, https://doi.org/10.1109/AQTR.2014.6857843.

3. Alcácer, V. and Cruz-Machado, V., Scanning the Industry 4.0: A Literature Review on Technologies for Manufacturing Systems. *Eng. Sci. Technol. Int. J.*, 22, 3, 899–919, 2019. https://doi.org/10.1016/j.jestch.2019.01.006.

4. Carnaz, G. and Nogueira, V.B., An Overview of IoT and Healthcare. *Actas Das 6as Jornadas de Informática de Universidade de Évora*, pp. 1–12, 2016, http://dspace.uevora.pt/rdpc/handle/10174/19998.

5. Ayaz, M., Ammad-Uddin, M., Sharif, Z., Mansour, A., Aggoune, E.H.M., Internet-of-Things (IoT)-based smart agriculture: Toward making the fields talk. *IEEE Access*, 7, 129551–129583, 2019. https://doi.org/10.1109/ACCESS.2019.2932609.

6. Rizvi, S., Kurtz, A., Pfeffer, J., Rizvi, M., Securing the Internet of Things (IoT): A Security Taxonomy for IoT. *Proceedings—17th IEEE International Conference on Trust, Security and Privacy in Computing and Communications and 12th IEEE International Conference on Big Data Science and Engineering, Trustcom/BigDataSE 2018*, pp. 163–168, 2018, https://doi.org/10.1109/TrustCom/BigDataSE.2018.00034.

7. Rajab, H. and Cinkelr, T., IoT based Smart Cities. *2018 International Symposium on Networks, Computers and Communications, ISNCC 2018, June*, pp. 1–4, 2018, https://doi.org/10.1109/ISNCC.2018.8530997.

8. Tweneboah-Koduah, S., Skouby, K.E., Tadayoni, R., Cyber Security Threats to IoT Applications and Service Domains. *Wireless Pers. Commun.*, 95, 1, 169–185, 2017. https://doi.org/10.1007/s11277-017-4434-6.

9. Sima, V., Gheorghe, I.G., Subić, J., Nancu, D., Influences of the industry 4.0 revolution on the human capital development and consumer behavior: A systematic review. *Sustainability (Switzerland)*, 12, 10, 1–28, 2020. https://doi.org/10.3390/SU12104035.

10. Dai, H.N., Wang, H., Xu, G., Wan, J., Imran, M., Big data analytics for manufacturing internet of things: opportunities, challenges and enabling technologies. *Enterp. Inf. Syst.*, 14, 1279–1303, 2019. https://doi.org/10.1080/17517575.2019.1633689.

11. Balaji, S., Nathani, K., Santhakumar, R., IoT Technology, Applications and Challenges: A Contemporary Survey. *Wireless Pers. Commun.*, 108, 1, 363–388, 2019. https://doi.org/10.1007/s11277-019-06407-w.

12. Cohen, Y., Faccio, M., Pilati, F., Yao, X., Design and management of digital manufacturing and assembly systems in the Industry 4.0 era. *Int. J. Adv. Manuf. Technol.*, 105, 9, 3565–3577, 2019. https://doi.org/10.1007/s00170-019-04595-0.

13. Prencipe, A., Aircraft and the third industrial revolution. *The Third Industrial Revolution in Global Business, January 2010*, pp. 168–199, 2010, https://doi.org/10.1017/CBO9781139236706.006.

14. Nangia, S., Makkar, S., Hassan, R., IoT based Predictive Maintenance in Manufacturing Sector. *SSRN Electron. J.*, 1–7, April, 2020. https://doi.org/10.2139/ssrn.3563559.

15. Pramanik, P.K.D., Upadhyaya, B.K., Pal, S., Pal, T., Internet of things, smart sensors, and pervasive systems: Enabling connected and pervasive healthcare, in: *Healthcare Data Analytics and Management*, (Issue November), Amsterdam, Netherlands, Elsevier Inc, 2019. https://doi.org/10.1016/b978-0-12-815368-0.00001-4.

16. Cioffi, R., Travaglioni, M., Piscitelli, G., Petrillo, A., De Felice, F., Artificial intelligence and machine learning applications in smart production: Progress, trends, and directions. *Sustainability (Switzerland)*, 12, 2, 1–26, 2020. https://doi.org/10.3390/su12020492.

17. Sethi, P. and Sarangi, S.R., Internet of Things: Architectures, Protocols, and Applications. *J. Electr. Comput. Eng.*, 2017, 1–25, 2017. https://doi.org/10.1155/2017/9324035.

18. Nordrum, A., The Internet of Fewer Things. *Specthrum. IEEE. Org.*, 53, 12–13, 2016.

19. National Academy of Medicine, *Artifical Intellingence in Healthcare*, United States of America, National Academy of Medicine, 2018.

20. Elijah, O., Rahman, T.A., Orikumhi, I., Leow, C.Y., Hindia, M.N., An Overview of Internet of Things (IoT) and Data Analytics in Agriculture: Benefits and Challenges. *IEEE Internet Things J.*, 5, 5, 3758–3773, 2018. https://doi.org/10.1109/JIOT.2018.2844296.

21. Masoud, M., Jaradat, Y., Manasrah, A., Jannoud, I., Sensors of smart devices in the internet of everything (IOE) era: Big opportunities and massive doubts. *J. Sens.*, 2019, 1–26, 2019. https://doi.org/10.1155/2019/6514520.

22. Adapa, A., Nah, F.F.H., Hall, R.H., Siau, K., Smith, S.N., Factors Influencing the Adoption of Smart Wearable Devices. *Int. J. Hum. Comput. Interact.*, 34, 5, 399–409, 2018. https://doi.org/10.1080/10447318.2017.1357902.

23. Seneviratne, S., Hu, Y., Nguyen, T., Lan, G., Khalifa, S., Thilakarathna, K., Hassan, M., Seneviratne, A., A Survey of Wearable Devices and Challenges. *IEEE Commun. Surv. Tutorials*, 19, 4, 2573–2620, 2017. https://doi.org/10.1109/COMST.2017.2731979.

24. Farhan, L., Kharel, R., Kaiwartya, O., Quiroz-Castellanos, M., Alissa, A., Abdulsalam, M., A Concise Review on Internet of Things (IoT)-Problems, Challenges and Opportunities. *2018 11th International Symposium on Communication Systems, Networks and Digital Signal Processing, CSNDSP*, 2018, February, https://doi.org/10.1109/CSNDSP.2018.8471762.

25. Khayyam, H., Javadi, B., Jalili, M., Jazar, R.N., Artificial Intelligence and Internet of Things for Autonomous Vehicles, in: *Nonlinear Approaches in Engineering Applications*, 39–68, 2020.

26. Al-Mayouf, Y.R.B., Mahdi, O.A., Taha, N.A., Abdullah, N.F., Khan, S., Alam, M., Accident Management System Based on Vehicular Network for an Intelligent Transportation System in Urban Environments. *J. Adv. Transp.*, 2018, 1–11, 2018. https://doi.org/10.1155/2018/6168981.

27. Ghasempour, A., Internet of things in smart grid: Architecture, applications, services, key technologies, and challenges. *Inventions*, 4, 1, 1–12, 2019. https://doi.org/10.3390/inventions4010022.

28. Mostafavi, S.A., Dawlatnazar, M.A., Paydar, F., *Edge Computing for IoT: Challenges and Solutions*, Journal of Communications Technology, Electronics and Computer Science, January, 2020.

29. Dauwed, M. and Meri, A., IoT Service Utilisation in Healthcare, in: *Internet of Things (IoT) for Automated and Smart Applications: Vol. i*, 2012, (Issue tourism, p. 38) https://doi.org/10.1016/j.colsurfa.2011.12.014.

30. Dorri, A., Kanhere, S.S., Jurdak, R., Gauravaram, P., Blockchain for IoT security and privacy: The case study of a smart home. *2017 IEEE International*

Conference on Pervasive Computing and Communications Workshops, PerCom Workshops 2017, March, pp. 618–623, 2017, https://doi.org/10.1109/PERCOMW.2017.7917634.

31. Henriques, V., Malekian, R., Capeska Bogatinoska, D., Mine safety system using wireless sensor networks. *2017 40th International Convention on Information and Communication Technology, Electronics and Microelectronics, MIPRO 2017—Proceedings*, vol. 4, pp. 515–520, 2017, https://doi.org/10.23919/MIPRO.2017.7973480.

32. Saiz-Rubio, V. and Rovira-Más, F., From smart farming towards agriculture 5.0: A review on crop data management. *Agronomy*, 10, 2, 1–21, 2020. https://doi.org/10.3390/agronomy10020207.

33. Khurpade, J.M., Rao, D., Sanghavi, P.D., A Survey on IOT and 5G Network. *2018 International Conference on Smart City and Emerging Technology, ICSCET 2018*, pp. 4–6, 2018, https://doi.org/10.1109/ICSCET.2018.8537340.

34. Kurni, M. and K, S.R., Internet of Things (IoT) in Agriculture, in: *Multidisciplinary Functions of Blockchain Technology in AI and IoT Applications*, pp. 88–117, Pennsylvania, United States, IGI Global, 2021, https://doi.org/10.4018/978-1-7998-5876-8.ch005.

35. Farooq, M.S., Riaz, S., Abid, A., Abid, K., Naeem, M.A., A Survey on the Role of IoT in Agriculture for the Implementation of Smart Farming. *IEEE Access*, 7, October, 156237–156271, 2019. https://doi.org/10.1109/ACCESS.2019.2949703.

36. Romeo, L., Petitti, A., Marani, R., Milella, A., Internet of robotic things in smart domains: Applications and challenges. *Sensors (Switzerland)*, 20, 12, 1–23, 2020. https://doi.org/10.3390/s20123355.

37. Valdés, R.A., Comendador, V.F.G., Sanz, A.R., Castán, J.P., Aviation 4.0: More Safety through Automation and Aviation 4.0: More Safety through Automation and Digitization, in: *Aircraft Technology: Vol. i*, Issue tourism, p. 38, 2012. https://doi.org/10.1016/j.colsurfa.2011.12.014.

38. Hammi, B., Khatoun, R., Zeadally, S., Fayad, A., Khoukhi, L., IoT technologies for smart cities. *IET Networks*, 7, 1, 1–13, 2018. https://doi.org/10.1049/iet-net.2017.0163.

39. Faraji, S.J. and Nozar, M.J., Smart parking :an efficient approach to city's smart management and air pollution reduction. *J. Air Pollut. Health*, February, 4, 53–72, 2019. https://doi.org/10.18502/japh.v4i1.603.

40. Adi, E., Anwar, A., Baig, Z., Zeadally, S., Machine learning and data analytics for the IoT. *Neural Comput. Appl.*, 32, 20, 16205–16233, 2020. https://doi.org/10.1007/s00521-020-04874-y.

41. Rghioui, A., Internet of Things: Visions, Technologies, and Areas of Application. *Autom. Control Intell. Syst.*, 5, 6, 83, 2017. https://doi.org/10.11648/j.acis.20170506.11.

42. Park, H., Kim, H., Joo, H., Song, J.S., Recent advancements in the Internet-of-Things related standards: A oneM2M perspective. *ICT Express*, 2, 3, 126–129, 2016. https://doi.org/10.1016/j.icte.2016.08.009.

43. Marjani, M., Nasaruddin, F., Gani, A., Karim, A., Hashem, I.A.T., Siddiqa, A., Yaqoob, I., Big IoT Data Analytics: Architecture, Opportunities, and Open Research Challenges. *IEEE Access*, 5, March, 5247–5261, 2017. https://doi.org/10.1109/ACCESS.2017.2689040.

44. Botta, A., De Donato, W., Persico, V., Pescapé, A., Integration of Cloud computing and Internet of Things: A survey. *Future Gener. Comput. Syst.*, 56, 684–700, August 2018. https://doi.org/10.1016/j.future.2015.09.021.

45. Ahmed, A.H., Omar, N.M., Ibrahim, H.M., Secured Framework for IoT Using Blockchain. *Proceedings—2019 IEEE 9th International Conference on Intelligent Computing and Information Systems, ICICIS 2019*, pp. 270–277, 2019, https://doi.org/10.1109/ICICIS46948.2019.9014853.

46. Alam, M.F., Katsikas, S., Beltramello, O., Hadjiefthymiades, S., Augmented and virtual reality based monitoring and safety system: A prototype IoT platform. *J. Network Comput. Appl.*, 89, March, 109–119, 2017. https://doi.org/10.1016/j.jnca.2017.03.022.

47. Kumar, V. and How, A.I., 5G and IoT are accelerating market growth of network analytics. *Anal. Insight*, 2019. https://www.analyticsinsight.net/ai-5g-iot-accelerating-market-growth-network-analytics/.

48. Oro, D., *10 Case Studies for the Industrial Internet of Things*, IoT Central, 2016, https://www.iotcentral.io/blog/10-case-studies-for-the-industrial-internet-of-things.

12

Reliance on Artificial Intelligence, Machine Learning and Deep Learning in the Era of Industry 4.0

**T. Venkat Narayana Rao[1], Akhila Gaddam[1],
Muralidhar Kurni[2]* and K. Saritha[3]**

*[1]Department of Computer Science and Engineering, Sreenidhi Institute of Science
and Technology, Hyderabad, India
[2]Department of CSE, Anantha Lakshmi Institute of Technology & Sciences,
Ananthapuram, India
[3]Sri Venkateswara Degree & PG College, Ananthapuram, India*

Abstract

As the days pass, the amount of work to do increases day by day, so there is a considerable need to automate the work. This necessity has led to the invention of a new technology named Artificial Intelligence. Artificial Intelligence or Machine Intelligence is a branch of science that deals with a machine's ability to learn, understand, think, and act like humans. The main goal of Artificial Intelligence is making machines to learn from the environment and make them capable of doing the given tasks successfully, that helps in maximizing their goal achievements. Artificial Intelligence is interdisciplinary, which has subfields such as Machine learning, Deep Learning, and others. Machine learning makes the machines automatically learn from their experience; it is done with computer programs that access the given data and uses it for learning for themselves. Deep Learning is a subfield of Machine Learning that processes or filters information in the same way as the human brain. Here, it uses a computer model that takes the input and filters it through different layers to predict and classify the information. These three fields Artificial Intelligence, Machine Learning, and Deep Learning, made many advancements in technology in every sector that transformed the world into a new dimension.

Corresponding author: muralidhar.kurni@gmail.com

SK Hafizul Islam and Debabrata Samanta (eds.) Smart Healthcare System Design: Security and Privacy Aspects, (281–300) © 2021 Scrivener Publishing LLC

Keywords: Artificial intelligence, machine learning, deep learning, Industry 4.0

12.1   Introduction to Artificial Intelligence

The world is changing, and many new technologies are emerging; one of the most prominent and essential technologies which made a significant transformation in this modern era is *Artificial Intelligence*. Artificial Intelligence is a branch of Computer Science that deals with machines; it is also called as Machine Intelligence. Artificial intelligence's main idea is to extend and supplement machines' capacity and efficiency for doing human tasks such as problem-solving, decision making, and others through learning [1]. Many people gave their definitions for Artificial Intelligence based on their study and research, but according to the leading AI textbooks, it is defined as a study of *Intelligent agents* [2]; the detailed study of these agents will be explained further. In simple terms, we can define AI as making a machine capable of making its own decision for particular goal achievement through learning from the environment without human intervention [3, 4]. The ultimate goal of AI is to make humans and machine coexist harmoniously [5].

12.1.1   History of AI

Artificial Intelligence (AI) was coined in 1956 at the Dartmouth college campus by McCarthy [6]. Before 1956, there were many myths and stories on the machines that possess intelligence as humans. However, after the invention of the programmable Digital computer in 1940, a group of scientists from various fields discussed the possibilities of creating a digital, artificial brain. This led to AI's evolution in 1940; Warren McCulloch proposed the first work on *artificial neurons*. Later, few updates were made by Donald Hebb using the *Hebbian Learning rule*. In 1950, Alan Turing proposed a *Turing test* that can check the machine's intelligent behavior [7]. The first Artificial Intelligence program was created by Allen Newell and Herbert A. Simon in 1955 [8]. Later, algorithms were developed that solved mathematical problems. In 1970, the first humanoid robot named WABOT-1 was built [9]. The emergence of Intelligent agents in 1993 brought a major change in the world, where AI came into the Business field, and companies like Netflix, Twitter, Facebook started using AI.

12.1.2   Views of AI

Figure 12.1 shows four main views of Artificial Intelligence [10].

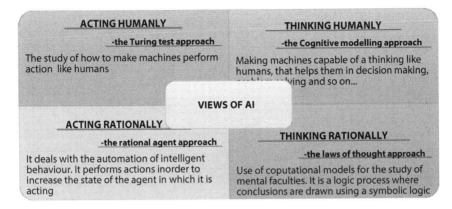

Figure 12.1 Views of AI [10].

12.1.3   Types of AI

The AI is broadly classified into seven different types based on its abilities and functionalities [11]. They are shown below in the following Figure 12.2.

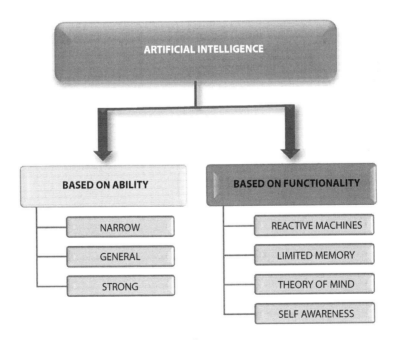

Figure 12.2 Different types of artificial intelligence.

The first type of AI is *Based on its Abilities:*

i. *NARROW AI:* Narrow or Weak AI is the most common AI; currently, it can perform a specific intelligence task. However, it cannot perform beyond its limits because it is trained only for a dedicated task. Hence it is termed as a Weak AI. Examples: image recognition, speech recognition, playing chess.

ii. *GENERAL AI:* The main aim of General AI is to build a system that can perform any task efficiently as humans with its intelligence. Currently, no such type of system exists; researches are going on in this field.

iii. *SUPER AI:* Developing systems that can perform more efficiently than humans come under the category of Super AI; it is a theoretical concept of AI. It includes some essential characteristics such as learning, planning, thinking, ability to make decisions, solving problems, etc.

The second type of AI is *Based on its Functionalities:*

i. *Reactive Machines:* Reactive machines are the basic types of AI that do not store any past data for future actions; they only emphasize the current activity and react accordingly. Example: IBM's Deep Blue system.

ii. *Limited Memory:* These systems can store past data or experience only for a limited period. Example: Self-driving car, it can store only recent information.

iii. *Theory of Mind:* The idea of Theory of Mind AI is to build a system that can understand human emotions, beliefs and enable them to interact socially as humans do.

iv. *Self Awareness:* It is a theoretical concept and is considered the future of Artificial Intelligence, where machines act smarter than humans.

12.1.4   Intelligent Agents

An Intelligent is an autonomous entity that performs actions through learning or observing from the environment with the help of consequent actuators and sensors to achieve its goals [12, 13]. It is similar to a computer program and can also be defined as a program that can perform

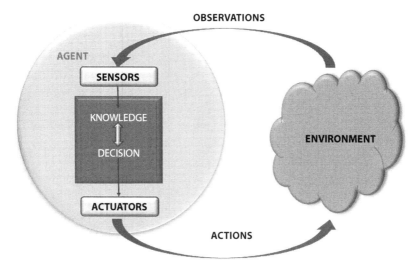

Figure 12.3 Intelligent agent.

actions based on its environment, experiences, and inputs. The following Figure 12.3 shows an intelligent, simple agent.

Types of Intelligent Agents:

The following are the various types of intelligent agents [14].

i. *Simple Reflex Agents:* These agents perform actions only based on the current state, ignoring history. Its response is based on the event-condition-action (ECA rule), where a user initializes an event, and the agent tests whether the condition is satisfied or not. If the condition is satisfied, then the agent can proceed with the action, else he cannot.

ii. *Model-based reflex agents*: Model-based agents deal with partial usability, which operates by keeping track of the current situation.

It has two essential factors:

a. Model: It refers to the knowledge of "how things happen in the world."

b. Internal State: History-based representation of the current state.

These agents perform actions based on the model by updating its state.

iii. *Goal-based agents:* These agents expand Model-based agent capabilities by providing a factor called "goal" information; they perform and choose the actions that help them in achieving their goal. It checks all the possible actions before making a decision; these are names as searching and planning. This makes the goal-based agents proactive.

iv. *Utility-based agents:* Utility-based agents act on their goals and try to find the best possible way to achieve their goals. It measures the utility of a state using a utility function.

v. *Learning agents:* These agents can learn from past experiences, analyze their performance, and improve their performance. In the beginning, they act with the necessary knowledge they possess; later, they adapt and act through learning.

It has four main components:

a) Learning element: It is responsible for making changes by learning.

b) Critic: Produces feedback used by the learning element, which helps agents modify the performance element for better results in the future.

c) Performance element: Its responsibility is to select the external actions.

d) Problem generator: It suggests actions that result in new and informative experiences.

12.2   AI and its Related Fields

Artificial Intelligence is interdisciplinary. It combines different areas, such as philosophy, mathematics, economics, neuroscience, psychology, computer theory, linguistics, and control theory [15]. These all disciplines together make AI more efficient [16]. Figure 12.4 express various disciplines of AI [15, 16].

a. *Philosophy:* The study of fundamental things of knowledge, existence, mind, values, and language.

b. *Economics:* Related to the production, distribution, and consumption of goods and services.

c. *Control Theory:* Control of dynamical systems in machines and processes.

d. *Neuroscience:* Study of structure and functionality of the nervous system.

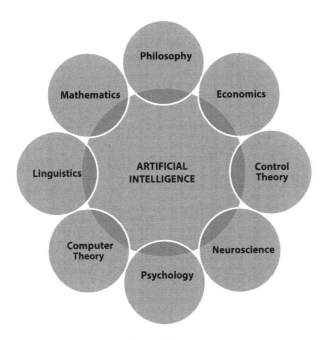

Figure 12.4 Various disciplines of AI [15, 16].

   e. *Psychology:* Study of mind and behavior.
   f. *Computer Theory:* Study of logics, microprogramming, file structures, compilers, programming languages, and system architecture.
   g. *Linguistics:* Study of language.
   h. *Mathematics:* Study of number theory, geometry, algebra, and so on.

Artificial Intelligence consists of many sub-fields [17]; among them, a few sub-fields are being upgraded day-by-day.

   a. *Natural Language Processing:* NLP helps develop methods that enable us to communicate with the machines using our natural language. These are used in dialogue systems, information retrieval, and machine translation systems.
   b. *Robotics and motion:* They aim to create a robot that has four main features.
      a. Vision: Detection and Recognition of objects.
      b. Grasp: Ability to determine the position and orientation to grasp an object.

   c. Motion control: Enable obstacle avoidance and dynamic interaction to maintain high productivity.

   d. Data: Ability to comprehend the data and act accordingly.

  c. *Computer vision*: The science of making a machine analyze and understand an image, just like how human vision acts.

  d. *Planning and Optimization*: Planning and Optimization build systems that can generate better solutions with limited resources. It determines what steps to be taken and when to perform it to achieve a given goal. The process of planning includes: **A** (action to be performed), **I** (initial state), **G** (Goal state)

  e. *Voice Recognition*: Building a system that helps in identifying a person when voice is given as input.

  f. *Knowledge Capture*: Conversion of knowledge from tacit to explicit form.

The other significant sub-fields that are highly used and implemented are Machine Learning and Deep Learning. Further, we will discuss these topics in detail. Figure 12.5 shows the relationship between AI, ML, and DL.

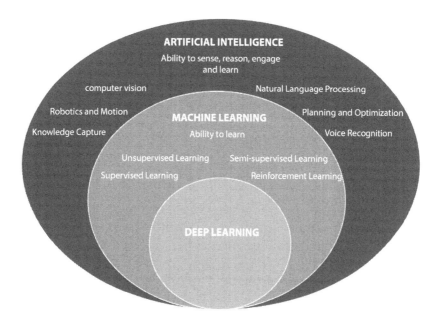

Figure 12.5 The relation between AI, ML, and DL.

12.3   What is Industry 4.0?

Today, the world is changing day, and we have to adapt to new innovations in order to thrive, one such technology that plays a vital role is Industry 4.0. Industry 4.0 is the fourth Industrial Revolution that has contributed to the digital transformation of industry-related value development and production/production processes [18]. It is a new phase based primarily on data from automation, interconnectivity, and real-time. It is also often referred to as the Industrial Internet of Things (IIoT). It aims to develop technologies that improve manufacturing processes' efficiency, thus helping in the organization's real growth or business. It also includes cyber-physical systems, cloud computing, the Internet of things, and creating a smart factory.

12.4   Industrial Revolutions

The change in the world is because of technological change. An increase in demand and need of people lead to the invention of technologies. This is called the Industrial Revolution. People use the technology that is currently available and bring it to the next level. According to the studies, there are four Industrial revolutions [19]. Figure 12.6 shows Industry 4.0 [19]. Now, we are in the fourth generation of the Industrial Revolution—Industry 4.0. The four Industrial Revolutions that took are given below in Figure 12.7.

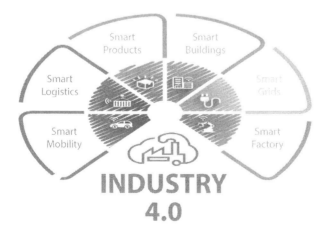

Figure 12.6 Industry 4.0 [19].

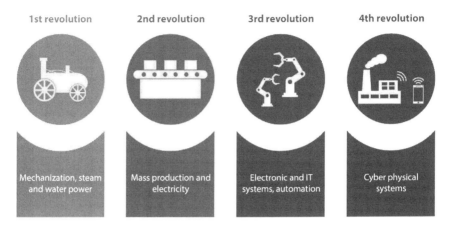

Figure 12.7 Types of industrial revolutions.

12.4.1   First Industrial Revolution (1765)

From the end of the 18th century to the beginning of the 19th, the first industrial revolution began. The modifications arising from this revolution were in the form of mechanization. This mechanization leads to the industry's replacement of agriculture as the backbone of our country's economy. Later, the steam engine's invention resulted in creating a new type of energy that helped speed up the manufacturing process.

12.4.2   Second Industrial Revolution (1870)

Second Revolution is the most important one because automobiles and planes began only in this period. It took almost a century for the Second revolution to start. It started at the end of the 19th century. Much technological advancements took place during this period in the industry; it led to the emergence of another new energy source using oil, electricity, and gas. The creation of the Combustion engine was asignificant result of this revolution. It also leads to the development of chemical synthesis and methods of communication and demand for steel.

12.4.3   Third Industrial Revolution (1969)

Again, a century after the Second revolution, Third Revolution came into existence. It leads to the emergence of Nuclear energy. It also resulted in the rise of telecommunications, computer courses, and electronics. The invention of Programmable Logic Controllers and Robots lead to the evolution of high-level automation.

12.4.4   Fourth Industrial Revolution

The fourth Industrial Revolution or Industry 4.0, is the revolution that we are currently experiencing. It aims at the digital transformation of the value creation process.

12.5   Reasons for Shifting Towards Industry 4.0

The digitalization and automation of work through Industry 4.0 has attracted many industries and people to adopt it. There are huge benefits that can be made out the Industry 4.0; below are some of the critical points where companies get benefited from Industry 4.0 [20].

a. *Increased Efficiency and Productivity:* Industry 4.0 can manufacture various products with high quality in less time, increasing production, thus improving the supply chain and distribution facilities. It is estimated that around 45–55% of production can be increased using Industry 4.0. Many companies such as Cisco, Airbus, and Siemens have already adopted Industry 4.0 and deployed IoT assisted production to increase their production.

b. *Revenue Gain:* Big data analytics in companies can gain a deeper knowledge of the customers' behavior. This helps understand their needs and product development, thereby strengthening customer interactions and earning profits [21].

c. *Machine Downtime Reductions:* Equipment failure can be detected before its occurrence using Predictive maintenance. ML-based systems can identify the repetitive pattern, which indicates failure occurrence. These systems also learn from experience over time, making them more accurate and fast spotting the failure [21].

d. *Improved Supply/Demand Matching:* Advancements in Industry 4.0 lead to a new conceptual model, "Digital Supply chain." This helps deliver the content (digital media content) from the content provider to the customer by electronic means. This can be anything like music or video.

e. *Minimize Human/Manual Errors:* Since human intervention is significantly less, the chance of error will also be less. This results in more efficient output compared.

12.6   Role of AI in Industry 4.0

AI is a significant part of Industry 4.0 [22]. Several small-scale industries use both machine learning and artificial intelligence in order to automate the work. A considerable amount of data will be collected and analyzed, and used according to their requirement.

Some of the use cases of AI in Industry 4.0 [23]:

- *AI for Growth Hack:* AI is the death of growth hacking. The main aim of growth hackers is to acquire a large number of customers with the least investment. As many companies are using AI inbuilt software, these systems' result rate is the same as growth hackers. Moreover, these systems can determine significant growth and scale using automated strategies with just a few clicks. These systems are efficient and result oriented.
- *AI for Digital Monitoring and Controlling:* Many monitoring that assist people and help in decision making are being invented to help people. They train the systems; deep analysis occurs during this process; some pattern will be drawn out of the data. Any irregular patterns indicate that something odd occurs, then it informs and assists the admin/user.

12.7   Role of ML in Industry 4.0

One of the important aspects of business and study is machine learning. The word Machine Learning was coined by Arthur Samuel in 1959 [24]. It is a sub-field of Artificial Intelligence that without explicit instructions, allows a computer or machine to learn and develop its experience. Using sample data, called training data, it uses algorithms to construct a mathematical model; with this training information, one can predict or make decisions for a given input. The goal of Machine Learning is to understand the data structure and fit the knowledge into models that people can understand and use.

Things that make companies shift towards Industry 4.0 [25]:

- Machine learning made a significant impact on small-scale and large-scale industries; many industries are making benefits out of the algorithms or ML software that consolidate and evaluate data for future predictions.
- It also helps find out the relations among the data, which further helps analyze the data.

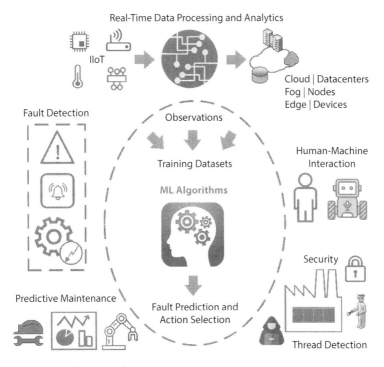

Figure 12.8 Role of ML in Industry 4.0.

This automation will help predict failures more accurately, predict Employees required and their payrolls, and detect and anticipate problems to achieve Zero Error or Fault. Figure 12.8 gives a clear picture of the role of ML in Industry 4.0 [26].

12.8   Role of Deep Learning in Industry 4.0

Deep Learning is a subset of Machine learning in Artificial Intelligence, which can learn and model a vast amount of data sets. The learning process in Deep Learning can be semi-supervised, unsupervised, or supervised [27]. It uses multiple layers to extract the required information from input data. The inspiration behind the architecture of Deep Learning is the Biological neural network (human brain), which consists of multiple layers of Artificial neural networks that are made up of hardware and GPUs.

Deep learning is one of the essential and emerging technologies in industries. It plays a vital role in industries like automotive, hospitality, manufacturing, digital assistants (IoT).

Some of the applications where Deep Learning is widely used in Industries [28]:

- Vision for Self-Driving Cars or Automobiles
- Drone Delivery
- Image colorization and Detection
- Facial recognition
- Making of Medicine and pharmaceuticals
- Translations.

12.9   Applications of AI, ML, and DL in Industry 4.0

The following are the various applications of AI, ML, and DL in Industry 4.0 [26, 29, 30]:

i. *New production process: "Smart Manufacturing"*: It is a new manufacturing technique that involves computer integrated manufacturing, digital transformation technology and is highly flexible and adaptable. It is the combination of various solutions and technology that are together implemented in manufacturing.

ii. *Self-driving vehicles and automated machines:* These machines use vast amounts of data from image recognition systems and develop a system with ML and neural networks that help develop autonomous systems. These systems work with any human intervention. Researchers are still trying to make advancements in these areas [31].

iii. *Quality control:* Quality control is another major thing in Industries. It takes much time for manual inspection during the quality check process. However, with ML algorithms and data mining techniques, one can easily predict the quality [27].

iv. *Demand prediction:* To meet customer needs, it is essential to know the demand in the market. Demand prediction using ML and DL made it a straightforward process. The patterns are studied from the available data, and the conclusions are drawn out of it. Figure 12.9 represents challenges in Industry 4.0 [29, 30].

v. *Chatbots and service bots:* With the help of Chatbots, the customer service process has become a straightforward and

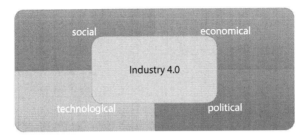

Figure 12.9 Challenges in Industry 4.0 [29, 30].

automated process. It interacts with the customers automatically based on its training [32].

12.10   Challenges

The four main challenges that can be observed in Industry 4.0 are [21]:

a. *Technological challenges:* Technological challenges are related to the different challenges that are used to develop a system. These are further subdivided into:
   i. *Collaboration challenge:* Maintaining proper planning and control in order to operate in a well-defined manner.
   ii. *Data sharing:* It may consume more time in transfer and a massive amount of data.
   iii. *Interaction Feature:* A cyber-physical device offers a more holistic view of the system, which is why careful calibration of the architecture for multi-use features is necessary.
b. *Social challenges:* Social challenge is the second most challenges that affect people, especially employees. The use of smart manufacturing may have a significant impact on jobs. People may lose their jobs because of the automation of work.
c. *Economic challenges:* Huge amount has to be invested in order to move towards Industry 4.0.
d. *Political challenges:* The government needs to manage the I4.0 migration and assist with strategic support, facilitating the process or grants.

12.11   Top Companies That Use AI to Augment Manufacturing Processes in the Era of Industry 4.0

There is a significant impact on AI in the Manufacturing Industry. In order to get effective and accurate outputs, many industries have adopted AI.

The firms that use AI to augment manufacturing [33]:

a. Uptake (Chicago): Involves in the design and development of AI software for various industries.

b. Veo Robotics (Waltham): Manufacture robots integrated with 3d sensing, AI, and computer vision. It aims to manufacture advanced robots that help its clients.

c. Mythic (Austin): This company aims at developing IPUs for supporting AI robots and drones.

d. Sight Machine (San Francisco): It creates analytics platforms that help manufacturers gain valuable insights into the production of their products and enhance their business operations.

e. Automation Anywhere (San Jose): It builds Robotic process automation (RPA) platforms.

f. Invisible AI (San Francisco): It helps in providing better visibility in the manufacturing process.

g. Sparkbeyond (New York): It develops tools that enable detecting patterns in complex datasets.

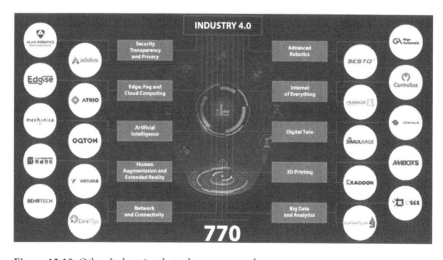

Figure 12.10 Other Industries that adopt new trends.

h. OQTON (San Francisco): It aims to provide production guidelines and a combination of different machines to increase productivity.

i. Fero Labs (New York): It uses AI and ML in their Intelligent AI app that helps in detecting hidden element that contains production volume

j. Landing AI (Palo Alto): develops AI platforms that help solve all the manufacturing process needs.

Figure 12.10 given below gives information about other companies that adopted the latest trends.

12.12 Conclusion

As technology advancements are taking place continuously, many new techniques and tools are coming into the world. These resulted in the growth of different industries. The manufacturing industry will be no more about producing products. It will be a collection of various other elements. The productivity increases rapidly and gives enormous profits to the companies. The next era of manufacturing will emerge with AI and ML technologies [33]. The changes in the process of production and also distribution will occur with the use of modern technologies. This also helps in the faster growth of the firm.

References

1. Jarrahi, M.H., Artificial intelligence and the future of work: Human–AI symbiosis in organizational decision making, in: *Business Horizons*, vol. 61, no. 4, pp. 577–586, 2018. https://doi.org/10.1016/j.bushor.2018.03.007.

2. Feldman, J., Artificial Intelligence in Cognitive Science. *Int. Encycl. Social Behav. Sci.*, 9, 792–796, 2001. https://doi.org/10.1016/b0-08-043076-7/01613-2.

3. Perez, J.A., Deligianni, F., Ravi, D., Yang, G.-Z., *Robotics Camp; Autonomous System*, UK-RAS NETWORK, London, UK, 2018, https://arxiv.org/ftp/arxiv/papers/1803/1803.10813.pdf.

4. Yeung, K., *Responsibility and AI*, The Council of Europe, European Union, 2019.

5. Waters, R., *Artificial intelligence: When humans coexist with robots*, Financial Times, China, 2018, https://www.ft.com/content/bcd81a88-cadb-11e8-b276-b9069bde0956.

6. Mijwel, M.M., History of Artificial Intelligence Yapay Zekânın T arihi. *Comput. Sci.*, 3–4, April 2015.

7. Copeland, J. and Proudfoot, D., Turing's Test: A philosophical and historical guide. *Parsing the Turing Test: Philosophical and Methodological Issues in the Quest for the Thinking Computer*, pp. 119–138, 2009, https://doi.org/10.1007/978-1-4020-6710-5_9.

8. Dick, S., Artificial Intelligence Concepts, in: *HDSR*, 2019, https://doi.org/10.1162/99608f92.92fe150c.

9. Takanishi, A., Historical Perspective of Humanoid Robot Research in Asia. *Humanoid Rob. Reference*, 35–52, 2019. https://doi.org/10.1007/978-94-007-6046-2_145.

10. Liu, J., Kong, X., Xia, F., Bai, X., Wang, L., Qing, Q., Lee, I., Artificial intelligence in the 21st century. *IEEE Access*, 6, 34403–34421, 2018. https://doi.org/10.1109/ACCESS.2018.2819688.

11. Joshi, N., 7 Types of Artificial Intelligence. *Forbes*, 1–7, 2019. https://www.forbes.com/sites/cognitiveworld/2019/06/19/7-types-of-artificial-intelligence/#b69f9bb233ee.

12. Balaji, P.G. and Srinivasan, D., An introduction to multi-agent systems, in: *Studies in Computational Intelligence*, vol. 310, pp. 1–27, 2010, https://doi.org/10.1007/978-3-642-14435-6_1.

13. Vermesan, O., Bröring, A., Tragos, E., Serrano, M., Bacciu, D., Chessa, S., Gallicchio, C., Micheli, A., Dragone, M., Saffiotti, A., Simoens, P., Cavallo, F., Bahr, R., Internet of robotic things-converging sensing/actuating, hyperconnectivity, artificial intelligence and IoT platforms, in: *Cognitive Hyperconnected Digital Transformation: Internet of Things Intelligence Evolution*, pp. 97–155, 2017.

14. Soliman, M. and Guetl, C., Evaluation of intelligent agent frameworks for human learning. *2011 14th International Conference on Interactive Collaborative Learning, ICL 2011—11th International Conference Virtual University, VU'11, September*, pp. 191–194, 2011, https://doi.org/10.1109/ICL.2011.6059574.

15. Laird, J.E., Lebiere, C., Rosenbloom, P.S., A standard model of the mind: Toward a common computational framework across artificial intelligence, cognitive science, neuroscience, and robotics. *AI Magazine*, 38, 4, 13–26, 2017. https://doi.org/10.1609/aimag.v38i4.2744.

16. Gil, Y. and Selman, B., A 20-Year Community Roadmap for Artificial Intelligence Research In The Us. *arXiv*, abs/1908.02624, 1–112, 2019.

17. Singh, N., Artificial Intelligence and Sub-Fields. *Medium*, 2018. https://doi.org/10.4018/978-1-7998-5068-7.ch015.

18. Vaidya, S., Ambad, P., Bhosle, S., Industry 4.0—A Glimpse. *Procedia Manuf.*, 20, November, 233–238, 2018. https://doi.org/10.1016/j.promfg.2018.02.034.

19. Koleva, N., Industry 4.0's Opportunities And Challenges For Production Engineering And Management. *Int. Sci. J. "Innovations,"*, VI, 1, 17–18, 2018.

20. Horváth, D. and Szabó, R.Z., Driving forces and barriers of Industry 4.0: Do multinational and small and medium-sized companies have equal

opportunities? *Technol. Forecasting Social Change*, 146, May, 119–132, 2019. https://doi.org/10.1016/j.techfore.2019.05.021.

21. El Hamdi, S., Abouabdellah, A., Oudani, M., Industry 4.0: Fundamentals and Main Challenges. *International Colloquium on Logistics and Supply Chain Management, LOGISTIQUA 2019*, pp. 1–5, 2019, https://doi.org/10.1109/LOGISTIQUA.2019.8907280.

22. Lee, J., Singh, J., Azamfar, M., Industrial artificial intelligence. *ArXiv*, abs/1908.02150, 2019.

23. Balamurugan, E., Flaih, L.R., Yuvaraj, D., Sangeetha, K., Jayanthiladevi, A., Kumar, T.S., Use Case of Artificial Intelligence in Machine Learning Manufacturing 4.0. *Proceedings of 2019 International Conference on Computational Intelligence and Knowledge Economy, ICCIKE 2019*, pp. 656–659, 2019, https://doi.org/10.1109/ICCIKE47802.2019.9004327.

24. Bhavsar, P., Safro, I., Bouaynaya, N., Polikar, R., Dera, D., Machine Learning in Transportation Data Analytics, in: *Data Analytics for Intelligent Transportation Systems*, pp. 283–307, Elsevier Inc, Netherlands, 2017, https://doi.org/10.1016/B978-0-12-809715-1.00012-2.

25. Ansari, F., Erol, S., Sihn, W., Rethinking Human-Machine Learning in Industry 4.0: How Does the Paradigm Shift Treat the Role of Human Learning? *Procedia Manuf.*, 23, 2017, 117–122, 2018. https://doi.org/10.1016/j.promfg.2018.04.003.

26. Angelopoulos, A., Michailidis, E.T., Nomikos, N., Trakadas, P., Hatziefremidis, A., Voliotis, S., Zahariadis, T., Tackling faults in the industry 4.0 era—A survey of machine-learning solutions and key aspects. *Sensors (Switzerland)*, 20, 1, 1–33, 2020. https://doi.org/10.3390/s20010109.

27. Control, Q. and Industry, I.N., Quality control in industry. *Nature*, 202, 4935, 857, 1964. https://doi.org/10.1038/202857b0.

28. Ing. Kuric I., Ing. Zajačko I., Ing. Císar M., Tomáš Gál, *Application of Artificial Intelligence for the Implementation*, vol. 123, no. 3, pp. 120–123, International Scientific Journals, Bulgaria, 2018.

29. Cioffi, R., Travaglioni, M., Piscitelli, G., Petrillo, A., De Felice, F., Artificial intelligence and machine learning applications in smart production: Progress, trends, and directions. *Sustainability (Switzerland)*, 12, 2, 1–26, 2020. https://doi.org/10.3390/su12020492.

30. Woschank, M., Rauch, E., Zsifkovits, H., A review of further directions for artificial intelligence, machine learning, and deep learning in smart logistics. *Sustainability (Switzerland)*, 12, 9, 1–23, 2020. https://doi.org/10.3390/su12093760.

31. Jain, G. and Pai, M., *The rise of autonomous vehicles*, Wipro Digital, India, 2015, https://dig.watch/trends/rise-autonomous-vehicles.

32. Lawton, J., *The Role Of Robots In Industry 4.0*, pp. 2018–2020, Forbes; Jersey City, NJ, 2019.

33. There, H. and Learning, D., *Industry 4.0—Top 10 Companies That Use AI to Augment Manufacturing Processes. Ml*, pp. 1–23, USM Systems; USA, 2020.

13

The Implementation of AI and AI-Empowered Imaging Systems to Fight Against COVID-19—A Review

Sanjay Chakraborty[1]* and Lopamudra Dey[2]

¹CSE, JIS University, Kolkata, India
²CSE, Heritage Institute of Technology, Kolkata, India

Abstract

COVID-19 has already affected the world with this deadly virus, resulting in over 3.5 lakh deaths. The behavior of this virus is extraordinarily peculiar and mutates frequently. So, the scientific community faces the problems to analyze and forecast the virus's growth and transmission capability. The combined effort of powerful Artificial intelligence and Image processing techniques to predict the initial pattern of COVID-19 disease identifies the most affected areas in each country through social networking information and predicts drug–protein interactions for making new drugs vaccines. However, AI-empowered X-Ray and computed tomography image acquisition and segmentation techniques help us identify and diagnose the COVID-19 affected patients with minimal contact. In this chapter, our primary motivation is to sum up the essential roles of some AI-driven techniques (Machine learning, Deep learning, etc.) and AI-empowered imaging techniques to analyze, predict, and diagnose against COVID-19 disease. An essential set of open challenges and future research issues on AI-empowered procedures for handling COVID-19 are also discussed in this chapter.

Keywords: Artificial intelligence, COVID-19, diagnosis, image processing, machine learning

*Corresponding author: sanjay.chakraborty@jisuniversity.ac.in

SK Hafizul Islam and Debabrata Samanta (eds.) Smart Healthcare System Design: Security and Privacy Aspects, (301–312) © 2021 Scrivener Publishing LLC

13.1   Introduction

In the present situation, the coronavirus pandemic is one of the most important diseases to diagnose (WHO). For healthcare systems worldwide, it causes tremendous strain and stress. At the end of 2019, the new case of the narrative coronavirus was identified in Wuhan City, China. Table 13.1 shows that its deadly consequences are now threatening the world as a whole from Europe to America [1]. The SARS-CoV-2 family is a disease that is lethal. Genomic research has shown that COVID-19 is related to bat diseases close to SARS. The potential cause of viral replication [2] could therefore be bats. Pangolins have also been observed as a possible transitional host of COVID-19 [3]. The typical indication of COVID-19 patients influenced is cold, temperature and multiple organ failure [4]. The hereditary individuality of the Coronavirus should be well known in order to protect against this disease. The coronavirus is a solitary-trapped RNA virus ranging in diameter from 65–125 nm with a particle size of approximately 27–32 kb, a general representation of protein particles from the COVID-19 disease.

Here the contributions from this survey can be described as follows:

An early, rapid review of AI's potential contribution to the fight against COVID-19 disease is provided in given chapter. We describe how some state-of-the-art ML and Deep Learning (DL) models could assist health experts in controlling the current epidemic with a stable judgment of COVID-19. However from their X-Ray and CT images, we also discuss the impact of image acquisition and segmentation technologies to detect COVID-19 patients. We also demonstrate how the AI, ML and DL instruments help predict the patterns of the COVID-19 diseases from X-Ray and CT images effectively and accurately. The pictorial representation of the preliminary transmission of COVID-19 based on the virus's possible

Table 13.1 Country-wise statistical table for affected area.

Country name	Confirmed cases	Death cases
United States	5,361,131	169,161
Brazil	3,170,474	104,263
India	2,411,547	47,274
Russia	907,758	15,384
South Africa	568,919	11,010

symptoms and a rapid detection using AI-empowered image processing tools is shown in Figure 13.1. It shows the patients' preliminary screening is often done by identifying some symptoms related to COVID-19 disease. COVID-19 pneumonia patients may have oxygen saturation as low as 50%, whereas normal patients have oxygen saturation within the range of 94–100%. It should be performed on the positive COVID-19 patients, and therefore the remainder of the negative symptoms patients will undergo a rapid antibody testing performed in each 7 days interval. As a result, we will send the COVID-19 affected patients for early quarantine/isolation/treatment resulting in the prevention of transmission within the near future [5].

AI-empowered image processing technologies were used to predict, analyze and diagnose COVID-19. Section explains the discoveries of some possible treatments and cures against COVID-19 up to date. Section 13.4 discusses some significant challenges and open research issues. In section, the survey work is wrapped up in the form of a set of conclusions. The researchers will get some useful references for their future researches in the reference section of this chapter.

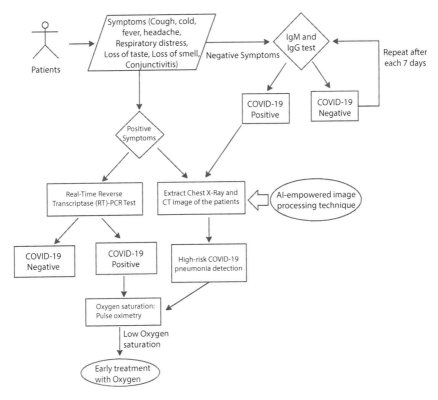

Figure 13.1 Preliminary screening of COVID-19 patients.

13.2   AI-Assisted Methods

We believe that fast and accurate identification of COVID-19 with the help of AI models can save lives and limit the multiplying of the ailment. In this work, we divide the entire methodology into two subsections [6]. The first subsection explains the role of AI tools such as ML, ANN, expert systems and DL techniques to predict and investigate the patterns of COVID-19 from various heterogeneous datasets (social networking data, public protein–protein interaction datasets, etc.). However, the second subsection describes the role of AI techniques to improve image processing tools' performance to diagnose the COVID-19 virus from patient's X-Ray and CT images. A series of published research works on these areas are explained in brief in this survey.

13.2.1   AI-Driven Tools to Diagnose COVID-19 and Drug Discovery

It is possible to predict the COVID-19 pattern and its saturation time with the help of Artificial Intelligence. There are some areas in which AI can contribute to COVID-19 fighting [7].

- Alerts and early warnings.
- Tracking, prediction and the finding of patterns.
- Controlling dashboards of information through social networking sites.
- Diagnosis and forecast
- Cures and treatments.

In the last few months, the most frequently searched words in various social networks and search engines are 'CORONA', 'COVID-19' and 'Pneumonia' [8]. So, AI and data processing techniques (classification [22], clustering [23], feature selection [24], etc.) help us to understand the longer term effect of COVID-19 by mining intelligent social networking data supported some specific keywords. However, this type of study helps the government in preparing the medical facilities to resist such an epidemic situation at the first stage. Besides that, the social networking data (like Twitter data) are often used to identify epicenters of COVID-19 efficiently and during a faster way without consuming a large amount of resources. A region-based geographical heat map is often generated from Twitter data to keep track of the epicenters of COVID-19 [9].

SARS was obtained from Uniprot proteomes by Ong *et al.*, according to the SARS-CoV-2 NCBI series. The Vaxign Reverse Vaccinology pipeline then analyzes these proteins. Then the positive and negative samples of protein are collected using the Vaxign-ML process [10]. Within the resulting dataset, the proteins are annotated with biological and physicochemical attributes. AI-driven instruments and their suitable COVID-19 train and test models are being introduced by Santosh *et al.* Active learning is used in this paper in the presence of field experts, rather than focusing on one form of data, through the use of multitudinal and multimodal data and an active learning approach, and various types of data are required to be used [19]. Dey *et al.* validate their findings by some biological studies (Gene Ontology pathway of GO and KEGG) [21]. In this prediction model, progression-based data of individual proteins such as the masterpiece of amino acids, the masterpiece of pseudo amino acids, and the conjoint triad are used. Ensemble-based voting classifiers and a deep neural classifier play a key role in predicting 1,326 potential human target proteins in this paper. A summary of a few important works on AI-assisted diagnosis and drug discovery of COVID-19 have been discussed in Table 13.2.

Table 13.2 AI-assisted diagnosis of COVID-19 and drug discovery.

Literature	Modality	Methods	Task
Avchaciov *et al.*	Gene expression signatures	Deep neural network	Drug discovery of SARS-CoV-2
Rao *et al.*	Mobile data	Machine learning	Pattern finding of COVID-19 viral spread
Gao *et al.*	SMILES strings	Gated recurrent unit (GRU) based encoders and decoders	Drug discovery of COVID-19
Ong *et al.*	S, nsp3, and nsp8 proteins	Reverse vaccinology tool & Vaxign-ML	COVID-19 vaccine candidates
Dey *et al.*	SARS-CoV-2 and human proteins	Ensemble and deep neural classifiers	Predict potential human target proteins and anti-COVID drug discovery

13.2.2   AI-Empowered Image Processing to Diagnosis

The goal of this research is to converse the position of AI-enabled medical imaging in the battle against COVID-19 in detail, which will be encouraging [13]. These medical imaging techniques based on AI are expected to provide guidance in the future for researchers and radiologists [14]. For diagnosis and prognosis, the role of image segmentation, edge detection and enhancement. In the case of COVID-19, patients with chest X-ray and CT images are commonly used in high-risk patients for the judgment of early stage COVID-19 pneumonia. COVID-19, which can infect all normal patients near it, is one of the most dangerous airborne viruses. However this X-Ray and CT image-based diagnosis offers a contactless and automatic workflow of detection since many modern X-ray and CT devices are fitted. Furthermore, in all hospitals, X-ray and CT imaging devices are available that greatly boost the issues of portability, scaling and affordability [15]. The separation of COVID-19 from other pneumonias and from healthy subjects was examined. A SqueezeNet structure with Bayesian optimization additive is used by Ucar *et al.* [15] for the diagnosis of COVID-19. This experiment includes a complete 5,949 poster anterior chest radiography images for 2,839 patient cases, the COVID chest X-ray data collection, and the Kaggle chest X-ray pneumonia dataset are combined [16]. The experimental results show that the deep Bayes-SqueezeNet improves the detection accuracy to 98.3% for single COVID-19 recognition (among regular, pneumonia and COVID cases) and 100% (among other classes). Researchers strengthen the perception of deep learning outcomes in this paper and encourage a more AI-based decision-making process. A composite structure of different deep learning models on chest X-Ray datasets is explained by Chowdhury *et al.* It utilizes sgdm-SqueezeNet with 98.3% precision for the COVID-19 classification [17].

A Bayesian Convolutional Neural Network is being introduced by Ghoshal *et al.* to predict COVID-19. It collected lung X-Ray images from an online COVID-19 dataset of 70 positive patients and images of non-COVID patients from Kaggles Chest X-Ray Images (Pneumonia). This enhances the VGG16 model's detection precision to 92.9%. A ResNet-based model for perceive COVID-19 from X-ray images is proposed by Zhang *et al.* It also performs anomaly detection along with the COVID-19 classification. To optimize the score of COVID-19 used for classification, anomaly detection is used. For the purpose of the experiment, 70 COVID and 1,008 X-Ray images of non-COVID patients were used. It achieves 96.0%

precision, along with an AUC of 0.952. Li and Zhu present a COVID-Xpert architecture based on DenseNet for the classification of chest X-ray images. They use transfer learning and gain 88.9% overall accuracy. A special CNN model tailored to the diagnosis of COVID-19 from X-Ray images is used by Wang and Wong. A machine-driven design is used, however in order to enhance the model architecture. 92.3% overall classification accuracy is achieved by this approach. A capsule network-based deep learning model using a four-class dataset is proposed by Afshar *et al.* In the classification of COVID-19, their model achieved 95.7% overall accuracy [18].

These experiments are primarily based on publicly available images of 70 COVID-19 patients that are insufficient to assess the techniques' efficiency and robustness. Ozkaya *et al.* used deep fusing and ranking features to detect COVID-19 from CT images in the early phase. From 150 CT images, two subsets are generated (16 × 16 & 32 × 32). There have been 3,000 patch images labeled as CoVID-19. Then, this models that are used in transfer learning classify the processed data. The experimental outcome indicates that it achieves 98.27% precision. The unique RF-based severity assessment is proposed by Tang *et al.* for the treatment planning model of COVID-19. First using deep VB-Net, the lung image is divided into anatomical sub-regions (e.g., lobes and segments). The quantitative features calculated from infection volumes and ratios of each anatomical sub-region are then used to train the RF-model. The result shows that the classification accuracy is 87.5% [19].

13.3   Optimistic Treatments and Cures

Many laboratories and information centers have previously designate that they are engage AI individuals and building efficient infrastructure to search for COVID-19 treatments and vaccines. Scientists and doctors are collaboratively working to determine an innovative drug against COVID-19 by recombining the existing drugs [11]. AI processes and tools help them to accelerate their process of discovering. Beck *et al.* and Stebbing *et al.* report that the existing drugs such as atazanavir and Baricitinib (used against rheumatoid arthritis and myelobrosis) could be an impending behavior for COVID-19. Dong *et al.* summarize a list of possible drugs for the behavior of COVID-19. This paper discusses the use of IFN-α drug through vapor inhalation for 10 days. Then it represents the use of Lopinavir/ritonavir and Arbidol through oral intake for 10 days. Then it also explains the intake of Ribavirin drug through intravenous infusion for 10 days [20].

13.4   Challenges and Future Research Issues

The work for studying the COVID-19 follow-up is still at an early stage and remains. Different image processing techniques such as segmentation, edge detection, diagnosis, classification, and morphological changes effectively monitor the enlargement of the COVID-19 AI-empowered follow-up study. Below, certain open challenges and future research questions have been discussed. Integrated use of medical imaging, AI, NLP, oncology and combination may promote from the measurement process for COVID-19. Natural language processing AI helps to crunch enormous amounts of data that would be impossible to process for humans. AI can help us track the spread, patterns, trends, and changing behaviour of the SARS-CoV-2 virus with statistical analysis and form a cluster of symptoms leading to a new treatment or drug discovery path [12]. AI and NLP-based chatbot systems can be built to answer patient queries by reading the database's tens of thousands of scholarly articles, ranking them and generating response snippets and summaries. Even deep learning can help to search databases quickly for intellectual purposes. We could focus on distinguishing patients with mild symptoms that may not be accurately visualized on X-rays or CT images instead of focusing on patients with pneumonia symptoms alone. Machine learning (ML) techniques implemented to enhance data of low eminence that would make biased and erroneous forecast for instances of COVID-19. Using different ML techniques (like Regression), insufficient time series data can also be improvised and analyzed. Deep learning CNN based models (ResNet, DenseNet, etc.) are preferred to be used to manage imbalance dataset of medical image data and decrease long training time. A dynamic programming approach can be useful to effectively manage large datasets of genomic or proteomic sequences and the help of a supervised deep learning method. We can use deep learning models along with NLP tools to handle low-quality, multidimensional, and highly unstructured satellite images of areas and social media data.

13.5   Conclusion

This research explains how COVID-19 and drug development can be predicted, diagnosed and categorized by AI-driven methods and AI-empowered imaging explanations. The smart AI instruments, deep learning strategies and AI-empowered imaging appliances are discussed in detail. These are primarily focused on demonstrating the efficiency of AI-enabled medical imaging for COVID-19, i.e., X-ray and CT. It is noted that when clinical manifestations and laboratory test findings are coupled with these AI-empowered methods, improved uncovering and analysis of COVID-19 is possible. In addition, enhanced AI-based image processing techniques for chest X-Ray and CT images may be built to more accurately and quickly diagnose high-risk COVID-19 pneumonia in the near future. Thus the methods of qRT-PCR and antigen detection may be well supported. The quantitative real-time polymerase chain reaction (qRT-PCR) technique is used to detect SARS-CoV-2 nucleic acid in upper and lower respiratory samples. In swabs taken from the mouth or nose, qRT-PCR can sense as little as one virus particle. The effective ML algorithms can built for sentiment analysis based on social networking data. Artificial intelligence can help to predict the effects of different drugs more rapidly. However in this report, along with some potential COVID-19 therapies and cures, some fascinating AI-driven drug discovery methods are also discussed.

References

1. Ucar, F. and Korkmaz, D., COVIDiagnosis-Net: Deep Bayes-SqueezeNet based Diagnostic of the Coronavirus Disease 2019 (COVID-19) from X-Ray Images. *Med. Hypotheses*, 140, 109761, 2020.

2. Ibrahim, I.M., Abdelmalek, D.H., Elshahat, M.E., Elfiky, A.A., COVID-19 spike-host cell receptor GRP78 binding site prediction. *J. Infect.*, 80, 554–562, 2020.

3. Kassani, S.H., Kassasni, P.H., Wesolowski, M.J., Schneider, K.A.R., Automatic Detection of Coronavirus Disease (COVID-19) in X-ray and CT Images: A Machine Learning-Based Approach. arXiv preprint arXiv:2004.10641, 1, 1–10, 2020.

4. Kumar, R., Arora, R., Bansal, V., Sahayasheela, V.J., Buckchash, H., Imran, J., Raman, B., Accurate Prediction of COVID-19 using Chest X-Ray Images through Deep Feature Learning model with SMOTE and Machine Learning Classifiers. medRxiv, 1, 1–10, 2020.

5. Salman, F.M., Abu-Naser, S.S., Alajrami, E., Abu-Nasser, B.S., Alashqar, B.A., Covid-19 detection using artificial intelligence, in: *AUG Repository*, 2020.

6. Horry, M.J., Paul, M., Ulhaq, A., Pradhan, B., Saha, M., Shukla, N., X-Ray Image based COVID-19 Detection using Pre-trained Deep Learning Models. EngrRxiv, 1, 1–13, 2020. https://doi.org/10.31224/osf.io/wx89s.

7. Barstugan, M., Ozkaya, U., Ozturk, S., Coronavirus (COVID-19) classification using ct images by machine learning methods. arXiv preprint arXiv:2003.09424, 2020.

8. Wang, L. and Wong, A., COVID-Net: A tailored deep convolutional neural network design for detection of COVID-19 cases from chest radiography images. arXiv preprint arXiv:2003.09871, 2020.

9. Ozkaya, U., Ozturk, S., Barstugan, M., Coronavirus (COVID-19) Classification using Deep Features Fusion and Ranking Technique. arXiv preprint arXiv:2004.03698, 11, 1581, 2020.

10. Ong, E., Wong, M.U., Huffman, A., He, Y., COVID-19 coronavirus vaccine design using reverse vaccinology and machine learning. *Front. Immunol.*, 11, 1581, 2020.

11. Gysi, D.M., Valle, D., Zitnik, M., Ameli, A., Gan, X., Varol, O., Barabsi, A.L., Network Medicine Framework for Identifying Drug Repurposing Opportunities for COVID-19. arXiv preprint arXiv:2004.07229, 2020.

12. Ge, Y., Tian, T., Huang, S., Wan, F., Li, J., Li, S., Cheng, L., A data-driven drug repositioning framework discovered a potential therapeutic agent targeting COVID-19. bioRxiv, 1, 1–62, 2020.

13. Batra, R., Chan, H., Kamath, G., Ramprasad, R., Cherukara, M.J., Sankaranarayanan, S., Screening of Therapeutic Agents for COVID-19 using Machine Learning and Ensemble Docking Simulations. arXiv preprint arXiv:2004.03766, 2020.

14. Bullock, J., Pham, K.H., Lam, C.S.N., Luengo-Oroz, M., Mapping the landscape of artificial intelligence applications against COVID-19. arXiv preprint arXiv:2003.11336, 2020.

15. Ardabili, S.F., Mosavi, A., Ghamisi, P., Ferdinand, F., Varkonyi-Koczy, A.R., Reuter, U., Atkinson, P.M., COVID-19 Outbreak Prediction with Machine Learning, Algorithms, 13, 10, 249, 2020.

16. Desautels, T., Zemla, A., Lau, E., Franco, M., Faissol, D., Rapid in silico design of antibodies targeting SARS-CoV-2 using machine learning and supercomputing. bioRxiv, 1, 1–14, 2020.

17. Shi, F., Wang, J., Shi, J., Wu, Z., Wang, Q., Tang, Z., Shen, D., Review of artificial intelligence techniques in imaging data acquisition, segmentation and diagnosis for COVID-19. *IEEE Rev. Biomed. Eng.*, 14, 4–15, 2020.

18. Naudé, W., Artificial intelligence vs COVID-19: limitations, constraints and pitfalls. *AI & Soc.*, 35, 3, 761–765, 2020.

19. Santosh, K.C., AI-driven tools for coronavirus outbreak: Need of active learning and cross-population train/test models on multitudinal/multimodal data. *J. Med. Syst.*, 44, 5, 1–5, 2020.

20. Rahmatizadeh, S., Valizadeh-Haghi, S., Dabbagh, A., The role of Artificial Intelligence in Management of Critical COVID-19 patients. *J. Cell. Mol. Anesthesia*, 5, 1, 16–22, 2020.

21. Dey, L., Chakraborty, S., Mukhopadhyay, A., Machine learning techniques for sequence-based prediction of viral–host interactions between SARS-CoV-2 and human proteins. *Biomed. J.*, 43, 5, 438–450, 2020.

22. Chakladar, D.D. and Chakraborty, S., Feature extraction and classification in brain-computer interfacing: Future research issues and challenges, in: *Natural Computing for Unsupervised Learning*, pp. 101–131, Springer, Cham, 2019.

23. Goswami, S., Chakraborty, S., Saha, H.N., An univariate feature elimination strategy for clustering based on metafeatures. *Int. J. Intell. Syst. Appl.*, 9, 10, 20, 2017.
24. Goswami, S., Das, A.K., Guha, P., Tarafdar, A., Chakraborty, S., Chakrabarti, A., Chakraborty, B., An approach of feature selection using graph-theoretic heuristic and hill climbing. *Pattern Anal. Appl.*, 22, 2, 615–631, 2019.

14

Implementation of Machine Learning Techniques for the Analysis of Transmission Dynamics of COVID-19

C. Vijayalakshmi[1]* and S. Bangusha Devi[2]

*[1]Department of Statistics and Applied Mathematics,
Central University of Tamil Nadu, Thiruvarur, Tamil Nadu, India
[2]Department of Science and Humanities, JP College of Engineering,
Tenkasi, Tamilnadu, India*

Abstract

This paper mainly deals with the design of Machine Learning model for the analysis of transmission dynamics of Covid 19. The entire globe is affected because of Corona virus. Ventilator dependent, Severe Acute respiratory and quarantine care ICU patients frequently face difficulties for their most basic human interactions, namely communication due to either respiratory illness, language problem or intubated. ICU patients have serious implications with respect to physical and psychological due to non communication problems. Researchers have developed different types of services like Speech language Pathologist so that Augmentative and alternative communication assistance can be given to all health professionals and caretakers. A probabilistic model is designed to analyse the new cases and death cases. Using machine learning approach Regression model is designed and future predications are displayed. The adequacy of the model is discussed along with the residuals of new cased and death cases. PCF and APCAF are obtained. This paper mainly deals with a probabilistic model to analyse and predict the new cases and deaths of covid 19. A new transformation of analyzing stationarity is carried out and based on this forecasting is executed.

Corresponding author: vijayalakshmi@cutn.ac.in; ORCID 0000-0002-0848-1289

SK Hafizul Islam and Debabrata Samanta (eds.) Smart Healthcare System Design: Security and Privacy Aspects, (313–350) © 2021 Scrivener Publishing LLC

Keywords: Statistical model, COVID-19, global, pandemic, ARIMA, regression analysis

14.1   Introduction

COVID-19 is currently a deadly disease disturbing all countries worldwide due to different symptoms. Flow chart for this disease is depicted in the Figure 14.1.

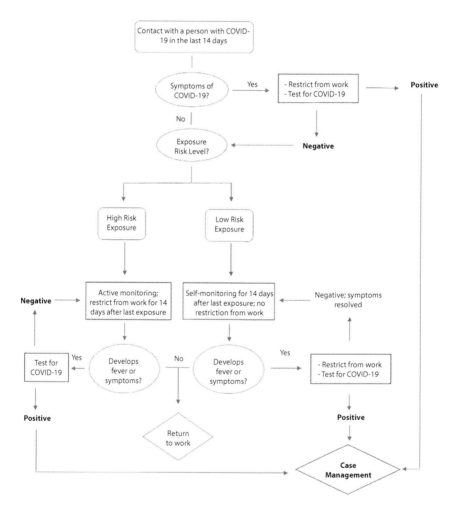

Figure 14.1 Flow chart—symptoms of COVID-19 and predictive measures.

14.2   Data Analysis

Data being collected from the WHO and the same has been analyzed using Statistical Techniques. Data has been pre-processed and normalized by using the existing Statistical techniques.

14.3   Methodology

14.3.1   Linear Regression Model

(i) Identification of Model
Firstly, scatter plot of the predictor variable and regressors are used to identify the relationship among them. It is visualized in two-dimensional geometry. The data points are plotted and the Linear Regression model is defined as

$$Y = b_0 + b_1 X + \varepsilon$$

where Y is the response variable, b_0 is the intercept, b_1 is the regression coefficient, X is the predictor variable, and ε is the error term [10, 13].

For the realization of the response and predictor variables, the model can be determined by obtaining the estimates to the unknown parameters or regression coefficients. The regression coefficients can be estimated using the method of least squares subject to the following assumptions:

   i. The relationship between the response variable Y and the regressor X is approximately linear.
   ii. The error term has zero mean and constant variance
   iii. The error terms are normally distributed and
   iv. The errors are uncorrelated.

(ii) Estimation of parameter
The method of least square is used to estimate β_0 and β_1. To estimate the model parameters first calculate, the following terms,

$$S_{xx} = \sum_{i=1}^{n} x_i^2 - \frac{\left(\sum_{i=1}^{n} x_i \right)^2}{n}$$

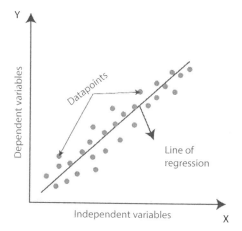

Figure 14.2 Linear regression model.

$$S_{xy} = \sum_{i=1}^{n} x_i y_i - \frac{\left(\sum_{i=1}^{n} y_i\right)\left(\sum_{i=1}^{n} x_i\right)}{n}$$

$$\hat{\beta}_1 = \frac{S_{xy}}{S_{xx}} \text{ and } \hat{\beta}_0 = \bar{y} - \hat{\beta}_1 \bar{x}$$

Mathematically the ith residual is

$$e_i = y_i - \hat{y}_i = y_i - (\hat{\beta}_0 + \hat{\beta}_1 x_i), i = 1, 2, ..., n.$$

The above Figure 14.2 represents the data points along with the lines of Regression based on the Independent and Dependent variables. The sum of squares and the residual analysis is being carried out.

(iii) Studying Adequacy of the Model
Residual estimated is used to analyze the adequacy of the fitted regression model. The normality assumption can be verified from Normal P–P plot. The assumption of non-correlation on residuals can be tested by applying Durbin–Watson test. It is also called as the test for autocorrelation. The term autocorrelation refers to the relationship between the successive

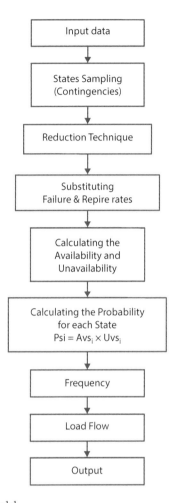

Figure 14.3 Adequacy model.

values of a random variable. The adequacy of the regression model is depicted in Figure 14.3. If ρ represents the coefficient of autocorrelation, then the hypothesis is tested and the test statistic is as follows:

$$d = \frac{\displaystyle\sum_{i=2}^{n} (e_t - e_{t-1})^2}{\displaystyle\sum_{i=1}^{n} e_t^2}$$

14.3.2   Time Series Model

(a) Testing the Stationarity of Time Series: Principles of stationarity is depicted in Figure 14.4 with respect to time dependent mean, variance and covariance.

By using the method of second differencing non stationary is changed to stationary so that future predictions are carried out. The existing techniques are Auto Regressive (AR), Moving Average (MA) and Auto Regressive Moving Average (ARMA) [1, 7–9].

(b) Autocorrelation Function

The degree of similarity between given infographic data and a lagged version of itself over successive intervals are being depicted in Figure 14.5 which is non-stationary in mean.

$$r_k = \frac{\sum_{t=k+1}^{n} (Y_t - \bar{Y})(Y_{t-k} - \bar{Y})}{\sum_{t=1}^{n} (Y_t - \bar{Y})^2}$$

(c) Partial Autocorrelation Function (PAF)

The summary of the relationship between an observation in the current predicted values with the previous time steps by removing the intervening observations as displayed in Figure 14.6.

$$Y_t = b_0 + b_1 Y_{t-1} + b_2 Y_{t-2} + \ldots + b_k Y_{t-k} \quad k = 1, 2, \ldots$$

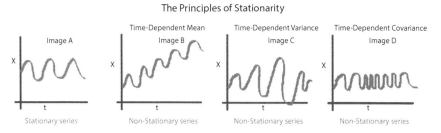

Figure 14.4 Stationarity analysis.

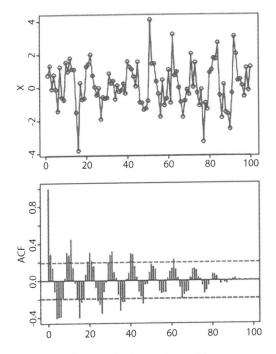

Figure 14.5 Auto correlation functional values—time and lag.

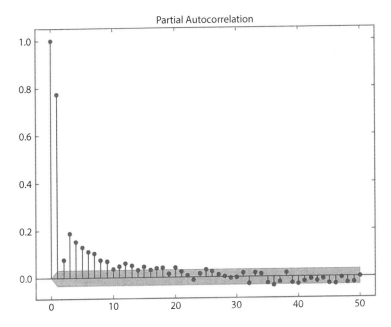

Figure 14.6 Partial autocorrelation.

14.4   Results and Discussions

Based on the stationarity, the plot of COVID-19 new cases and new deaths from Jan. 22, 2020 to 31 May 2020 is shown in the figure below. As per Figure 14.7 the new cases increases and due to preventive, corrective measures fluctuations are there in new death cases (Figure 14.8).

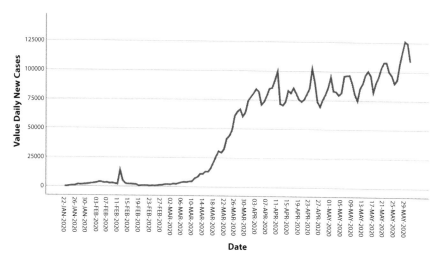

Figure 14.7 Time plot of daily COVID-19 new cases in the world during 22-Jan 22-2020 to 31-May-2020.

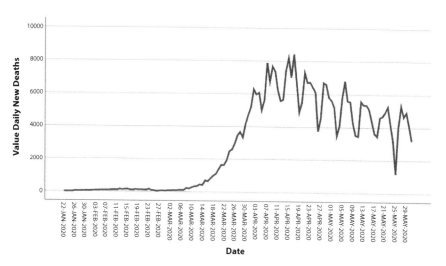

Figure 14.8 Time plot of daily COVID-19 new deaths in the world during 22-Jan-2020 to 31-May-2020.

From the figures it is observed that there is a variation changes over time. It points out that mean of the daily affected cases and deaths are not set and its changes over time. These details reveals that daily affected are non-stationary in both mean and variance.

Figures 14.9 and 14.10 represent the ACF and PACF values against 16 time lags. The non stationarity in mean also be observed from Figures 14.9 and 14.10. It can be noted from the ACF plots, all the spikes are lying outside the confident limits. The time lags at 1 is very large and lying outside the confidence limits. Figures 14.11 and 14.12 represent the ACF and PACF values against 16 time lags. The non-stationarity in mean can also be noted from Figures 14.11 and 14.12. It can be observed from the ACF plots, all the spikes are lying outside the confident limits. From PACF the times lags 1, 3, 5, 6, 8 are very large and lying outside the confidence limits.

So it is necessary that to transfer the non-stationary data to stationary data. Because Figures 14.9, 14.10, 14.11 and 14.12 confirm the non-stationary in mean. So that process of differencing is carried out in the data to eliminate the non-stationary. To remove the non-stationary in mean the technique of second differencing is applied. After two times differencing is carried out, it can be observed from the following results that stationary is maintained with respect to mean and variance.

Autocorrelations and Partial autocorrelations with standard error are depicted below.

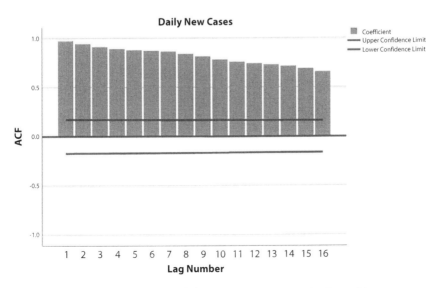

Figure 14.9 Plots of ACF values for daily COVID-19-new cases in the world.

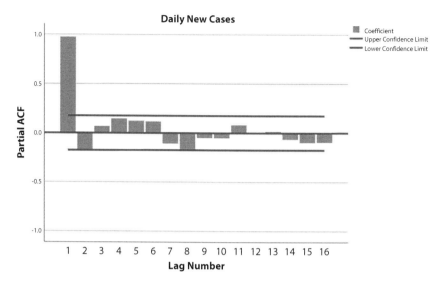

Figure 14.10 Plots of PACF values for daily COVID-19 new cases in the world.

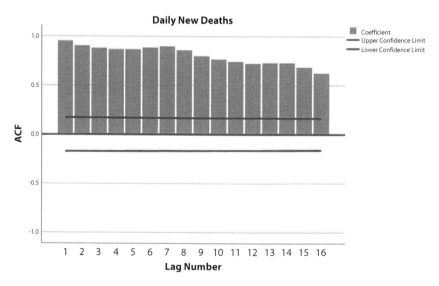

Figure 14.11 Plots of ACF values for daily COVID-19 deaths in the world.

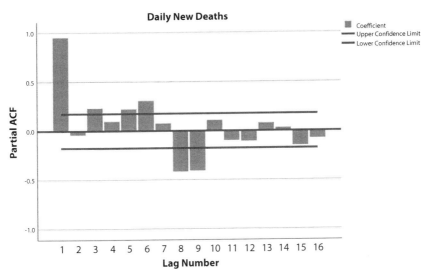

Figure 14.12 Plots of PACF values for daily COVID-19 new new deaths in the world.

After taking second order differencing, from Figures 14.13 and 14.14, it can be diagnosed that the second level differences series may be stationary. Figures 14.15, 14.16, 14.17 and 14.18 are respectively represents the ACF and PACF values against 16 time lags. From Tables 14.1 and 14.3, it is observed that Box–Ljung statistic value increases when the lag number increases. From Table 14.2 and 14.4, it is also noted that PACF standard error is constant irrespective of the number of lag. The value of ACF and PACF of 16 lags are maximum falling inside to the confident limits and also not so far from the central value. Hence based on the graphical representations it can be concluded that the observations are stationary when the second differencing is carried out. The models AR or ARMA model can be able to fit only to the stationary time series. In this case, the observations are converted into stationary time series by using second ordered differencing [11]. So that ARIMA model can be built to this second ordered differencing time series data. Hence the appropriate ARIMA model can be determined by using this stationary time series and the model can be used to yield forecast.

14.4.1   Model Estimation and Studying its Adequacy

From stationarity on second differences of daily new cases and daily new deaths time series data an ARIMA model is fitted to the data. We considered nine different ARIMA models and choose the best model which has minimum Normalized BIC.

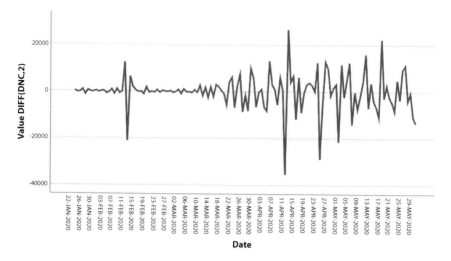

Figure 14.13 Time plot of new cases across the globe during 22 Jan-2020 to 31-May-2020.

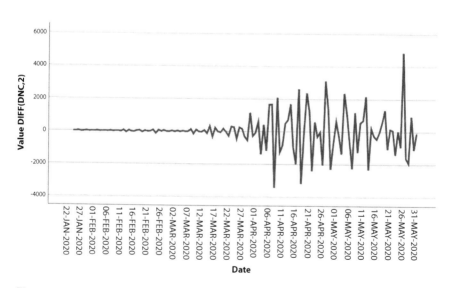

Figure 14.14 Time plot of second differencing for new cases and deaths in the world during 22 Jan-2020 to 31-May-2020.

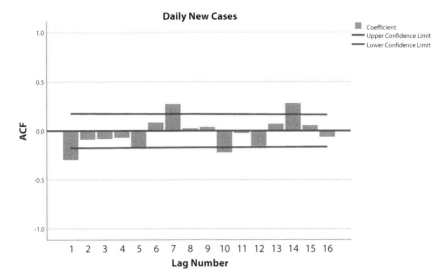

Figure 14.15 Plots of ACF values of second differencing of daily new cases in the world.

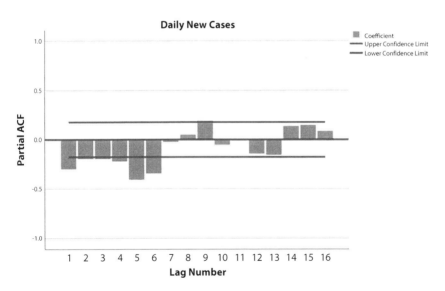

Figure 14.16 Plots of PACF values of second differencing of daily new cases in the world.

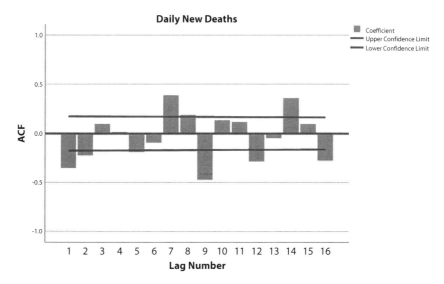

Figure 14.17 Plots of ACF values of second differencing of daily new deaths in the world.

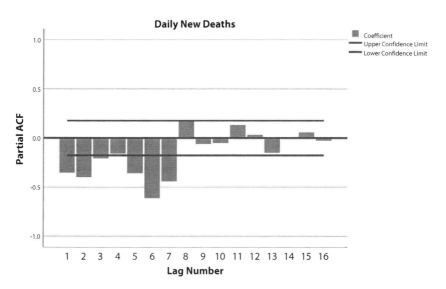

Figure 14.18 Plots of PACF values of second differencing of daily new deaths in the world.

Table 14.1 Auto correlation of second differenced daily new cases.

Autocorrelations					
			Box-Ljung statistic		
Lag	Autocorrelation	Std. error[a]	Value	df	Sig.[b]
1	−0.297	0.087	11.652	1	0.001
2	−0.091	0.087	12.748	2	0.002
3	−0.082	0.086	13.646	3	0.003
4	−0.07	0.086	14.309	4	0.006
5	−0.179	0.086	18.664	5	0.002
6	0.086	0.085	19.677	6	0.003
7	0.271	0.085	29.865	7	0
8	0.026	0.085	29.959	8	0
9	0.04	0.084	30.182	9	0
10	−0.221	0.084	37.141	10	0
11	−0.025	0.084	37.232	11	0
12	−0.155	0.083	40.708	12	0
13	0.07	0.083	41.413	13	0
14	0.28	0.082	52.949	14	0
15	0.056	0.082	53.421	15	0
16	−0.063	0.082	54.019	16	0

The normalized Bayseian Information Criteria values are listed in Tables 14.5 and 14.6 respectively. From Tables 14.5 and 14.6, it is observed that the most suitable model is ARIMA (2, 2, 2) and ARIMA (0, 2, 1) because of having the minimum Normalized BIC values.

The predictors count, R squared values along with the Bayesian normalized values are being obtained for daily new cases and daily new deaths across globe which is depicted in Tables 14.7 and 14.8.

The ARIMA model is designed for the significance of new cases and new deaths with standard error and it reveals to the fact that it is highly significant as displayed in Tables 14.9 and 14.10.

Table 14.2 Partial auto correlation of second differenced daily new cases.

Partial autocorrelations		
Lag	Partial autocorrelation	Std. error
1	−0.297	0.088
2	−0.196	0.088
3	−0.197	0.088
4	−0.219	0.088
5	−0.407	0.088
6	−0.344	0.088
7	−0.024	0.088
8	0.049	0.088
9	0.19	0.088
10	−0.055	0.088
11	−0.012	0.088
12	−0.143	0.088
13	−0.155	0.088
14	0.136	0.088
15	0.147	0.088
16	0.086	0.088

The ARIMA model ARIMA (2, 2, 2) and ARIMA (0, 2, 1) is fitted to the second difference series of daily new cases and daily new deaths respectively. The adequacy of this model is also studied on the analysis of residuals.

From the normal P–P plot (Figures 14.21 and 14.22) for estimated residuals; we infer that the distribution of residuals may be normal. Therefore, the given model may be used for forecasting purpose [3, 4, 6, 12].

Figures 14.19 and 14.20 show that maximum values of ACF and PACF are lying within the confidence limit. Hence, from all the studies, the estimated ARIMA model ARIMA (2,2,2) and ARIMA (0,2,1) are found to be

Table 14.3 Autocorrelation with second differenced values are obtained by transforming non stationary to stationary with respect to daily new deaths using Box Ljung Statistic.

Autocorrelations					
			Box-Ljung statistic		
Lag	Autocorrelation	Std. error[a]	Value	df	Sig.[b]
1	−0.353	0.087	16.45	1	0
2	−0.224	0.087	23.12	2	0
3	0.099	0.086	24.43	3	0
4	0.016	0.086	24.47	4	0
5	−0.19	0.086	29.38	5	0
6	−0.094	0.085	30.58	6	0
7	0.388	0.085	51.42	7	0
8	0.19	0.085	56.45	8	0
9	−0.472	0.084	87.84	9	0
10	0.134	0.084	90.38	10	0
11	0.119	0.084	92.4	11	0
12	−0.285	0.083	104.2	12	0
13	−0.047	0.083	104.5	13	0
14	0.36	0.082	123.6	14	0
15	0.097	0.082	125	15	0
16	−0.278	0.082	136.5	16	0

[a]Standard error analysis
[b]Significance in second differenced values

adequate and therefore model can be used for forecasting reason of daily COVID-19 new cases in the world and COVID-19 new deaths in the world. Forecasting values are given in Tables 14.11 and 14.12. These values are presented diagrammatically in Figures 14.23 and 14.24.

Table 14.4 Partial auto correlation of second differenced daily new deaths.

Partial autocorrelations		
Lag	Partial autocorrelation	Std. error
1	−0.353	0.088
2	−0.398	0.088
3	−0.206	0.088
4	−0.158	0.088
5	−0.357	0.088
6	−0.614	0.088
7	−0.44	0.088
8	0.177	0.088
9	−0.063	0.088
10	−0.051	0.088
11	0.132	0.088
12	0.032	0.088
13	−0.149	0.088
14	−0.002	0.088
15	0.057	0.088
16	−0.027	0.088

14.4.2   Regression Model for Daily New Cases and New Deaths

A simple linear regression model is fitted by considering daily new deaths as the response variable and daily new cases as the predictor variable [2, 5].

The scatter plot for daily new cases against daily new deaths is given in Figure 14.25. It shows the linear relationships between the daily new cases and daily new deaths. Hence, a LR model is an appropriate to find out the relationship between daily new cases and daily new deaths which is highly significant. The output presented in Table 14.13 shows the appropriate LR model. The fitted model is as

Table 14.5 ARIMA models and normalized BIC value for daily new cases in the world.

ARIMA(p,d,q) model	Normalized BIC value
(0,2,0)	18.120
(1,2,0)	17.980
(0,2,1)	17.618
(1,2,0)	17.610
(0,2,2)	17.612
(2,2,0)	17.980
(2,2,2)	**17.467**
(1,2,2)	17.663
(2,2,1)	17.614

Table 14.6 ARIMA models and normalized BIC value for daily COVID-19 new deaths in the world.

ARIMA(p,d,q) model	Normalized BIC value
(0,2,0)	14.105
(1,2,0)	14.017
(0,2,1)	**13.543**
(1,2)	13.683
(0,2,2)	13.668
(2,2,0)	13.888
(2,2,2)	13.822
(1,2,2)	13.615
(2,2,1)	13.564

Table 14.7 Model statistics of daily new cases in the world.

Description	Predictors count	Statistics analysis		
		R-squared (STS)	R-squared	Bayesian information criteria-normalized
Daily new cases-Model_1	1	0.525	0.983	17.467

Table 14.8 Model statistics of daily new deaths in the globe.

Description	Predictors count	Statistics analysis		
		R-squared (STS)	R-squared	Bayesian information criteria-normalized
Daily new deaths-Model_1	1	0.455	0.908	13.543

$$Y = 78.818 + 0.058X$$

which is simple linear regression model for daily COVID-19 new deaths on daily COVID-19 new cases.

The stanadarized and unstandardized coefficient values along with errors are displayed in Table 14.14. This reveals to the fact that it is highly significant with the acceptance of Null hypothesis

The significant probability 0.000, calculated in testing the nullity of the co-efficient of daily COVID-19 new cases indicates the significant presence of water daily new cases. Rises of daily new cases makes 0.058 changes in the daily new deaths. The value of coefficient of determination, $R^2 = 0.801$, shows the relevance of this linear relationship. The adequacy of the model can be analyzed from the residuals. From Table 14.15, it is found that the mean residual is zero. The value of Durbin–Watson test statistic d is 0.34. Since, this value is less than the d_L value it is observed that there is +ve autocorrelation in the errors. The other model assumptions can be verified using the residual plots. The

Table 14.9 ARIMA model parameters of daily new cases in the world.

Daily new cases-Model_1[a]	Daily new cases	No transformation	Constant		Estimate	SE	t	Sig.
					−119.031	294,867.5	0	1
			AR	Lag 1	0.898	0.09	9.959	0
				Lag 2	−0.489	0.086	−5.681	0
			Difference		2			
			MA	Lag 1	1.805	0.057	31.752	0
				Lag 2	−0.887	0.054	−16.285	0
	Date	No transformation	Numerator	Lag 0	9.53E−09	2.14E−05	0	1

Table 14.10 ARIMA model parameters of daily new deaths in the world.

Daily new deaths-model_1	Daily new deaths	No transformation			Estimate	SE	t	Sig.
		Constant			−7.031	36400.68	0	1
		Difference			2			
		MA	Lag 1		0.912	0.077	11.785	0
	Date	No transformation	Numerator	Lag 0	4.28E−10	2.64E−06	0	1

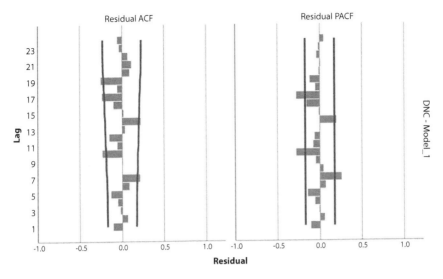

Figure 14.19 Plotting of ACF and PACF values for estimated residuals of daily new cases in the world.

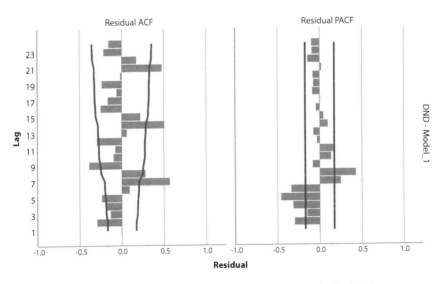

Figure 14.20 Plotting of ACF and PACF values for estimated residuals of daily new deaths in the world.

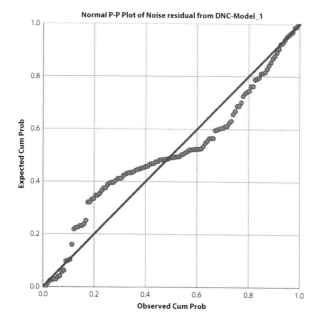

Figure 14.21 Normal P–P plot of estimated residual daily new cases.

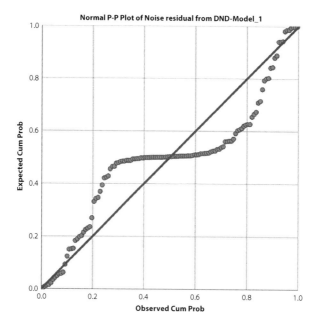

Figure 14.22 Normal P–P plot of estimated of residuals of daily new deaths.

Table 14.11 Forecasting values of daily new cases in the world (June 2020–August 2020).

Date	Predicted daily COVID 19 new cases	LCL	UCL	Date	Predicted daily COVID 19 new cases	LCL	UCL
01-Jun-2020	105,530	94,563	116,497	17-Jul-2020	211,130	–82,020	504,281
02-Jun-2020	110,995	94,748	127,242	18-Jul-2020	213,494	–88,840	515,828
03-Jun-2020	118,649	100,340	136,959	19-Jul-2020	215,870	–95,742	527,482
04-Jun-2020	123,919	104,754	143,083	20-Jul-2020	218,259	–102,726	539,243
05-Jun-2020	125,982	105,961	146,003	21-Jul-2020	220,660	–109,790	551,110
06-Jun-2020	126,341	104,714	147,967	22-Jul-2020	223,074	–116,933	563,081
07-Jun-2020	126,742	102,410	151,075	23-Jul-2020	225,501	–124,154	575,156
08-Jun-2020	128,025	100,169	155,880	24-Jul-2020	227,940	–131,453	587,334
09-Jun-2020	130,084	98,366	161,802	25-Jul-2020	230,392	–138,829	599,614
10-Jun-2020	132,419	96,741	168,096	26-Jul-2020	232,857	–146,281	611,995
11-Jun-2020	134,627	94,889	174,365	27-Jul-2020	235,334	–153,808	624,477
12-Jun-2020	136,596	92,604	180,588	28-Jul-2020	237,824	–161,409	637,058
13-Jun-2020	138,418	89,909	186,926	29-Jul-2020	240,327	–169,084	649,738

(Continued)

Table 14.11 Forecasting values of daily new cases in the world (June 2020– August 2020). (*Continued*)

Date	Predicted daily COVID 19 new cases	LCL	UCL	Date	Predicted daily COVID 19 new cases	LCL	UCL
14-Jun-2020	140,233	86,938	193,528	30-Jul-2020	242,843	−176,831	662,516
15-Jun-2020	142,121	83,802	200,440	31-Jul-2020	245,371	−184,651	675,392
16-Jun-2020	144,086	80,547	207,625	01-Aug-2020	247,911	−192,542	688,365
17-Jun-2020	146,091	77,162	215,020	02-Aug-2020	250,465	−200,504	701,433
18-Jun-2020	148,102	73,622	222,583	03-Aug-2020	253,031	−208,536	714,598
19-Jun-2020	150,107	69,914	230,301	04-Aug-2020	255,609	−216,637	727,856
20-Jun-2020	152,110	66,043	238,178	05-Aug-2020	258,201	−224,808	741,209
21-Jun-2020	154,123	62,023	246,223	06-Aug-2020	260,805	−233,046	754,656
22-Jun-2020	156,152	57,867	254,437	07-Aug-2020	263,422	−241,352	768,195
23-Jun-2020	158,199	53,583	262,816	08-Aug-2020	266,051	−249,725	781,827
24-Jun-2020	160,261	49,172	271,350	09-Aug-2020	268,693	−258,164	795,550

(*Continued*)

Table 14.11 Forecasting values of daily new cases in the world (June 2020– August 2020). (*Continued*)

Date	Predicted daily COVID 19 new cases	LCL	UCL	Date	Predicted daily COVID 19 new cases	LCL	UCL
25-Jun-2020	162,336	44,638	280,035	10-Aug-2020	271,348	−266,669	809,365
26-Jun-2020	164,422	39,980	288,865	11-Aug-2020	274,015	−275,239	823,270
27-Jun-2020	166,520	35,202	297,838	12-Aug-2020	276,695	−283,874	837,265
28-Jun-2020	168,629	30,307	306,952	13-Aug-2020	279,388	−292,574	851,350
29-Jun-2020	170,752	25,298	316,206	14-Aug-2020	282,094	−301,336	865,524
30-Jun-2020	172,888	20,179	325,597	15-Aug-2020	284,812	−310,163	879,786
01-Jul-2020	175,036	14,951	335,121	16-Aug-2020	287,543	−319,051	894,137
02-Jul-2020	177,197	9,617	344,778	17-Aug-2020	290,286	−328,002	908,575
03-Jul-2020	179,371	4,178	354,565	18-Aug-2020	293,042	−337,015	923,100
04-Jul-2020	181,557	−1,364	364,479	19-Aug-2020	295,811	−346,089	937,711
05-Jul-2020	183,756	−7,006	374,519	20-Aug-2020	298,593	−355,223	952,409
06-Jul-2020	185,968	−12,748	384,684	21-Aug-2020	301,387	−364,418	967,193

(*Continued*)

Table 14.11 Forecasting values of daily new cases in the world (June 2020–August 2020). (*Continued*)

Date	Predicted daily COVID 19 new cases	LCL	UCL	Date	Predicted daily COVID 19 new cases	LCL	UCL
07-Jul-2020	188,192	−18,587	394,971	22-Aug-2020	304,194	−373,673	982,061
08-Jul-2020	190,429	−24,522	405,380	23-Aug-2020	307,014	−382,987	997,015
09-Jul-2020	192,679	−30,551	415,908	24-Aug-2020	309,846	−392,360	1,012,052
10-Jul-2020	194,941	−36,673	426,555	25-Aug-2020	312,691	−401,792	1,027,174
11-Jul-2020	197,216	−42,887	437,318	26-Aug-2020	315,549	−411,282	1,042,379
12-Jul-2020	199,503	−49,191	448,197	27-Aug-2020	318,419	−420,830	1,057,668
13-Jul-2020	201,803	−55,584	459,190	28-Aug-2020	321,302	−430,435	1,073,039
14-Jul-2020	204,116	−62,064	470,296	29-Aug-2020	324,198	−440,097	1,088,493
15-Jul-2020	206,442	−68,631	481,514	30-Aug-2020	327,106	−449,815	1,104,028
16-Jul-2020	208,780	−75,283	492,843	31-Aug-2020	330,028	−459,590	1,119,645

Table 14.12 Forecasting values of daily new deaths in the world (June 2020–August 2020).

Date	Predicted daily COVID 19 new deaths	LCL	UCL	Date	Predicted daily COVID 19 new deaths	LCL	UCL
01-Jun-2020	3,066	1,406	4,725	17-Jul-2020	-3,930	-41,066	33,207
02-Jun-2020	2,940	487	5,393	18-Jul-2020	-4,109	-42,220	34,001
03-Jun-2020	2,813	-323	5,949	19-Jul-2020	-4,290	-43,383	34,803
04-Jun-2020	2,685	-1,089	6,459	20-Jul-2020	-4,472	-44,556	35,611
05-Jun-2020	2,556	-1,836	6,948	21-Jul-2020	-4,655	-45,737	36,427
06-Jun-2020	2,426	-2,577	7,428	22-Jul-2020	-4,840	-46,928	37,249
07-Jun-2020	2,294	-3,316	7,905	23-Jul-2020	-5,025	-48,128	38,078
08-Jun-2020	2,161	-4,060	8,383	24-Jul-2020	-5,212	-49,337	38,913
09-Jun-2020	2,028	-4,809	8,864	25-Jul-2020	-5,400	-50,555	39,756
10-Jun-2020	1,893	-5,566	9,351	26-Jul-2020	-5,589	-51,782	40,604
11-Jun-2020	1,756	-6,331	9,844	27-Jul-2020	-5,779	-53,018	41,460
12-Jun-2020	1,619	-7,107	10,345	28-Jul-2020	-5,971	-54,262	42,321
13-Jun-2020	1,480	-7,892	10,853	29-Jul-2020	-6,163	-55,516	43,190

(Continued)

Table 14.12 Forecasting values of daily new deaths in the world (June 2020–August 2020). (*Continued*)

Date	Predicted daily COVID 19 new deaths	LCL	UCL	Date	Predicted daily COVID 19 new deaths	LCL	UCL
14-Jun-2020	1,341	-8,688	11,370	30-Jul-2020	-6,357	-56,778	44,064
15-Jun-2020	1,200	-9,495	11,895	31-Jul-2020	-6,552	-58,049	44,945
16-Jun-2020	1,058	-10,313	12,429	01-Aug-2020	-6,748	-59,328	45,832
17-Jun-2020	914	-11,143	12,972	02-Aug-2020	-6,945	-60,616	46,725
18-Jun-2020	770	-11,983	13,524	03-Aug-2020	-7,144	-61,912	47,625
19-Jun-2020	624	-12,835	14,084	04-Aug-2020	-7,343	-63,217	48,531
20-Jun-2020	478	-13,699	14,654	05-Aug-2020	-7,544	-64,531	49,442
21-Jun-2020	330	-14,573	15,233	06-Aug-2020	-7,746	-65,852	50,360
22-Jun-2020	181	-15,459	15,820	07-Aug-2020	-7,949	-67,182	51,284
23-Jun-2020	30	-16,356	16,417	08-Aug-2020	-8,154	-68,521	52,214
24-Jun-2020	-121	-17,265	17,022	09-Aug-2020	-8,359	-69,867	53,149
25-Jun-2020	-274	-18,184	17,636	10-Aug-2020	-8,566	-71,222	54,091
26-Jun-2020	-428	-19,114	18,259	11-Aug-2020	-8,774	-72,585	55,038

(Continued)

Table 14.12 Forecasting values of daily new deaths in the world (June 2020–August 2020). (*Continued*)

Date	Predicted daily COVID 19 new deaths	LCL	UCL	Date	Predicted daily COVID 19 new deaths	LCL	UCL
27-Jun-2020	−583	−20,056	18,890	12-Aug-2020	−8,983	−73,956	55,991
28-Jun-2020	−739	−21,008	19,530	13-Aug-2020	−9,193	−75,335	56,950
29-Jun-2020	−896	−21,971	20,179	14-Aug-2020	−9,404	−76,722	57,914
30-Jun-2020	−1,055	−22,945	20,835	15-Aug-2020	−9,617	−78,118	58,884
01-Jul-2020	−1,215	−23,929	21,500	16-Aug-2020	−9,830	−79,521	59,860
02-Jul-2020	−1,375	−24,924	22,174	17-Aug-2020	−10,045	−80,932	60,841
03-Jul-2020	−1,537	−25,930	22,855	18-Aug-2020	−10,261	−82,351	61,828
04-Jul-2020	−1,701	−26,946	23,544	19-Aug-2020	−10,479	−83,778	62,821
05-Jul-2020	−1,865	−27,972	24,242	20-Aug-2020	−10,697	−85,212	63,819
06-Jul-2020	−2,031	−29,009	24,947	21-Aug-2020	−10,916	−86,655	64,822
07-Jul-2020	−2,197	−30,055	25,661	22-Aug-2020	−11,137	−88,105	65,831
08-Jul-2020	−2,365	−31,112	26,381	23-Aug-2020	−11,359	−89,563	66,845
09-Jul-2020	−2,534	−32,179	27,110	24-Aug-2020	−11,582	−91,028	67,864

(*Continued*)

Table 14.12 Forecasting values of daily new deaths in the world (June 2020–August 2020). (*Continued*)

Date	Predicted daily COVID 19 new deaths	LCL	UCL	Date	Predicted daily COVID 19 new deaths	LCL	UCL
10-Jul-2020	−2,705	−33,256	27,846	25-Aug-2020	−11,806	−92,502	68,889
11-Jul-2020	−2,876	−34,343	28,590	26-Aug-2020	−12,032	−93,983	69,919
12-Jul-2020	−3,049	−35,439	29,341	27-Aug-2020	−12,259	−95,471	70,954
13-Jul-2020	−3,223	−36,545	30,100	28-Aug-2020	−12,486	−96,967	71,994
14-Jul-2020	−3,398	−37,661	30,866	29-Aug-2020	−12,715	−98,470	73,040
15-Jul-2020	−3,574	−38,787	31,639	30-Aug-2020	−12,945	−99,981	74,091
16-Jul-2020	−3,751	−39,922	32,419	31-Aug-2020	−13,177	−101,500	75,146

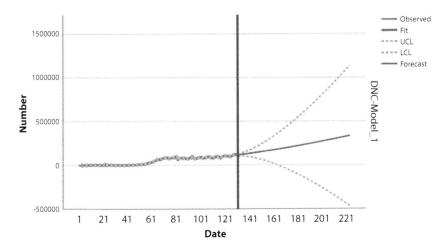

Figure 14.23 Forecast graph of daily new cases in the world.

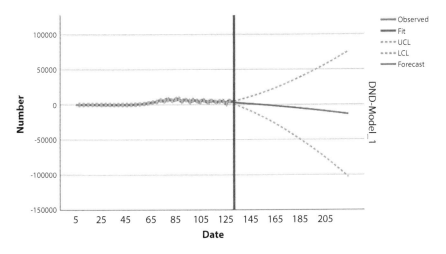

Figure 14.24 Forecast graph of daily new deaths in the world.

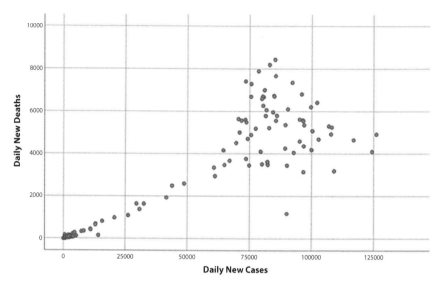

Figure 14.25 Scatter plot of daily new cases vs daily COVID-19 new deaths.

Table 14.13 Statistical measures.

Description	Value-R	Value-R square	Value-adjusted R square	Value-Std. error of the estimate	Durbin–Watson
1	.895[a]	0.801	0.799	1212.759	0.34

Table 14.14 Coefficients.

Description		Values-unstandardized coefficients		Values-standardized coefficients	Value-t	Sig.
		B	Std. error	Beta		
1	(Constant)	78.818	161.585		0.488	0.627
	Daily New Cases	0.058	0.003	0.895	22.776	0

residual for this model can be defined as e = $X_1 - \hat{X}_2$. The residuals are calculated and plotted to verify the above statistical assumptions.

The plots are given in Figure 14.26. From the residual plot 26, it is observed that the normality assumption is moderately satisfied.

Table 14.15 Residuals statistics.

	Value-minimum	Value-maximum	Value-mean	Value-Std. deviation
Predicted Value	78.82	7,415.17	2,857.39	2,422.644
Residual	−4,136.204	3,397.069	0	1,208.085
Std. Predicted Value	−1.147	1.881	0	1
Std. Residual	−3.411	2.801	0	0.996

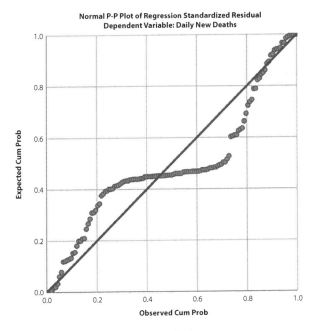

Figure 14.26 Normal P–P plot of estimated residuals.

14.5   Conclusions

This study aims at forecasting the daily new cases, new deaths and also finds out the relationship between daily deaths and daily new cases using time series and regression model respectively. We developed ARIMA and LR model for COVID-19 data. The best result is obtained by using ARIMA (2, 2, 2) and ARIMA (0, 2, 1) model for daily nee cases and daily new deaths respectively. The first major finding of the study is that new cases will increase in future if the same monitoring scheme is continued and the death rate will not go for danger zoon in future. So we can conclude that the death rate is controlled by proper treatments. Linear Model results revealed that if the new COVID-19 cases will not increase, daily new deaths cases will not increase gradually. This helps the healthcare monitoring department to develop new scheme to monitor the COVID-19 problem.

References

1. Box, G.E.P. and Jenkins, G.M., *Time Series Analysis: Forecasting and Control*, San Francisco: Holden Day (revised ed. 1976), 44, 575, 1970.
2. Cook, R.D., Detection of influential observations in linear regression. *Technometrics*, 1, 15–18, 1977.
3. Pankratz, A., *Forecasting with Univariate Box–Jenkins Models: Concepts and Cases*, John Wiley & Sons, New York, 1983.
4. Cummins, J.D. and Griepentrog, G.L., Forecasting Automobile Insurance Paid Claims Using Econometric and ARIMA Models. *Int. J. Forecasting*, 1, 203–215, 1985.
5. Montgomery, D.C., Peck, E.A., Geoffrey Vining, G., *Introduction to Linear Regression Analysis*, Fifth Edition, John Wiley & Sons, Inc, Hoboken, New Jersey, 2012.
6. Volkan, S., Edigera, A., Sertac, U., Berkin, Forecasting production of fossil fuel sources in Turkey using a comparative regression and ARIMA model, in: *Energy Policy*, vol. 34, pp. 3836–3846, 2005.
7. Cooray, T.M.J.A., *Applied Time Series: Analysis and Forecasting*, Narosa Publishing House, New Delhi, 2008.
8. Box, G.E.P., Jenkins, G.M., Reinsel, G.C., *Time Series Analysis, Forecasting and Control*, 4th edition, John Wiley & Sons, Inc., New Jersey, 2008.
9. Naill, P.E. and Momani, M., Time Series Analysis Model for Rainfall Data in Jordan: Case Study for Using Time Series Analysis. *Am. J. Environ. Sci.*, 5, 5, 599–604, 2009.

10. Bianco, V., Manco, O., Nardini, S., Linear Regression Models to Forecast Electricuty Consumption in Italy, in: *Energy Sources, Part B: Economics, Planning, and Policy*, vol. 8, no. 1, pp. 86–93, 2013.
11. He, Z., Chin, Y., Huang, J., He, Y., Akinwunmi, B.O., Yu, S., Zhang, C.J.P., Ming, W.-k., *Meteorological factors and domestic new cases of coronavirus disease (COVID-19) in nine Asian cities: A time series analysis*, Cold Spring Harbor Laboratory Press. 2020.
12. Voumik, L.C. and Smrity, D.Y., Forecasting GDP Per Capita In Bangladesh: Using Arima Model. *Eur. J. Bus. Manage. Res.*, 5, 5, 1–5, 2020.
13. Argawu, A.S., *Regression Models for Predictions of COVID-19 New Cases and New Deaths Based on May/June Data in Ethiopia*, Cold Spring Harbor Laboratory Press, 2020.

Index

Printed and bound by CPI Group (UK) Ltd, Croydon, CR0 4YY